ASPECTS OF ARISTOCRACY

ASPECTS OF ARISTOCRACY

Grandeur and Decline in Modern Britain

DAVID CANNADINE

YALE UNIVERSITY PRESS
New Haven & London
1994

Set in Linotron Bembo by Best-set Typesetter Ltd.,
Hong Kong, and printed and bound in Great Britain
by St Edmundsbury Press

Library of Congress Cataloging-in-Publication Data
Cannadine, David, 1950–
Beyond the country house: aspects of aristocracy in modern
Britain / David Cannadine.
p.   cm.
Includes bibliographical references (p.   ) and index.
ISBN 0-300-05981-7
1. Aristocracy—Great Britain—History.   2. Upper classes—Great
Britain—History.   3. Nobility—Great Britain—History.   4. Great
Britain—History—1789–1820.   I. Title.
HT653.G7C357   1994
305.5'2'0941—dc20   93-40460
                                                                     CIP

For Jan and Martin

Contents

viii   Contents

Acknowledgements

ONE OF THE PLEASURES of completing another book is the opportunity it affords for saluting the many people who have helped in its making. My first thanks are to the owners and custodians of the papers and collections which I have consulted: the Trustees of the Chatsworth Settlement, the Trustees of the Bedford Estates, the Fitzwilliam Trustees, the Partners of Hoare's Bank, the Court of Governors of the Royal Exchange Assurance Company, and the archivists and staff of the Bodleian Library, Oxford University, the British Library, the Butler Library of Columbia University, Cambridge University Library, the India Office Library, the Kent Archives Office, the Norfolk Record Office, Norwich City Library, Oxford City Library, the Public Record Office, Sheffield City Library, the Sterling Memorial Library of Yale University, Somerset House, and the University of East Anglia Library.

I am also especially grateful to the many individuals who have helped me along the way: Dr Paul Addison, Professor T.C. Barker, Professor Christopher Bayly, the Lord Blake, Professor Peter Clarke, Professor Roy Church, Mr R.L. Colley, the Hon. Miss Beryl Cozens-Hardy, Mr John Cozens-Hardy, Mr Ivan Cresswell, Dr Mark Curthoys, Mr Peter Day, Mr Michael De-la-Noy, the Lady Antonia Fraser, Mr Raymond Frostick, the Hon. Mr David Gilmour, Dr Erik Goldstein, Dr Brian Harrison, Professor Eric Hobsbawm, Dr Janet Howarth, Mr S.S.F. Hornor, Ms Eleanor John, Mr R.T.B. Langhorne, Ms Nomi Levy, Professor William Roger Louis, Dr Peter Mathias, Professor Sir John Plumb, Dr David Reynolds, Professor Duncan Robinson, Mr Paul Rutledge, the late Professor Eric Stokes, Sir Keith Thomas, Professor F.M.L. Thompson, Mr John Trevitt, and Mr James Tueller.

In the case of certain of these essays, acknowledgements are also due of a rather broader kind. Chapter 1 began life as a travelling paper, and I recall with appreciation the comments and suggestions I received when I presented it at seminars at Cambridge, London, Harvard and Columbia Universities. An earlier version of chapter 2 appeared in the *Economic*

History Review (1977), and I thank the editors for their permission to reproduce sections of it here. Chapter 6 grew out of a paper presented at an unforgettably agreeable conference held at the University of Texas at Austin in March 1991, and I am most grateful to the participants for their warm comments on that occasion. A much-abridged version has subsequently been published in R. Blake and W.R. Louis (eds.), *Churchill* (1993). Chapter 7 originally appeared in the *Agricultural History Review* (1977), whose editors I also thank for permission to reprint, with subsequent alterations and additions.

My last debts are far greater than those aristocratic accumulations about which I have written in chapter 2, and are much more difficult to repay, not least because they show every sign of increasing at an alarming and unrestrainable rate. To my agent, Mike Shaw, I owe thanks for constant support and boundless enthusiasm, unfailingly displayed. To my editor, publisher, and friend, John Nicoll of Yale University Press, I can express only gratitude and admiration which increase with the years. And the fact that my final acknowledgement is once again to my wife, Linda Colley, is the customarily inadequate thank you for her life and her love.

DNC

1 *August 1993*

Aspects of Aristocracy

THE ESSAYS COLLECTED HERE have been accumulating during the last sixteen years, and were completed before, during and after the period when I was primarily concerned with writing *The Decline and Fall of the British Aristocracy* (1990). Some were attempts to sort out particular problems which I needed to get clear before tackling the larger survey; some sought to look in more detail at an individual or a dynasty than was possible in a general and generalised account; and some were written out of curiosity and for pleasure, and for no other reason. Assembled together, these occasional pieces cover the period from the late eighteenth century to our own day. They encompass Britain and Ireland, and parts of the Empire that was once beyond the seas. They deal with great families and lesser known clans, with ducal opulence and genteel poverty, and with the multiple identities of patricians as landowners, statesmen, proconsuls, businessmen, professionals, authors – and horticulturalists. And they are concerned with abiding aristocratic preoccupations: fame and fortune, power and prestige, place and office, rank and title, ancestor worship and family pride.

Read as a whole, these essays explore the grandeur of high status and individual accomplishment, and the ambiguities and uncertainties of a class in decline. They have been grouped here under three headings, and thus exemplify some of the different approaches which can be taken to the study of the modern British aristocracy. Part One is concerned with themes and questions which related to the traditional landowning classes as a whole. Part Two looks at some famous aristocratic individuals, but seeks to locate them more historically in their broader patrician milieu. Part Three explores that most fundamental unit of upper-class existence: the family and the sense of interconnection between the generations dead, living and yet unborn, which Edmund Burke regarded as being the very essence of aristocracy. At the same time, each of these essays was also written for a particular purpose and under particular circumstances, and it might be useful to mention what they were.

One of my aims in writing *The Decline and Fall of the British Aristocracy* was to produce an authentic piece of *British* history, which was as much concerned with Wales, Scotland and Ireland as it was with England. Since the late-nineteenth-century aristocracy was a recognisably supra-national phenomenon, this did not prove to be too difficult a task. But it did beg the question of when and how this titled, territorial and trans-national elite had itself come into being. The essay on the making of the British upper classes is an attempt to provide an answer. It concentrates on the years either side of 1800, and suggests that it was at this time that the traditional landed establishments of the British Isles were fundamentally re-made and re-formed. All too often, we tend to suppose that the upper classes stand for tradition, and the lower classes for change. But we should never forget that one of the greatest strengths of the British aristocracy has been its capacity to present itself as venerable, while constantly evolving and developing. The period from the 1780s to the 1820s was one in which such evolution and development were especially marked.

A significant characteristic of this new British aristocracy was a relatively high degree of indebtedness, and I was drawn to this subject early in my researches, because it had recently been the focus of an appropriately genteel controversy between two professors by whose work I was much influenced and inspired: David Spring and F.M.L. Thompson. Since then the debate has rumbled on, and I have revised this essay to take account of writing which has appeared since it was first published. The subject of mortgages, interest payments, estate rentals and land values may not sound especially appealing, but the world today is characterised by unprecedented levels of individual, corporate and governmental debt, and there may be something to be learned from those patricians who pioneered this rather constrained way of living. As we all know, there are many reasons why spending may outrun income, and it is possible to bear relatively high levels of indebtedness, provided that the interest payments can be maintained, that there is enough left over to live on, and that the assets on which the loans are secured retain or increase their value. But we also know what happens if interest payments get too high, if there is insufficient money left to live on, and if the value of the equity suddenly and unexpectedly declines. The woes of late-twentieth-century householders in the south east of England were vividly anticipated by late-nineteenth-century land-owners across the length and breadth of the British Isles.

In the years before and after the First World War some aristocrats sought to salvage their finances by going into business, and while some burned their fingers as badly as many Lloyds names have done in recent years, others joined reputable firms and made an adequate if not spectacular living. Railway companies were particularly notable for their boards groaning with patrician directors, and for their engines bearing noble names. Yet earlier in the nineteenth century, many owners were supposed to have been hostile to railways being laid across their lands, and I was curious to find out when and how (and if) their attitudes had changed. Having looked into these matters, I was naturally drawn into those two other areas of post-equine transport with which the aristocracy has been connected, albeit less influentially: cars and aeroplanes. Who was the Hon. C.S. Rolls of Rolls-Royce? Why did some inter-war aristocrats like to be thought 'air-minded'? And why – to return to railways once more – did Viscount Whitelaw's father have several steam engines named after him? The answers are to be found below in chapter 3.

While biographers are conscious of the things that make their subjects unique, historians are more concerned with seeing individuals in the context of their times and their class, and the essays grouped together in the second section exemplify that approach. For many good reasons, Lord Curzon has been extensively biographied. But too much attention has been given to his superiority of manner, to the funny stories which gathered around him, and to his ultimate political failure. As a result, he is often made to appear less substantial and less significant than he actually was. Moreover, he lived at a time when the empire in which he believed so passionately was in many ways at its zenith, and when British life was becoming more ceremonial and ornamental. He himself played a great part in both of these developments, and as an historian of pageantry and spectacle I was eager to write about Curzon from this angle. It proved to be a very rewarding task. Curzon's theories of ceremonial were well developed and brilliantly articulated, and he was at the centre of four great pageants, two of which he planned himself. And even he could not have been indifferent to the contrast between the imperial hubris of his Delhi Durbar and the bleak desolation of his Remembrance Day observances.

Ever since I was an undergraduate, I had wanted to write something about Lord Curzon; but the essay on Lord Strickland originated under very different circumstances. I was holidaying in Malta some years ago, and visited the cathedral at Mdina. There I came upon a magnificent memorial slab, not just to a Maltese nobleman, as the others were, but to a man who had also been made a British peer: Gerald, first and last Baron Strickland of Sizergh, and sixth Count della Catena in the nobility of Malta, who had died in 1940. On closer investigation it turned out that Strickland was a fascinating figure, whose stormy life had touched the history of the British aristocracy at many points. He was descended from a long line of proud but poor Westmorland landowners; he made a career for himself as a turn of the century proconsul; he dabbled in British politics; and he was Prime Minister of Malta. As such, he provided an unexpected opportunity for a further exploration of the imperial dimension to the late-nineteenth- and twentieth-century British aristocracy – a dimension that deserves much more study than it has thus far received.

By contrast, Winston Churchill has been more than amply studied. Yet as a twentieth-century historian I have found the temptation to write about him irresistible. In the pages of *The Decline and Fall of the British Aristocracy*, he appeared as a member of his class rather than as a great man of history, not because I do not think him a great man, but because that was how the conception of the book required that I treat him. The invitation to give a paper on Churchill's family background at the Austin conference gave me the opportunity to explore his aristocratic antecedents and attitudes more fully. Most biographers of Churchill begin – as he himself did with the life of his father, Lord Randolph – by mentioning Blenheim Palace and his ducal forbears. But then they move on to the brightly lit drama of his life, and the broader (and often disreputable) history of the Churchill family is largely disregarded. It was that history which I tried to uncover, both for its intrinsic interest, and also to see what impact it had, not just on Churchill himself, but and on contemporary perceptions of him. On the whole, it is not an edifying story. But at least it should oblige future biographers to address a question thus far neglected: how did Churchill manage to rise above it all?

Of the dynastic essays, the first written was on the Dukes of Devonshire, partly as the by-product of some early research I undertook on their development of Eastbourne, which appeared in *Lords and Landlords: The Aristocracy and the Towns, 1774–1967* (1980). I needed to find out how the investment and return on their seaside resort fitted into the broader financial picture, but this also led me into a subject which had a fascination all its own, not least because the evidence I uncovered suggested that the conventional wisdom about the Devonshires' nineteenth-century financial history was often mistaken. The sixth duke was indeed a spendthrift: but the full details had never been known, nor the part played by his gardener, Joseph Paxton. It was widely believed that the seventh duke had rescued the estates from the brink of ruin: in fact, his massive and ill-advised over-investment in Barrow-in-Furness had made the family finances worse, not better. But the most unexpected result of my investigations was the discovery that the shrewdest business head was to be found on the shoulders of the eighth duke, the Devonshire usually regarded as in-corrigibly vague and lethargic. In revising this essay, I have brought the account as far into the twentieth century as it is possible to come: almost one hundred years after the death of the seventh duke, the Devonshires' finances are now much healthier, though of course the Cavendishes have long since ceased to play the prominent part in politics that they did a century ago.

By comparison with the Dukes of Devonshire, the Cozens-Hardys were never a big-time dynasty; but to the historian of the aristocracy, they are scarcely less fascinating. As with Lord Strickland, my interest in them was accidently aroused. Our summer house in Norfolk is but a few miles from Letheringsett, the village which the family owned until quite recently. In Norwich itself, Cozens-Hardy and Jewson remains one of the city's most respected firms of solicitors. How, I wondered, had the family managed to be so important in both the country and the town, in agriculture and in the law? Within the county and the city, my researches led me far and wide: to estate ownership and management, to parliamentary politics, to the mustard-making firm of J.J. Colman, to the glass-making firm of Pilkingtons, to the charities of Norwich, to a long-serving newspaper editor, and to a remarkable Norfolk historian. The resulting essay does more than tell the story of one family: it also throws light, not just on the accumulation of wealth and the exercising of power in nineteenth- and early-twentieth-century Norfolk, but also on the broader issues of 'gentlemanly capitalism' with which historians are now very much concerned.

The final essay takes a lengthy look at two of Britain's most famous upper-class gardeners: Harold Nicolson and Vita Sackville-West. They were, of course, many other things besides, but it is as the creators of Sissinghurst that they are today best jointly known. He is also remembered and read as one of the finest diarists of the century, and her unconventional love-life has recently attracted a great deal of attention. My intention in writing this essay was to get behind the plants and the personalities, the buddleias and the bed-hopping, to try to set Nicolson and Sackville-West in a broader historical perspective. I wanted to see them in the context of their very different and very influential family histories; to look at Nicolson as the patrician and diplomat he always at heart remained; to read Sackville-West's works as she had written them, as an aristocrat and a countrywoman; and to try to understand why they were so snobbish and self-satisfied, yet at the same time so aware that they were both, ultimately, second-rate. The resulting essay may make them appear less heroically individualistic; but I believe it also makes them more interesting and historically credible figures.

These, then, are my nine aristocratic essays. They could be read to bear out a remark made by one of Tom Stoppard's characters in *Arcadia*: 'with scholarly articles as with divorce, there is a certain cachet in citing a member of the aristocracy'.[1] But that is not how or why they have been composed or collected. They have been written with a mixture of sympathy and detachment, with sceptical interest and ironic fascination, and I hope they bear witness to the continuing importance of aristocracy in modern British history and modern British historiography, to the many forms and varieties which aristocracy has always assumed, and to some of the different approaches which need to be adopted if aristocracy is to be treated in a satisfactorily scholarly way. I have enjoyed writing these essays, and I hope that by turns they will inform, entertain, stimulate and (just occasionally) provoke. And if, in addition, they encourage other historians to delve more deeply and more originally into the modern British aristocracy, they will more than have fulfilled their purpose.

PART ONE

PROCESSES AND PROBLEMS

I

The Making of the
British Upper Classes

DURING THE LAST TEN YEARS OR SO, it has become commonplace to argue that between the restoration of the monarchy in 1660 and the outbreak of the First World War, something called the 'old regime' survived and persisted in England much more successfully than was previously supposed.[1] Instead of stressing, as had an earlier generation of scholars, the inexorably declining aristocracy, the inevitably rising middle class, and the proletariat actively making itself in the furnace-fire of the Industrial Revolution, historians have become increasingly impressed by the resilience of the traditional landowning elite, by the weaknesses and divisions of the bourgeoisie, and by a working class which never fulfilled the heroic revolutionary role that Marx had prescribed and predicted for it. In many ways this is a salutary change of interpretation and emphasis: it helps to explain some things about the history of England during the last three centuries which were otherwise unclear; and it has brought the aristocracy to the centre of the historiographical stage, which is where it belongs, and where it should remain.

But these largely undifferentiated notions of patrician 'persistence' and aristocratic 'survival' are not without their own difficulties.[2] In the first place, they tend to be myopically Anglocentric, ignoring the separate but increasingly convergent histories of the aristocracies of Wales, Scotland and Ireland, and indifferent to the claims of *British* history, claims which have been advanced with considerable cogency and conviction in recent years.[3] By definition, the traditional territorial classes owned most of the land, not just of England, but also of the rest of the British Isles. To be sure, it is possible to write distinct – and distinguished – histories of these separate English, Welsh, Scottish and Irish landed establishments. But by the nineteenth century, the men and women who belonged to them had no doubt that they belonged also to something bigger and broader called the British aristocracy, and they were quite correct to believe that they did. Yet the history of the formation and the functioning of that integrated and supranational class remains largely unwritten, at least before the last quarter of the nineteenth century.

This leads, in turn, to a second objection to the approach which stresses 'persistence' and 'survival', namely that it is insufficiently sensitive to the many ways in which the traditional landed elites actually developed and evolved over time. Of course, the balance between continuity and change is never easy to strike, and it has certainly been valuable to stress the tenacity of the so-called old regime to a greater degree than was once fashionable. But there is a danger in giving, as a result, too static, too un-nuanced, and too uninflected a picture, which unthinkingly accepts the aristocracy's own (and often deliberately misleading) self-image of antiquity and permanence, and which thus fails to recognise its remarkable capacity to renew, to re-create and to re-invent itself over time. This essay seeks to investigate one such crucial period of renewal, re-creation and re-invention, which lasted from the 1780s to the 1820s, and which not only saw a remarkable series of changes in the English aristocracy, but also witnessed the creation of a truly British titled and territorial class.

It hardly needs saying that the era of the American War of Independence, of the climacteric conflicts with France, and of the Industrial Revolution was a challenging time for landowners throughout the British Isles. Their dominance was threatened at home and abroad. There were alarms and anxieties aplenty, of which Edmund Burke's renditions were undoubtedly the most eloquent and influential.[4] But as radicals like Thomas Paine, John Wade and William Cobbett recognised and constantly complained, the great landowners and the country gentlemen were in fact doing very well for themselves.[5] As R.R. Palmer was later to argue, Britain was the most successful counter-revolutionary nation in Europe, where 'the elites of birth, rank, wealth and fashion, of government, the church, the army and navy, of the universities, the law and the learned professions' fused 'into a generalised upper class'.[6] Put another way, it was precisely the years between the American Declaration of Independence and the introduction of the Great Reform Bill which saw the landowners of England, Wales, Scotland and Ireland become more rich, more powerful, more status-conscious and more unified. In short, these were the decades which saw the making of the British upper classes.

I

One fundamental reason for this was that between the 1780s and the 1820s the structure of landownership in the British Isles changed significantly, and those lucky enough to consolidate, to possess or to acquire broad acres found themselves enjoying unprecedented prosperity. To begin with, there was a marked trend towards territorial amalgamation, sometimes in particular localities, sometimes in massive supra-national empires, the effect of which was that the hitherto separate territorial elites of England, Ireland, Scotland and Wales gradually merged into a new, authentically British landed class. The process whereby this transformation occured was neither simple nor deliberately planned. Suffice it to say that it was largely the consequence of the demographic crisis which had hit landowners through-out the British Isles during the first half of the eighteenth century.[7] The result was that many ancient families died out in the male line (something, incidentally, which William Cobbett deeply lamented),[8] there was an unprecedented number of heiresses on the marriage market, and estates were consolidated in the hands of a smaller number of landowners. This, in turn, gave rise to a territorial elite which was more wealthy, more cosmo-politan and more British in its circumstances and its outlook.

Such a transformation has been traced in counties from Essex to Merioneth, Yorkshire to Anglesey, as old families died out, and their estates passed, via the female line, to other dynasties which often lived far away.[9] As heiresses were obliged – or encouraged – to marry more distantly and more adventurously, the result was the consolidation of extended territorial empires, often straddling the borders of England, Scotland, Ireland and Wales.[10] In the case of Glamorgan, the demographic decline of the ancient Tudor and Stuart gentry meant that the county elite was both re-made and supra-nationalised during the reign of George III. One by one, Glamorgan estates passed by marriage to major out-of-county landowners, such as the Butes, the Dunravens, the Dynevors and the Windsors. All these families already held land in England, and some were major owners in Scotland and Ireland also. The result of such mergers was to incorporate the Glamorgan elite into the new British elite. Put another way, this meant that one half of the great nineteenth-century owners in the county had entered it only between 1760 and 1810, by marrying heiresses of older but now extinct families. In short, the old, localised, Welsh-speaking gentry had been replaced by a new, supra-national British aristocracy.

As estates were brought together in this way, this also led to the creation of a distinct group of new super-rich grandees, at the very apex of the structure of British landownership. The Dukes of Norfolk found their English holdings twice augmented by inheritance – in 1777 on the death of the ninth duke, and again in 1815 on the death of the eleventh duke, since both were without direct male heirs, and the ducal titles and estates passed to collateral branches of the family already endowed with their own lands. The Dukes of Buccleuch inherited the estates of the Douglas family in 1810, which enhanced their position as Scottish super-powers, and meant they also acquired extensive estates in England.[11] Some Irish families were equally successful. The future second Marquess of Downshire made a spectacularly successful marriage in 1786 to Mary Sandys, which eventually extended the family's Irish holdings by nearly twenty thousand acres, and also brought them English estates in Worcestershire and Berkshire. Their great rivals, the Londonderrys, did equally well, for in 1819 the future third Marquess married Frances Anne Vane-Tempest, thereby linking his lands in Ireland with her acres and colleries in Durham. But the greatest heiress hunters were the Butes, who successfully ensnared four in three generations, and so piled estate on estate in England, Scotland and Wales.[12]

The Butes were not the only once-obscure family who transformed themselves, through successful marriages, into transnational territorialists of the first rank. In 1752 the second Earl Temple inherited estates, including stowe, from his mother; in 1788 his nephew, who had succeeded him as third earl, inherited lands in Ireland, Essex and Cornwall from his father-in-law; and in 1796 the third earl married off his son to the daughter and heiress of the third Duke of Chandos, who would one day inherit lands in Hampshire, Queen's County, Somerset and Jamaica.[13] The Leveson-Gowers were equally fortunate. In 1785, the third Earl Gower, already a substantial landowner in Staffordshire and Shropshire, married the Countess of Sutherland, who brought with her more than eight hundred thousand acres from her titular county in the Scottish Highlands. From 1803 until 1833 the family also enjoyed the massive income from the Bridgewater Trust, thanks to an earlier marriage as far back as 1748 between the second Earl Gower and Lady Louisa Egerton.[14] With the Leveson-Gowers as with other families, the impact of earlier inheritance often made itself felt only at the end of the eighteenth century and at the beginning of the nineteenth.

This process of amalgamation and internationalisation was both inexorable and cumulative, and in consequence a genuinely British landed elite came into being at this time on the ruins of a decaying local squirearchy. But not all estates passed by inheritance when the male line died out. In some cases, there were no relatives of either sex, however distant, to whom the lands could pass, in which case the estate would be put on the market. And there were many old – and new – men of wealth who were able and willing to buy. In Norfolk, it was reported that between 1809 and 1812, 'a number of characters in high life . . . , peers, courtiers, statesmen, nabobs, royal physicians, naval and military commanders', were purchasing their way in as estates came up for sale. Contrary to what was once thought, the late-eighteenth and early-nineteenth-century land market seems to have been a busy one. Indeed, so great was the demand for land during this period that it outstripped supply, and the price was driven up from 23 to 28 years' purchase between the 1780s and the 1800s. 'Terramania' was the name popularly given to this phenomenon.[15]

The catalogue of Norfolk buyers was well composed, aptly enumerating those who, by acquisition rather than by inheritance, were further changing the structure of British landholding. There were rich landowners, extending their estates, like the first Lord Dudley, the Strutts of Terling, and Coke of Norfolk. There were self-made men of commerce and industry: the Guests, Crawshays and Baileys in Glamorgan; merchants and Indian 'nabobs' in Renfrewshire; Samuel Whitbread in Bedfordshire;

the Peels at Tamworth; and the Arkwrights in Herefordshire.[16] And there were the men who had done the state some service, who received ample financial reward, and who ploughed much of it into the land. Lord Eldon spent £500,000 building up a great estate in the north of England, and the Duke of Wellington lavished a similar amount on the purchase of Stratfield Saye in Hampshire. Lord Nelson's elder brother spent the £100,000 posthumously voted to the hero of Trafalgar on a place in Wiltshire. Lords Exmouth and St Vincent survived to enjoy the lands they had acquired, and even Lord Sidmouth managed to accumulate enough money to hand on to his descendants an estate as well as a title.[17]

One of the reasons why land was being bought so eagerly at this time was that the wars with France brought unprecedented prosperity to agriculture throughout the British Isles. From the 1790s, the price of wheat rose impressively and inexorably: forty-five shillings a quarter in 1789, eighty-four shillings by 1800, and it averaged one hundred and two shillings between 1810 and 1814 – prices never attained before, and never equalled since. On English estates, rentals increased by between seventy and ninety per cent. In Wales, they rose by at least sixty per cent, and sometimes by almost three times that much. In Ireland, the increase averaged ninety per cent, and in Scotland it was probably eightfold between 1750 and 1815.[18] Thanks to this 'unexampled prosperity', the economic experiences of landowners throughout the British Isles became increasingly uniform, as the incomes of the previously poorer Celtic proprietors began to catch up with those of their English cousins; and even during the post-Waterloo slump, most of the burden of falling prices was borne by the farmers and the labourers, and rentals settled down in the late 1820s at roughly double the pre-1790 figure.[19]

Consolidated estates and enhanced rentals not only served to merge and mould the historically-separate landed elites of England, Scotland, Ireland and Wales into an increasingly prosperous and increasingly homogeneous British territorial class: they also provided the opportunity and the incentive for landowners throughout the British Isles to act as major agents in agricultural change. During the first three-quarters of the eighteenth century, large farmers had been in the vanguard of improvement in England, while on the still-impoverished Celtic fringe there had been little activity to report. But from the 1780s to the 1820s the picture changed dramatically as landowners throughout Britain, driven by the competitive desire to increase their incomes, sought to make agriculture more progressive and more profitable. The structure of tenure was fundamentally altered; there was a shift from communal to individual husbandry; and heaths, moors, commons and wastes were sub-divided into separate holdings.[20] In short, a new British elite was promoting a new British agriculture.

For English landowners, the main instrument of agricultural change was parliamentary enclosure. Between 1760 and 1780, there were only nine hundred acts passed; but from 1793 to 1815 there were two thousand, as well as many private agreements which, like the acts themselves, were usually the result of the local landowner taking the initiative. Farms were rationalised, spending on drainage was increased, crops and rotation were more carefully controlled, and the cultivated area was extended, all of which resulted in increased output, enhanced productivity and augmented rental.[21] In Wales, agriculture was more backward and capital less abundant, which gave even greater scope for landowners – aware of fashions and developments in England – to play a major role. As in England, there was a marked upsurge in parliamentary enclosure in the 1790s and 1800s. Large areas of waste, common and sheep-walks were taken over, walled in, and became private property. Landowners like Sir Watkyn Williams Wynn, Sir Stephen Glynn and Lord Penrhyn invested heavily in improved drainage, better breeding and new crops. They sponsored agricultural societies, gave prizes at agricultural shows and, in the case of Thomas Johnes of Hafod, wrote improving agricultural manuals.[22]

In Ireland, the changes were on the same scale, and again resulted from the landlords' desire to create a more rational, more efficient, more capitalistic agriculture. As in England and Wales, great magnates like Lords Donegall, Hertford and Downshire were pioneers in improved breeding, cultivation and drainage. In Ulster, the landlords reclaimed waste, drained bogs, promoted the new husbandry, and instituted shorter leases. A series of Ejectment Acts passed between 1816 and 1820 gave landlords sweeping powers of eviction to help them create a more efficient and capitalistic agriculture.[23] The same was true in Scotland, where owner-led improvement advanced from the southern uplands, via the central lowlands, to the highlands themselves, culminating in the notorious 'clearances'. The Duke of Argyll presided over the Highland Society of Edinburgh, which was founded in 1784 to promote agricultural improvement. Sir John Sinclair, the author of the *Statistical Account of Scotland*, was from 1793 President of the Board of Agriculture. And by the 1800s, the Sutherlands, Breadalbanes, Montroses, Lovats, Hamiltons and Camerons began to transform their vast highland holdings into large-scale sheep farms.[24]

Viewed in this broader British perspective, the Highland clearances were but English enclosure writ large, writ Scotch and writ controversially – the local variation of the general impulse which gripped landowners throughout the British Isles at this time: to improve, to rationalise, to increase profits. In this period, agriculture remained the flywheel of the British economy, and it was the initiative and investment of the landlords which made that flywheel go round. But there was more to the efficient exploitation of broad acres than agricultural improvement. During the classical age of the Industrial Revolution, a great deal of activity centred on the non-agricultural exploitation of the land: getting minerals from underneath it, building docks and harbours on the edge of it, cutting canals through it, and constructing houses on top of it. For British landowners, increasingly alert to new investment opportunities, it was but a short step from agricultural to industrial development. Once again it was often enclosure which was the essential pre-condition. It confirmed mineral rights, it rationalised surface boundaries, which made for more efficient exploitation of the resources beneath, and it divided up common rights to the advantage of the largest owner.[25]

The greatest mineral resource to which ownership and enclosure gave access was coal, most of which was to be found below ground held by the aristocracy. In Scotland, the Duke of Buccleuch was dominant in Midlothian and Dumfries, the Duke of Hamilton in Lanark, and the Duke of Portland in Ayrshire.[26] In Wales, the Marquess of Bute and Lord Windsor were the major owners of the Glamorgan coalfield. In England, the Dudleys, Dartmouths, Hathertons, Sutherlands, Portlands, Rutlands and Clevelands were supreme in the Midlands; the Derbys, Seftons and Crawfords in Lancashire; the Norfolks, Devonshires and Fitzwilliams in Yorkshire; and the Londonderrys, Wharncliffes, Scarbroughs and Durhams in the north-east.[27] Between 1775 and 1830, the output of coal in Britain soared from nine to thirty million tons. Much of the investment which made this possible was undertaken by the landowners, as families like the Fitzwilliams, the Lonsdales and the Lambtons committed large capital sums. And there can be no doubt that it paid. The Duke of Northumberland's revenue from coal royalties increased tenfold between 1790 and 1830. By the 1800s the Dudleys were drawing £17,500 and the Lonsdales £30,000 a year. And not for nothing was the first Earl of Durham known as 'His Carbonic Majesty'.[28]

The products of coal mines, like the products of farms, needed transporting, and this led many British patricians to play a prominent part in transport innovation and investment. The first large-scale canal had been built between 1759 and 1763 by James Brindley for the Duke of Bridgewater, so that an aristocrat could ship his coals. And where Bridgewater led, other landowners followed. Between 1776 and 1785, Lord Dudley was the driving force behind the Stourbridge Navigation, the Dudley Canal and the Dudley Tunnel, all of which were designed to make it easier to move his minerals to market.[29] When the Grand Junction Canal was floated in 1793, the promoters included the Marquess of Buckingham, the Duke of Grafton, and the Earls of Clarendon and of Exeter. But as transport moguls, they were far surpassed by the Marquess of Stafford, who not only drew a massive income from the Bridgewater Canal Trust, averaging considerably more than £45,000 a year between 1806 and 1826, but also invested heavily (and profitably) in the Birmingham and Liverpool Junction Canal and the new Liverpool and Manchester Railway. By the mid 1820s, he was indisputably the greatest – and richest – transport magnate in the country.[30]

As with agriculture, so with minerals and transport, the greater the distance from London, the greater the part played by the landowners. In north Wales, the promotors and shareholders of both the Ellesmere Canal and the Montgomery Canal included most of the local notables: the Duke of Bridgewater, Sir Watkyn Williams Wynn, Lord Powis and Lord Clive. In south Wales, it was Lord Bute who decided, in 1825, to finance and construct Cardiff Docks, a decision which was to have momentous consequences for the region. In Ireland, the local grandees were no less in evidence as initiators and subscribers of local projects: the Marquess of Abercorn (the Strabane Canal), the Duke of Devonshire (Lismore Canal), the Marquess of Downshire (Newry Navigation), the Marquess of Donegall (Lagan Navigation), and Lords Drogheda and Lansdowne (the Grand and the Royal Canals).[31] In Scotland, the Earl of Eglinton, a major Ayrshire coal owner, built a canal and harbour at Ardrossan. The Duke of Buccleuch constructed his own port at Rosyth. The Duke of Argyll built sea walls, a harbour and a fishery on the island of Tiree, and was also a leading figure in the British Fisheries Society, the purpose of which was to establish ports and harbours along the Highland coast.[32]

From the fishing villages of Sutherlandshire to the squares and stucco of Belgravia, Britain's landowners were also closely and lucratively involved in the urbanisation process, and this at a time when towns and cities were expanding throughout the British Isles, thanks to the unprecedented growth of population and the economy, as never before. In Ireland and in Scotland, landowners took the initiative in the planning and construction of estate villages, and their activity was at its peak between the 1780s and the 1820s.[33] In the provinces, the Calthorpes (Birmingham), the Norfolks (Sheffield), the Pembrokes and Longfords (Dublin), the Butes and Windsors (Cardiff), and the Derbys and Seftons (Liverpool), were only the most famous ground landlords of what soon became extremely valuable building estates. In London much of the West End took shape in this period, again under aristocratic auspices: Thomas Cubitt completed Bloomsbury for the Bedfords, and developed Belgravia and Pimlico for the Grosvenors, and nearby the Portlands and Portmans began to turn their country fields into city streets. As a result, these families were soon drawing tens of thousands of pounds a year from ground rents, which helped make them among the richest aristocrats in the country.[34]

As John Wade, the author of *The Black Book*, rightly pointed out, 'whatever tended to enhance the value of land directly augments aristocratic incomes', and the period from the 1780s to the 1820s saw aristocratic incomes, throughout the length and breadth of the British Isles, being augmented by this means to an altogether remarkable extent. The degree to which the British aristocracy should be praised (or blamed) for their contribution (or lack of it) to agricultural improvement and industrial development remains a source of controversy among economic historians.[35] But for historians of the aristocracy, the important point is that at this time more landowners were more involved in the more profitable exploitation of their estates than ever before. Coming to advantageous terms with both the agricultural and the industrial revolutions was one of the most distinctive characteristics of the new British territorial elite which was gradually forming during these years. To a much greater extent than had been true of their predecessors, these great proprietors were capitalists and commercial potentates of the first rank.

But John Wade's main aim, in the pages of *The Black Book*, was not so much to draw attention to the much-enhanced revenues enjoyed by the landowners directly and indirectly from their estates. Rather, he was concerned to show how many of them were augmenting their burgeoning incomes still further from the pensions, prizes and sinecures which aristocratic governments awarded to themselves. For radical critics, 'Old Corruption' was the most unacceptable aspect of patrician pre-eminence: a rapacious aristocracy, 'a prodigious band of spongers', irresponsibly feasting off the state at the taxpayer's expense – men like the Duke of St Albans, who enjoyed £2000 a year as Hereditary Grand Falconer, and Lord Auckland who drew £1900 per annum as Auditor of Greenwich Hospital.[36] One explanation for this may be the dominance, between 1783 and 1830, of the Tory Party, many of whose members were drawn from among the lower echelons of the landed classes, and were particularly keen to augment their wealth. But it also seems clear that the radical critics overstated the extent to which Old Corruption thrived: much of their information was inaccurate, misleading or out of date.[37]

Nevertheless, there can be no doubt that a certain segment of the aristocracy did extemely well for themselves in these years out of what remained of Old Corruption. Second-ranking commanders from the French wars, such as St Vincent, Collingwood and Duncan, received pensions of £3000 a year. In the aftermath of Trafalgar, Nelson's elder brother was given a parliamentary grant of £100,000, and a pension of £5000 which was paid every year to his descendants until 1947. The Duke of Wellington was given £600,000 by a grateful nation, and his brothers were also well rewarded: William drew £12,450 a Master of the Mint and Joint Remembrancer of the Court of the Exchequer; Henry was Ambassador to Madrid at a salary of £10,000; and Richard saved £100,000 while Governor General of India, and received a pension of £5000.[38] Less deserving – though scarcely less successful – than the Wellesleys were the Grenvilles, and the members of that extended clan were drawing more than £20,000 a year in sinecures and pensions during the 1800s. As *The Black Book* put it, with perhaps pardonable exaggeration, 'within the last thirty years . . . the Grenville and Wellesley families must have absorbed each at least one million and a half or two millions of public money'.[39]

From this account of territorial aggrandisement and acquisition, increased income from rentals, the non-agricultural exploitation of estate resources, and the profits and perquisites of Old Corruption, two points bear emphasising and repeating. The first is the growing uniformity of landowners' economic experience, behaviour and outlook, throughout the British Isles. The second is the remarkable extent to which their incomes were being enlarged and augmented. Among the middlingly well-off, landowners still impressively outnumbered those whose wealth came from other sources. It was also in this period that the landed super-rich consolidated their unrivalled position as the wealth elite, which they were to maintain for the next half-century.[40] The most opulent of their number was the first Duke of Sutherland, whose income derived from investments in Consols, canals and railways, from massive estates in England and Scotland, and from the Bridgewater Trustees. As Charles Greville correctly observed on his demise in 1833, 'He was a leviathan of wealth. I do believe he was the richest man who ever died.'[41]

II

In what became, during this period, the unified aristocratic kingdom of Great Britain and Ireland, land was not only wealth: it was also power. And just as a new British wealth elite was formed out of the old and separate territorial orders of England, Scotland, Ireland and Wales, so a correspondingly new British power elite came into being as well. In terms of parliamentary representation, as in terms of estate accumulation, the trend throughout the British Isles was emphatically towards the enhancement of patrician importance. As English landowners became richer, and consolidated their estates, they tightened their hold on the rotten boroughs. In 1761, 224 such seats were influenced by patrons; by 1790 the figure was still rising. At the same time, a limited number of landed families came to monopolise the representation of county constituencies as varied as Warwickshire and Huntingdonshire, Sussex and Wiltshire.[42] Many of these were traditional gentry. But by the 1790s and the 1800s there was growing criticism of the high-handed way in which aristocratic families were increasingly intruding into the county constituencies as well as the boroughs; and what was true for England also held good for Wales.[43]

In Scotland, by contrast, the system created by the Act of Union in 1707 was already so exclusive that it could scarcely become more so. By the 1750s, the total Scottish electorate was only 2662 for 33 counties, and 1250 for the 15 burghs. Landed control was overwhelming, but it was still Scottish rather than British. The merging of this oligarchic representational structure with that of England was duly accomplished for the younger Pitt at the end of the century by Sir Henry Dundas. By 1784, he was already the master of 22 seats, and during the next ten years he won over some of the greatest Scottish peers, including Buccleuch (Midlothian), Fife

(Aberdeen), and Eglinton (Ayr). By 1796, only nine Scottish MPs were outside his power, and neither Pitt's demise nor Dundas's subsequent disgrace threatened the machine thus created: from 1807 to 1827, it was run by his son, the second Lord Melville, who controlled 24 out of 45 MPs. Thus were the Scottish landowners, who dominated their representational system, incorporated into the broader British political elite.[44]

It was essentially the same story in Ireland. In the pre-Union parliaments, the trend towards oligarchy was as pronounced as in England and Wales, and between 1777 and 1800 electoral influence was concentrated in the hands of fewer landowners than at any previous time, of whom the Elys, Shannons, Beresfords and Downshires were pre-eminent.[45] In 1785, a Belfast petition noted that the 'Commons House' was 'distrusted by the nation', because it had 'become the representative of an overbearing aristocracy'. Pitt's decision, thirteen years later, to promote Anglo-Irish Union may be seen in this context as the culmination of the century-long tendency in Irish politics and representation towards oligarchy. Sixty-four borough seats were abolished so as to merge the landed polity of Ireland with Britain. Borough proprietors were generously compensated: Downshire received £52,000 for the loss of seven seats, Ely £45,000 for six, Shannon £37,000 for five, and Granard, Belmore, Clifden, Devonshire and Abercorn £30,000 for four each. Pruned of its most venal boroughs, and grafted on to the British Parliament, the Irish electoral system went on very much as before: of the hundred MPs returned to the British House of Commons, seventy-one were controlled by patrician proprietors.[46]

In short, the combination of demography, territorial accumulation, increased wealth, political management, and the Act of Union resulted in a representational structure which became more exclusive and more British between the 1780s and the 1800s. It is worth stressing three features of this new, supra-national political system. In the first place it was extremely Anglocentric: of the 658 MPs in the post-1801 British House of Commons, 24 represented Wales, 45 Scotland, 100 Ireland, and the remainder (489) England. In the second place, it was a system over which the electorate wielded minimal (and declining) influence: by 1800, scarcely one adult in ten voted in England and Wales, one in twenty in Ireland, and fewer than one in a hundred in Scotland.[47] But in the third place, while the power of the electorate diminished, the power of the landowners further increased. Contemporaries were clear, and correct, in believing that it was growing throughout the closing decades of the eighteenth century, and in 1816 T.H.B. Oldfield calculated that 140 peers and 120 commoners influenced or determined the return of almost three-quarters of the lower house. Far from representing the majority of the people, the Commons was increasingly representing only the patricians: over three-quarters of all MPs had close landed connections.[48]

More precisely, the Commons was increasingly representing the peers. In part this was because the new, supra-national grandees developed appropriately supra-national networks of nomination. The Butes were influential both in their titular county in Scotland, and in Cardiff boroughs in Glamorgan. The Sutherlands nominated two MPs in the north of Scotland, and also five in Staffordshire. It was also because some great titled families used their increased wealth to buy up boroughs. The eleventh Duke of Norfolk controlled only four MPs in 1784, but by 1796 he controlled nine. In 1774, the much-sinecured and much-titled Buckinghams had only three seats in their gift, but by 1818 they boasted seven.[49] And the influence of the nobility in the lower house was further increased as a result of Pitt's policy of giving peerages to commoner borough-mongers. Between 1784 and 1801, he ennobled 21 men who dominated 41 seats. Some were relatively minor figures, like Sir Henry Gough-Calthorpe, who controlled one seat at Hindon in Wiltshire and another at Bramber in Sussex, and was created Lord Calthorpe in 1796. But others operated on a much larger scale, the most famous being Sir James Lowther, who returned nine MPs (known as the 'ninepins') and was made Earl of Lonsdale in 1784.[50]

Inevitably, as the peerage became more powerful, and as the more powerful commoners became peers, the result was a lower house increasingly full, not only of the clients, but also of the relatives, of the members of the upper house. In 1734, only 13 per cent of MPs were sons of peers; but by the 1800s the figure was 22 per cent; and after the 1826 election it reached its peak of 25 per cent.[51] If more distant relatives of peers are included, the trend was even more pronounced: in 1820, according to *The Black Book*, 222 MPs, or one-third of the house, were related to the peerage. 'If it be an infringement', it observed, 'of the privileges of the Commons for peers to interfere in the election of members, it must be a higher infringement of their liberties to thrust their relatives into the House itself.' For, as John Cartwright explained (and complained), this meant there were 'two hereditary houses of parliament instead of one'.[52]

The result was an overwhelmingly propertied and patrician polity: as William Cobbett lamented, with only slight exaggeration, there was 'one house filled wholly with landowners, and the other four fifths filled with their relatives'.[53] Yet it was not just that the peerage increasingly dominated the Commons, both by nomination and by connection. It was also that, as a result, they were as pre-eminent in the executive as in the legislature. Of the great political leaders of this period who served in the Commons, Pitt, Fox, Perceval, Castlereagh and Grey were all younger sons of peers: only Addington and Canning were outsiders – and their careers and reputations suffered accordingly. Pitt's second administration of 1804, and Perceval's of 1809, were entirely composed of peers and sons of peers. Liverpool's government was the first to be led successfully for long periods from the Lords, but as such was very much a portent of things to come. In 1830, every former Prime Minister still living was in the upper house: Grenville, Sidmouth, Goderich and Wellington; and nine former Foreign Secretaries were there as well. Even Earl Grey's cabinet, the great reforming act, contained thirteen peers or sons of peers, and one commoner who was also a major landowner.[54]

Here was a formidable concentration and consolidation of political power in the hands of the landowning classes – exactly reflecting, and in part brought about by, their formidable concentration and consolidation of territorial power.[55] Inevitably, this resulted in some blatant examples of self-interested class legislation, the most notorious being the Game Laws, which reserved to the grandees and gentry the right to kill a wide range of animals and birds, and which became progressively more severe from the 1770s. In 1803 the Ellenborough Act made resisting arrest for poaching a capital offence, and between 1816 and 1827 additional legislation made them even more savage.[56] Equally self-interested were the Corn Laws. For many land-owners, flushed with high rents in the boom years of the 1800s, the prospect of falling prices in the next decade was alarming. In 1815, they forced Lord Liverpool to pass a measure which meant that no foreign corn could be imported until the domestic price reached eighty shillings a quarter. Whatever may have been the Prime Minister's intention, the pressure of the aristocracy meant that there was no substantial modification until 1828. 'Perish commerce, let the landed interest live!', was how one radical summed it up.[57]

With the structure of representation, the personnel of government, and the pattern of legislation so dominated by the British landowners, it almost inevitably followed that they would also control the administration of the state. But there were other reasons why this was so, and became more so, at this time. In the aftermath of the demographic crisis, the size of landed families increased during the later eighteenth century, which meant that the number of patricians seeking jobs also went up.[58] Moreover, these were not just the well-born of England, but also those from Ireland, Scotland and Wales, who saw in state service one of the best opportunities of consolidating their position as members of the new British upper class. At the same time, the unprecedented challenges of war and peace led to the creation of a new ethos among these genteel state servants. In a manner conspicuously different from their forebears, they were trained from an early age to take their place among the ruling elite: at public school, at Oxford and Cambridge, and at the Inns of Court. They wore military uniforms or plain, well-cut civilian clothes, and they saw themselves as men of affairs, disinterestedly and heroically doing their best for the country.[59]

From the 1780s to the 1820s, they had ample scope to display such new-found virtues. To begin with, the state bureaucracy underwent massive and irreversible expansion as a result of wartime pressures and demands. Between 1784 and 1794, the Home Office was established, the

Board of Trade revived, and the Secretaryship of War resurrected. From 1783 to 1815, the amount of work done at the Treasury increased seven-fold, and the number of positions available went up at a corresponding rate. The Colonial Office expanded under Lord Bathurst between 1815 and 1827, as it took over the administration of seventeen new colonies retained after the war with France. But this enlargement of the government bu-reaucracy took place within the traditional framework of aristocratic patronage and family connection, which meant that the new recruits were drawn, as their predecessors had been, from among the relatives, friends and clients of the aristocracy. The civil service remained a patrician pre-serve. Indeed, for men like Lord Grenville, the Duke of Portland, Lord Howick or Spencer Perceval, much of the appeal of high office was the patronage which it gave them.[60]

Landed participation – and preponderance – was even more marked in the armed forces. Fighting was the aristocratic profession par excellence, and between the 1790s and the 1810s there was a great deal of it to be done, not just in Europe, but throughout the world. As a result, more patricians than ever were involved in both the armed services. In the Navy, the number of officers rose from 1800 to 8400 between 1792 and 1826, and 40 per cent came from landed backgrounds, a higher proportion than before or since. In the Army, the officer corps increased from 2000 in 1780 to 19,000 by 1823, but the proportion with landed connections actually went up, from 40 per cent to 53 per cent. And at the very top, patrician dominance was even greater.[61] Between 1750 and 1800, 124 peers and sons of peers had served in the Life Guards, the Blues, the First Foot Guards and the Scots Guards. During the next half century, 228 did so. Of the fifteen generals who obtained peerages in the reign of George III, eleven were from noble or landed backgrounds; and in 1830, 78 per cent of all generals were from aristocratic or landed families. 'My notion of the army', observed the future King William IV, 'is very aristocratic. I wish to have all the men of fashion brought forward in the service. The country is safest when they are engaged in it.'[62]

But it was not just that the aristocracy and country gentry were doing the state some service – indeed, more service – than ever before. It was also that they were increasingly drawn, not only from England, but from through-out the British Isles. Indeed, it was the influx of Celtic landowners and their relatives which was the most pronounced phenomenon, and which further helped to consolidate the new, and genuinely British, power elite. In Wales, almost all the members of the surviving resident Glamorgan gentry could boast a general or an admiral in their family by the 1790s, something that would not have been so two generations before. Among Anglo-Irish families, the Wellesleys provided the most famous dynasty of well-placed (and well-rewarded) state servants: Arthur was a soldier and subsequently a politician, Richard was a proconsul, and Henry an ambassador.[63] And from Scotland, the demand for jobs was equally as great, which helps to explain how Henry Dundas, in his capacity as President of the Board of Control, brought about what Lord Rosebery memorably described as 'the Scottisization of India'. As Dundas explained to Sir Archibald Campbell, the Governor of Madras, 'It is said that with a Scotchman at the head of the Board of Control, and a Scotchman at the Government of Madras, all India will soon be in their hands.' He was not far wrong, for overseas jobs were as sought after by British patricians as home postings.[64]

By the late eighteenth century, almost all the major diplomatic posts abroad were held by well-connected Scotsmen, such as Sir Robert Murray Keith in Vienna, Sir William Hamilton in Naples, and Sir Robert Ainslie at Constantinople. One Earl of Seaforth died at sea on his way to India with his regiment in 1781; his heir expired in India two years later of wounds received in a battle with the Marhattas; and his successor became a colonial governor in the West Indies. Before he went as Ambassador to Constantinople in 1799, and became embroiled with the marbles to which he gave his name, the Earl of Elgin had already been on diplomatic missions to Vienna, Brussels and Prussia. The Earl of Aberdeen led a mission to Vienna to re-open diplomatic relations in 1813.[65] Sir John Sinclair, having completed his *Statistical Account of Scotland*, sought to get himself appointed Governor of the Cape of Good Hope in 1813. He did not succeed. But many others did: Lord Charles Somerset in South Africa, Lord William Cavendish-Bentinck in Madras, and Sir Charles Fitzroy in the Leeward Islands. Indeed, during the early nineteenth century, the government of the British Empire was patrician in personnel and grandiose in style to a degree that was not to be seen again until the 1880s and 1890s.[66]

It was not only the British state, the British armed forces, and the British Empire in which there was a marked aristocratic resurgence at this time. Some notables rose to the highest level in the Church of England, thereby tying it more closely to the establishment than ever before. From the Restoration to the middle of the eighteenth century, most bishops had been of relatively humble origin; but during the reign of George III, and especially the second half, the number of patrician prelates dramatically increased. Between 1660 and 1790, only 39 per cent of bishops were from landed backgrounds; but from 1791 to 1830, the figure was nearly 60 per cent.[67] Here was the Church of England newly established as an out-work of the aristocracy. The see of Durham was occupied successively by relatives of the Duke of Bridgewater, Lord Thurlow, and Lord Barrington. In 1805, a grandson of the third Duke of Rutland was made Archbishop of Canterbury, and two years later a younger son of Lord Vernon was appointed Archbishop of York. George III was especially pleased: 'He judged fitness for high station', noted Lord Holland, 'by rank rather than by talent, and he hailed the appointment of two archbishops, who from their connexions he called gentlemen, as a triumph for the church and a consolation for himself.'[68]

Lower down the ecclesiastical hierarchy, there was an equally unprecedented merging of the church and the state, the spiritual and the temporal, the ecclesiastical and the landed interests. Enclosure made many livings more attractive, rectories were extended and rebuilt, and it became increasingly common for the local landowner to appoint one of his younger sons to the living in his gift. The most impressive evidence of this new convergence was the growth in the number of clerical magistrates in England and Wales. As late as the 1760s, fewer than ten per cent of JPs were clergymen; but by the early nineteenth century, clerics provided nearly one quarter of the bench.[69]. They were firmly on the side of property, patriotism and order. According to Cobbett, the clergy had 'laid down the Bible, and taken up the statute book'. Put another way, this new alliance between church and state, mediated and promoted by the exercise of aristocratic patronage, was central to the making of the new and extended British upper class. As William Scott explained, comfortable livings were now 'family provisions for the sons of nobility and gentry' who, having entered the church, 'connect the safety of its interests with those of other great establishments of our ancient constitution'.[70]

As the growth in the number of patrician clergymen and clerical magistrates suggests, the final realm of activity which saw the increasing assimilation of English, Welsh, Scottish and Irish landowners into the new British territorial elite was that of local government. By the late eighteenth century, they were more actively involved than they had been in generations. During the stresses and strains of the Napoleonic Wars, the responsibility for order and for local defence rested entirely upon them. An English grandee like the Duke of Northumberland found the powers and burdens of local administration so great that he refused to consider any offer of a position in London.[71] The concentration of local influence in a Welsh landowner like Thomas Johnes of Hafod was equally impressive: in Cardiganshire he was a major landowner, county MP, and Lord Lieutenant; and in Carmarthen, he was head of the militia, which he clothed and fitted out at his own expense. In 1793, a militia was set up in Ireland, to be followed four years later by Scotland. Once again, the burden of county defence, and county recruitment, was placed on the aristocracy. By the 1800s, 77 peers were either Lords Lieutenant or Colonels of Militia or both: without them, the British Isles could not have been defended.[72]

Nor was the contribution of landowners to local affairs confined to the countryside: they were also unprecedentedly involved in the towns, and with industry. The Butes dominated both the government and the representation of Cardiff, as did the Donegalls in Belfast. In unrepresented towns like Sheffield and Birmingham, it became customary to entrust parliamentary petitions to peers (or their relatives in the Commons) with close territorial connections: Viscount Milton in the one case, Lord Calthorpe in the other.[73] Many grandees also gave their support to new industries and new industrialists: Lord Gower for Wedgwood, Lord Fitzwilliam for the Yorkshire woollen manufacturers, Lord Dartmouth for Boulton and Watt, are but the most famous examples of peers interceding with parliament and with government. As Michael McCahill notes, 'over the course of the late eighteenth century, peers extended their patronage across the face of England, to new trades and old, to small producers and the greatest factory owners.' They, and they alone, could work the system. After all, they were the system.[74]

With power as with wealth, it is important to get clear the general trends in the making of this new British upper class. Once again, there was the gradual melding and blending of the separate elites of England, Scotland, Wales and Ireland into a new supra-national formation. But in other ways, the developments were less uniformly consistent. On the one side, there was a growing degree of aristocratic power in the constituencies and in parliament, which appeared to imply a contempt for ordinary people and a self-interested delight in plunder, patronage and control. On the other, there was a new cult of dutiful and disinterested state service by many landowners and their relatives, which seemed to embody a very different set of values, and which was memorably saluted and proclaimed by Sir Kenelm Digby in his book, *The Broad Stone of Honour*, which was addressed, significantly, to 'many lords and divers gentlemen, as well of this realm of England, as of those famous kingdoms of Ireland and Scotland, now happily united'.[75] The gradual resolution of these contradictory attitudes and images will be dealt with later. Meanwhile, it is time to turn from examining the new British elite in terms of wealth and power, and to look at it finally from the standpoint of status.

III

These new agglomerations of supra-national wealth and power necessarily had their effect on the status structure of late-eighteenth and early-nineteenth-century Britain. For as the separate aristocracies of England, Ireland, Scotland and Wales merged into a new British elite of wealth and power, this inevitably brought with it major changes in the lives these people led, in the ways they spent their money, and in the titles and honours which they awarded to each other. Enlarged income made possible increased expenditure, especially as the new rich sought to catch up with the old, and the landowners of the Celtic fringe sought to emulate and to rival their cousins in England who had previously been so much wealthier. And this scramble for spending was paralleled by a scramble for honours, as the newly rich, the newly powerful and the newly assimilated sought titles to set the seal on their arrival. In turn, this lead to the creation and codification of the first authentically British system of titles and rewards for what was becoming the first authentically British upper class.

The most obvious expression of competitive and conspicuous consumption, throughout the British Isles, was the construction of country houses. For England, the quantitative evidence suggests that the years from the 1780s to the 1820s saw a major upsurge in the building and extension of great mansions: Chatsworth and Belvoir, Ashridge and Ickworth, Lilleshall and Lowther, Panshanger and Lambton. With enlarged incomes, broadened horizons, and the desire to prove themselves the equal of any English aristocrat, many Celtic owners followed suit, able for the first time to compete and indulge in lavish display.[76] In Ireland, the period witnessed the construction of some of the country's most massive mansions: Castle Coole in County Fermanagh for the Earl of Belmore, Lyons in County Kildare for Lord Cloncurry, and Ormeau House, near Belfast, for Lord Donegall. In Glamorgan, only five new houses had been built by the old and decaying gentry between 1640 and 1760; but between 1760 and 1810 the newcomers to the county constructed more than three times as many. And in Scotland many families now possessed, for the first time, both the wealth and the wish to build. Robert Adam designed Melville Castle for Dundas and Culzean Castle for Lord Lochinvar; William Atkinson constructed Scone Castle for the Earl of Mansfield and Dalmeny House for the Earl of Rosebery, and extended Taymouth Castle for the Earls of Breadalbane.[77]

Throughout the British Isles, these new great houses were surrounded by parks of unprecedented size, often created by Capability Brown or Humphrey Repton. At Panshanger, the fifth Earl Cowper built a lake of thirteen acres, and six new miles of roads to replace those he had closed off when making his park. The eleventh Duke of Norfolk made a park at Greystoke in Cumberland of five thousand acres, designed to shame the Lonsdales whose park at nearby Lowther Castle was a mere four thousand. Again, this was not just an English but a British trend. Brown never got to the Celtic fringe, because he had too much to do in England, but by the 1800s both Repton and John Loudon were much more widely in demand.[78] The transformation of the policies at Inverary Castle between 1771 and 1790 inaugurated a new fashion for emparking and landscaping, which soon spread throughout Scotland and to Ireland. Indeed, it was partly to record all these changes that John Preston Neale published his *Views of the Seats of Noblemen and Gentlemen in England, Wales, Scotland and Ireland* in eleven volumes between 1818 and 1823, the first great supra-national survey of British country houses and their grounds.[79]

This massive outlay on houses and parks in the country was paralleled by unprecedented spending on London town palaces, as the new super-rich vied with each other in splendour, and as new supra-national families stormed the metropolis in the most ostentatious way possible. Cleveland House was completely remodelled for the third Duke of Bridgewater between 1795 and 1797; Burlington House was bought and refurbished by Lord George Cavendish for £120,000; and in the early part of the nineteenth century Breadalbane, Spencer, Hertford, Dudley and Argyll Houses were constructed or much improved.[80] In 1806, the Grosvenors bought Grosvenor House for £20,000, and spent more than that again on alterations and extensions. The Londonderrys lavished £33,000 on Holdernesse House in 1822, and a further £200,000 on its renovation. And in 1827 the Sutherlands bought, then rebuilt, Stafford House, at a total cost of more than £200,000. Meanwhile, Park Lane was completed and Hyde Park improved: an appropriately grand environment for the metropolitan display of aristocratic wealth.[81]

These unprecedentedly splendid London palaces provided the setting for further displays of conspicuously competitive consumption, as their owners adorned them with Old Masters which had suddenly become available in the aftermath of the French Revolution, which had obliged many impoverished continental nobles to sell their treasured works of art. In 1798 the Orléans collection was bought for £43,000 by a syndicate comprising the Duke of Bridgewater, the Earl of Carlisle and Lord Gower.[82] The driving force was the Duke of Bridgewater, who later left his pictures to the Marquess of Stafford, who in turn opened the gallery in which they were housed to the public. Equally acquisitive was Earl Grosvenor, whose purchases included the Agar Collection in 1806 for £31,000, four large Rubens religious paintings bought from the Danish Envoy in 1818 for £9000, and Reynolds' 'Mrs Siddons as the Tragic Muse' from the Watson Taylor sale in 1823 for 1750 guineas. To display them, he built a new picture gallery at his London house in 1817–19, and spent £23,000 on further extensions a decade later. By the time John Young was able to publish his *Catalogue of the Pictures at Grosvenor House* in 1831, the collection amounted to 143 items.[83]

Like housebuilding, the purchase or patronage of art was widely indulged in by British landowners. Among the super-rich, Lords Cowper, Lansdowne, Dudley, Fitzwilliam and Londonderry all purchased continental masterpieces at this time. Richard Payne Knight, a Shropshire country gentleman, acquired a large collection of coins, medals, sculptures, bronzes, and old master drawings. Samuel Whitbread II was a considerable patron of British art and British artists. Sir George Beaumont, who owned lands in Leicester and Essex, purchased Old Masters, and left sixteen to the National Gallery in 1826. Sir John Leicester, whose estates were in Cheshire, and who was created Lord de Tabley in 1827, collected only English artists.[84] The second Earl Spencer and the eleventh Duke of Norfolk collected books, the fifth Duke of Marlborough rare botanical plants, and the first Marquess of Lansdowne ancient Roman marbles. The greatest collector, connoisseur and patron of them all was the third Lord Egremont, who purchased compulsively from the 1780s until his death in 1837. He bought portraits by Reynolds and Gainsborough; he supported Constable and Blake; and he was J.M.W. Turner's greatest benefactor.[85]

All this competitive and ostentatious expenditure on country houses, town palaces, landscaped parks, and works of art provided the elaborate backdrop for day-to-day living, which itself reached new heights of extravagance. The gambling mania, which lasted from the 1770s to the 1820s, was one aspect of this, and Whig politicians like Charles James Fox, the Earl of Carlisle, and Georgiana, Duchess of Devonshire, paid dearly for their extravagance, not just in financial terms, but also in the damage that such indulgence did to their public reputations.[86] Even for those who did not gamble to excess, the cost of London living was higher than ever before. In the 1790s, Lord Verulam's metropolitan expenses were £1000 a year, and by the 1820s, Lord Fitzwilliam's expenditure was averaging £3500. Even these wealthy grandees were outdone by the Marquess of Stafford, the future 'leviathan of wealth', whose expenditure, according to Lady Beaumont in 1810, 'exceeded anything in this country, no one could vie with it'. Thus did the relatively parvenu Leveson-Gowers storm the citadel of metropolitan exclusiveness.[87]

Equally expensive and ostentatious was fox-hunting, which was developed and perfected throughout the British Isles at precisely this time. By the 1790s, the shires had become the centre of the sport; the Prince of Wales patronised it; books such as Beckford's *Thoughts on Hunting* appeared; and in 1792 the *Sporting Magazine* was published for the first time.[88] In the late eighteenth century, hunting spread first to Wales, and then to Scotland and Ireland. Great magnates, already dominant in their counties as landowners, as political tycoons, and as Lords Lieutenant, further enhanced their positions by becoming Masters of Fox Hounds. As the owners of packs of hounds and horses, they spent with astonishing lavishness. For many, the construction of stables and kennels was but another aspect of the building mania, and the scale was scarely less grand. 'It is not right to see hounds lodged better than human beings', lamented one observer after seeing the kennels and stables at Badminton.[89]

Electioneering was another expensive pastime for this new British landed elite, and the costs seem to have reached unprecedented heights in this period, as old-established and newly-rich dynasties were prepared to go to extreme lengths to get their way. In Norfolk, the families fighting for the control of the county were few in number, but that did not prevent them from spending £160,000 on five contests between 1768 and 1817. At the elections of 1790 and 1805 in County Down, the Marquess of Downshire lavished £30,000 on each occasion. The Fortescues paid £10,000 to contest Devon successfully in 1818, and £6000 to defend it unsuccessfully two years later. In Westmorland, the challenge by Brougham to the

Lowthers' hegemony in 1818, 1820 and 1826 cost him £31,000 and them £120,000.[90] In Sussex, Lord Ashburnham, Lord Egremont and Lord George Cavendish paid out more than £50,000 between them in 1820. In 1826 the Marquess of Waterford spent £15,000 yet lost his titular county, and in 1830 the Marquess of Hertford offered his candidate in County Antrim a float of £20,000 and whatever future help he might need.[91]

This nationwide competition by members of the British upper class in spending and extravagance was exactly paralleled by competition over titles and honours, the other − and more formal − expression of status. It is not at all coincidence that during this period there was a massive proliferation in knighthoods. The Order of the Bath, founded in 1725 with only 36 knights, was extended to 250 in 1815. The Order of St Michael and St George was created in 1818, and further extended in 1832. The Irish Order of St Patrick was established in 1783 with 15 knights, and enlarged to 21 in 1821 and 25 in 1831. The Scottish Order of the Thistle was augmented by one third between 1821 and 1827. The English Order of the Garter was increased in 1786, 1805, and 1821. As their titles suggest, these orders were created or extended partly to reward men of government and of military distinction, and partly to assimilate patricians from the Celtic fringe into a new British system of titles and rewards.[92] They were supra-national honours for the new supra-national territorial elite.

Equally noteworthy and unprecedented was the extension, diversification and codification of the peerage. Between 1700 and 1775, new creations had averaged only two a year, and had barely kept up with the rate of extinction during the period of elite demographic crisis. But between 1776 and 1830 some 209 United Kingdom peerages were created, and the House of Lords was increased from 199 to 358, a quite extraordinary enlargement and transformation.[93] And unprecedented ennoblements were accompanied by unprecedented rates of promotion. In 1784, there were only two English marquesses, but by 1801 there were nine, and by 1837 there were twenty three. As Michael McCahill observes, 'by the late eighteenth century, the British aristocracy had become acutely sensitive to questions of rank. The clearest manifestation of this obsession is what can only be described as a peerage mania.'[94] Put another way, the new patterns in the distribution of peerages resulted in the creation of a new and genuinely British nobility. Altogether, there were six developments, which need to be described in some detail.

The first category of recipients were those who became very rich during this period, and expected their status to be correspondingly adjusted. The Butes obtained a clutch of titles in 1796, as if to recognise their clutch of estates: Viscount Mountjoy, Earl of Windsor and Marquess of Bute. The Grosvenors had added a barony to their baronetcy in 1761, obtained a viscountcy and earldom in 1784, and received a marquessate in 1831. The Leveson-Gowers became Marquesses of Stafford in 1786 and Dukes of

Sutherland in 1833, as well as obtaining a barony, a viscountcy and two earldoms for cadet branches of their family. Nor did the Londonderrys, who were rich, Anglo-Irish, and did the state some service, lag far behind. In the Irish peerage, they acquired a barony (1789), a viscountcy (1795), an earldom (1796) and a marquessate (1816); and in the United Kingdom peerage they obtained a barony (1814) and an earldom (1823).[95]

The second claim to ennoblement or promotion was political clout – borough-mongering, influence with the government of the day, or power wielded more directly. The Grenvilles were the most accomplished players of this game – rich through sinecures and intermarriage, well endowed with rotten boroughs, and at the very centre of political affairs. The third Earl Temple obtained an Irish earldom for his father-in-law in 1776, a marquessate for himself in 1784, the Garter in 1786, and an Irish barony for his wife in 1800. His brother, William, was made a baron in 1790; one brother-in-law, Fortescue, was made a United Kingdom earl in 1789; another, Carysfort, an Irish earl in 1789 and a UK baron in 1801; and a cousin, James, was made a baron in 1797. Finally, in 1822, as the price of giving his support to the Liverpool government and abandoning the Whigs in opposition, the son of the third earl and first marquess was made Duke of Buckingham and Chandos. Nine years later, Creevey saw 'stately Buckingham going down to the Lords just now', and speculated as to how he viewed the prospect of losing some of his rotten boroughs in the Reform Bill. 'He would never have been a duke without them', Creevey concluded, 'and could there be any better reason for their destruction?'[96]

The third group who obtained peerages were those who, in civilian or military capacity, had been servants of the state: indeed, between 1801 and 1830, half of the new peerages created went to such men, many of whom, though having close landed connections, were not rich in their own right.[97] One or two, such as Dundas or Eldon, made enough money out of government office to support the dignity of their title. But many needed lump sums or pensions to enable them to keep up a suitably noble style and state. When Speaker Allot and Speaker Onslow were awarded peerages on their retirement, they were also given pensions appropriate to their rank. Lord Cornwallis accepted a marquessate, but refused a dukedom, on the grounds that his resources were inadequate to sustain the greater dignity. Nelson was made a viscount and (posthumously) an earl. Wellington was created successively baron, viscount, earl, marquess and duke. Many lesser commanders and captains also were ennobled and pensioned: St Vincent, Duncan, Collingwood, Blake and Exmouth in the navy; and Beresford, Hope and Hill among the generals.[98]

The fourth development was the amalgamation of the hitherto separate and inferior Scottish peerage into the new, supra-national British nobility – apt recognition of their increasing wealth, power, importance, equality and assimilation. In 1782, the Duke of Hamilton successfully petitioned against the standing order of 1711, which meant that those Scottish peers who already possessed post-Union UK titles could now sit in the upper house, from which they had previously been debarred. In turn, this led to a growing demand by Scottish peers for new UK titles, so that they, too, might sit in the Lords – a demand skilfully exploited by Dundas as he consolidated his power over the Scottish nobility. Between 1780 and 1830, 23 Scottish peers were given UK titles, and thus incorporated into the new British peerage.[99] They included Lord Aberdeen, who had hankered after a UK peerage since Pitt's time, and who finally obtained a viscountcy in 1814 after his diplomatic mission to Vienna the year before. But not all Scottish importuners did equally well. Five times, between 1801 and 1824, Lord Elgin begged for a UK peerage as a reward for his efforts in obtaining the Greek marbles for the British nation; but he was unsuccessful. 'To a Scotch peer', he wrote revealingly to Spencer Perceval in 1811, 'nothing could be so desirable as a British peerage.'[100]

The fifth new trend – which closely, but not exactly, paralleled the assimilation of the Scottish peerage – was the incorporation of the Irish peerage into an authentically British nobility. There had never been restrictions preventing Irish peers from sitting in the British House of Lords, and between 1783 and 1800 the younger Pitt gave seven UK peerages to holders of Irish titles. Moreover, the Union itself could be carried only by giving UK peerages to some of the greatest borough-mongers, such as Shannon, Tyrone and Donegall. And the abolition of the Irish parliament made it imperative to provide other ways in which to assimilate the Irish peerage to Westminster. Unlike their Scottish cousins, they were allowed to seek election to the British House of Commons, and in addition 28 Irish representative peers were added to the House of Lords.[101] Since they sat for life from the time of their appointment, this made them virtually indistinguishable from the majority of peers with UK titles. In addition, there was a further hand-out of UK titles, and 16 more Irish peers were put in the Lords between 1801 and 1828. The result was that by 1830 nearly half of the old, separate Irish peerage had gained admission to the British House of Lords, either as the holders of UK titles, or as Irish representative peers.[102]

Taken together, these changes betokened a massive upheaval, extension, and eventually rationalisation of the honours system. Those among established peers who were already very rich, very powerful and very grand (like the Dukes of Norfolk, Rutland, Bedford or Devonshire) looked on with disdain as their inferiors and the parvenus fought it out. But inevitably – and this was the sixth and final development – there were those with ancient titles of less exalted rank who were put out by this peerage mania, and who tried to keep ahead of the glut of new creations by themselves obtaining promotions. The seventh Earl of Salisbury applied successfully for a marquessate when he learned that peers who had once been his juniors were to be put above him. Lord Scarsdale asked for an earldom when his younger brother was made a viscount. Lord Bristol dressed up his request for a marquessate by saying that he had spent £120,000 on roads and improvements. The Earl of Ailesbury's son urged him to join the general scramble for marquessates, because it was 'the rank in the peerage to which your immense estates, long attachment to the government, and your party interest entitle you.'[103]

The end result, after several decades of frantic ennoblement, assimilation and promotion, was that by the 1820s the peerage had been re-structured and rationalised as a status group: rank was better matched to wealth, power and general consequence; the three separate peerages of England, Scotland and Ireland were more closely integrated; and a new, supra-national status group, an authentically British peerage, thus came into being. And it was appropriately – and innovatively – recorded. For most of the eighteenth century, reference books about the nobility had confined themselves to the English, or to the Scottish, or to the Irish peerage. But from the early nineteenth century, new reference books appeared which were comprehensively concerned with the British peerage as a whole: John Stockdale's *The Present Peerage of the United Kingdom* in four volumes in 1808, and a revised and augmented version of *Collins Peerage* in nine volumes in 1812. More lastingly, John Debrett produced the first edition of his supra-national *Peerage of England, Scotland and Ireland* in 1802, and arranged the entries in alphabetical order, regardless of the particular national nobility to which they belonged; by 1832 it was in its nineteenth edition.[104]

This widespread struggle for status by members of the British land-owning classes shows them at their most competitive, yet also at their most cohesive and most supra-national. For the spur to competition was emula-tion, the desire to enjoy, to share, and to surpass their rivals, whether in the material accoutrements of patrician life, or in the titles of honour that went with them. Among the mass of evidence about enhanced ambitions – sometimes fulfilled, sometimes thwarted – it is the convergence and uni-formity of status aspirations on the part of English, Irish, Scottish and Welsh landowners which most vividly and significantly stand out. Inevitably, the whole process was cumulative, interlocking and self-reinforcing: increased wealth lead to increased expenditure, just as unprecedented state service was unprecedentedly rewarded. But the links also ran the other way. Welsh or Scottish or Irish landowners were driven to enlarge their incomes, so that they could compete with their more prosperous English neighbours, and those who sought titles of honour were obliged to find ways of proving themselves worthy, or making themselves indispensable. By whatever process, and for whatever reasons, the result was a newly-conscious and newly-created British elite, in which prestige mattered as much as wealth and power, and was the honorific expression of them both.

IV

Whatever else they may – or may not – have witnessed, it seems clear that the years from the 1780s to the 1820s saw a consolidation of the nation's top personnel into a new British upper class, with a heightened sense of privilege and extended sense of identity. The formerly separate landed elites of England, Ireland, Scotland and Wales gradually fused, as their economic interests, their political ambitions, and their status aspirations converged, melded and coalesced. The result, as R.R. Palmer so perceptively spotted, was that 'the most class conscious class'[105] in late-eighteenth and early-nineteenth-century Britain was the traditional – but transformed – landed elite. In opposition to the challenges which it faced, it may have stood for permanence, for order, for stability, for inertia, for history and for tradition, as aristocracies always claim to do. But as the evidence presented here makes plain, that same landed class was being wrought anew, and was also making itself anew, during these restful and eventful decades.[106]

Here are three instructive ducal examples. The ninth Earl of Abercorn succeeded to his titles and estates in 1789, and was made a marquess in the following year. Appropriately enough for the only peer with titles in all three kingdoms, he married three times, and his first wife was English, his second Irish, and his third Scottish. Eighty years later, his grandson was made an Irish duke. The sixth Duke of Beaufort, by comparison, was an authentic English grandee, although he also held extensive estates in Wales, and his wife was a daughter of the Anglo-Scottish Marquess of Stafford, who later became first Duke of Sutherland. During the 1810s, the great Beaufort house at Badminton was refurbished, and the chandeliers were decorated in a truly British style, with branches of the oak, the thistle, and the shamrock.[107] Finally, there was Lord George Bentinck, whose father was the fourth Duke of Portland, and whose mother was a Scottish heiress. This may explain why, when speaking against the repeal of the Corn Laws, Bentinck adopted a broad, British perspective, describing the prospect of an end to agricultural protection as 'a measure which . . . a great majority of the landed aristocracy of England, of Scotland or Ireland imagine fraught with deep injury, if not ruin to them.'[108]

In each case, members of these three ducal dynasties were thinking and behaving in a much more British way than their forbears would – or could – have done. Here was something recent, something novel, some-thing new. But as so often with aristocracy, it was presented as something old. Consider those giant, gothic, foreboding castles, with their towers, their battlements and their gatehouses, which were built by many land-owners across the length and breadth of the British Isles in this period. The number constructed, the scale of the building, and the homogeneity of the style make them powerful and visible expressions of the new, cohesive, supra-national elite.[109] Yet in fact they were elaborate and flamboyant exercises in parvenu self-concealment. Rich and recently-ennobled coal-owners, like the Lowthers, the Lambtons and the Liddells, enfolded themselves in all the romantic extravagance of a spurious antiquity. In Glamorgan, new industrialists and interloping British landowners con-structed castles and abbeys at Cyfarthfa, Clyne, Margam and Hensol with much the same illusionary historical purpose in view.[110]

Nowhere was this new elite more fittingly commemorated than by Sir Thomas Lawrence, the most dazzling and stylish portrait painter of the age. Between 1790 and 1830 he was painter laureate to the British upper classes. There is the Hon. Shute Barrington, youngest brother of the second Viscount Barrington, Bishop successively of Llandaff, Salisbury and Durham, who sits vain, proud, berobed and well preserved. There is the future first Earl Granville, a jaunty, handsome, self-confident youth: the very embodiment of a swagger portrait. There is John, Lord Mountstuart, eldest son of the Marquess of Bute, the quintessential Byronic hero. There is the future third Marquess of Londonderry, bemedalled and beribboned, in his Hussar uniform.[111] Here, and in numerous other portraits, Lawrence invested his subjects with incomparable vivacity and allure, and with antiquity, too, as he harked back to Michaelangelo, Rubens and Van Dyck, and to classical poses. He memorialised them all: Whigs and Tories, Scots and Irish, soldiers and state servants, men and women – every one brilliantly coloured and richly ornamented. No wonder he was so avidly and so widely patronised: for he was the ideal artist to record, to celebrate, and to assist an elite in the process of re-making and re-presenting itself.[112]

The ultimate paradox of Britain's so-called ancien regime was thus not that it was so old, but rather that it was so new. In its essential and constituent elements, it may be summarised as follows. There were English families, some noble, some country gentry, which had managed to sur-vive the eighteenth-century demographic crisis. There were also Welsh, Scottish or Irish landowners, similarly lucky, who increasingly found them-selves tied to their English cousins by marriage and connection. There were self-made merchants, nabobs and industrialists, who bought their way in and gradually established themselves as bona-fide landowners. There were state servants (often, but not always, with patrician connections), who did not become, as in most European nations, a separate (and inferior) service nobility, but were themselves fitted out with all the accoutrements of landed aristocracy. Together, these disparate, separate and varied elements were assimilated and homogenised into a new British landed class. Thus renewed, extended and recreated, this old–new elite successfully preserved itself through much of the Victorian era, and even on into the twentieth century.

After all, it is easy to forget, but essential to remember, that most of the very wealthiest landed families in Victorian Britain traced their riches back no further than to the late eighteenth and early nineteenth centuries. Those who had been well heeled before, such as the Devonshires, Norfolks, Bedfords, Derbys and Northumberlands, became a great deal more prosperous at this time, thanks to advantageous marriages and the bountifulness of the Industrial Revolution. And, for essentially the same reasons, there were many families which joined the ranks of the super-rich only during this period: the Westminsters, the Sutherlands, the Fitzwilliams, the Dudleys, the Londonderrys, the Portmans and the Downshires. In the middle of the eighteenth century they had been relatively obscure and only middlingly rich; it was because of the developments which took place between the 1780s and the 1820s that they found themselves projected into the ranks of the very rich, where they were to remain for the next hundred years and beyond. Thus described, the wealth elite of Victorian Britain was much more new than old.

The same was true of the power elite. Leaving aside Disraeli, every nineteenth-century prime minister came from a family whose circumstances had been changed and improved between the 1780s and the 1830s. Of those from old and august dynasties: Lord John Russell was a Bedford, and his father benefitted greatly from the development of Bloomsbury; Lord Derby depended on the coals and ground rents of Lancashire; and the Salisbury money and Marquessate had been obtained during precisely this period. Two more were Anglo-Scottish: Lord Aberdeen, who fought so hard for his UK peerage in the 1800s, and Lord Rosebery, whose UK title dated from 1828. Two were Anglo-Irish: Wellington, a much-rewarded and much-honoured patrician from the Napoleonic Wars; and Lord Palmerston, who only sat in the Commons thanks to the terms of the Act of Union. Two were Whigs who, for all the cliquish snobbery of their clan, were men of recent title: Melbourne, whose viscountcy dated from the 1780s, and Grey, whose earldom went back only to the 1800s. And two were descendants of businessmen, whose forbears had bought their way into the landed elite during the classical phase of the Industrial Revolution: Sir Robert Peel (a great patron, incidentally, of Sir Thomas Lawrence) and Mr Gladstone. Thus described, the men of power were as new and as British as the men of wealth.

So, inevitably, were the men of status. In 1826, John Burke published his *Genealogical and Heraldic History of the Peerage and Baronetage of the United Kingdom* which, like *Debrett*, arranged the British nobility alphabetically, thereby assimilating the new supra-national peerages on the page as it had recently become in reality. In the third edition, Burke announced that he was also preparing a directory of the landed gentry as a companion work, which duly appeared, as the *Genealogical and Heraldic History of the Commoners of Great Britain and Ireland*, in four volumes, between 1833 and 1838. Here was a complete directory of the new British landed classes, which was not only a monument to the changes which had taken place during the previous half century, but was also the work of reference in which almost anybody who was anybody in the British Isles was to be found during the next half century. While the traditional titled and territorial classes of Britain continued supreme in their riches, their power and their prestige, no other handbook was necessary. Not until the 1880s did new, alternative elite directories begin to appear, such as the *Directory of Directors* and *Who's Who*, emphatic evidence that new, alternative non-landed elites were coming into being.

Before then, however, this newly-made British landed class, which had been created, and which had created itself, between the 1780s and the 1820s, continued to hold sway. Assuredly, it did not go unchallenged during its years of creation or of survival. In the light of its unprecedented wealth, its newly-consolidated power, and its enhanced prestige, it is hardly surprising that there was so much criticism, so much opposition. For in truth, radicals like Paine, Cobbett and Wade had much to be exercised about. But what stands out most significantly in retrospect is the very limited nature of the concessions and the accommodations which this new elite was forced to make. The most selfish upper-class traits – gambling and Old Corruption – were gradually given up, and more time and effort were given to the dutiful and disinterested administration of the country in the national interest. Works of art, which had been so acquisitively purchased or commissioned, were made available for public viewing, or in some cases left to the nation.[113] There was a mild degree of parliamentary reform, which made the Commons less subordinate to the Lords and more responsive to the people, by abolishing so many rotten boroughs, and by extending the franchise. And the repeal of the Corn Laws removed the last notorious piece of self-interested class legislation, which had given the middle and working classes legitimate grounds for complaint.

Such limited concessions merely served to consolidate the British landed elite's position: renewed, re-created, re-invented, and re-legitimated, it carried on so securely and so successfully that its very novelty was soon forgotten. No wonder, during the mid-Victorian years, that Cobden and Bright and their friends were so dismayed and so disappointed.[114]

2

Aristocratic Indebtedness in the Nineteenth Century

DURING the 1950s, while the 'storm over the gentry' raged and thundered, there took place another debate about the British landowning classes, more genteel and thus less well known. Its chief protagonists were Professors David Spring and F.M.L. Thompson, and the subject of their disagreement concerned the origins, extent, and consequences of aristocratic indebtedness in nineteenth-century Britain. In a pioneering and provocative article, Professor Spring drew attention to the 'widespread financial embarrassment' and the 'heavy indebtedness' which he believed were 'often to be found among the older landed families' during the first half of the century, resulting from heavy and accumulated family charges, from electoral extravagance, from the expense of house-building, and from the high living of the Regency period. But, he argued, by mid-Victorian times the aristocracy had become more restrained, more sober, and more aware of their obligations. Gambling, house-building, and excessive spending on high politics were curtailed and reduced, and retrenchment and recovery were successfully accomplished: the spendthrifts of one era were replaced by a 'generation more careful about how its money was spent, and more informed about how it was earned'. Thus was the threat of 'imminent disaster' averted. By 1880, he concluded, 'many of the big estates saw their encumbrances fall markedly away'. Revived, retrenched, and restored, the aristocracy enjoyed a new and prolonged lease of life.[1]

This somewhat melodramatic view was contested by Professor Thompson who, while admitting that 'some debt was characteristic of great estates', questioned whether it was overwhelming in its weight or mortal in its consequences. 'Debts', he noted, 'require careful handling as evidence: they may easily indicate increasing prosperity as increasing adversity, intelligent use of available resources as wayward appropriation.' Pointing out how few peers actually went bankrupt, he thought it 'extremely doubtful whether ruinous indebtedness was rife amongst the landed aristocracy of early Victorian England'. On the contrary, he argued that a high level of debt was often sustained by aristocratic families over a long period of time, and that the crucial issue was not the absolute size of encumbrances but rather the actual amount of income which was appropriated to servicing them. Only when 'interest charges equalled and even exceeded disposable income', he suggested, did 'indebtedness become disastrous', and this he insisted was a relatively infrequent occurrence.[2]

There in the late 1950s the debate halted.[3] Nevertheless, despite the retirement from the fray of the two chief combatants, the views which they expressed have passed into the conventional wisdom of modern British history. Ironically – given that he did not have the last word – this has been more generally true of Spring's arguments than of Thompson's. His picture of the early-nineteenth-century aristocracy as being spendthrift and self-indulgent has been taken up and embellished by Professors Hobsbawm and Perkin, the one depicting Regency peers as inhabiting a fox-hunting, pheasant-shooting, mansion-building paradise, the other taking pains to show how the landed governing classes 'abdicated their responsibility' to the social groups beneath.[4] Likewise, the assumed shift from early-nineteenth-century dissipation and debt to mid-Victorian sobriety and solvency has been oft repeated. A changed pattern of aristocratic behaviour, so the argument runs, led to a changed pattern of aristocratic finance; loose morals and loose spending were replaced by good manners and good business. Such in essence has become the standard interpretation.[5]

The purpose of this essay is to re-examine this consensus view about aristocratic finance and behaviour, and the controversy from which it originally derived, in the light of subsequent research. How, today, can we answer the questions which another historian posed nearly thirty years ago:

Were these landowners, as a class, threatened in the first half of the century by the disaster which overtook the second Duke of Buckingham in 1848? Were the vast debts, which many heirs inherited, evidence of a highly precarious financial position or, rather, of expenditure which was ultimately to be more than repaid by increased income?[6]

Despite the immense amount of inquiry which this subject has attracted in the intervening years, this essay is inevitably no more than another interim report.[7] Generalisations about social classes are notoriously suspect, and the aristocracy of nineteenth-century Britain is no exception to the rule. The section immediately following discusses the indebtedness of specific families, and of the landed elite as a whole. Thereafter, the sources of patrician credit will be explored and the uses to which it was put will be investigated, and in the final section an attempt will be made to relate these findings to the aristocracy's weakened position at the end of the nineteenth century.

I

How far did aristocratic indebtedness in the early years of the nineteenth century represent a departure from the state of affairs which had prevailed hitherto? In general it seems that it did not. Debt was a constant feature of life for the early modern aristocracy, the only means by which expenditure and income, both of which fluctuated, but rarely together, could be reconciled. It seems to have been between the years 1580 and 1610 that the nobility first became heavily dependent on credit, and by 1641 the total indebtedness of the peerage amounted to approximately £1.5 million.[8] Thereafter, no aggregate figures are available, though it is probable that the aristocracy were, collectively, becoming more, rather than less, indebted in the second half of the seventeenth century. During the eighteenth century, legal refinements in the terms of mortgages, the decline of the rate of interest, the evolution of the 'West End' banks, the advent of insurance companies, the development of the provincial mortgage market, and the professionalisation of estate management, made it much easier for the landowner to borrow. Although within a single family the extent of debt at any given time might depend on the quirks of personality (was the tenant for life who held the estate responsible or spendthrift?) and the accidents of biology (how many children were there to provide for?), the consensus seems to be that total aristocratic indebtedness increased as the century advanced, especially after the 1770s, as consumption became ever more conspicuous and family charges accumulated.[9]

Accordingly, it seems probable that for many early-nineteenth-century landed families, from the Salisburys, Seftons and Myddletons at one extreme to the gentry of Merioneth, Pembrokeshire and Essex at the other, some degree of indebtedness was a familiar condition for themselves, their immediate ancestors, their relatives, or their friends.[10] And recent research suggests that this continued to be the case throughout the nineteenth century, not just for the first fifty years or so. To be sure a few great names, buoyed up with extensive non-agricultural sources of revenue, managed to avoid long-term mortgages altogether. Despite extensive and protracted expenditure on houses, land and non-industrial developments, families such as the Dudleys, Sutherlands and Westminsters were obliged to resort only to occasional short-term mortgages or bridging loans from their bankers when spending temporarily outran income.[11] Even among the super-rich, however, these lucky few seem to have been exceptional.

At the other extreme came those landowners completely ruined or very severely embarrassed by accumulations of debt, the most famous example being the second Duke of Buckingham and Chandos, who went bankrupt in 1848 with encumbrances in excess of £1.5 million, £950,000 of which had been borrowed between 1839 and 1845.[12] Such cases of complete financial collapse, where payments to service the debt actually exceeded current disposable income, were indeed rare, and were not confined to the earlier part of the century. The fourth and last Marquess of Hastings, the 'King of Punters', who was accustomed to start the day with a breakfast of mackerel bones cooked in gin, went rapidly to his ruin and death following the notorious Derby of 1867. Less spectacular examples of dangerous insolvency seem also to be equally distributed either side of the Great Exhibition. In the late 1840s the Earl of Mornington and the Duke of Beaufort were severely embarrassed, and in the 1870s the Duke of Newcastle, the Earl of Winchilsea, and Lord De Mauley were all before bankruptcy courts.[13]

Between these extremes of mortal and trivial indebtedness come the majority of families whose finances have so far been studied. Some of them succeeded in lessening their encumbrances very substantially. Early in the century, the fourth Duke of Portland launched a massive assault on his inherited debt, reducing it from £512,000 to £162,000. Between 1822 and 1842, the Cokes of Norfolk cut their encumbrances from more than a quarter of a million pounds to less than ten thousand. During the 1840s and early 1850s, the Duke of Bedford completely liquidated his inherited debts of more than half a million pounds. Over a slightly longer period, from the 1840s to the 1880s, the Earls of Durham reduced their mortgages from more than £600,000 to £100,000.[14] Between 1868 and 1892, Lord Carrington paid off £300,000 of the debts he had inherited from his father. Substantial reductions were undertaken during the 1870s and 1880s by the Dukes of Hamilton and of Marlborough, and in the 1880s and 1890s by the Earls of Carnarvon.[15] If these few examples are any guide to more general trends, then it is clear that debt reduction took place throughout the nineteenth century, and was not concentrated during the earlier period, as was once supposed.

How were these debts paid off? In some cases there was certainly more prudent financial management, and the Bedfords and the Durhams enjoyed burgeoning incomes from their already extensive non-agricultural resources. But in most cases, it does seem as though sales of land were more important than Professor Spring was originally prepared to allow. Distant properties, to which there was little sentimental attachment, were usually first to go. Outlying portions of the heartland estate were sold more rarely, and occasionally there were windfall gains resulting from compulsory sales to railways or other public utilities. The Dukes of Portland sold part of their Cumberland estate, Coke of Norfolk sold out in Buckinghamshire, the Duke of Bedford sold some of his Bloomsbury acres, the Duke of Marlborough sold his Waddesdon estate, and Lord Carrington sold extensively in Wales and Bedfordshire. And there were other assets which could be realised, especially after the passing of the Settled Lands Act in 1882. The Dukes of Hamilton and of Marlborough parted with paintings and other family heirlooms, thereby establishing a pattern of patrician dispersal which has become much more familiar in the hundred years since then.

But while some families achieved significant debt reduction during the nineteenth century, it is difficult to believe that the class as a whole was as successful in this endeavour as was once thought. For many landed dynasties, sustained indebtedness was part of the immutable order of things.[16] It might rise or fall, dramatically or imperceptibly, or it might stay unchanged for decades. But it was not eradicated. The Grahams of Netherby and the Earls of Lisburne were in debt for most of the century. The Sneyds of Keele Hall, the Lords Hatherton, and the Earls of Scarbrough increased their encumbrances substantially in the decades after 1850. The Downshires' debts on their Irish estates fluctuated between £250,000 and £400,000. The Butes' mortgages on their Welsh and English properties had surpassed half a million pounds by the 1870s. The Fitzwilliams' debts were considerably greater. And the total encumbrances of the Dukes of Devonshire increased from half a million to two million pounds between the 1800s and the 1880s. In no case was this ruinous debt: but in each instance the cost of sustaining it was a substantial element in the family's annual expenditure.

Of course, this is no more than a handful of examples. But it includes those with and without non-agricultural sources of revenue, the gentry as well as the great grandees, and landowners with estates in all parts of the British Isles. The full extent of aristocratic encumbrances in the nineteenth century will probably never be known. Landowners themselves were disinclined to publicise their level of indebtedness, and it was very often extremely difficult to calculate the total sum. For different reasons, both the friends and the enemies of the landed interest were inclined to exaggerate the aggregate figure: allies so as to stress the burdens borne by landowners; critics so as to claim that agriculture under the system of great estates was intrinsically inefficient and uneconomical.[17] Nevertheless, the total amount of debt secured on landed estates in the nineteenth century was certainly substantial, and was probably on the increase for much of the time, especially during the prosperous mid-Victorian years. It seems to have been greater in Wales and Ireland than in England and Scotland, and the burden weighed more heavily on small estates than on greater accumulations of land.[18] In the late nineteenth century, these differences in the extent and location of encumbrances were to be of considerable – and sometimes critical – importance.

II

What were the reservoirs of credit on which so many aristocratic families were able to keep afloat from the Regency to the Victorian era? They were many and varied – much more so than those available to the most successful or well-connected businessman. To begin with, there were the surplus funds of unencumbered relatives or prosperous friends. In 1825 the Marquess of Stafford (later to become the first Duke of Sutherland) had £60,000 out on mortgage to the Duke of York, and £100,000 to Lord Reay. Part of the massive debt left by the first Earl of Durham was held by landed neighbours, including £30,000 from Sir John Swinburn. In 1906 the seventh Earl Fitzwilliam mortgaged one of his estates to the Marquess of Zetland and the Earl of Dalkeith for £121,000.[19] But such arrangements between relatives or friends might become difficult if the borrower defaulted on his payments, or if the lender abruptly demanded his money back, and on the whole patricians preferred to place, or to obtain, their money elsewhere.[20]

The funds controlled by local attorneys provided a rich and reliable source. Many country solicitors were responsible for investing money held in trust funds of one sort or another, and as one of their number, R.A. Ward, noted in a book obviously designed as a guide for his colleagues, 'a first mortgage on ample real property is unquestionably one of the safest investments that can be had'.[21] True, the returns were not spectacular, declining from a peak of $4\frac{1}{2}-5$ per cent in the 1820s and 1830s to 4 per cent in the 1850s, and even lower by the 1880s. But for those seeking regular income rather than spectacular dividends or capital appreciation, such an investment was ideal. On a first mortgage, money was usually advanced only to the extent of two-thirds of the value of the land being used as security, which meant that many must have felt as did Trollope's widow in *The Last Chronicle of Barset* (1867) who had 'every shilling laid out in a first class mortgage on land at four per cent. That does make one feel so secure! The land can't run away.'[22]

Many landowners thus turned eagerly to local solicitors and local funds. Until the 1870s the loans secured on their Irish estates by the Downshires were obtained in precisely this way. Between 1801 and 1811, £96,500 was raised on seven mortgages, four of which were held by Belfast merchants, and two by neighbouring gentry. Later mortgages were held by similar people, as well as by rentiers, well-to-do manufacturers, estate agents, and even employees. 'So far as loans on mortgage security are concerned,' the historian of their estates concluded, 'Irish sources were local and personal rather than institutional.'[23] The same was often true in England. During the mid-Victorian period, as their Edgbaston building estate began to yield a handsome return, the Calthorpes entered the long-term mortgage market for the first time. They, too, stayed within their own locality: between 1852 and 1880, they took out thirteen mortgages, none of them for more than £35,000, and all of them arranged by their Birmingham solicitor.[24]

As well as finance from family and friends, or arranged through their professional contacts, the aristocracy were able to obtain some support from country banks. This might be no more than an ordinary loan, as in the case of the third Lord Calthorpe, who ran up an overdraft of £6500 with Spooners, his Birmingham bank, which was suddenly and inconveniently called in in the December panic of 1825.[25] Or it might be a more formal arrangement for a larger amount. In the same year that Lord Calthorpe had to pay off his loan, one half of the Marquess of Londonderry's debt was held by bankers, including local firms such as Backhouse and Son of Sunderland and Darlington. In Scotland, landed estates had been acceptable security for such advances since the 1770s, so that by the 1820s loans in excess of £100,000 to grandees such as the Duke of Buccleuch and Lord Belhaven were not uncommon.[26]

Although the advantages of status and connexion no doubt favoured the aristocracy, the financial world thus described was open to many aspiring entrepreneurs. But other sources of credit were more restricted. At the very top came the Bank of England itself, which lent more than £1.5 million to landowners in the 1820s. Although this policy was never repeated, some of the loans remained outstanding for many years, that to the Duke of Rutland until 1869–70.[27] Slightly lower in the financial firmament, but a more important and sustained source of funds, came those old-established West End banks, such as Hoare's, Child's, Gosling's and Coutts', which much preferred titled and landed clients to 'mercantile men', and whose managers were precisely described by Walter Bagehot as possessing 'a certain union of pecuniary sagacity and educated refinement which was scarcely to be found in any other part of society.'[28]

The account books of Hoare's bank suggest that there were three types of financial support which such institutions gave to the aristocracy.[29] In the first place, there were bridging loans to tide a peer over a temporary shortage, as when the Duke of Beaufort borrowed £24,000 on 14 February 1842, only to repay it four days later. Second were those ostensibly short-term loans which, through constant renewal, became the instruments of long-term finance. The debt of the Duke of Northumberland comes under this heading, having been negotiated in the 1820s and carried through, with only a slight reduction, until the 1850s. Finally, there were formalised mortgages, bearing fixed interest, sustained over a long period of time, with land as security, such as the £104,000 lent by Hoare's to the Ailesbury Trustees in 1832.[30]

These activities were completely eclipsed in magnitude by those of the great insurance companies. Already by the eighteenth century the combined advances of two of them, the Equitable and the Sun Fire Office, amounted to more than Hoare's were to lend out on mortgage at any time up to 1877. Indeed, by the end of the century, half the counties of England and Wales contained some land mortgaged to one or other of these two companies, and their list of clients included five dukes: Newcastle,

Chandos, Leeds, Marlborough and Bedford.[31] With the fall in the yield of Consols after Waterloo, mortgages became an increasingly attractive investment, and firms like the Royal Exchange, which had hitherto shunned such activity, joined in. By the 1840s the Dukes of Devonshire, Bedford and Buckingham were substantially indebted to insurance companies; the Earl of Durham owed the London Life Co. £115,000; the Marquess of Bute owed the Equitable £185,000; and Sir James Graham owed the same company £200,000.[32]

Thereafter, the picture is less straightforward. As a proportion of all insurance-company investments, mortgages declined as the century advanced; and as a proportion of mortgages, loans secured on real property also fell.[33] But, given the dramatic expansion in the total investable funds held by insurance companies, it seems unlikely that the amount lent to landowners diminished in absolute terms. The Earl of Charlemont owed the Royal Exchange £150,000 in 1851. By 1892 the figure had increased to £205,000 and the loan was not fully paid off until 1902. Likewise, the Butes remained heavily indebted to the Equitable, owing £190,000 in 1868, and £550,000 ten years later.[34] It must have been examples such as these which caused Walter Bagehot to remark in 1879 that 'a large part of the titles of our richest landowners are mortgaged . . . to insurance offices who have much money constantly to lend.' And, in addition to direct advances such as these, the funds of those many land improvement companies active in the mid-Victorian years of 'High Farming' were in large measure provided by insurance houses.[35]

Broadly speaking, there were thus two sources of credit available to the aristocracy during the nineteenth century: that from within their own closed circle of relatives, friends, and bankers, and that from the world outside, those private, decentralized, middle- and working-class savings which were channelled in their direction by solicitors and insurance companies. On the basis of those families whose mortgages have been examined in detail, this second source seems to have been the more important, especially as the nineteenth century advanced, and finance became increasingly institutionalised. As the final report of the *Royal Commission on Agricultural Depression* put it, describing those halcyon mid-Victorian years vanished beyond recall, land was seen as 'the most safe and improving security for *the vast industrial and commercial savings of the country*'.[36] In other words, it was not just that the aristocracy benefited from industrialisation by the profits which they drew from involvement in non-agricultural forms of estate development. It was also that 'the savings of the commercial, industrial and shopkeeping classes of the community' helped 'in a significant manner to finance the economy of the English landed estate'.[37] Whether this was an appropriate allocation of scarce capital resources depends on what, in turn, the aristocracy did with the substantial sums thus obtained.

III

How, then, did the landowners spend their borrowed largesse? Or, to pose the question slightly differently: why did a high aggregate level of aristocratic encumbrances persist? In part, it continued because it was not easy to reduce a large pile of inherited debt without substantial windfall gains, spectacular increases in revenue, or extensive land sales. Economy of living might make some impact but, as the experience of the Ailesbury Trustees showed between 1832 and 1856, it was rarely enough by itself.[38] Servicing debt out of current income was one thing: reducing it from the same source was quite another. Indeed, provided it could be sustained without too much discomfort, why should the tenant for life bother to try? What was the point of putting away a few thousand pounds each year, which would hardly make any impression at all, when he could spend it on himself, and pass on the debt to his successors? What sense did it make, at a time when the social and political value of land was still high enough to outweigh its low economic return, to sell it to pay off mortgages? An unencumbered but reduced landowner was a lesser person than one indebted but with broad acres.[39]

Yet it was not just that accumulated debts were often carried over from one generation to the next. It was also that the basic aristocratic problem of reconciling income and expenditure, which fluctuated independently of one another, persisted throughout the nineteenth century. Old debt was sustained, and new debt incurred. The gambling extravagances of the days of Charles James Fox, and the excesses of pre-Reform Act electioneering, may not have been repeated. But many aristocrats habitually lived beyond their means, so that debt grew inexorably over the years. And there were additional items of 'lumpy' expenditure which could be financed only by borrowing. It is worth glancing at five of these: family portions, house-building, the purchase of land, agricultural improvement, and involvement in non-agricultural enterprises.

Of these, family charges rank as the most predictably unavoidable. From the second half of the seventeenth century, the evolution of strict settle-ment meant it had become customary to make portions for younger sons and daughters first charges on the estate.[40] Under normal circumstances, this burden appeared every generation, as the younger children of the tenant for life either reached the age of twenty-one or married, and then became entitled to their money. Thus may be explained much of the ups and downs in the Scarbroughs' and Lisburnes' debts, as the portions of each generation were accumulated and discharged.[41] The increase in the Hathertons' encumbrances in the 1880s can be attributed to the same cause, and in the case of William, third Earl of Radnor, portions amounting to £80,000 resulting from his two marriages in 1801 and 1814 were not discharged until after his death in 1869.[42] In Ireland and Wales the weight of family charges seems to have been especially burdensome. Conversely, among the super-rich such as the Durhams and the Fitzwilliams, it was less significant.[43] There were other reasons why they got into debt.

House-building offers one explanation. It used to be generally believed that the last great phase of country-house construction – in terms of both quantity and quality – terminated somewhere between 1815 and 1830, and that thereafter the aristocracy, 'however wealthy, seldom did more than add wings or ornaments to existing mansions'.[44] But recent quantitative evidence casts doubt on this view. Mark Girouard has taken a sample of five hundred country houses which were either built or remodelled in the years 1839–89, and has shown that for established dynasties (those owning a substantial family seat for more than two generations) house-building activity remained relatively high until 1880, peaking in 1870–4, exactly the same time as for the *nouveaux riches*. Jill Franklin's more restricted analysis suggests that between 1835 and 1874 traditional landowners were responsible for well over half of the mansions that were built. And the Stones' elaborate survey of three English counties confirms that there was a renewed upsurge in the mid-Victorian era.[45] It was the agricultural depression at the end of the century, rather than restraint and respectability in the middle, which put an end to house-building as a general activity, though some very rich families like the Butes and Norfolks continued even in those latter years.

How much of this was financed out of loans it is not possible to say with any degree of precision. The Northumberlands were able to spend £320,000 on the rebuilding of Alnwick in the 1850s without needing to borrow at all.[46] But even the Westminsters were obliged to resort to loans for the rebuilding of Eaton Hall, and for lesser families it seems that the considerable short-term strain could rarely be borne without recourse to external assistance. George Cornwallis-West recalled how his grandfather, owner of Ruthin Castle in Wales, was not satisfied with the existing house, 'mortgaged the property, pulled down most of the second edition, and erected, in 1850, the huge mansion which now exists'. Other Welsh landed families behaved in a similarly extravagant manner from mid-century onward, creating simultaneously heavy debts and hideous houses which their successors were to find an aesthetic, as well as a financial burden.[47] Back in England, the fifth Lord Calthorpe lavished some £40,000 of his borrowed money on the creation of a stud farm and house at Newmarket in the 1870s and 1880s. At the same time, part of the money which the Lisburnes and the Scarbroughs raised went on embellishing their ancestral seats. And Lord Beaumont's decision to entrust the rebuilding of Carlton Towers to E.W. Pugin and Francis Bentley in the 1870s left him with a debt of £250,000 by the end of the decade.[48]

Like family portions and country-house building, the purchase of land was a traditional patrician activity, which increased indebtedness and continued well into the nineteenth century. Once again, there were a few super-rich families, such as the Northumberlands, who could finance such expenditure out of current income. But, for all except the smallest purchases, most acquisitive landowners were obliged to borrow, especially those set on building up their limited acres into a large estate. The chief cause of Lord Hatherton's debts was that, since 1812, he had added 2500 acres to the (previously modest) family holdings. Between 1814 and 1826, the second Marquess of Bute bought £150,000-worth of land in Glamorgan, which he could finance only by extensive borrowing. A large part of the debt that Ralph Sneyd had accumulated by 1848 resulted from buying two thousand acres during the previous twenty years.[49] And although the rate of purchase and accumulation slowed down at mid-century, there remained some ambitiously acquisitive families. Between the 1850s and 1880s, the Calthorpes and Harrowbys spent, and borrowed, so as to extend and consolidate their scattered estates.[50]

Not only was land still being bought: it was also still being improved. This provides the fourth major item of debt-financed outlay, 'the gathering momentum of expenditure on repairs and improvements from the 1830s to the 1870s': in the age of 'High Farming' and the 'Second Agricultural Revolution'. This 'Golden Age of English Agriculture' was made possible by the widespread drainage of hitherto soggy fields, by the increased use of purchased feed and artificial fertilisers, by the evolution of integrated, market-oriented production techniques, and by the gradual shift of emphasis, within a mixed-farming system, from arable to livestock.[51] The exact nature and extent of these changes are still a source of some controversy. But they certainly involved the landlord in unprecedented expenditure on drainage and building – in part because a greater proportion of investment in fixed capital in agriculture was borne by the landowner; in part because the actual costs of improvement (at least £5 an acre) were much greater than they had been in the classical age of Parliamentary enclosure (between £1 and £2 an acre).[52]

While some of this expenditure was financed by such magnates as the Dukes of Bedford and Sutherland out of current income, many lesser proprietors were obliged to resort to loans to begin or complete improvements. Indeed, borrowing for such purposes dated back at least to the classical era of enclosure. What was new about this second phase of activity was that new sources of finance suddenly became available in the mid-Victorian period. The Public Money Drainage Act (1846), the Private Money Drainage Act (1849) and the Improvement of Land Act (1864) enabled tenants for life in Britain to borrow money for agricultural investments, and made Treasury funds available for the purpose. The initial statute was a palliative offered to the landed interest to sweeten the bitter pill of Corn Law repeal; and similar legislation, with similar provisions, was passed for Ireland in the aftermath of the Famine. In turn, this meant that a clutch of companies came into being, often financed by the great insurance houses, to make additional funds available to land-owners, including the General Land Drainage and Improvement Company and the Lands Improvement Company.[53]

The result was borrowing on an unprecedented scale. Sir John Clapham has estimated that in the thirty years after 1846 some £24 million was applied to the improvement of British agriculture, of which £4 million came from the government, £8 million from private companies, and the rest from landowners' 'own resources'. Of the £4 million advanced by the British government, £2.2 million went to landowners in Scotland, £1.8 million to landowners in England, and £100,000 to landowners in Wales. In Ireland the Board of Works advanced a further £3 million between 1847 and 1880.[54] Of the families already mentioned, the Harrowbys borrowed from land companies in the 1850s and 1870s, the Scarbroughs were lent £16,000 from the Lands Improvement Company between 1864 and 1882, and the Earls of Lisburne borrowed £20,000 in 1874 and a further £17,000 in 1882.[55] Indeed, it seems that as spending on new land lessened, invest-ment in the improvement of land already held increased, and loans pro-vided much of the finance for both types of undertaking.

The final item of debt-enlarging expenditure was investment in non-agricultural enterprises: the increasing of encumbrances in the short run in the hope of securing long-term gains in income. As an aristocratic activity, this was nothing new in the nineteenth century.[56] What *was* new was the number of families involved, and the scale of their activities. Much of the indebtedness of the Durhams, Londonderrys and Fitzwilliams in the middle years of the nineteenth century was as a result of their extensive invest-ment in mining. In the 1860s and 1870s, the Earl of Radnor borrowed in excess of £13,000 'for the purpose of applying the same in and about the improvement of the estates and hereditaments at Folkestone'.[57] Of the £120,000 mortgage raised by the Earl of Scarbrough in 1878–9, £53,000 went on the creation of Skegness. The Londonderrys' development of Seaham Harbour, the Butes' investment in Cardiff Docks and the Devonshires' outlay on Barrow-in-Furness were all costly ventures which involved very substantial borrowing indeed.[58]

Taken in aggregate, this debt-increasing expenditure by the landowning classes may be divided into two categories. The first was spending which had as its objective the enhancement of the social prestige and the fulfill-ment of the traditional responsibilities of the landowner. This included the costs of living, of portions, of house-building, of the purchase of agricul-tural land (which rarely gave a return of more than three per cent), and of investment in High Farming (where the return was even lower).[59] None of these ventures, with the possible exception of outlay on agricultural im-provement, was undertaken by the aristocracy with the maximisation of profit as its objective. To the extent that such self-indulgent activities were financed from middle- and working-class savings, which were channelled in the direction of the titled and territorial classes by solicitors, banks, insurance companies and government agencies, this definitely amounted to a 'haemorrhage of capital', a 'misallocation of scarce resources', as funds from urban and industrial Britain were diverted to underpin the indulgence of the landed order.[60]

The second category of debt-inducing expenditure was more productive, in that it involved the exploitation of non-agricultural estate resources. Here the aim was certainly profit, and here the borrowed funds drawn from the urban and industrial sector were recycled in a more constructive way. The sinking of coal mines, the creation of urban estates and seaside resorts, and the development of docks and harbours, undoubtedly contributed to the expansion of the nineteenth-century economy. In such cases, the landowner could obtain and commit large sums of money, sums much greater than mere businessmen would have been able to secure. It has been argued that such investment was of great strategic importance to the economy, and in some cases it undoubtedly was. But the Devonshires at Barrow and the Butes at Cardiff also provide examples of increasingly unjustified and unprofitable expenditure on the basis of a misguided or excessive sense of paternalism. Whether, on balance, such aristocratic spending of loanable funds was more creative than 'eccentric', more profitable than 'idiosyncratic', has still to be determined.[61]

IV

The argument advanced thus far seems to be internally consistent, in that the evidence concerning the extent of debt, the sources of credit and the uses to which the money thereby obtained was put seems to cohere. Whatever might have been the financial state of individual families, it seems clear that the landed aristocracy *as a class* was in debt throughout the first three-quarters of the nineteenth century. In Ireland and Wales, where the pressure was greater, encumbrances were primarily the result of family portions and expenditure on house building. In England and Scotland, they may have been more the result of the purchase and improvement of land, and of substantial investment in non-agricultural ventures. Despite these variations, the overall conclusion must be that in the nineteenth century, as in the eighteenth, debt was a commonplace feature of estate management and patrician finance. And this in turn helps us to understand the collective aristocratic anguish which was so much in evidence from the 1880s onwards. In retrospect, it may, perhaps, seem overdone. But there was no mistaking its intensity at the time, and of the many reasons for it, the impact of indebtedness was undoubtedly one.

To begin with, the decline in rentals associated with the agricultural depression clearly assumed more ominous proportions for those families

whose estates were bearing jointures or fixed interest charges (which had
often been incurred on the assumption – easily made in the relatively balmy
days of the 1850s, 1860s, and early 1870s – that rentals would at worst
remain static, and at best continue to rise). Nor should the compulsory
reductions by the Land Commissioners in Ireland be forgotten.[62] Gross
income, previously large enough to allow such payments, fell by between
one-quarter and one-third; and disposable income, hitherto adequate, now
became much reduced. As a result the third Lord Hatherton was left
in 1888 with no more than £1000 to spare for the payment of household expenses.[63] The proprietor of a four-thousand-acre arable estate in
Cambridgeshire was equally hard pressed. Between 1875 and 1885, his
gross rental averaged £7152, of which 41 per cent went in interest payments; but, from 1885 to 1894, his income fell to £5343 a year, of which
the same charges gobbled up nearly 75 per cent. Only because he drew
ground rents from land in central London in the region of £4000–6000 a
year was the situation rendered tolerable; and only by extensive sales of land
in the years 1915–24 were the mortgages paid off.[64]

But it was not just that the agricultural depression squeezed *current*
incomes of which a fixed amount was earmarked for servicing debt. It also
undermined the entire basis of aristocratic borrowing. As with rentals, so
with the *capital* value of land, a static or rising trend had been presupposed
but, with the depression, the capital value of land fell everywhere by about
thirty per cent, thereby often wiping out the entire margin which had
customarily been left between the size of the first mortgage and the assessed
value of the land to be used as collateral. 'No security', observed *The
Economist*, 'was ever relied on with more implicit faith, and few have lately
been found more sadly wanting than English land.'[65] Under such circumstances, it was hardly surprising that companies like the Royal Exchange
began to review their mortgages. And while old loans were constantly
being scrutinised and called in by solicitors as well as by insurance companies, new loans became harder to obtain on the security of land whose
future value could not be precisely predicted. 'Lawyers', noted a Herefordshire attorney, 'have grown very careful about advancing money upon a
mortgage of land, since such extreme caution had to be exercised that the
investment was rarely worth the anxiety.'[66]

Events in Ireland served only to darken the picture still further. The bad
harvests and falling world prices of the late 1870s and 1880s hit there as hard
as anywhere, and to add to this the agrarian violence of the 1880s and the
compulsory reductions in rents by the Land Commissioners meant that
Irish land became an even more unreliable asset than land in England. As
one authority put it in 1898: 'I imagine that at present, unless in specially
favourable cases, it is a matter of some difficulty to induce an English or
Scottish capitalist to lend money upon security of land in Ireland.'[67] Indeed,
the institutional lenders at whom these remarks were directed went further

and reviewed their mortgages on Irish land much more sceptically than those held in England, and in many cases actually requested repayment of loans or the provision of alternative, English collateral. Between 1866 and 1880, the Scottish Widows' Company lent out no less than £1.2 million secured on Irish land, but in that latter year it was decided to begin calling these loans in, and by 1894 £846,560 had been repaid.[68]

The combined impact of the fall in rentals, the decline in the capital value of land, and the Irish troubles thus lessened very considerably the room in which indebted landowners might conduct their financial manoeuvres. Interest payments, bearable in normal times, became increasingly burdensome; disposable income, adequate before, shrank alarmingly; mortgages, safe hitherto, became dangerously large in relation to the value of the property on which they were secured; loans, easily available in days past, were now much more difficult to obtain. To make matters worse, this was at the very time when families needed to borrow more urgently and extensively than ever, to meet a new and unprecedented form of large-scale expenditure destined soon to eclipse all others: death duties. First introduced in 1894, they hardly represented a mortal blow to an unencumbered estate, being levied initially at the rate of only 10 per cent on property assessed in excess of £1 million. Small sales of land or limited mortgages could easily be arranged to meet such contingencies. But on an estate which was *already* heavily encumbered the effect might be out of all proportion to the absolute size of the demand. Additional mortgages would be hard to obtain; if land was sold, there might be no surplus once the old debts had been discharged; and with disposable income so reduced, there would be no possibility of setting up a sinking fund. In circumstances such as these, death duties might well come as the last straw.

Accordingly, in assessing landowners' capacity to respond to the increasingly hostile financial environment which developed at the end of the nineteenth century, it is necessary to consider not only the size of their incomes but also the extent of their inherited encumbrances. If a landlord was possessed of especially broad and valuable acres or of extensive sources of non-agricultural revenue, then he might well have considerable scope for re-ordering his affairs to advantage, heavy mortgages and death duties notwithstanding. From the 1870s until the 1930s, financial super-powers such as the Sutherlands, the Butes, the Bedfords, the Devonshires and the Westminsters all behaved in this way, selling agricultural land, urban property or their London town houses, paying off encumbrances (if they had any), meeting death duties, and investing the residue in shares and government bonds, thereby enjoying an income larger and more secure than that which they had drawn from land in the years before the First World War.[69] By shifting their assets with such dexterity, and by fortuitously avoiding major deaths in the inter-war years, many of the great landed families were able to win for themselves a further generation in

high society and high politics which was not brought to an end until the
Second World War or after.[70]

Those with smaller gross incomes – between £10,000 and £50,000 a
year – were not able to weather the storm so easily. The Calthorpes entered
the twentieth century unencumbered, but following the death of the sixth
Lord in 1910 were forced to sell their outlying East Anglian estates and to
mortgage their remaining holdings to the extent of £230,000. Other
families fared even less well, suffering at the end of the century for the
mortgages which had been raised earlier. 'Oh,' wailed the third Lord
Hatherton in 1891, 'what a dreadful thing it is to inherit a debt.' How right
he was. Spending was cut, participation in politics dispensed with, land
purchase virtually abandoned. Nearby at Keele Hall, Ralph Sneyd also
found the burden of debt harder to support in such straitened times, and let
his house to a Russian grand duke for seven years.[71] Even more drastic
measures were adopted by the Lisburnes, who began large-scale selling
of their estates in the 1880s, and by George Cornwallis-West, who was
obliged to go into business 'to endeavour to make sufficient money to
pay off the mortgages on my family estates'. Over the mountains in
Herefordshire, the Arkwrights were finding life even harder, burdened
with loans from land improvement companies, the attempts to repay which
in the 1880s and 1890s were 'a serious, perhaps the fatal, charge on the
estate during the great depression'.[72]

Retrenchment, sales of land, new or enlarged debts, the abdication of
traditional paternal and political roles, the search for extra and alternative
sources of income, both at home and abroad: all these activities characterised aristocrats of moderate means in the years from the late 1870s and
1880s. For the squirearchy and minor gentry beneath – those with incomes
from £1000 to £10,000 a year – the pressure of debt was greater, the
impact of depression more marked, and decline in consequence more rapid
and complete.[73] How could mortgages be paid off or death duties met by
the owners of estates so small that no parts could be lopped off for sale?
Either the whole estate had to go under the hammer or none of it. What
prospects were there for a Worcestershire squire like Joseph Jones, when
on an estate of 3519 acres producing £4860 a year gross he was obliged to
make a 20 per cent rent abatement? Small wonder that by the time of the
1937 edition of Burke's Landed Gentry, one-third of the families were listed
as landless, as old gentry moved out and nouveaux riches moved in.[74] Indeed,
one best-selling inter-war novelist, Francis Brett Young, who set his
stories in the Severn Valley, was able to people them with decayed squires
and aristocrats like the Pomfrets, the Abberleys, and the d'Abitots: poor,
mortgaged, without heirs, and doomed to extinction.

Reality provided many similar examples, most numerous in Wales and
Ireland where the burden of debt was greatest, where the market for land
was most vigorous, and where the 'passing of the squires' was correspond-

ingly most pronounced. In Wales, such families as the Tylers of Mount Gernos, the Lloyds of Bronwydd, the Lisburnes of Crosswood, the Powells of Nanteos and the Pryses of Gogerddan were overwhelmed by their accumulated encumbrances. Lands were sold, houses were let, expenses were cut: but rarely was it to any avail.[75] In Ireland a succession of Land Acts, beginning in 1871 and ending in 1909, encouraged many families to sell, especially from amongst the most hard pressed. What hope was there for Captain Newton of County Carlow, whose estate yielded £1688 gross, of which outgoings (including interest payments of £800) absorbed £1374? In the early 1880s, his rents were compulsorily reduced by 30 per cent by the Land Commission. For him, as for many Irish landowners, the only chance was to hang on until slightly better times, then to sell out on the best terms available under the Land Purchase Acts, and hope that there might be a small surplus left over, after the debts were cleared off.[76]

V

How far does the picture painted here support or undermine those views of nineteenth-century aristocratic debt which were contested in the 1950s, some of which have become historical commonplaces since? As far as individual families are concerned, the best that can be offered by way of generalisation is to say that at almost any time in the century some were getting into debt and others getting out, some bearing fluctuating debt, some servicing unchanging levels of encumbrances. But, collectively, this and other evidence seems to reinforce the view that the size of the debt alone is no adequate basis on which to assess the financial condition of any family; that the distinction between early-Victorian crisis and mid-Victorian recovery has been overdrawn; and that debt, but not ruinous debt, was a common feature of life for many landed families. There may have been changes in the pattern of landed behaviour between the early nineteenth century and the mid-Victorian period, but it is not clear that there were any significant changes in the structure of landed finance or any significant reduction in the extent of landed indebtedness.

If a pivotal period *is* therefore to be suggested, it seems much more appropriate to draw attention to the late 1870s and 1880s than to the 1840s and 1850s, and to stress the internal unity of the seventy-year periods both before and after. In the years up to the late 1870s, debt was incurred (with some modifications) for essentially the same reasons that it had been during the eighteenth century and before: because building houses, buying and improving land, and investing in non-agricultural ventures required large sums of money which could rarely be found out of current income. But in the seventy years which came after, declining revenue and eroded confidence brought almost all such ventures to an end. Old debts were harder to bear, and new ones were rarely incurred voluntarily. Incurred they were, nonetheless, as money had to be found for the newest and most reluctant form of patrician expenditure: death duties. Encumbrances, hitherto internally generated by a relatively buoyant, confident, expansive and optimistic landowning class, were superseded by burdens externally imposed by a predatory state on a landed interest increasingly on the decline and defensive. In the depressed 1880s and 1890s – the decades of Home Rule, of local government reform, of the Third Reform Act – is it any wonder that the landed classes were so pessimistic?[77]

Very generally, it seems that the greater and more diverse their sources of income, and the smaller their burden of inherited debt, the longer a landed family might hope to survive unscathed from the nineteenth into the twentieth century. And, since it was the super-rich who were most likely to be unencumbered in the first place, fortune tended to favour those already well placed and advantaged. The result was that from the 1880s the owners of land in the British Isles became an increasingly fragmented social group, as the distance between rich and poor became wider, as the sales of estates gathered pace in Ireland and Wales in the late nineteenth century, and as England and Scotland followed suit in the years immediately before and after the First World War. In that process of survival, adaptation, decline and decay, the pressure of accumulated and sustained indebtedness, and the widespread anxiety to which it gave rise, merit as much attention as the better-examined theme of agricultural depression. For many nineteenth-century landowners, and especially during the late-Victorian years, the capital account was at least as important – and at least as worrying – as the current account.

3

Nobility and Mobility in Modern Britain

IN TRADITIONAL WESTERN SOCIETIES, the horse was the very emblem of aristocratic wealth, power and status. 'All pre-eminence', an Arab emir noted of the Franks, 'belongs to horsemen. They are in truth the only men who count. Theirs is to give counsel; theirs to render justice.'[1] For more than a millenium, this remained the case: the ownership of horses was largely confined to the patrician elite, their dependants and their servants. From the Norman Conquest to the nineteenth century, an English gentleman who did not possess a safe seat in the saddle was almost a contradiction in terms. The breeding and racing of horses were quintessentially aristocratic hobbies, and fox-hunting became a favourite recreation of most landowners. The limits to county society were set by the distance a horse could comfortably travel in a day, and the cavalry, not the infantry, was the most glamorous and exclusive element in the army. The horse was thus an apt symbol of a rural, ordered, hierarchical and aristocratic world, and the 'men on horesback' towered above the rest of society, in their material resources, in their political power, and in their enjoyment of life.[2]

But the transport revolution which eclipsed the horse was itself an integral part of those broader economic, political and social changes which undermined and eventually marginalised the aristocracy. In the long run the advent of the train, then of the motor, and finally of the aeroplane helped to consolidate the triumph of the town over the country, of the mass over the elite, of industrial riches over landed wealth, and of speed over repose. As Lord Brabazon of Tara recorded in his autobiography, the two most significant developments during his lifetime had been changes in what he called 'mechanical things', and 'the complete revolution in the social structure of our country.'[3] But the impact of these developments in transport on aristocratic decline was more varied and more nuanced than it is often fashionable to suppose, and the changing relationship between the traditional landed elite and the railway, the automobile, and the heavier-than-air machine deserves more detailed and sustained examination than, for the most part, it has thus far received.

I

In a famous and oft-quoted remark, Thomas Arnold welcomed the steam train as 'heralding the downfall of the aristocracy. I rejoice', he continued, 'to see it, and think that feudality is gone for ever.' As headmaster of Rugby School (once disparagingly dismissed by Lord Peter Wimsey as little more than a railway junction), Arnold may well have been making a virtue of a necessity, but in essence he was correct. The railway brought noise and smoke into the sequestered quietude of the countryside; its lines compulsorily crossed lands considered inviolate by their owners; and it enabled masses of ordinary people to travel distances hitherto undreamed of. It was the most potent symbol of the new age of the Industrial Revolution, and it portended major changes in the structure of business and of wealth-holding.[4] In short, it cut the aristocracy down to size. As Walter Bagehot observed, 'our companies, our railways, our debentures, our shares', had 'come up', while 'the aristocracy have come down'. In the old days, grandees had journeyed in magnificent carriage processions, while land-ladies and waiters bowed before them. But on the trains they were virtually indistinguishable from other wealthy travellers, and at large railway stations they often went almost unnoticed.[5]

During the first phase of railway building, when the major trunk lines were being constructed between 1825 and 1850, many landowners did all they could to protect their parks and their estates from what they regarded as this new and outrageous invasion of their privacy. When the Liverpool and Manchester Railway was first promoted, it was opposed by Lords Derby and Sefton on just these the grounds, and in 1830 the line of the London and Birmingham Railway was resisted by Lords Clarendon and Essex for precisely the same reason.[6] The Great Northern Railway was criticised by Lord Exeter, because it went too near Burleigh, and by Lord Fitzwilliam, who feared it would lead to 'the separation of some woods [near Peterborough] which in a hunting point of view are inseparable'. The Duke of Wellington, having initially insisted that there should be no railway station within five miles of Stratfield Saye, eventually relented, and allowed one at Mortimer – fully three miles distant. Some grandees carried their opposition to yet further lengths. Even after the London to Norwich line had been completed, Lady Suffield always drove from Blickling to the metropolis in her carriage, 'rather than rub shoulders with other people in trains'.[7]

It was not just the privacy of their parks and houses that patricians sought to protect from the intrusion of the railway: it was also their high-class building estates in London and their suburban developments in the provinces. The Bedfords succeeded in keeping the London and North Western Railway out of their Bloomsbury estate, but the amount of traffic generated by the nearby Euston station nevertheless led to a marked decline in the social tone of the area. During the 1870s and early 1880s, the Calthorpes sought unavailingly to prevent the construction of a main line from Birmingham to Bristol through Edgbaston, and had to settle for restrictions on sidings and a total ban on factory buildings adjacent to the line.[8] At Folkestone, the Earl of Radnor was more successful in preventing the South Eastern Railway from promoting an extension scheme which would have undermined his attempts to develop a high-class resort. When the Great Central came to Marylebone, in the 1890s, Lord Portman imposed 'burdensome and expensive restrictions': the track was to be put in tunnels or concealed behind high walls; there were to be no advertisements or working-class housing close to the main line; all coal yards had to be roofed in; and all buildings were to be seemly and ornamented.[9]

Nevertheless, as the British aristocracy was well aware, there were occasions when timely concession could be more profitable than intransigent opposition, and the attraction of selling agricultural land to railway companies at written-up development value was undoubtedly considerable. Indeed, Robert Stephenson believed that 'the charge for land was greatly augmented by the enormous and unreasonable compensation required by some proprietors beyond the correct value of the land', and recent research has confirmed this opinion.[10] The most famous example was Lord Petre, who received £120,000 from the Eastern Counties Railway for lands reputedly worth £5000. This seems to have been an exception, but other landowners clearly did well for themselves. The Marquess of Ailesbury obtained £19,000 from the Great Western Railway, and George Lane-Fox, an indebted Yorkshire country gentleman, was happy to sell off land to fourteen English and Irish railway companies.[11] Sales of urban land could be even more lucrative: between 1864 and 1892, the Derbys obtained £483,408 for small plots in Liverpool, after the major sales had already been made. In London, families like the Camdens, Somers, Southamptons and Westminsters also obtained large sums of money from the same source.[12]

From the late 1840s onwards, many landowners were prepared to take a more positive view of local railways, as an essential instrument in the exploitation of their non-agricultural estate resources. The Earls of Dudley were keen promotors of mineral lines in the west Midlands, and the Marquesses of Bute backed the Rhymney Railway as a means to bring their Glamorgan coal to their Cardiff docks. Earl Fitzwilliam supported the South Yorkshire Railway, because it would help his collieries, the Duke of Northumberland invested in the Border Counties line because it opened up his iron ore at Bellingham and his coal at Plashetts, and the Duke of Norfolk built a branch line to link Glossop with the Manchester and Sheffield Railway.[13] Sir Peter Hesketh-Fleetwood promoted the Preston and Wyre Railway in the hope it would lead to the growth of the resort to which he gave his name, and the Earl of Burlington (the future seventh Duke of Devonshire) persuaded the Brighton and Hastings Railway to build a branch line to Eastbourne. In collaboration with the Duke of Buccleuch, he was also a founding father of the Furness Railway, which later became the most profitable mineral line in the country.[14]

By the mid-Victorian period it had also become clear that branch lines could greatly enhance the value of agricultural estates, and landowners began to support local railways out of a traditional sense of *noblesse oblige* mingled with self-interest. The Earls of Yarborough encouraged lines in Lincolnshire, and the Earls of Leicester invested in the Wells and Fakenham Railway and the West Norfolk Junction Railway. In Northumberland the Wansbeck Valley Railway was almost entirely financed by two local land-owners, Sir Walter Trevelyan and the Earl of Carlisle.[15] On a larger scale, the Duke of Devonshire invested heavily in the Lismore and Dungavron Railway, in the hope that it would benefit his Irish estates: by 1873 his shareholdings were £117,810, and by 1885 they had almost doubled. The third Duke of Sutherland was even more lavish in his expenditure, laying out £266,000 on the construction of railways in his Highland fiefdom. He was, notes Eric Richards, a man 'besotted by steam trains, fire engines and gadgets', who was 'guided by anachronistic notions of a Highland princedom to such an extent that they became extensions of the aristocratic ego'.[16]

Inevitably, this meant that by the mid-Victorian period it was 'quite common for members of the peerage to appear on the boards of railway companies, though these were usually lines of local importance to particular estates'.[17] Having invested heavily in the South Yorkshire Railway, it seemed only natural that Earl Fitzwilliam should eventually become its chairman. The Duke of Devonshire was chairman of the Furness Railway, and most of his co-directors were Cavendishes or Buccleuchs or their associates. The Duke of Sutherland was chairman of the Sutherland and Caithness Railway, the Earl of Mansfield of the Perth and Dunkeld line, the Earl of Carlisle of the Malton and Driffield Junction Railway, and the Earl of Yarborough of the Manchester, Sheffield and Lincolnshire. Untitled country gentlemen were also to be found occupying the same positions. From 1847 to 1865, the chairman of the Bristol and Exeter Railway was James Wentworth Buller, a West Country squire, who was followed by the twelfth Earl of Devon.[18]

During the first three-quarters of the nineteenth century, aristocratic involvement with railways thus followed a recognisable pattern. On the whole, they were not especially enthused about main lines and trunk routes: they regarded them as dangerous speculations, indulged in by irresponsible financiers who had no interest in the countryside they were crossing.[19] As a result, patrician investment was relatively meagre: the massive holding by the Dukes of Sutherland in the LNWR was the exception which proved the rule (it derived from their early investment in the Liverpool and Manchester Railway, itself the product of local considerations).[20] Their main concern was in fostering branch lines, which sometimes paid handsomely if they were mineral-bearing, but which often did not. They were happy to become chairmen, but this was out of a sense of local obligation, rather than because of any desire to go into business. Once again, the few exceptions prove the rule. From 1853 to 1861, the third Duke of Buckingham was chairman of the LNWR, partly because he urgently needed to repair the family fortunes, and partly because the directors wanted an appropriate counterpoise to the excessive influence of the Duke of Sutherland in the company's affairs. And from 1868 to 1872, Lord Cranborne (later Lord Salisbury, and Queen Victoria's last Prime Minister) was chairman of the Great Eastern. Like Buckingham, he needed the salary. But he, too, did well. He took over an ailing company, was determined to nurse it back to health, showed a firm grasp of business essentials, and did much to restore confidence.[21]

During the last quarter of the nineteenth century, the relationship between the landowners and the railways changed fundamentally, and in a variety of ways. As the engineering profession became more respectable, a small trickle of patricians began to go into the railway workshops.[22] G.J. Churchward's ancestors had been squires of Stoke Gabriel in south Devon since 1457, but after an apprenticeship on the South Devon Railway he spent his life in the service of the GWR. From 1902 to 1921, he was Superintendent of Locomotives and Carriages, and designed both the Stars and the Saints, the prototypical Great Western 4-6-0s, as well as the only Pacific ever built by the GWR, the Great Bear.[23] Even more genteel was the second Lord Montagu of Beaulieu, who had been sent down from New College, Oxford, and was apprenticed at the London and South West Railway's workshop at Nine Elms, London, where he was known as John Douglas, and earned 11s 6d for a 48-hour week. For a time he drove expresses on the London to Bournemouth line, and he did so again during the strikes of 1919 and 1926. 'I'm glad', one railwayman remarked to him, 'that you're driving the train, my lord – I know that you will return it in perfect condition.' And so he did: at the end of one of these journeys, a passenger gave him sixpence: 'Well done, young man,' he observed, 'I am so glad you are defying your union.'[24]

More generally, many aristocrats now began to see the railway companies of Britain as appropriate places in which to place extensive investments. The amalgamations of the mid-Victorian years meant that by 1900 the biggest railway companies were among the largest and (at least in the case of preference and debenture shares) most secure businesses in the land. As aristocrats began to move into the stock market, such railway shares beckoned alluringly – initially at home, and subsequently abroad.[25] Before 1870 the railway investments of the Earls of Leicester had been confined to the £15,000 they had placed in local Norfolk lines. During the 1870s, they invested £50,000 in the Great Eastern, the North Eastern, the GWR and the LNWR, as well as £40,000 in Indian lines; and in the next decade they bought a further £110,000-worth of British railway shares, and also made substantial investments in lines in Canada, the United States and South America. By then, indeed, this was a general trend. During the 1880s Lord Salisbury invested extensively in railway stock debentures, and during the following decades other illustrious investors in such home and overseas companies included the Dukes of Portland, Devonshire, Bedford and Sutherland.[26]

But it was not just as investors that grandees (and gentry, too) were associating themselves with railways in a new way: they also were joining the boards of these great companies with an alacrity that had been con-spicuously absent in earlier years. Landowners hard hit by agricultural depression eagerly sought directors' fees, and to be on the board of a railway company was to join the most elect group of all – partly because of the size and stability of these great undertakings, partly because of their unique position as prototypical public utilities, and partly because directors enjoyed the right of free travel throughout the whole of the national rail network.[27] Again, local connections helped. The Earl of Dudley, whose Black Country collieries depended on the railway, was a director of the GWR, as was Walter Long, a Wiltshire country gentleman and Tory Party potentate. The NER recruited its board even more assiduously from the local notability: at the turn of the century, its directors included Lords Grey, Wenlock and Londonderry, as well as Sir Matthew Ridley and Sir Edward Grey.[28]

This sudden proliferation of titled directors of great railway companies inevitably lead to a marked increase in the number of titled chairmen. Among the longest serving were Lord Colville of Culross at the GNR (1879–95), Lord Cawdor at the GWR (1895–1905), Lord Stalbridge at the LNWR (1891–1912), and Lord Cottesloe at the London Brighton and South Coast Railway (1896–1908). When Viscount Ridley died in 1904, after three years as chairman of the NER, he was replaced by Sir Edward Grey, who felt obliged to resign when the Liberals gained office only two years later.[29] Other patrician chairmen in the decade before the First World War included Lord Bessborough (LBSCR), Lord Knaresborough (NER), Sir William Hart Dyke (LCDR), Lord Stuart of Wortley (GCR), Viscount Churchill (GWR), and William Whitelaw (Highland Railway and NBR). The most famous aristocratic chairman was probably Lord Claud Hamilton, second son of the first Duke of Abercorn. He became a director of the GER in 1872, at the age of twenty-nine; he was vice-chairman from 1874 to 1893; he was chairman from 1893 until the com-pany disappeared in 1922; and he had named after him one of the loveliest class of locomotives ever built.[30]

Most of these upper-class chairmen were younger sons or landowners of limited resources: Sir Edward Grey, whose Fallodon estate yielded a mere £4000 a year, was certainly grateful for the £2000 salary he briefly drew as chairman of the NER. The contribution that the railways made to aristocratic finances is clear: what the aristocracy did for the railways in return is rather less apparent. Coincidentally, the era of patrician predominance on the boards of these great companies was a difficult period in railway history: reduced profits, declining dividends, rising costs, increased government regulation and growing labour troubles.[31] These problems was so deep rooted, and so pervasive, that it seems unlikely that patrician (or even non-patrician?) management was primarily to blame. In any case, most companies were under the de facto control of the general manager: the NER, though groaning with grandees, was effectively run (and very innovatively and efficiently run) by Sir George Gibb.[32]

Nevertheless, it was widely believed that aristocratic directors and chairmen did not know much about running a company. In a time of growing labour unrest, it was increasingly inappropriate that they should look on themselves as paternal employers, regard their staff as 'servants', and remain implaccably hostile to trades unions.[33] When Lord Colville of Culross retired as chairman of the GNR, it was partly because the company's recent performance had been distinctly unimpressive, and he was replaced by W.L. Jackson, who was significantly described as 'a man of practical commercial training'. Lord Stuart of Wortley's motto was 'Hold Fast by the Past', and this also seems to have been his maxim as regards business practice.[34] In his later years, Lord Knaresborough increasingly felt 'that the times were out of joint, and that he had little in common with current trends'. Lord Claud Hamilton was equally inflexible and out of date, and was described by his *Times* obituarist as 'not a conspicuously able man of business, and his judgement was not infrequently at fault'.[35]

With the major re-grouping of 1921–3, the number of railway directors was drastically reduced, from 600 to 80, and the aristocratic connection was inevitably much weakened. Neither the London Midland and Scottish Railway, nor the Southern Railway, opted for landed chairmen, although lords continued to appear on the board: Rockley, Clinton, Folkestone and Courthope in the case of the SR.[36] At the GWR, Viscount Churchill carried on as chairman until his death in 1934, and at the London and North Eastern Railway, William Whitelaw took charge when Sir Edward Grey made it plain that he would not accept. But again it was the general managers who were very much the dominant figures, and the problems of air and motor competition, of inadequate capital and delayed electrification, largely passed the chairmen by. Churchill was 'perplexed and ill at ease' during the strike-ridden inter-war period and was replaced by Viscount Horne, who had much more experience of business, politics and industry. And Sir Eric Geddes once dismissed Whitelaw as representing 'the byegone feudal system of railway management, when railway directors regarded the general manager much as they would their bailiff or game-keeper'. Appropriately enough, Whitelaw resigned as chairman in 1938 in order to devote himself to his family estates in Scotland.[37]

In a similar manner to Lord Claud Hamilton, these two notables both received fitting recognition from the companies they had served. When the GWR decided that it would produce no more Pacific locomotives, Churchward's Great Bear was rebuilt as a 4-6-0, and was re-named Viscount Churchill. And one of Sir Nigel Gresley's famous A4 Pacifics was called William Whitelaw – at least the second engine which was named after the LNER chairman. But it was Gresley himself who most triumphantly sustained the dwindling tradition of patrician involvement with railways into the inter-war years. He was the grandson of the Rev. Sir Nigel Gresley, ninth baronet, and the bearer of one of the oldest names in the country. In the 1890s, he trained at the LNWR workshops at Crewe, and for most of the inter-war years he was chief locomotive engineer of the LNER. In 1928, he introduced the Flying Scotsman, which ran non-stop from London to Edinburgh; in 1935 he put on the streamlined Silver Jubilee service; and in 1938 the Mallard became the fastest steam locomotive in the world. How different were Gresley's social origins from those of George Stephenson. As was remarked on his retirement, he was 'a great Englishman, whose ancestors fought at Agincourt'.[38]

II

In certain quarters, the aristocratic reaction to the motor-car in the two decades before the First World War was even more hostile than it had been to the steam engine during the second quarter of the nineteenth century. Unlike the railway, the automobile was explicitly conceived as a horse substitute: not for nothing was it initially called the 'horseless carriage', and firms like Mulliners, which had previously made carriages, soon turned to the building of motor-car bodies.[39] The motor was also the most potent symbol of the irresponsible and corrosive plutocracy by which the patricians felt themselves threatened from the 1880s onwards. By definition, motorists were vulgar, selfish and inconsiderate, 'simply rich people enjoying a new excitement'. They drove 'recklessly, and without proper consideration for other users of the road'. As they hurtled through the countryside, indifferent to tradition or to locality, they seemed to epitomise 'wealth's intolerable arrogance'. They abused their privileges 'with an inconsiderate insolence' which merely served to demonstrate 'the extent to which the wealth of England, during the past half century, has passsed away from the hands of gentlemen'. If the horse was the apt symbol of landed supremacy, then the motor-car was the sure and certain sign that that supremacy was coming to an end.[40]

More precisely, the car threatened three of the landed elite's most cherished institutions. The first was the very ideal of the county community, which presupposed a settled and leisurely country existence. But the car effectively destroyed this stable and self sufficient mode of life, by making country houses more accessible, and by making possible that new and quintessentially plutocratic custom, the weekend house party.[41] The second was fox-hunting, which was the most potent symbol of county solidarity; but the noise of the motor frightened the horses, and the smell put the hounds off the scent. Many hunt committees forbade their members from driving to meets in cars; one master of foxhounds described the car as 'the invention of the evil one': and Lord Willoughby de Broke thought it was 'quite out of harmony with the sport of fox-hunting'.[42] The third institution which was undermined by the motor was the cavalry: by 1914 it was clearly anachronistic, and during the inter-war years the British army was belatedly mechanised. Even as late as the 1930s, a patrician officer like Major-General Howard-Vyse was prepared to defend the 'constant association' with 'that comparatively swift animal, the horse', because he thought it resulted in a 'quickness of thought and an elasticity of outlook which are almost second nature'. But by then, the battle had long since been lost.[43]

Not surprisingly, then, 'early motorists', as Lord Brabazon later recalled, '. . . were a community rather disliked by the horsey element, and had to stick together'.[44] But as in the case of the railway, there were some aristocrats who from the very outset were well disposed to this new form of transport, especially among the super-rich, those landowners who most approximated to the new plutocracy in both their income and their outlook. Among famous owners of racehorses, both Lord Derby and Lord Rosebery were early motoring enthusiasts. So was Lord Lonsdale, arguably the most renowned horseman of his generation, who was President of the Automobile Association from 1910 until 1944.[45] Among the more restless landowners of Cheshire, the second Duke of Westminster, Lord Rocksavage and the Hon. Maurice Egerton were eager motorists; and during the First World War Westminster equipped, at his own expense, a unit of twelve armour-plated Rolls-Royces, which saw service on the Western Front and in north Africa.[46] Arthur Balfour was the first motoring Prime Minister, and drove up from the country to attend cabinet meetings. When he resigned in November 1905, he used a car to move his chattels out of 10 Downing Street; and on his eightieth birthday, his friends bought him a new Rolls-Royce.[47]

But some aristocrats also played a more active part, in the early days of the motor-car, as propagandists and publicists. The Hon. Evelyn Ellis was a younger son of the sixth Lord Howard de Walden, and brother of one of the courtiers of the Prince of Wales.[48] In 1894 he purchased a Panhard in Paris, and he brought it to England in the following year, driving it from the south coast to the Cotswolds, passing through Windsor on the way. By making the first recorded motor journey in England, he aimed to draw attention to the unreasonable restrictions imposed by the Locomotive Acts of 1865 and 1878, which limited all road vehicles to four miles per hour, and required that a man should walk in front carrying a red flag. Ellis deliberately flouted this law, by dispensing with the red flag and driving above the speed limit, and so helped to bring about the Locomotives and Highways Act of 1896, which did away with the red flag and raised the speed limit to fourteen miles per hour. Thanks to his courtly connections, he also persuaded the Prince of Wales to take his first drive in a motor in 1896, at Warwick Castle.[49]

Ellis was outshone by Lord Montagu of Beaulieu, who soon changed his interests from driving trains to driving cars, and energetically exploited his social and political contacts in support of this new cause. He bought his first car in 1896, and paid his first motoring fine three years later. In 1899 he became the first MP to appear in a car in New Palace Yard, in the following year he was the first MP to use a motor in a general election campaign, and in 1902 he took Edward VII for his first drive as King. He contibuted to the *Book of Motoring* in the *Badminton Library of Sports and Pastimes*, was chairman of the Parliamentary Automobile Committee, and did much to facilitate the passing of the 1903 Motor Bill, which raised the speed limit to 20 m.p.h.[50] But Montagu's greatest impact was through his journalism. In 1902, he began to publish *Car Illustrated*, which boasted a message of support from Arthur Balfour, and ran a series of articles entitled 'Cars and Country Houses'. As a friend of Alfred Harmsworth's, Montagu was a regular contributor to *The Times* and the *Daily Mail*, for whom he wrote a series of motoring articles on a wide range of subjects.[51]

The third patrician propagandist in these early pioneering years was Hugh Fortescue Locke-King, a country gentleman who owned a 3500-acre estate at Brooklands near Weybridge in Surrey. In 1907, he opened a two-and-three-quarter-mile race track, to publicise British cars and to enable British drivers to reach much higher speeds than were allowed on the road.[52] Until the Second World War, Brooklands was the mecca for British motoring, and it long retained signs of its aristocratic origins. Hugh Allen of the Jockey Club was the starter, the entry fees and prize money were in sovereigns, and the results were run up on a telegraph board at the end of each race. In the early years, the cars were un-numbered, like horses, and drivers wore coloured smocks, like jockeys, by which they expected to be identified. Even after this practice was abandoned, amateur drivers still talked of 'stabling their mounts' at garages near the track, and throughout the inter-war years the club committee remained dominated by grandees.[53]

Although there were many motoring enthusiastists and propagandists among the aristocracy and gentry, few of them became closely involved in investment or in management. Before the First World War, four hundred companies were set up to manufacture motor cars in Britain. Almost all of them operated on a very small scale, and by 1914 scarcely a quarter of them were still in being. Compared with railway debentures or preference shares, these were decidedly risky undertakings, and there were very few instances of aristocratic investment.[54] In the early 1900s, the Hon. Evelyn Ellis invested £13,000 in Daimler debenture shares, and this infusion of capital probably kept the company from collapsing completely. Better documented is the connection between the Earl of Macclesfield and William Morris. They first met in a motor-car collision in Oxford (where Macclesfield was an undergdraduate) in 1905. In August 1912, Macclesfield invested £4000 in preference shares in Morris's new company, and in 1919, when Morris reorganised his business, Macclesfield took £25,000-worth of seven per cent preference shares. Again, this support seems to have been crucial for the survival of Morris's early enterprises.[55]

Since aristocratic investment in the motor industry was minimal, aristocratic directors and chairmen were rarer still. In the investment boom of the mid 1890s, many companies were promoted connected with tyres, bicycles and cars, especially by Harry Lawson and E.T. Hooley. One technique they employed to persuade the public to invest in their uncertain undertakings was to deck out their lists of directors with titled names. Lord de la Warr was chairman of Dunlop, and Lord Winchilsea was chairman of the Great Horseless Carriage Company.[56] Other peers who were involved in such companies, either as chairmen or directors, included Lords Aylesford, Lonsdale and Albemarle. These men were among the more disreputable members of the peerage, who eagerly (and foolishly) accepted cash payments from Hooley and Lawson in exchange for allowing their names to be used. When the companies collapsed, the result was public humiliation, and thereafter titled directors in the car industry were very rare indeed. Before 1914, the most conspicuous exception was the Earl of Shrewsbury and Talbot, who in 1903 became chairman of a syndicate formed to sell Clement cars in England, and which later sold Talbot cars, made in Ladbroke Grove, Kensington.[57]

The closest connection between the motor industry and the aristocracy was forged by the Hon. C.S. Rolls, younger son of Lord Llangattock, a Monmouthshire landowner. Rolls had bought his first car in 1896, and was one of the earliest patrician enthusiasts.[58] In 1902, he set himself up in London, selling high-class cars to high-class people, and by ruthlessly exploiting his aristocratic connections established a reputation as a brilliant salesman and demonstrator. By 1903, he numbered Lord Rosebery, Lord Willoughby d'Eresby and the Duke of Sutherland among his clients, and by the following year his customers included foreign princes, two dukes, two earls, one viscount, seven barons and three baronets. Initially, Rolls was obliged to sell foreign motors, but his ambition was to sell a high-class English car. In 1904, he met the engineer Henry Royce, and two years later the company of Rolls-Royce was registered, with Royce making the cars, and Rolls making the sales.[59] By the time of Rolls's death in 1910, the Silver Ghost was already established as 'the best car in the world'. Only Daimler, with close royal connections, which lasted until the death of Queen Mary, and with the early financial support provided by the Hon. Evelyn Ellis, offered any serious competition in this high-status market.[60]

By the inter-war years the links between the aristocracy and the motor-car had become noticeably weaker. In part, this was because the sale of great estates, and the increasing impoverishment of many landowners, meant that they no longer made up such an important element in the quality market for cars as they once had. This, at least, was Lord Cottenham's opinion:

A great deal of money has changed hands of late years, but not always for the better. Where the Rolls-Royce, the Daimler or the Sunbeam in days gone by might well have been occupied by those to whom the well-being of their tenants and their servants was as important as the upbringing of their own children, today, these cars are occupied far too often by the war profiteer, to whom, after the manner of their kind, the maintenance of their 'dignity' and the satisfying of their appetites alike are gods. The squire is constantly seen driving a little car, nowadays.[61]

There were also major changes in the industry itself. It no longer meant sport for the few, so much as transport for the many. Large firms like Morris and Austin took over many of their rivals, and concentrated on mass-produced vehicles for a mass market.[62] The aristocracy played no part in this transformation. William Morris bought out Lord Macclesfield's shareholding in February 1922, and thereafter never had dealings with him again. Only at Rolls-Royce did the patrician connection linger, where Lord Herbert Scott, a younger son of the Duke of Buccleuch, was chairman between 1936 and 1944.[63]

Some notables also continued in their self-appointed task as publicists and propagandists. From 1921 until his death in 1929, Lord Montagu was motoring correspondent of *The Times*, and in 1922–3, he vainly tried to set up a syndicate to construct a motorway network connecting all the major British towns.[64] The sixth Earl of Cottenham raced cars for Alvis and Sunbeam during the 1920s, and wrote a succession of books dealing with almost every aspect of the past, present and future of the car: *Motoring Without Fears* (1928), *Motoring Today and Tomorrow* (1928), and *Steering Wheel Papers* (1932). Thereafter, he became motoring adviser to the Metropolitan Police and the Home Office.[65] Viscount Curzon, later fifth Earl Howe, took up competitive driving in 1928 at the age of 44, on the advice of a magistrate who was bored with fining him so often for speeding. He became president of the British Racing Drivers' Club, and edited the volume on *Motor Racing* in the *Lonsdale Library*.[66]

The most famous upper-class motorist during the interwar years was probably the Hon. Mrs Victor Bruce, the daughter of Lawrence Petre of Coptfold Hall in Essex, who married the fourth son of the second Lord Aberdare in 1926.[67] She was the first women to ride a motor cycle, the first to be in an accident, and the first to be summonsed for speeding. In 1927, she won the Ladies Cup in the Monte Carlo Rally, having driven for 72 hours, non-stop. In the same year, she drove to the Arctic Circle and back (and was granted an audience by the King of Denmark on the way). With her husband, she drove non-stop round the track at Montlhéry, covering 15,000 miles in ten days at an average of 68 miles per hour. In 1929 she drove round the same track for 24 hours, at an average speed of 90 m.p.h., establishing a new world record for the greatest non-stop run by a single-handed driver. True to her aristocratic origins, she always drove wearing a string of pearls. In 1939 she came first in the open jumping class at the Royal Horse Show, Windsor. 'Speed', she recalled in her autobiography, 'has always fascinated me since my first pony bolted. Going slowly always makes me tired.'[68]

III

Compared with the train or the car, the aeroplane was less negatively viewed by the aristocracy, at least during its early years. Ever since the time of Sir George Cayley, titled dilettantes had shown an interest in the problems of flight, and during the last quarter of the nineteenth century ballooning had enjoyed extensive aristocratic patronage. 'To go up in a balloon', Lord Brabazon later recalled, 'is the only way to go into the air like a gentleman.'[69] Nor, in its pre-jet manifestation, did the aeroplane threaten the sanctity of landowners' broad acres, or the peace and quiet of the countryside, in the way that the steam train or the car did. Above all, there was something appealingly chivalric about the early pioneers of powered flight. In peacetime, it was daring, dangerous, almost buccaneering, to take to the air in these frail and flimsy machines. In wartime, these latter-day knights of the skies duelled and jousted in aerial tournaments, elevated above the earth-bound and plodding infantry in much the same way that the men on horseback had been in earlier eras.

For many patricians, interest in the aeroplane was the natural extension of their interest in the motor car. Rolls was an ardent balloonist (he eventually made 170 ascents), and in 1903 he had founded the Aero Club to promote the sport, significantly described as 'the Jockey Club of flying'. He then shifted his attention to cars, but once Rolls-Royce was established turned again to the air, this time as an eager champion of powered flight. In 1908 he visited Le Mans to study Wilbur Wright's aeroplane, and soon bought one of his machines for his own use. In June 1910 he set a new record by flying the English Channel both ways in his Wright aeroplane.

By this time his reputation was at its peak, and he began to be concerned about the government's indifference to the military implications of flying, and the precarious finances of many of the British aeroplane producers.[70] But in July 1910 he took part in a flying tournament at Bournemouth, and was killed when his plane crashed following the collapse of the tailplane, thus becoming the first Englishman to be involved in a fatal aero accident.

Among Rolls's closest friends was J.T.C. Moore-Brabazon, scion of a famous Irish landed family, who after leaving Cambridge, where he had briefly read engineering, was apprenticed for a year as a mechanic at the Darracq company in Paris, and became an international racing driver. In 1907, he won the Circuit des Ardennes in a Minerva, but by then he had already taken up ballooning, and soon turned his attention to flying. In May 1909, he became the first Englishman to make a powered flight in the United Kingdom. On the Isle of Sheppey, he flew a Voisin for a little over one minute, and ended with a crash that nearly killed him. But as a result, he obtained the first pilot's certificate given out by the Royal Aero Club (Rolls was given the second). In October of the same year, he piloted a Short Brothers machine, and won the £1000 prize offered by the *Daily Mail* for the first English aircraft to fly one mile. Like Rolls, he began to establish himself as a pundit and propagandist, but after Rolls's fatal crash he stopped flying altogether.[71]

Other notables were not so easily deterred. Maurice Egerton, Sir Archibald Sinclair, Lord Edward Grosvenor, Lord George Wellesley and the Marquess of Tullibardine were among the earliest pilots to qualify in the years before 1914. Like the Automobile Association and the Royal Automobile Club, the Royal Aero Club was laden with grandees among its presidents and committee men. Hugh Locke-King made Brooklands into a centre for aviation, and Lord Montagu of Beaulieu opened a training school in the grounds of his country house.[72] He gave generous coverage to flying in *Car Illustrated*, and began to take an interest in the military implications of powered flight. In 1909, he established the Aerial Defence Committee, and initiated the first-ever parliamentary debate on the subject. Until 1914 he was a severe critic of the government's lack of interest, and throughout the First World War he campaigned vigorously for the amalgamation of the Royal Flying Corps and the Royal Naval Air Service, and for the setting up of a proper Air Ministry.[73]

With very few exceptions, this was sum of the aristocracy's involvement with flying in its formative years: adventure and propaganda, augmented by a little politicking. As with the motor industry, there were a large number of small producers, whose finances were exceptionally precarious.[74] But there are only two recorded cases of financial assistance along the lines of Ellis with Daimler, and Macclesfield with Morris. Lady Howard de Walden recalled that her husband helped to finance one such venture, although she does not specify which. It proved to be a failure, as the plane flew only once, briefly and unsuccessfully; but for years afterwards the silk with which the wings had been covered 'produced shirts galore' for de Walden's 'various godsons'. More significant was the Blair Atholl Syndicate, which was created to support the efforts of John William Dunne. The Duke of Westminster, the Marquess of Tullibardine, Earl Fitzwilliam and Lord Rothschild each subscribed £1000. Although initially his experiments prospered more than those of Lord Howard de Walden's unknown pioneer, Dunne eventually ran out of ideas, and left aviation for good in 1914.[75]

Under these circumstances, it is perhaps not surprising that the aristocratic contribution to the airborne war of 1914–18 was decidedly meagre. Moore-Brabazon joined the Royal Flying Corps, and became expert in aerial photography and reconnaissance. The young Oswald Mosley served briefly during 1915. Other patricians who flew include Lord Edward Grosvenor, Lord Hugh Cecil and the Master of Sempill.[76] But the most famous British aces – Albert Ball, James McCudden and Mick Mannock – were from a much lower social stratum, while the high command was very much in the hands of Hugh Trenchard. Unlike the war on the western front, there was no 'lost generation' of doomed patrician flyers. There was no English equivalent to the German ace, von Richthofen, a Prussian aristocrat with a passion for hunting, who brought down eighty allied pilots, and was idolised in Germany is a knight of the air, a chivalric crusader. The British public shared this view: they christened him the Red Baron, and when he was finally shot down, in the spring of 1918, he was saluted by *The Aeroplane* as 'a brave man, a clean fighter, and . . . a courageous nobleman'.[77] No such figure emerged from the thin ranks of Britain's flying aristocracy.

During the inter-war years the Royal Air Force was subjected to severe economies until 1934, Imperial Airways was starved of funds, and the plane-makers suffered accordingly.[78] To the extent that aristocrats were still involved, their connection was the familiar amalgam of recreation and propaganda, topped off by politics. The 'Flying' Duchess of Bedford took to the air because she was stone deaf, and because the change in atmospheric pressure alleviated the buzzing in her ears. She qualified as a pilot in her sixties, and made much-publicised round trips to India and the Cape of Good Hope. In March 1937 she took off from Woburn on a routine flight, and was never seen again. It was later discovered that the word WOBURN had been painted in large letters on the roof of the house, for her benefit, and this caused mild embarrassment when the secret service moved there during the Second World War.[79] Predictably more flamboyant was Mrs Victor Bruce, who embarked on a round-the-world solo flight in 1930, only eight weeks after having gained her pilot's licence. In order to lighten her plane, she dispensed with the parachute. She crashed in the Arabian desert, caught malaria in Indo-China, and when flying over

Hong Kong on 11 November stopped her engine in mid-air to observe the two minutes' silence. She later joined a flying circus, and subsequently ran an air despatch company.[80]

The foreword to her account of her round-the-world flight was written by the Master of Sempill, who was as much a propagandist for air travel as Lord Cottesloe was for the motor car. After serving in the RFC, he undertook many overseas missions to advise other governments on the setting up of their air forces. He competed for the King's Cup each year between 1924 and 1930, and made many long flights abroad. He was President of the Royal Aeronautical Society and of the Gliding Association, aviation correspondent of *The Field*, and in 1931 published *The Air and the Plain Man*.[81] Even more adventurous was the Marquess of Clydesdale, who later became fourteenth Duke of Hamilton. In 1933, he successfully led an expedition to take the first photographs of the summit of Mount Everest, an adventure which he later described as 'the only one original flight worthwhile.'[82] Like Sempill, Clydesdale prided himself on being – in the language of the time – 'airminded'. In essence, this meant being well disposed to modernity and to technological progress. For members of the inter-war aristocracy, constantly afraid that their day was done, the attractions of proclaiming their 'airmindedness' were very great indeed.[83]

This may partly explain why it was that during the inter-war years the Air Ministry was almost consistently in patrician hands. In 1919, the Secretary of State for War and Air was Winston Churchill; the Under-Secretary of State was his cousin, Lord Londonderry; and his Parliamentary Private Secretary was Moore-Brabazon. For almost the whole of the period 1922–9 the Secretary of State was Sir Samuel Hoare, a Norfolk country gentleman, who was one of the best shots in the land, and had married a daughter of Lord Beauchamp.[84] Between 1922 and 1924, Hoare's Under-Secretary was the Duke of Sutherland, one of the last dukes to hold high political office. From 1931 to 1935 the Air Ministry was held by Lord Londonderry, whose wife staged lavish receptions for the National Government at Londonderry House, and was a close friend of Ramsay MacDonald. And Londonderry was followed by Philip Cunliffe-Lister, another landowner, who soon went to the Lords as Viscount Swinton.[85]

At a time when the aristocratic contribution to politics was in steep decline, this disproportionate concentration in one ministry deserves attention. For much of the inter-war period, the Air Ministry was a marginal and low-spending department, and thus an appropriate billet for second-ranking notables. The patricians in charge of it were either lightweight or accident-prone, or both. Samuel Hoare was in the shadow of Trenchard, the Chief of the Air Staff, and saw himself in the subordinate role as 'the prophet's interpreter to a world that did not always understand his dark sayings'.[86] Londonderry owed his job to Macdonald's favouritism, and he was described by J.C.C. Davidson as 'not really equipped for thinking... not really fit for Cabinet rank'. When the government's policy was abruptly altered in 1934–5, he was clearly out of his depth, and Baldwin soon got rid of him. By contrast, Swinton was a much more able minister – who drove ahead the re-armament programme with vigour and success – but a maladroit politician, ill at ease in the Commons, and then marginalised in the Lords, who alienated Neville Chamberlain without conciliating the anti-appeasers.[87]

In fact, the major contribution of these genteel ministers was made at the social rather than the political level, as they used their connections and their prestige in promoting the cause of 'airmindedness'.[88] The Duke of Sutherland was 'a leading patron of aviation', endowed a prize for light aircraft, organised an International Air Congress in London, was chairman of the Royal Aero Club from 1924 to 1925, and president of the Air League from 1921 to 1944. Sir Samuel Hoare did his utmost to interest the royal family in the RAF, visited India in 1926 to launch the new Imperial Airways route, and flew to South Africa three years later.[89] The Marquess of Londonderry was the most 'ardent flying enthusiast' of them all. In order to identify himself with the RAF, he learned to fly at the age of 55, thereby earning a letter from the king's private secretary which was revealing in the comparison it drew: 'It is a fine performance at your age', Sir Clive Wigram wrote, 'to pilot an aeroplane as well as you do a horse.' He went on extended tours of inspection overseas, promoted an airport in Northern Ireland, regularly flew his plane between his estates in Durham and County Down, and wrote and lectured extensively on aviation matters.[90]

The Second World War vividly demonstrated what remained of this aristocratic connection with flying. Throughout Churchill's great coalition, the Secretary of State for Air was another notable, Sir Archibald Sinclair, Lord Lieutenant of Caithness, MP for the county (and the direct descendant of the great agricultural improver, Sir John Sinclair). For a short time, Moore-Brabazon was Minister of Aircraft Production, where his close contacts with the industry enabled him to restore order after the piratical idiosyncrasies of Lord Beaverbrook's regime.[91] Senior commanders in the RAF included the Duke of Hamilton, the Earl of Bandon, and the future sixth Earl of Gosford. Three of Hamilton's brothers also served, and the Duke himself was the embarrassed object of Rudolph Hess's peace mission in 1941.[92] Lord Londonderry, embittered at his dismissal from power, encouraged flying in Northern Ireland. And after her aircraft had been requisitioned and her despatch-pilots called up, Mrs Victor Bruce set up a factory in Cardiff to repair battle-damaged plane wings. They were brought to the factory in converted horse-boxes.[93]

But the weakness of the aristocratic-aeronautic link inevitably meant that the patrician contribution to the war in the air was distinctly limited. As Secretary of State, Sinclair failed to stand up to the prime minister or the service chiefs, and being what one admirer called 'a great gentleman with a total incapacity for departing from the rules of truth and honour' was a grave handicap in his dealings with Beaverbrook. After only a few months at the MAP, Moore-Brabazon was obliged to resign, having made some indiscreet and uncomplimentary remarks about the Russians.[94] Among the RAF high command, Dowding, Portal, Harris and Tedder were distinctly non-patrician. Only Sholto Douglas could claim distant aristo-cratic ancestry, but when he was made a peer in 1948 he took the Labour whip. Among the pilots, there was no knightly cult of chivalry comparable to that which was deliberately fostered in the German and Japanese air forces. Even Churchill noted, with slight but pardonable exaggeration, that 'none of the aristocracy chose the RAF – they left it all to the lower middle classes'. As G.M. Trevelyan put it in his *English Social History*, the Battle of Britain was won, neither on the playing fields of Eton, nor the village greens of England, but in the primary and secondary schools of the great cities.[95]

IV

In the last decade of the nineteenth century, a Yorkshire breeder made this confident prediction: 'I don't think for one moment that all the cycles and motor cars in the world, after the novelty is gone, will ever cause our English gentry, or their sons and daughters, to turn their backs on a beautiful typical riding or driving horse.'[96] To the extent that many mem-bers of the aristocracy remain attached to the outdoor life, and to country pursuits, this prophecy has undoubtedly been fulfilled. At a deeper level, however, it has not been borne out by subsequent events: the horse has not survived as the pre-eminent mode of transport any more than the aristoc-racy has survived as the pre-eminent elite. In part this has been because what the Countess of Minto described as 'incessant motion, high-speed motor cars, perpetual rush and hurry' has inevitably undermined the stability and hierarchy so essential for the survival of a traditional territorial aristocracy.[97] And in part it is because the patricians themselves have not loomed large in the histories of the railway, the car or the plane. Even as inter-war celebrities, Lord Cottenham, Lord Sempill and Mrs Victor Bruce could not compare with Seagrave, Campbell, Lindbergh or Amy Johnson.

But while recent developments in transport can be studied with virtually no reference to the aristocracy, it is clear that accounts of the aristocracy should not ignore recent developments in transport. For, as so often in the history of the nineteenth- and twentieth-century landed classes, these agents of decline were also the means of adaption. In the case of the railways, the aristocracy came to a very profitable accommodation: not just through selling their land, but later as shareholders in the major companies, as directors and as chairmen. Some of them welcomed the motor and the plane with at least as much enthusiasm: partly because they genuinely saw these new machines as super-charged versions of the horse; partly because they provided new scope for aristocrats to display their traditional characteristics of bravery, foolhardiness and a sense of adventure; and partly because they offered opportunities for a declining and anachronistic class to present itself as modern and fully up to date. Not surprisingly, many notables viewed these innovations in transport with at least as much enthusiasm as regret. As Lord Dunraven once delightedly exclaimed: 'Goodness! What changes in locomotion I have seen.'[98]

Nor has this connection between nobility and mobility entirely disappeared in post-war Britain. As a result of the Transport Act of 1953, Donald Cameron of Lochiel, bearer of one of the most historic names in Scotland, became a part-time Transport Commissioner, and chairman of British Rail's Scottish Area Board. Two of Mrs Thatcher's senior ministers, William Whitelaw and Nicholas Ridley, were the direct descendants of notables who were themselves chairmen of railway companies.[99] The Duke of Richmond built a motor-race track in the grounds of Goodwood, and the third Lord Montagu of Beaulieu opened his vintage car museum, which soon became world-famous. Another Tory grandee, Lord Carrington, was once a trainee manager at De Havilland's, the aircraft manufacturers, and the Duke of Leinster, whose forebears were among the greatest landowners in Ireland, runs a flying school near Oxford.[100]

These individual examples are not the only way in which transport, like so much else in Britain, remains enfolded in what has been called the 'aristocratic embrace'.[101] For those who cannot afford to fly the Atlantic First Class, but aspire to mark themselves off from the mass of travellers going Tourist, most airlines offer an intermediary category. American companies described it as Business Class – but on British Airways it is called Club.

PART TWO

INDIVIDUALS IN CONTEXT

4

Lord Curzon as Ceremonial Impressario

THE LAST QUARTER of the nineteenth century and the years before the First World War witnessed a remarkable flowering of ceremonial and spectacle in Europe and the United States, and throughout those parts of the globe where the great powers held sway. Though they were novel pageants in many ways, self-consciously planned and developed, the aim of those who stage-managed them was to create feelings of security, cohesion and identity, in an era of anxiety, uncertainty and social dislocation. As a result, old rituals were refurbished, and new traditions were invented, in the churches, in the armed services, in schools and universities, in towns and cities, in republics and monarchies.[1] At all levels of society, Britain and its dominions fully shared in these developments. The Delhi Durbar of 1877, the Golden Jubilee of 1887 and the Diamond Jubilee of 1897 portended a new interest in spectacle and display, which contrasted vividly with the drabness and incompetence of the mid-Victorian era. As Lord George Hamilton noted in 1902, 'until recently, we had allowed ceremony and pageant to play far too small a part in our national life, and we reduced all functions to the smallest scope, divested of all picturesqueness, at the instance of the Utilitarian or Manchester school party'.[2] But since the late 1870s, all that had changed.

The recipient of this letter, George Nathaniel Curzon, at that time serving as Viceroy of India, wholeheartedly agreed that the transformation from mid-Victorian austerity to late-Victorian grandeur was a distinct improvement. Nor should this be surprising, since he was himself a child of this more stately, more theatrical, more ceremonially-conscious age. He was born in 1859, became a Member of Parliament in 1886, was sent to India as Viceroy in 1898, was appointed Lord Privy Seal in 1915 and Foreign Secretary four years later, and died in 1925. To his contemporaries, he was the grandest and most caparisoned statesman of his day. 'No public man of our time', one journalist remarked, early in Curzon's career, 'has a greater innate love of display than he.' 'In the spectacular sphere', Sir J.A.R. Marriott wrote in a corroborative obituary notice, 'Lord Curzon was unsurpassed. He had a genuine and a well-grounded belief in the value of ritual and ceremonial.'[3] Indeed, he possessed unrivalled skill and imagination as a master of ceremonies, as a stage-manager of spectacle, as an inventor of traditions. For Curzon was not only good at making history: he was even better at making his version of it come alive. To him, history was a pageant, and pageantry was history. In his mind, the two were inseparable.

I

To his critics, Curzon's love of pomp and circumstance was merely the inevitable extension of his own stateliness of manner and insufferable sense of superiority: not for him 'the sordid policy of self-effacement'. His Indian Viceroyalty was a by-word for splendour and show remarkable even by the standards of the Raj. At the Coronation of King George V, Curzon bore the Banner of India in Westminster Abbey, and 'processed as if the whole proceedings were in his honour: the aisle was just wide enough for him'.[4] He lived in four magnificent homes: 1 Carlton House Terrace in London, Kedleston in Derbyshire, Montacute in Somerset, and Hackwood near Basingstoke.[5] In the course of his career, he was loaded with honours: an Irish barony, a British earldom and marquessate, the Royal Victorian Chain, the two Indian orders, and the Garter. He helped to establish the Order of the British Empire in 1917, and was closely involved in decisions concerning etiquette and jurisdiction at the royal court. On one occasion, he observed that it was the 'insatiable appetite' of the British people 'for titles and precedence' which helped explain why Britain won the First World War.[6] It was an appetite he himself fully shared.

    Yet there was much more to Curzon's love of ceremony and pageantry than his unbridled egotism and sense of superiority. Nor did he accept Walter Bagehot's view that there was a distinction between the 'dignified' and 'efficient' parts of the constitution, to the detriment of the latter. On the contrary, he believed that spectacle and display an integral part of the life and the history of the nation. He explained this to the citizens of Dover in his first speech as Lord Warden of the Cinque Ports:

We English are a people who combine a love for progress and a faculty for ordered change with a most passionate attachment to our ancient institutions, and a scrupulous reverence for those forms and customs whose roots are embedded in our history, and whose evolution has been typical of our national growth. We are always living half in the present and half in the past. In the conditions, and still more in the ceremonies, of our public life, the two are blended together with peculiar harmony, so that we cannot quite say where the one ends and the other begins, and the spirit of the past seems to be a part of the atmosphere we breathe.[7]

He made the same point again in 1910: King George V's Coronation, he insisted, was not just 'some great pageant or procession', empty of deeper or more profound meaning: it was 'one of the great historic landmarks in the history of the British people', in which 'the history, the tradition, the poetry, the romance of untold centuries', would be 'summed up in that great ceremonial'.[8]

As these remarks imply, Curzon's belief in the importance of ritual and spectacle was deeply felt, carefully thought out, cogently articulated, and (when necessary) vigorously defended. In part, his devotion to human ceremonial was but an extension of his exceptional sensitivity to the pageantry of nature. Curzon was one of the most indefatigable travellers of his age, both in Europe and in Asia, and his early books and letters record his vivid reactions to natural phenomena: to blazing sunsets, to intimidating mountain peaks, and to the thunder and spray of waterfalls.[9] For Curzon, much of the attraction of nature lay in its theatrical properties and sensational displays: unforgettable vistas, magnificent colours, the tension between movement and repose, and the contrasts between sounds and silence. Here, in their natural form, were the essential ingredients of ceremonial effect – most vividly displayed by the great waterfalls of the world, which combined beauty and power, setting and sound, majesty and movement, which brought forth feelings of 'awe' as well as 'admiration', and which provided 'a unique experience and imperishable memory'.[10] This was his response to one of nature's wonders: it was also his response to man-made spectacle.

Curzon's passion for nature was especially indulged in the distant lands of Asia, to which he became addicted during his travels, and which continued to haunt him all his life.[11] Like many contemporary travellers, he was captivated by the alliterative combination of splendour and squalor, dignity and decay, which seemed to characterise the Orient. He was fascinated too by the ancient monarchies of the east: Korea, Japan, Persia, China, Afghanistan, and Hue. In his books and letters, he provided vivid vignettes of royal palaces, royal regalia, royal etiquette. He described the powers, the functions and the characters of these oriental potentates, and he left unforgettable accounts of his own audiences with several of them.[12] He feared – or in some cases, hoped – that these despotic regimes were gradually crumbling under the impact of the west. Only India seemed destined to survive, thanks to the Raj: 'a country famed for its lavish ostentation, its princely wealth, and its titled classes'. By comparison with such oriental magnificence, the British seemed 'dingy and unimaginative'.[13] But the rituals and romance of 'the gorgeous east' held Curzon in fee and in thrall all his life.

His love of ceremonial and show was further reinforced by his powerful sense of the past, by his 'reverence for the ancient and historic', which was, he believed, 'the surest spring of national self-respect'. At Oxford, he was steeped in Greek and Roman history, and he wrote prize essays on the Emperor Justinian and Sir Thomas More. As the result of his great travels in Asia, he was remarkably well informed about the 'blazoned histories' of

Egypt, Mesopotamia, Russia, Persia, China and Japan, which took up large parts of his early travel books. He was an accomplished amateur archaeologist, a Fellow of the British Academy, an Honorary Fellow of the Royal Institute of British Architects, and an energetic Trustee of the National Gallery and of the British Museum.[14] He was drawn to study the great houses he owned, or had purchased, or inhabited officially: the circumstances in which they were built; the individuals who had lived in them; and the 'almost human personality' which the buildings themselves possessed. 'If these stones could speak', he wrote of Government House, Calcutta, which was itself modelled on Kedleston, 'what a tale they might tell.' Here was the 'fascination and romance of the past', something of which Curzon never tired.[15]

This love of history, combined with his delight in works of art and beautiful things, made Curzon one of the earliest, most active and most creative conservationists. He bought and restored Tattershall and Bodiam Castles, and donated them to the National Trust. He spent extensively on renovating Montacute, Hackwood and Kedleston. He opposed the sale of Old Masters to the United States, supported legislation designed to protect ancient monuments, and deprecated the spoliation of the countryside by suburban development.[16] In India, he was appalled at the neglect and decay of ancient buildings and historic monuments, and created a new Archaeological Department, so as to make possible their scientific conservation and repair. For they were, Curzon believed, 'documents just as valuable in reading the records of the past as is any manuscript or parchment deed'. It was these feelings which inspired the two great monuments he created on two continents: the memorial chapel to his first wife, built at Kedleston between 1906 and 1913, and the Victoria Memorial Hall, constructed at Calcutta between 1906 and 1921.[17] In the grandest manner possible, Curzon commemorated the Queen's reign, and celebrated the long story of the Anglo-Indian connection. As such, it was not just a museum to past deeds: here, for Curzon, was history reconstructed in tanglble, visible, arresting form.

Curzon's exceptional sensitivity to natural splendour, his delight in oriental pageantry, his prodigious scholarship, his passion for conservation, and his vivid sense of the links which bound the past and the present together, meant he was possessed of an astonishingly powerful historical imagination. He could not project himself inside the minds and hearts of other men, but the glimpse of a building or a ruin with past associations set his imagination free. In Rome, the mere sight of the Forum caused him to think of Cato and Caesar, Cicero and Pompey. The battlements of Bodiam lead him to visualise 'a train of richly-clad knights, falcons on their wrists, with their ladies mounted on gaudy, caparisoned palfreys, suddenly to emerge from the barbican gate, for the enjoyment of the chase'.[18] At Government House in Calcutta, the effect of 'sitting, as successive Viceroys do, in the rooms where a long series of great men have lived and worked', meant that he thought 'of them so often that their shades almost seem to rise before one's eyes', as a 'company of fellow workers and counsellors, who had done the same thing that I was trying to do, and who, from the stores of their experience or wisdom, offered to me invaluable advice or warning'.[19]

Curzon's remarkable creative imagination found two important outlets in his public life, which were closely related. The first was in his oratory. From his years at Eton he developed an elaborate, Latinate style of rhetoric, so spacious, so majestic, so studied, so ornamented and so polysyllabic that the Master of Balliol, Benjamin Jowett, took him aside, and warned him against the dangers of excessive prolixity. Even Churchill, himself scarcely a man of few words, thought Curzon sometimes overdid it; but he was impervious to such suggestions. As he made plain in his Rede Lecture on *Modern Parliamentary Eloquence*, he would have been happier in the eighteenth century, the last age of classical oratory, when Greek and Latin quotations were thrown back and forth, and when 'imagery, metaphor, antithesis, alliteration, trope' were all an accepted part of the orator's art and craft.[20] At his best, as in his threnody for Alfred Lyttelton, or in his speech announcing the Allied victory in the House of Lords in November 1918, Curzon could rise to great heights of eloquence and feeling. At his worst, he sounded pompous and unconvincingly verbose. One by no means unappreciative figure, Harold Nicolson, compared a Curzon speech in full flow to 'some stately procession proceeding orderly through *Arcs de Triomphe* along a straight wide avenue; outriders, escorts, bands; the perfection of accoutrements, the precise marshalling of detail, the sense of conscious continuity, the sense of absolute control'.[21]

In likening Curzon's oratory to a military parade or a richly-bejewelled procession, Nicolson not only did full and evocative justice to Curzon's brocaded and bespangled rhetorical style: he also mimicked one of Curzon's own favourite – and revealing – turns of phrase. For he often resorted to the language of ritual and ceremonial to describe people, events or activities which those of lesser imagination would not have seen in such terms. 'Too soon the procession had passed', he observed of a sunset in India in 1888, 'and the pageant was no more.' The life and death of Mrs Alfred Lyttelton left 'a sense of wonder and enchantment', which continued to 'thrill the heart of everyone who beheld the spectacle'.[22] Asquith's oratory he likened to 'some great military parade', as sentence followed sentence in 'rhythmical order' and 'to the roll of drums'. The 'singing sands' of the desert spoke 'in notes now as of harp strings, anon as of trumpets and drums', which echoed 'down the ages'. And in his more buoyant moments Curzon saw his own career as one long, stately and *noblimente* progress: 'So long as one is marching, I say, let the drums beat and the flags fly!'[23] As these words suggest, the metaphors of ceremony and spectacle permeated much that Curzon thought, said or did.

From his highly-coloured world of images, sensations, history, sounds and words, it was but a short step to the pomp and pageantry of ceremonial itself, Curzon's second contribution to the imaginative side of public life. Just as rhetoric was verbal advocacy, so ritual was visual advocacy: the opportunity to make a case, to impart a message, to impress an audience, to reinforce a sense of identity and of community, and to cement those links between past and present about which he cared so dearly. For Curzon was astonishingly well endowed with the ability to visualise a pageant. In 1903 he held a grand reception at Government House, Calcutta, to mark the centenary of the ball which his predecessor, Lord Wellesley, had given to celebrate the news of the Treaty of Amiens. Curzon was dressed as Wellesley, and all the guests wore period costume: thus was the past made to live again. As Lord Esher – himself no mean pageant-master – once observed, Curzon was possessed of an 'enormous capacity for work, a brilliant imagination, with supreme gift of expression'.[24] Lord George Hamilton recognised the same qualities: 'you have the imaginative conception necessary for the creation of an original scheme, and the administrative power required to look into every detail'.[25]

As his admirers all conceded, it was this rare combination of imagination and industry, magnificence and meticulousness, which made Curzon unrivalled as a ceremonial impressario. Having conceived and visualised his pageant – the setting, the actors, the audience, the movements, the colours, the sounds, the mood, the atmosphere – he possessed both the will and the energy to make it happen, to make it come alive. For Curzon's obsessive attention to detail was legendary. He hired his own footmen, scrutinised his household accounts down to the last farthing, and wrote the names for the places at dinner. When restoring Kedleston, in his last years, he personally got into each of the new baths that were being installed, 'lined first of all with copies of *The Times*, in order to discover they were the right shape from the inside'. The second Lady Curzon not only had her marriage service planned down to the last detail: her husband also left instructions as to where her coffin would be placed in the family vault.[26] This total inability to delegate was, at different times in Curzon's career, a terrible political disadvantage; but in the planning of great occasions, down to the very last detail, it was an essential skill. As Curzon said of Lord Wellesley, so it might be said of him: 'he elevated the spectacular to the level of an exact science'.[27]

Lord Selborne once remarked that Curzon's gift for taking himself seriously at a ceremonal function was 'un-British', 'invaluable' and 'splendid'. Precisely when he discovered this passion for pageantry, this lust for lustre, it is impossible to say. When scarcely out of adolescence, Curzon already knew the essentials of the matter: in 1881, at the age of seventeen, he observed the funeral accorded to Benjamin Disraeli, Earl of Beaconsfield, and was not impressed. It was, he noted, 'a somewhat jarring combination of public display and quiet modesty', which prevented it from being 'either impressive as a sight or moving as a function'.[28] Curzon's pageants never incurred such criticism. Even his critics, who could not bear his delight in grandeur, grudgingly admitted that his shows were both impressive and moving. For him, great ceremonials were 'pages of history', 'chapters in the ritual of the state'.[29] They were also chapters in the ritual of his life, and in the course of his career, he was closely associated with four of them: the Delhi Durbar of 1903; his installation as Lord Warden of the Cinque Ports in the following year; his admission as Chancellor of Oxford University in 1907; and the creation of the Remembrance Day observances in the aftermath of the First World War.

II

The Delhi Coronation Durbar of January 1903 was both the most spectacular and the most controversial episode in Curzon's career as a ceremonial impressario. Within two months of the death of Queen Victoria in January 1901, the Viceroy had obtained Edward VII's approval for his proposal that he should publicly proclaim the accession of the new Emperor to his Indian subjects. Curzon even dared to hope that the King might himself journey to India, to be present at his own Durbar. Edward VII feared this would oblige him to be absent from England for too long, though for a time he toyed with the idea of sending his son instead.[30] This scheme also came to nothing, and it was only in July 1902, by which time plans were well advanced, that it was unexpectedly announced that the king's brother, the Duke of Connaught, would visit India as his representative. Even so, the Duke was consistently outshone by the Viceroy himself, who combined in his own resplendent and magnificent personage the roles of instigator, planner, inspirer, philosopher, master of ceremonies and principal celebrity. 'You talked about stage management', Curzon wrote to his friend George Wyndham in May 1902. 'That is just what I am doing for the biggest show that India will ever have had'.[31]

In conceiving this grand pageant to celebrate the accession of the King-Emperor, Curzon was following – and elaborating – a recently-developed British tradition that was scarcely twenty-five years old.[32] During the early Victorian period, the British had cared as little for pomp in India as they had for pomp at home, despising the enfeebled and hollow ceremonials of the Mughal court, and contrasting 'their honest, plain black frock coats with the pretentious glitter of the oriental monarchs they controlled'. But in the aftermath of the Mutiny, the demise of the Mughal Emperor, the abolition of the East India Company, and the assumption by the Crown of full responsibility for the sub-continent, this policy was put into reverse.

Instead, the British now saw themselves as the legitimate successors of the Mughal emperors, and came to believe that their regime should project a suitably 'oriental' and 'imperial' image. So they set out to construct a new ritual idiom for the government of India, partly based on the appropriation of what they believed were traditional Mughal court ceremonials, and partly invented and developed by themselves, through which they could express their own authority, in terms which they thought the Indians – especially the native princes – would understand and appreciate.

Thus was gradually elaborated the British Raj, which was to reach the apogee of its splendour under Curzon himself. In 1876, Queen Victoria was made Empress of India, and her new style and title were proclaimed at the 'Imperial Assemblage' at Delhi the following year, which was master-minded by the Viceroy, Lord Lytton.[33] New orders of chivalry were established, for both the native princes and British administrators: the Order of the Star of India (1861), the Order of the Indian Empire (1878) and the Order of the Crown of India (1878).[34] It was even proposed that a college of arms and a privy council should be created for the native rulers on the British model. At the same time, the ceremonial surrounding the Viceroy, both in Calcutta and at Simla, and as he travelled around India, became increasingly splendid, ornate, elaborate and magnificent – far grander than the state in which British monarchs themselves lived at home. The justification for all this was that the British had convinced themselves that what they called the 'oriental mind' was especially susceptible to pomp and circumstance, to 'barbaric splendour', and this was a belief which Curzon himself fully shared. It is in the context of these invented and appropriated traditions that his Durbar of 1903 must be set and understood.

Before he could hope to carry his scheme through in India, Curzon had to obtain the consent of the Cabinet in London, and this proved to be both more difficult and more protracted than he expected. There were some who were doubtful about the very idea: if there was to be a separate coronation for India, perhaps each dominion might end up wanting one? Curzon scotched these objections imperiously: 'in the colonies', he wrote, 'it would be an anachronism and an absurdity; in India it is a feature of a hallowed system'. There were others who thought the whole idea as perposterous as it was dangerous: an ego-trip for the Viceroy which might go terribly and embarrasingly wrong.[35] Even when these objections were overcome, there remained one subject so contentious that it led to a major crisis between the Viceroy and the Cabinet. For Curzon wished to con-clude his proclamation speech with the anouncement of some remission, in accordance with eastern practice, preferably a large reduction in the salt tax. The Cabinet refused, on the grounds that it was a dangerous and inappropriate precedent. Curzon appealed personally to the king, which only made matters worse.[36] In the end, after threatening resignation, he obtained permission from the Cabinet to make a 'general committment of intention to reduce taxes'. But he was mortified, fearing that the absence of a substantive boon would reduce his Durbar to little more than a 'tamasha', 'an empty and futile pageant', in the eyes of the Indians.[37]

These were not Curzon's only worries at the English end of things, for the Liberal press and opposition were predictably hostile. They condemned the Durbar as a 'mere empty piece of pageantry, which will serve no useful purpose whatsoever', as a 'vulgar display provided to furnish a Viceregal holiday', as a 'Curzonation'.[38] In a land of irremediable poverty, which had recently suffered severe famine, the very idea of lavishing thousands of pounds on such a show and such a sham seemed indefensible. Curzon was unfailingly persistent and resourceful in his replies. The cost, he contended, would not be above £200,000, which would make it 'the cheapest state ceremonial on a great scale that had ever been seen', far less expensive, per head of population, than the British Coronation; and he insisted that the whole enterprise would be run on 'strictly business-like and economical lines'. Above all, he was convinced that the pageantry would serve an essential political and imperial function. 'The installation Durbar', he argued, 'is an accepted and acceptable feature of ceremonial life from one end of the country to the other.' It would bring together people from far-flung places, and make them aware of the unity of India. It would proclaim to the world the greatness of the Empire of which India was an integral part. In sum, it would be 'an act of supreme public solemnity, demonstrating to ourselves our union, and to the world our strength'.[39]

From beginning to end, Curzon kept the planning of the Durbar in his own hands. He had before him the detailed precedent of Lytton's earlier extravaganza; but he departed from that in three significant respects.[40] In the first place, the overall design and aesthetic motif was to be more 'Indo-Saracenic' than 'Victorian Feudal'. It would be a Durbar, not an 'Imperial Assemblage', and the coats of arms which Lytton had implausibly foisted on the Indian princes would be dispensed with. In the second place, the scale of the enterprise would be greatly enhanced. There would be nearly twice as many Indian princes present; the total number of people involved would be nearer 150,000 than the 68,000 who had appeared in 1877; and instead of lasting for a few days, the festivities would go on for nearly two weeks. In the third place, the Durbar would involve the Indians to a much greater degree than before. The ruling princes would be 'prominent actors in the ceremony, instead of mere spectators at it', and would be given an opportunity to pay homage which had been denied them by Lytton. There was to be an exhibition devoted to displaying and celebrating the greatest achievements of Indian art and handicrafts. Furthermore, Curzon hoped that the Durbar ceremony itself would be replicated, on a smaller scale, in every town and village throughout India.[41]

The Viceroy first seriously began to turn his attention to the planning of the Durbar early in 1902, and in April visited Delhi, on his way to the

North-West Frontier.[42] He decided to use the same site as in 1877, though naturally he needed more space for the more elaborate ceremonials he had in mind. With Lytton's notes beside him, and with the aid of the official account that had been written by J. Talboys Wheeler, Curzon outlined his own proposals in an elaborate Minute, extending to 77 paragraphs of print, which was published in May, to which was added a supplementary Minute, containing another 40 paragraphs, in October. Curzon proposed that the proceedings should last from the 27 December until 10 January, and outlined in detail the programme of events for each day. He listed the different categories of guests, from ruling chiefs and provincial governors to representatives of foreign states and neighbouring powers. He described his design for the Amphitheatre, resembling 'a gigantic horse-shoe', in which the main events would take place. He mentioned the camps that would have to be built to contain the guests, the princes, the troops and the journalists. Once again he justified the estimated cost 'as not ill but well expended in such a cause'.[43]

The work went forward at Delhi under the supervision of a local committee chaired by H.S. Barnes, but the Viceroy remained in complete and commanding control, making further extended visits in August, October and December to push the works along. For it was not just two weeks of ceremonial that Curzon was staging: he also had to create the infrastructure without which the pageant could not take place. Altogether, there were 70 camps, occupying the area of a substantial town; railways, water supply, sanitation, lighting, telephones and postal services had to be installed; the grounds had to be grassed and ornamented, and the amphitheatre constructed. Sofas, arm chairs, tables, book cases, pianos, and pictures had to be provided in the tents of the Viceroy's guests. In each case, the final decision lay with Curzon himself, as he explained to Lord George Hamilton, the Secretary of State for India:

You would be amazed at the questions that I have to decide: the design of a railing, the width of a road, the pattern of a carving, the colour of a plaster, the planting of a flower bed, the decoration of a pole – all this alongside of big questions affecting the movement or accommodation of tens of thousands of persons.[44]

Nothing was delegated, nothing was left to chance. 'We are', the Viceroy noted on another occasion, 'doing the whole thing with an elaboration and finish that have never previously been devoted, at any rate in British times, to an Indian celebration.'[45]

On Monday 29 December 1902 the Durbar formally began with the State Entry into Delhi.[46] The Viceroy and Vicereine arrived at the railway station, followed shortly after by the Duke and Duchess of Connaught. After official welcomes, the four took their place in the procession, some three miles long, which slowly and majestically wound its way through the streets of Delhi, 'like a spangled serpent glimmering through zones of light and shadow', and watched by a million people. First came the Dragoon Guards, the Horse Artillery, the heralds, the trumpeters, and the Imperial Cadet Corps. Then came Lord and Lady Curzon, riding an elephant lent by the Maharajah of Benares, previously used by Lord Lytton in 1877, covered with cloth of gold embroidered with lions rampant, and topped with a silver, boat-shaped howdah. There followed the Duke and Duchess of Connaught on an elephant scarcely less majestic, and then fifty ruling chiefs, magnificently caparisoned, processing two by two, 'a vision of blazing brilliancy'. According to *The Times* special correspondent, the effect was like 'a succession of waves of brilliant colour, breaking into foams of gold and silver, and the crest of each wave flashed with diamonds, rubies and emeralds of jewelled robes and turbans, stiff with pearls and glittering with aigrettes'. Or, as he put it more succinctly, the procession combined 'oriental exuberance' with 'western precision'.[47]

The climax of the proceedings was the Coronation Durbar itself, which took place in the Amphitheatre on Thursday 1 January 1903, and formed 'as brilliant a picture as ever a state pageant presented'. Altogether there were some sixteen thousand people assembled, including the ruling princes, the Viceroy's guests, and the representatives of the dominions, the empire and other nations, as well as another forty thousand soldiers out-side. At 11.15, the surviving veterans of the Mutiny, 'both European and Native', marched into the Amphitheatre, which brought the whole audience, cheering, to their feet.[48] Soon after, the Duke and Duchess of Connaught arrived, to the sounds of the National Anthem. Then came Curzon, who received a royal salute of 31 guns, mounted the dais in the centre of the arena, and took his seat on the throne, which was upholstered in red velvet and richly ornamented with a golden crown and silver lotus leaves. After a flourish of trumpets, the proclamation was read, announc-ing King Edward VII as Emperor of India. Curzon made his speech to loud cheering, even though many could not understand it, many more could not hear it, and he could speak only in vague terms of 'measures of financial relief'. The trumpeters sounded another fanfare, three cheers were given for the Emperor, the National Anthem was played again, and the ruling chiefs were presented. Thus ended a ceremony of 'impressive dignity proportioned to its deep significance'.[49]

The State Entry and the Proclamation were the two principal events, but before, between and after were a heady succession of gatherings, festivities and entertainments, while the Viceroy and Vicereine were hosts at great banquets every evening. 'For days', one journalist recalled, 'the eye was dazzled and the senses sated with the brilliance, colour and seemingly unending pageant.' There was the official opening of the exhibition of Indian arts and crafts, a firework display, and polo, hockey, football and cricket matches. There was a state ball for 4000 held at the Red Fort, and a chapter of the two Indian Orders, which 2500 attended. There was an evening party to the native chiefs and a state church service (at which Curzon refused to allow the singing of 'Onward Christian soldiers' because of the lines 'Crowns and thrones may perish, kingdoms rise and wane').[50] There was a mock battle, a review of native retainers, and a parade of British and Indian troops. Finally, on Saturday 10 January, the Connaughts and the Viceroy departed, and the Durbar was officially over. 'In a few weeks', *The Times* correspondent noted, in words mingling regret with relief, 'this great city of tents will have disappeared, and the multitude who filled it for a brief space with a life of rare intensity and brilliancy will have dispersed to all parts of India, and far beyond.'[51]

Yet Curzon himself remained convinced that the Durbar would 'not be forgotten'. 'The sounds of the trumpets have already died away; the captains and the kings have departed; but', he insisted, 'the effect produced by its overwhelming display of unity and patriotism is still alive and will not perish.' It was, he believed, 'a landmark in the history of the people, and a chapter in the history of the state', and it was also 'one of the most solemn and awe-inspiring ceremonials ever held'. As Curzon explained, in a letter of pardonable pride sent to Lord George Hamilton soon after the proceedings were over, 'It was by planning and scheming the whole thing myself, by superintending every detail of the execution, by overhauling every drawing and plan, by telling every officer exactly what he had to do, by going to Delhi four times myself, and seeing to everything on the spot, and finally by driving out to the scene of each ceremonial a few hours before it occurred, and issuing final instructions – that the whole thing went through'.[52] Throughout the proceedings, the regal bearing and commanding personality of the Viceroy had been pre-eminent. He had conceived and executed a pageant on an heroic scale, and breathed life into the stiff print of history. The Delhi Durbar was a one-man show and a one-man triumph.[53]

From many sides, Curzon was lavished with praise. The king acclaimed his 'magnificent success', and conferred upon the Viceroy the Royal Victorian Chain, a special mark of esteem which had been held by only one other non-royal person, the late Archbishop of Canterbury. His Private Secretary, Lord Knollys, wrote to say that 'all the arrangements were perfect and above praise'. Lord George Hamilton congratulated Curzon on 'a rare achievement, unique in many respects, and you have, as its creator and superintendent, every reason to be proud'.[54] Arthur Balfour opined that 'the show was the best show that ever was shown', while Asquith reported 'complete unanimity as to the splendour of your hospitalities and your unfailing tact and judgement'. 'By universal consent', declared Sir Schomberg McDonnell, 'nothing had ever been so wonderfully carried through.' For the Duchess of Marlborough, who was one of Curzon's personal guests, the Durbar had provided 'events as glamorous and gorgeous as those narrated in the tales of the Arabian Nights'. But it was left to Sir Arthur Godley, the Permanent Secretary at the India Office, to sum such opinions up in one word: it was, quite simply, Curzon's 'apogee'.[55]

As such, it also enjoyed a generally appreciative press in Britain and in the Anglo-Indian community: Curzon's decision to ensure that the artists, historians and journalists who were recording and reporting the Durbar were especially well housed was certainly a wise one. They lavished fulsome praise on the Viceroy himself: 'from the first the Durbar has been his own child'; 'everything you saw, you knew that Lord Curzon had done'; 'no one can ever hope to organise an assemblage that will rival it'.[56] They lavished even more extravagant prose − a 'river of description, immense and overpoweringly adjectival' − on their accounts of the 'sublime splendour' of the Durbar's 'splendid spectacles': 'the greatest ceremony the orient has ever witnessed'; 'the most georgeous pageant that has ever been devised by the imagination and ingenuity of mortal man to point a moral or adorn a tale'.[57] They were in no doubts that the Durbar had brilliantly achieved its objectives: it had brought the Indians together; it had proclaimed the power of the British Empire; and it had captured the imagination of the people in England. 'On the one hand it reveals India to herself; on the other it provides for the half-informed and not very imaginative public at home a surpassing demonstration of the magnitude and magnificence of the Empire in the East.'[58]

There were, however, other opinions in the British newspapers, some merely sceptical, others downright hostile. Even among Curzon's supporters, there were those who could not take pomp and spectacle quite seriously: 'we should never forget', opined *The Times*, 'that it is power not pageantry on which our imperial strength is based'.[59] Those who had been ill-disposed before the event were no less disapproving afterwards. There was criticism of Curzon, for being enslaved by 'the power of rhetoric', and for his excessive 'fondness for spectacular display'. There was hostility to the expense and extravagance of the Durbar, when compared with the 'misery and poverty' of India, with which the Viceroy's guests never came into contact. There was consternation that the people of India were largely ignored, and that too much trust was being put in the ruling princes: 'we are, as usual, backing the wrong horse'.[60] And there was deep scepticism as to whether anything important or lasting had been achieved: 'these Durbars have no real political significance, and leave no trace upon the problems of actual life . . . Lord Curzon's Durbar will not leave the Indian people less dissatisfied or the Indian frontier more securely guarded against foreign aggression'. In sum, the Durbar was 'a foolish, empty and expensive ceremony', the 'borrowed plumes or oriental barbarism', which 'had no more significance than the Lord Mayor's Show'.[61]

If this was the reaction of the radical British press, then how much more hostile were the native Indian newspapers. Both Curzon and Lord George Hamilton dismissed them as a 'microscopic minority', which were 'nothing

if . . . not spiteful'. But put another way, this meant that educated, nationalist opinion – especially in Bengal – was distinctly unimpressed.[62] By this
point in his tenure of office, the Viceroy himself had become decidedly
unpopular, and the expense, extravagance and self-glorification of the
'Curzonation' only served to reinforce these feelings. Far from proclaiming
the unity of India and the greatness of the British Empire, the Durbar
merely served to reinforce an unequal division of wealth, and to demonstrate that India was 'a nation ruled by others'. True, there had been many
local celebrations, but the idea that the Durbar would be 'talked over
for generations in every village in India' was simply not borne out by
subsequent events.[63] For it was not so much the 'native mind' that was
obsessed with pageantry: it was the British in general, and Curzon in
particular, with his 'inordinate love of pomp and show'. In short, the
'articulate public' of India was 'deeply condemnatory': for them, there was
no evidence that the Durbar had achieved any of the grandiose objectives
that Curzon had claimed for it. On the contrary, it was nothing more than
a 'tamasha', an empty entertainment.[64]

One newspaper, with what seems in retrospect to have been exceptional
prescience, dared to predict that 'the Durbar marks the beginning of Lord
Curzon's decline, and has made it impossible for him to end his term of
office on the same high note with which it began'.[65] And so, indeed, it
turned out to be. Increasingly ill and over-worked, the Viceroy alienated
friends in India and at home; there was the protracted disagreement with
Lord Kitchener; and eventually Curzon lost the support of the Cabinet in
London. Within three years, he was out of India and out of office, and
denied the British peerage to which he believed himself entitled. But these
defeats and disappointments did not prevent him from offering Lord
Hardinge much gratuitous advice about the planning of the next Durbar,
held in December 1911, at which the King-Emperor did indeed appear and
crown himself.[66] As such, it was an even more spectacular occasion than the
Durbar for King Edward VII, but no one personality dominated the
proceedings in the way that Curzon had in 1902–3, least of all the Viceroy.
In any case, it was the last of the line, the end of the tradition.[67] There
was talk of a Durbar for King Edward VIII, then for King George VI, in
1936–8, but the hostile state of Indian nationalist opinion, and the increasingly tense international situation, meant that the project was postponed
indefinitely.[68] In 1947, only 22 years after Curzon's death, India became
independent, and the Raj and its Durbars passed into history.

III

Despite its controversial reception and limited success, Curzon's Delhi
Durbar was not only his first great triumph as a ceremonial impressario: it
was also in many ways his most comprehensive and complete. Never again

would he be both the organiser of the show, and the star of the show, in the way that he was in India in January 1903. 'Curzonation' may have been a term of abuse, but there was more than a grain of truth in it. By comparison, the next two pageants with which he was connected possessed very different characters. They were British rather than Indian in their location, and parochial rather than imperial in their significance. And although he was the centre of attention in both cases, Curzon was neither the originating nor the controlling mind: the historical vision, the creative imagination, and the careful organisation were provided on these occasions by others rather than by him. Curzon collaborated, encouraged, interfered, acquiesced, did what he was told, performed as required, enjoyed himself, and later expressed his appreciative thanks – but, while he was still the chief actor, he was neither the stage-manager of the ceremonials nor the inventor of the traditions that went with them.

The first of these pageants was Curzon's installation as Lord Warden of the Cinque Ports at Dover in July 1904, an office to which he had been appointed by the sovereign on the nomination of the Prime Minister following the death of Lord Salisbury.[69] The post was one of genuine antiquity, dating back to Edward the Confessor and William the Conqueror. In medieval and early modern times the Lord Warden had been responsible for organising the defences of south-eastern England, and also presided at the Court of Shepway. By the late eighteenth century the office had lost most of its powers and responsibilities, and by the mid nineteenth it had lost most of its perquisites and emoluments as well, although Walmer Castle was still available as the official residence. In addition to Salisbury, previous Prime Ministerial holders had included the younger Pitt and the Duke of Wellington, who had died at Walmer in 1852. It had also been held by two former Viceroys of India: Lord Dalhousie and Lord Dufferin. With such illustrious forebears, and with such a long history attaching to it, the Lord Wardenship was an office which Curzon eagerly accepted, the more so as it was 'a mark of honour from the Crown'.[70] He looked forward, not only to his installation, but to studying the history of Walmer Castle and its occupants.

Yet, if an earlier generation had had its way, there would by then have been no Lord Wardenship left for Curzon to enjoy. On Wellington's death, Lord Dalhousie had been appointed; but he remained in India for four more years, returned home an invalid, and died abroad in 1860. He never resided at Walmer, was not even installed, and twice unavailingly tried to resign the office. Moreover, his eight years of absenteeism conicided with the high point of the mid-Victorian cult of retrenchment, economy, rationality and utilitarianism, and on Dalhousie's death it was suggested that this anachronistic non-job should be abolished altogether. Thus threatened, the leading citizens of the Cinque Ports sent a memorial to Queen Victoria, and a deputation to Lord Palmerston, not only urging that this ancient office be retained, but also that it should be occupied by the Prime Minister himself. After some deliberation, he eventually accepted, and further agreed 'to revive the old and quaint ceremony of installation'.[71] It was Palmerston's decision which kept the job in being, and which provided the immediate precedent for Curzon's own ceremonial installation, forty years later.

The individual to whom the credit seems single-handedly due for inventing – or, more properly, for re-inventing – the Lord Warden's installation pageant was Edward Knocker, a solicitor and local historian, who was also Town Clerk of Dover and Seneschal of the Cinque Ports.[72] In the early 1860s, he seems to have been one of the first men in Britain to notice something that the monarchy, the City of London, and Oxford University were later to discover: namely that the best way to repel reformers and deflect criticism, to justify what had previously regarded as an abuse, and to gain popularity and public support, was to create and unfurl grand and impressive ceremonial. As soon as Palmerston had agreed to accept the office, Knocker set out to persuade him to participate in a splendid public pageant. The last such recorded installation had been that of Lord Sydney, early in the 1690s, an account of which was to be found in Harris's *History of Kent*, and Knocker hoped Palmerston would accept a similar programme. But the Prime Minister was not 'disposed to go through all the ceremony, as it has so long fallen into disuetude', and preferred something less grandiose. Having made his views plain, he left it to Knocker to 'make the necessary arrangements'. And because there was so little by way of detailed precedent, Knocker found there was 'considerable work to do'.[73]

The ceremonial devised by Knocker for Lord Palmerston's installation in August 1861 was as follows. The Lord Warden was met in the forecourt of Dover Castle by the mayors, bailiffs and other officials of the Cinque Port towns, all clad in their most decorative and colourful robes, and by a contingent of troops and the Cinque Port Volunteers. They duly processed to Bredenstone Hill, overlooking the sea, where Lord Wardens had traditionally taken their oath of office and presided at the Court of Shepway. Palmerston refused to take the oath, but received instead an address of congratulation, and made an appropriate reply, in which he urged that 'we ought to respect ancient traditions'. Thereupon the assorted dignitaries processed to Dover Town Hall for lunch, toasts and speeches, and Palmerston re-affirmed his belief that 'there is nothing that more dignifies man than clinging to ancient and honourable traditions'. For Knocker in particular, the occasion had been a great personal triumph. Throughout the proceedings he was 'cool, imperturbable and dignified', and it was recognised that 'the whole function seemed to rest upon the Seneschal'. He shortly after published a history of the Lord Wardenship, which included a detailed account of Palmerston's installation, which he dedicated to the

Prime Minister, and which became the essential handbook for all subsequent installation ceremonies, Lord Curzon's included.[74]

While Edward Knocker was undeniably the inventor, it took several decades for the tradition of public installation to become established. Palmerston's successor was Lord Granville, appointed by Lord John Russell in 1865. Although born into the very centre of the Whig cousinhood, Granville was a poor man, and for him the appeal of the post was that it provided him with the country house he himself could not afford. He thus spent much time at Walmer, but he was never formally installed, the ceremonial having been cancelled in May 1866 because of the death of his brother-in-law and sister, Lord and Lady Rivers. Granville's successor, W.H. Smith, was appointed by Lord Salisbury in 1891; but he was already too ill to contemplate a public pageant, and he died within the year.[75] Only with Lord Dufferin, who was made Lord Warden in 1892, was the ceremonial installation revived, and the innovation of thirty years ago thus established as a tradition. By this time, Edward Knocker was dead, and had been succeeded in his many local offices by his son, Wollaston Knocker – like his father, a local solicitor and antiquarian of note. He wrote a history of the Dover corporation insignia, and an account of the town's celebrations of the coronation of Edward VII. Armed with the precedent established by his father, it was Sir Wollaston Knocker who created the tradition that Lords Warden of the Cinque Ports took up their office with public pomp and pageantry.[76]

Dufferin's installation took place in June 1892, and was generally judged a great success. Several months before, Knocker sent the new Lord Warden a copy of his father's book, and Dufferin agreed that the arrangements should be on essentially 'the same lines'.[77] Thanks to the precedents of 1861, the planning and organisation were more elaborate and assured: detailed files have survived concerning the military procession, the decorations and illuminations on the streets, and the banquet at the town hall. A church service was added at the beginning of the pageant, and a commemorative pamphlet was published at the end. Three years later, on Dufferin's resignation, Lord Salisbury was installed, and Wollaston Knocker was once more in charge. The proceedings followed the established pattern, except that the ceremonial took place on Dover College Close, instead of on Bredenstone Hill. Lord Dufferin, who was the only Lord Warden ever to witness the installation of his successor, wrote Knocker an admiring and appreciative letter. 'It interested me very much', Dufferin observed, 'to take part in those old world [sic] ceremonies, which I was too much preoccupied to observe minutely when I myself was the object of them.'[78]

Curzon's installation was Knocker's third, last and most successful pageant. The Viceroy returned from India in May 1904, worn out by the unceasing labours of his proconsular office, and worried about his wife's health. But he was captivated by the history, the drama, the romance and the traditions of the Lord Wardenship, and was prepared to spend money to make Walmer Castle a more comfortable habitation. All the detailed arrangements concerning his installation were made by Knocker: triumphal arches were constructed and the streets decorated with masts and flags; business was to be suspended between the hours of eleven and two o'clock; the police were given precise instructions as to their duties and the time-table; and the carriage procession was elaborately planned. The order of service for St Mary's in the Castle was arranged and printed; the agenda of the Court of Shepway was agreed; and the luncheon menu was fixed.[79] Knocker's attention to detail was worthy of Curzon himself, with the result that Curzon had very little to do. He went over the processional route, suggested the names of relatives and friends who might be invited, and wrote attentive and encouraging letters. But beyond that, he had 'no alterations to suggest': he knew a good pageant-master when he saw one.[80]

On the day itself, 2 July, the representatives of the Cinque Ports assembled in the Banqueting Hall of Dover Castle, and were given their instructions by Knocker, 'in tones which forbade the idea of anything but instant compliance'.[81] They walked in procession to St Mary's Church where, in the company of the Lord Warden and Lady Curzon, they heard the Bishop of Dover observe that 'memories of the past are ever linked closely with a great historical ceremony'. At the end of the service, a carriage procession formed in the castle yard, which drove through the town to the Dover College Close, where Curzon was duly installed and presided briefly over the Court of Shepway. Those present then repaired to the town hall for their celebratory lunch, where the Lord Warden's health was proposed by his friend George Wyndham, who was himself the MP for Dover and Irish Secretary. 'Coming as he did from India', Wyndham remarked, 'a land in which ancient traditions were cherished, Lord Curzon might be more able than any other man to understand why they of the Cinque Ports cherished the forms and ceremonies which clustered around the Lord Wardenship.' In his reply, Curzon spoke of the history of Dover, the importance of ceremonial, and the great burdens of Empire.[82] Thus ended the formal proceedings. That evening, the public buildings of Dover were illuiminated, and the Curzons entertained their guests to dinner in Walmer Castle.

By common consent, the occasion had been a triumph. One friend wrote to thank Knocker for 'the very best arranged function it has ever been my lot to witness: there was not a hitch anywhere'. The Dover Corporation congratulated him, as Town Clerk, on arranging an installa-tion which 'surpassed them all'. *The Times* wrote of the 'customary pomp and circumstance, insignificant, doubtless, compared with the splendid ceremonies to which a Viceroy of India is accustomed, but not without a picturesque interest of their own'. The Cinque Ports, it went on, may have lost their ancient functions and their curious privileges, 'but the forms survive, and are perhaps the more affectionately cherished because they are nothing more'.[83] Curzon himself wrote an appreciative and generous letter to Knocker, which echoed the commonplace view, that he was 'a past master of the art' of creating and planning a pageant:

I cannot let the day pass away without writing you a few words to say how greatly pleased I have been with the admirable arrangements that were made by you in connection with my installation. It could not possibly have gone off under better auspicies, with greater eclat, or with more successful results, and I am sure that in your long experiences of the Cinque Ports, you have never organised a celebration that gave greater satisfaction to those who took part in it, or that was entitled to give greater satisfaction to yourself.[84]

Here, in happy and fruitful partnership, were two men who shared what Ford Madox Ford called 'a just appreciation for the lessons of tradition'.[85] Yet even after these three successful installations, the tradition was not yet fully established. Soon after the ceremonials, Curzon's wife became ill, miscarried and almost died. The reason given was the insanitary condition of the drains at Walmer. As a result, Curzon turned against the Castle, which he now described as a 'charnel house, unfit for human habitation', and resigned the office of Lord Warden, after having held it for barely four months. The next Lord Warden, Prince George, the son and heir of Edward VII, held the office for little longer. He did not take kindly to the job; he refused to be installed, or to undertake any of the ceremonial duties associated with it, incurred great local hostility as a result, and resigned after less than two years.[86] Only with the appointment of Lord Brassey in 1908 was the tradition restored, when the installation arrangements were carried out by Sir Wollaston's son, R.E. Knocker. After spending extensively on the fabric of Walmer Castle, Brassey resigned in 1913, and was followed by Lord Beauchamp. His installation, and that of his successor, Lord Reading, in 1934, were both superintended by R.E. Knocker, and provided the precedents for the installations of Sir Winston Churchill, Sir Robert Menzies, and Queen Elizabeth the Queen Mother.[87]

IV

Curzon's experience as Lord Warden of the Cinque Ports was initially pleasurable, but subsequently deeply unhappy – although this did not prevent him from continuing to work on his history of Walmer Castle and its occupants, which was eventually published posthumously in 1927. His public admission as Chancellor of Oxford University was equally splendid and even more novel, but in this case his tenure was lifelong and agreeable. Like the Lord Wardenship of the Cinque Ports, the Oxford Chancellorship was an office of great antiquity, which was conventionally held by a statesman-grandee. Indeed, previous occupants had included Wellington and Salisbury, both of whom were also Lord Warden of the Cinque Ports. In theory – and in practice under Archbishop Laud – the Chancellor possessed considerable powers, but the office had been declining in authority and prestige since the Restoration.[88] By the nineteenth century, the Chancellor was little more than an absentee figurehead, rarely presiding even at Encaenia, and his admission, once a public pageant, had dwindled into a 'dull and indolent' domestic occasion. Wellington, Derby, Salisbury and Goschen were waited on in their own homes by a deputation from the University, and there was no ceremonial in Oxford at all.[89]

By the early 1900s, it seemed as though Oxford, like the Lord Wardenship of the Cinque Ports forty years earlier, was under threat from the reformers of ancient anomalies and abuses, whose cause was greatly strengthened following the Liberal landslide in the general election of 1906. Compared with German scholarship and science, the education offered by the University seemed amateur and superficial. The undergraduates were drawn from a very narrow social background, and there were scarcely any women. The college endowments were not always well managed, and the total funding was inadequate. That Oxford needed reforming was widely admitted, both inside and outside the University. In Oxford itself there were many who believed that the University should be allowed (and encouraged) to put its own house in order, while there were others who argued that Oxford was so complex in its organisation, so infirm in its purpose, and so riven by academic animosities, that the only solution was to appoint a Royal Commission to investigate its affairs, which would recommend drastic and far-reaching reforms that could then be forced upon the University by parliamentary legislation.[90]

It was against this disturbing and uncertain background that Curzon found himself a candidate for the Chancellorship early in 1907. Lord Goschen had been elected on the death of Lord Salisbury, and a long incumbency was confidently expected. However, Goschen died within three years of taking office and Curzon, now back from India, was urged to stand. Compared with his immediate predecessors, he was on the young side; but as a Balliol and All Souls man, an honorary graduand, and a former Viceroy, he was a loyal and distinguished son of Oxford. Even in its diminished state, the Chancellorship was an historic office, which might acquire new significance in the impending battle over University reform. At a meeting convened by the Vice-Chancellor, Herbert Warren, President of Magdalen, Curzon emerged as the preferred candidate, and made plain his eagerness to stand.[91] He was formally nominated on 26 February, supported by Lords Salisbury and Milner, the Warden of All Souls, the Master of Balliol, and a long list of prelates, politicians and other public men. Soon after, Lord Rosebery was put up as the Liberal candidate, but neither in Oxford nor outside was his support as strong or as well organised. The election took place on 14 March, and Curzon won by the substantial majority of 1101 votes to 440.[92]

If past precedent had been followed, Curzon would have been privately admitted to the Chancellorship in his own home by a deputation from Oxford. But the Vice-Chancellor had other ideas.[93] In part, this was because Warren was the first Magdalen Vice-Chancellor in one hundred and forty years, and was determined to make his tenure of the office both splendid and memorable; in part, because he was a person scarcely less superior than Curzon himself, who loved great men and great events with such snobbish and unsubtle ardour that he was much lampooned in Oxford because of it. Throughout his Presidency, which had begun long ago in 1885, Warren had sought to make Magdalen as aristocratic a place as Christ Church, shamelessly urging the great, the grand and the good to send their sons to his college. (He would achieve his supreme social triumph in 1912, when the Prince of Wales became an undergraduate at Magdalen, and for which he would be made a Knight Commander of the Royal Victorian Order by King George V.) Clearly Curzon was a magnificent figure much to Warren's liking and, although publicly obliged to be impartial as Vice-Chancellor, Warren had in fact played a large part in securing his election to the Chancellorship.

In fairness to Warren, he was also deeply concerned about the dangers of outside interference in the affairs of the University, and one of his reasons for supporting Curzon's candidacy was that he hoped the new Chancellor might be able to defend Oxford from the predators in Westminster and Whitehall. He also believed that the University's public standing must be raised, and that one way of doing this was by exploiting the ceremonial potential of its history, its buildings, and its officers. He dismissed the 'drawing-room admission' of previous Chancellors as 'quite unworthy of a great historic university, and one moreover which can set its stage in some of the most stately and appropriate buildings in Christendom'. Accordingly, Warren resolved that Curzon should be publicly and ceremonially admitted as Chancellor in the Sheldonian Theatre. Curzon himself agreed with the proposal – provided there were precedents. But in the imediate past there were none, which meant, as Warren later recalled, that 'the whole ceremony, mode and order of procedure, ritual directions, Latin formulae, had to be invented de novo'.[94] Here, in Oxford, in 1907, Herbert Warren was playing the same part that R.G. Knocker had played in Dover in 1861.

As was the case when Knocker invented the modern version of the installation of the Lord Warden of the Cinque Ports, there were distant precedents, but they were inadequately documented. The latest account of the public admission of the Chancellor was by Thomas Hearne, himself a University bedel, who had recorded the admission of the Earl of Arran in 1715. Hearne's musings had recently been published by the Oxford

Historical Society, and Warren reprinted them in the *Oxford Magazine* in May 1907, shortly before Curzon's own admission.[95] The ceremonial itself was vividly described: the colourful processions from St Mary's to the Sheldonian; the admission in the theatre of the Chancellor by the Vice-Chancellor; the ringing of bells and applause of spectators; and the dinner which took place after the proceedings were over. But Hearne reported very little of what was actually said by the principal participants to each other, which meant that Warren was forced to improvise. 'With the aid of the Latin Statutes, the Registrar, the Proctor, and the University Press', he later recalled, 'I drew up an order of proceedings which was printed and circulated and carefully followed out, at any rate without a hitch, was scenic and dramatic, and I believe was generally considered a thorough success.'[96]

On the day itself, 11 May 1907, the only disappointment was that Curzon was far from well – he was recovering from bronchitis – which meant that the colourful procession from St Mary's had to be cancelled. Otherwise everything went according to plan.[97] The Sheldonian was thronged with senior members of the University, and with undergraduates, who regularly interrupted the Latin proceedings with laughter or applause. The ceremonial began with the entry of the Vice-Chancellor, accompanied by the Proctors and Doctors wearing scarlet. Then followed the procession of the Chancellor, clad in his gold-embroidered robe, and attended by two train bearers. The instrument of election was read by the Registrar, the Insignia of the University were handed over, the oath was administered, and the Vice-Chancellor announced to the audience, 'Domini Doctores vosque Magistri Universititas, habetis Cancellarium'. After a speech by the Public Orator, Curzon replied, in Latin, and dwelt, as he had at Dover, but also with his eye on the reformers, on the interconnectedness of the past, the present, and the future. At the conclusion of his speech, Curzon conferred an honorary degree on the Prime Minister of Natal, the Vice-Chancellor thereupon closed the congregation, and the Chancellor returned to All Souls, escorted by the Vice-Chancellor, the Doctors, the Proctors and the Heads of Colleges.

By common consent, the occasion had been faultlessly planned and stage managed, and the 'high ceremonial of admitting a Chancellor' was 'an affair at once stately, impressive and picturesque', the 'most . . . impressive ceremony the University has witnessed for many a long day'. It was widely recognised that the occasion was at once old yet novel. The *Oxford Journal* noted, somewhat redundantly, that the spectacle 'must have been new to many there'. More appropriately, *The Times* welcomed the 'revival of the ancient practice' of a public installation. The *Oxford Magazine* praised the 'Vice-Chancellor's happy thought in restoring after two centuries a splendid piece of academic ritual', which only served to show that 'state ceremonies planned and executed with due regard to what history and a great and living tradition prescribe can convey lessons worth enforcing as well as memories pleasant to retain'.[98] Curzon himself wrote to Warren to thank him 'most warmly for all your admirable arrangements for the never-to-be-forgotten ceremony of yesterday. Its success was due to you.' As Warren had hoped, Curzon had also played his own part to perfection. He knew how to conduct himself with a dignity appropriate to the occasion, and 'bore himself throughout as one conscious that he was being invested with a great and historic office in a great and historic place'.[99]

Curzon's unprecedentedly grand installation was but the first step in the campaign to give Oxford a higher public and academic profile. Two months later, the Chancellor presided at a magnificent Encaenia, at which the recipients of honorary degrees were his own nominees, and Curzon chose as grandly as he could. Among those honoured were the Prime Minister, Prince Arthur of Connaught, Rodin, Kipling and Mark Twain and, as was intended, the publicity was immense. Shortly after, there was a grand pageant, in which town and gown together enacted colourful scenes from Oxford's past on the banks of the Cherwell.[100] Meanwhile, Curzon was turning his attention to ways in which he might ward off outside interference in Oxford's affairs by lobbying hard for reform from within. As Warren had hoped, he persuaded Asquith to let the University have the opportunity to put its own house in order. He took up residence in Oxford to find out for himself the true state of affairs. Two years later, he published a book entitled *Principles and Methods of University Reform*, and in the years before 1914 he vainly tried to persuade the University to accept and enact his recommendations. But the First World War brought his initiative to an end, and thereafter his proposals were swallowed up in the Royal Commission appointed in 1919.[101]

If Curzon was a thwarted reformer in Oxford, he was an outstanding success as a dignified and decorous Chancellor. As Warren had hoped, Curzon raised the public profile of the University, and the installation had provided a splendidly appropriate beginning. Warren himself wondered how long the new pageant, with its deliberate and archaic revival of Latin, would last. In fact, it provided the model for the subsequent installations of Lord Grey, Lord Halifax, Harold Macmillan and Lord Jenkins, and it has been appropriated or adapted by other universities, not only in Britain, but throughout the English-speaking world.[102] As the inventor, it was Warren's achievement; but as the principal actor, it was the Chancellor's, and it inaugurated a whole new era of ceremonial consciousness and ceremonial splendour in Oxford. 'To see Lord Curzon in his magnificent robes', one admirer later recalled, 'leading the procession of Doctors into the Sheldonian Theatre, was in itself a liberal education; and it was, moreover, an aspect of education sorely neglected in the careless and slovenly Oxford to which Lord Curzon was recalled.'[103]

V

The First World War brought Curzon back to power, after more than a decade spent in opposition. But it also brought the style of ceremonial that had been developed in the years before 1914 to an end: not just − as in Britain and the Empire − for the time being, but in certain countries, for ever. In Russia, in Germany and in Austria-Hungary, the overthrow of the royal houses meant the disappearance of the three great-power monarchies which had competed with the British in the golden era of pre-war 'invented traditions'. The advent of new regimes, both Communist and Fascist, in the 1920s and 1930s resulted in new-style rituals, more vigorous, up-to-date and technologically sophisticated, which were less inclined to cultivate anachronism and stress continuity with the past. The result, as Eric Hobsbawm has argued, was a transition from the operatic to the prosaic mode of spectacle.[104] In Britain, which kept its monarchy, there was no such change: new ceremonies were invented which remained very much in the style of the traditions established before 1914. But there was one exception, where the prosaic mode was brilliantly, poignantly and unforgettably adopted by Lord Curzon himself, as he conceived and planned the observances of Remembrance Day.[105]

By the time the First World War came to an end, Britain and its Empire had lost well over one million men on the battlefields: the conflict which had begun with the most buoyant and naive hopes that it would soon be over became, after five bleak and devastating years, a 'carnival of death', from which very few families in Britain were left unscarred and unscathed. To his abiding regret, Curzon himself had no sons, by either of his marriages, but at least he was spared the bereavement endured by many figures in public life, Asquith and Bonar Law being the most famous. Nevertheless, as his second wife later recalled, 'there was scarcely one of our friends who did not lose a son, a husband, or a brother', and for Curzon, as for many, writing letters of condolence soon became an almost full-time occupation.[106] As his eloquent tributes to George Wyndham and Alfred Lyttelton made plain, Curzon was deeply moved by the death of those who died too young, and whose promise had been unfulfilled, and never doubted that the price paid by Britain for victory over the Kaiser had been almost unendurably high. These were his feelings when he was called upon, early in 1919, to preside over the Cabinet Committee initially charged with making arrangements for celebrating the successful outcome of the Versailles Peace Conference, which was due to reach agreement during the summer.[107]

As the most ceremonially conscious and ceremonially experienced member of the Cabinet, Curzon was the obvious choice for this task. However, unlike the previous pageants with which he had been involved, Curzon had no precedents which he could follow and elaborate, and he had to try to devise rituals which would give effective expression to the contradictory feelings of triumph and tragedy which so haunted the nation and the people. By May 1919, Curzon's committee had provisionally decided on four days of celebrations to be held early in August, including a victory parade through the streets of London, a day of thanksgiving services throughout the land, a river pageant on the Thames, and popular festivities mounted by local authorities.[108] Curzon himself was especially keen on 'reviving the idea of a river pageant', something which during the early nineteenth century had been an integral feature of the Lord Mayor's procession each November. He was anxious also to ensure ample opportunity for 'general rejoicings . . . for the masses of the people'. Every effort, he believed, 'should be made to give them their due share in the celebrations', and children in particular should be entertained and amused. Above all, he was adamant that 'the whole festival should be as thoroughly democratic in character as possible. It was to be a popular celebration, and not a spectacle to be enjoyed by the wealthy classes only.'[109]

By June 1919 these arrangements seemed to be well in hand; but then, and apparently under pressure from the King, the government 'decided upon an all-round alteration of the Committee's original proposals, which they had provisionally accepted'. It was agreed to simplify the programme, and to bring it forward so that the celebrations might come as soon as possible after the treaty was actually signed.[110] Eventually, it was settled that a Thanksgiving Service would be held in London on 6 July, and the victory parade on 19 July. It was at the Cabinet meeting when these decisions were taken that Lloyd George proposed that there might be 'a catafalque at some prominent spot along the route selected for the military procession, past which the troops would march and salute the dead.' He went on to suggest that 'some prominent artist might be consulted on the subject'. At this stage, Curzon's personal response was unenthusiastic, but he agreed to refer the matter to his Committee, remarking, characteristically, that 'if the idea was properly carried out, it should prove very impressive; it was, perhaps, however, more essentially suitable to the Latin temperament'.[111]

Three days later, by which time Curzon's Committee had carefully considered Lloyd George's proposal, the Cabinet discussed the matter again.[112] Curzon reported that his Committee as a whole shared his scepticism:

There was considerable feeling against the idea of adapting the French proposal to have a catafalque on the processional route which would be saluted by the troops as they passed in honour of the dead. The king was not in favour of the idea, and objections had been raised in other quarters.

Curzon then went on to enumerate them more fully:

The reasons against the proposal were: that it was foreign to the customs and temper of the nation; that it might not be easy for the public to assume the properly reverential attitude; and, as the structure would be of a very temporary character, it must be carefully safeguarded, or it would be overturned and trampled in the crush.

But Lloyd George would not be dissuaded: 'He deprecated a national rejoicing which did not include some tribute to the dead.' Eventually, his proposal for the construction of a 'temporary pylon' was carried, and on the same day Sir Edwin Lutyens was asked to design a non-denonminational shrine, made out of wood and plaster, which could be constructed within two weeks. At Lutyens's suggestion its name was changed from catafalque to Cenotaph: the empty tomb.[113]

The celebrations held in London and in the provinces on Saturday 19 July were a great success: but the high point in the London ceremonial was the quite unexpected appeal of the Cenotaph itself.[114] The salutes of Pershing, Foch, Beatty and Haig to their dead comrades were captured in unforgettable photographs, which appeared in newspapers throughout the country, and at the end of the day, many of the bereaved placed wreaths at the base of the Cenotaph in remembrance of dead relatives or comrades.[115] No such response had been anticipated: the Cenotaph was envisaged as a temporary monument, which would soon be dismantled, after which no further official recognition of the war dead was intended. However, public opinion decreed otherwise. Indeed, so insistent was popular pressure that at the end of July, only eleven days after the Cenotaph had been unveiled, the Cabinet agreed to replace it with a permanent and identical structure on the same site, and to ask Parliament for the £10,000 necessary to finance the work. Accordingly, the old structure was dis-mantled early in January 1920, and work on its permanent replacement – again overseen by Curzon – was begun.[116]

It was agreed that the King should unveil the new Cenotaph on Armistice Day, 11 November 1920, and in October the Cabinet turned its attention to the matter.[117] Once more, a Committee was set up to make the arrangements, consisting of Lord Lee of Fareham, Winston Churchill and Walter Long, and once more Curzon was put in charge. Since the Cenotaph was rightly regarded as 'an Imperial monument, commemorating men of many races and creeds', it was thought 'undesirable that the unveiling ceremony should have any distinctive denominational flavour'. Accordingly, it was decided that the National Anthem should be played when George V arrived in Whitehall; that he should unveil the Cenotaph 'without ceremony'; that there should be two minutes' silence at eleven o'clock; that there should be the hymn 'O God our help in ages past'; and that the 'Last Post' should then be sounded. Here was a low-key, understated ceremonial, totally lacking in any form of ostentation or triumphalism, and once again, it was Curzon himself who insisted that 'fashionable society would be excluded', and that widows, ex-servicemen and members of the armed forces would be allowed to gather in Whitehall.[118]

No sooner had the Cabinet agreed this than it was confronted by a further proposal, emanating from Dean Ryle of Westminster Abbey.[119] His suggestion was that the body of an unknown soldier should be dis-interred from Flanders, brought by destroyer to England, and receive a state funeral in Westminster Abbey on the same day that the new Cenotaph was unveiled. This time, even the King was unenthusiastic, on the grounds that 'a funeral now might be regarded as belated, and almost, as it were, re-open the war wound which time was gradually healing'. However, after some debate the proposal was agreed to, and Curzon's Committee took over charge of the scheme.[120] Curzon himself at once grasped the importance and potential of the idea, and expounded it vigorously and sensitively to his colleagues:

The ceremony of bringing in the Abbey an unknown soldier, whose remains should be borne in honour through London, and then interred in the Nave, had not merely its emotional, sentimental and dramatic aspect, but would offer a worthy and highly-esteemed tribute to those who fell in the war, and strike a chord of deep feeling in the hearts of the nation.

He then went on to outline his 'rough scheme' for bringing back the body and burying it in the Abbey, which formed the basis of the detailed arrangements as they were eventually made.[121]

Once again, Curzon showed himself exceptionally sensitive to the prevailing mood, especially when it came to the delicate matter of allocating seats in Westminster Abbey, and deciding what sort of service should accompany the internment. Despite the objections of Lloyd George and Bonar Law, Curzon insisted that neither peers nor Members of Parliament had any prior claim on seats in the Abbey, unless they had 'lost a son or brother in the war'.[122] The majority of the places were given over to representatives of the armed forces, to the organisations of ex-servicemen, and to those who had been wounded in action. 'Any further available places' were to be allotted, 'not to society ladies or the wives of dignitaries, but to the selected widows and mothers of those who had fallen, especially in the humbler ranks.' Curzon also recognised 'the great emotional strain under which the relatives would be suffering' throughout the proceedings, and so decided against a long service in the choir of the Abbey. 'It would', he noted in what seems a very un-Curzonian sentence, 'detract from the simplicity of the ceremonial, and lend histrionic and pompous elements to a solemn service.'[123]

Despite the initial misgivings on the part of the Cabinet, the appeal of the rituals on the day itself greatly surpassed expectation. With predictable thoroughness, Curzon's Committee had made contingency plans, in case there was dense fog: but they were not needed. 'The ceremony of yesterday', noted *The Times*, 'was the most beautiful, the most touching, and the most impressive that in all its long, eventful story, this island has ever seen.' In Whitehall, the King and his family, the Cabinet and representatives of the Empire, the service chiefs and a great throng of the bereaved were gathered, and the overwhelming emotion of the occasion was vividly captured in *The Times*:

The first thundering strokes of Big Ben boomed out, louder it seemed, than ever one heard it even in the stillness of dawn. The King turned to face the Cenotaph and, by a touch on a button, released the flags. . . . They fell away, and it stood, clear and wonderful in its naked beauty. Big Ben ceased, and the very pulse of time stood still. In silence, broken only by a nearby sob, the great multitude bowed its head. . . . Then, suddenly, acute, shattering, the very voice of pain itself – but pain triumphant – rose the clear notes of the bugles of The Last Post.[124]

The first part of the ceremony having been thus completed, the coffin of the Unknown Warrior was conveyed down Whitehall on a gun carriage to Westminster Abbey, with the King as chief mourner, and with Haig, Beatty, French and Trenchard among the pallbearers. In the Abbey itself, where representatives of the armed services and the bereaved formed the majority of the congregation, the Unknown was laid to rest amid further scenes of intense and heart-breaking solemnity, best described in Dean Ryle's own words:

The great service virtually formed part of a single ceremony with the unveiling of the Cenotaph. In all its history, the Abbey can have witnessed no such moving spectacle. The congregation of nearly one thousand of those bereaved in the war, and one hundred nurses wounded or blinded in the discharge of their duty; the lines of soldiers, sailors and airmen who had won the Victoria Cross 'for valour' stretching down the nave, fifty on either hand; the long procession from the north transept to the west end of the nave, in which, as chief mourners, the king and princes of the blood followed the coffin with its nameless burden – a procession blessed, as it might seem, at its entry, by the effigy of the great Earl of Chatham, and greeted as it reached the graveside by the figure of his famous son: all this was to stir such memories and emotions as might have made the very stones cry out. The popular feeling matched the occasion. Outside the Abbey for a distance of a mile or more, stretched a long line of people eager to enter and pay their tribute to the heroic dead. For over ten hours, till it was necessary to close the doors at 11 p.m., they passed through the Abbey, in a ceaseless stream; and day by day throughout the following week, the grave was visited by thousands of those whom the Unknown and his friends had died to save.[125]

Indeed, by the end of the week, it was estimated that one million people had visited the Cenotaph and the graveside, and that no less than a hundred thousand wreaths had been laid either in the Abbey or in Whitehall. *The Times* produced a special four-page Armistice Day Supplement, and observed, quite correctly, that 'the authorities frankly admit that the extent to which the public imagination has been stirred has exceeded all their expectations'.[126]

With a permanent Cenotaph in existence, and with the signs of public feeling as strong and continuing as they were, it soon became clear that an annual ceremonial of remembrance must be devised, to be held for the first time on 11 November 1921. Once again, the Cabinet entrusted Curzon and his committee with the task – not, this time, with devising a unique ritual, as had been the case in the previous year, but with creating a service which would 'become a type for the future'. Once again, Curzon thought it 'undesirable that the ceremony should be too elaborate', and the final form as based largely on those elements of the Cenotaph observances of the previous year which could be appropriately repeated.[127] The King, the royal family, the Cabinet, the service chiefs and the representatives of the empire were present. Wreaths were laid at the base of the Cenotaph. The two minutes' silence was observed. 'O God our help in ages past' was sung. The Last Post was sounded, and the National Anthem played. The principal participants withdrew, leaving Whitehall and the Cenotaph to the soldiers, the ex-servicemen, and the war widows, who laid their wreaths in turn.

Here, in essence, was the ceremonial – stark but effective – which was soon to be observed at local war memorials throughout the nation and the Empire. It was, felt Curzon, his touch for once perhaps deserting him, 'not a day of national grief, but rather a commemoration of a great occasion in the national history', which meant it was 'undesirable to lay stress upon the idea of mourning'.[128] It was entirely in character that Curzon himself should regard Remembrance Day in that light; but it is difficult to believe that many of those who laid their wreaths and bowed their heads shared his view. Be that as it may, the Remembrance Day rituals, as devised by Curzon, soon became the most poignant occasion in the British calendar. To the observances which his committee had devised, were gradually added the wearing of Flanders poppies, the festival of Remembrance in the Albert Hall, and the Empire Field of Remembrance at Westminster Abbey. With these additions, the ceremonials of the inter-war years were complete – but it was the Cenotaph, and the service held there, which was central. As *The Times* observed in November 1923, 'there is nothing artificial in the annual observance at the Cenotaph. It has become part of the expected order of things.'[129]

Beyond any doubt, Remembrance Day was Curzon's most moving and most enduring ceremonial creation. In scale, it was nothing like the Delhi Durbar, but the challenges faced by his Committee were of an unusually demanding kind. There were no precedents. There was something to celebrate, but also much to mourn. There was not just one pageant to invent and stage-manage, but three in as many years, the last of which had to be simple enough for the smallest community to enact, yet solemn enough to bear repetition in subsequent years; and the Committee was constantly obliged to modify its proposals in the light of powerful and unexpected expressions of public opinion, changing Cabinet decisions, and altered royal preferences. Yet Curzon and his colleagues had succeeded in devising rituals and observances which met with almost universal approbation. After the unveiling of the Cenotaph and the burial of the Unknown Warrior, the Cabinet congratulated Curzon and his committee on the 'remarkable success' of their labours.[130] Lord Stamfordham wrote to convey the King's 'complete satisfaction with the admirable manner in which the committee, under your presidency, conceived and carried out all the arrangements' for the 'solemn and impressive ceremonies'. 'The King feels', he concluded, in words of appropriately Curzonian idiom, 'that their record will be an everlasting incomparable page in the history of our country'.[131]

As with every pageant with which he was closely involved, Curzon's mastery of detail was unrivalled. The planning of the unveiling of the Cenotaph and the interment of the Unknown Warrior was meticulous in every detail. What was more remarkable was the fact that for the only time in his career as a ceremonial impressario, Curzon had devised a ritual which caught and articulated a genuinely popular and deeply-felt mood. In seeking to exclude false pomposity, and to include as many ordinary people as possible, his judgement was unerring, and he displayed a common touch for which he was rarely given credit. As Lord Ronaldshay remarked in his official biography, 'It may, perhaps, surprise those who habitually picture him as a proud patrician, scornful of the claims of the people, and tenacious of the rights of rank, to learn that in all these projects he argued powerfully for the prominent participation of the masses.'[132] At the same time, he himself played no conspicuous part in the rituals and observances he had so feelingly and so fittingly devised. The Delhi Durbar may have been the supreme ceremonial ego-trip; at Dover and Oxford he was the ceremonial cynosure; but Remembrance Day was the ultimate in ceremonial self-effacement.

After his installation as Lord Warden of the Cinque Ports, and his admission as Chancellor of Oxford University, Curzon had sent letters to the two men who had been responsible for the arrangements, thanking them for all they had done. After the observances of November 1920, Curzon himself received a similar letter, from Lt-Colonel Launcelot Storr, the Secretary to the Committee, which must surely have pleased him:

It is curious that, with one exception – the *Pall Mall Gazette* last evening – the press have given no credit to those who organised the ceremonies. Possibly this negligence is due to the fact that the public were aware that the arrangements were in the hands of one with your unique experience, and so confidently expected that the organisation would prove unexceptionable. I hope the king and your colleagues recognise what is due to you in undertaking, as in carrying to a successful issue, this arduous and anxious task on the top of your other heavy labours. Yours was the conception of the way in which the Cabinet's wishes could best be carried out, and yours – triumphant – the directing and controlling mind.[133]

In 1903, Curzon had described the Delhi Durbar as 'one of the most solemn and awe-inspiring ceremonials ever held' and as 'a landmark in the history of the people and a chapter in the ritual of the state'.[134] For many reasons, this was an overstatement. But his words applied much more appropriately to the rituals he devised in London between 1919 and 1921.

VI

The fact that Curzon's greatest triumph was a pageant most people did not even know he had organised is only one of many ironies in his remarkable and varied career as an ceremonial impressario.[135] Another is that, while he regarded spectacle and pomp as the outward and visible expression of history, tradition, poetry and romance, and as an essential aspect of the life of a nation state, he certainly did not consider stage-management as the main business of government, or as the main impulse in his public life. Curzon never wanted to be just a 'great ornamental', an insubstantial pageant fading and leaving not a rack behind. On the contrary, for him the real business of life was summed up in his own epitaph: writing, exploring, administrating and ruling other men. Pageantry might be an essential adjunct to power; but it was power which ultimately mattered. In India, Curzon wielded astonishing power, such as he was never to know again; but in Britain, the supreme office eluded him, and in his own eyes, the fact that he was so outstandingly successful a pageant-master in no way atoned for the ultimate failure of his political career.

There is another, even more curious irony. For behind what *The Times* once described as 'the pomp and circumstance of Lord Curzon's official façade', there lurked a very different and perenially schoolboyish figure, who could never quite take ceremonial seriously at all.[136] His famous audience with the Amir of Afghanistan, when he wore orders and medals obtained from a London theatrical costumier, is one conspicuous example of this. Some of his best-written and most light-hearted reminiscences recount ceremonial disasters, especially in his time as Viceroy of India: horses which misbehaved, state entries which went wrong, speeches which could not be given, clothes which did not fit.[137] Even at King George V's Coronation, when he strutted upon the stage in a manner which infuriated others, he could not help noticing that the 'peers in their coronets' looked 'exquisitely ludicrous'. As one of the mourners at Bonar Law's funeral, where there was an urn with the ashes, and a sham coffin, his sense of the ridiculous overcame him again.[138] Contemporaries, biographers and historians have often had cause to mark on the unintegrated nature of Curzon's personality, and his curiously ambivalent attitude to ceremonial provides an excellent example.

Appropriately enough, Curzon's own funeral exactly reflected these contradictory views and uncertain opinions. The first part, held at Westminster Abbey, was as grand and as splendid as he could have wished: a vast and distinguished congregation; his many orders and honours borne in procession; representatives of the King and Queen and European royalty; and Stanley Baldwin, Ramsay MacDonald, Lord Asquith and Winston Churchill among the pall-bearers.[139] Yet the subsequent interment at Kedleston was conspicuously devoid of grandeur, and Curzon was buried, as his first wife had been, with 'no show'. The young Henry Channon, who had come to know Curzon in his later years, and was himself addicted to splendour and spectacle, was puzzled and dismayed:

I shall never forget the simple service and the great beauty of the bereft widow, the absence of ostentation and, also, the absence of friends. Where were the royalties he had served? Where were the statesmen he had made and terrified? Where were the oriental potentates he had cowed? Where were the companions of his Oxford days? No one. Only the Duke of Devonshire, who had come over from Chatsworth, and our little group from London.[140]

But then, Curzon was a much more complicated man than most people knew – even in his most public role as a ceremonial impressario.

5

Lord Strickland

Imperial Aristocrat and Aristocratic Imperialist

It is a commonplace of history that between 1877, when Queen Victoria was proclaimed Empress of India, and 1947, when the Raj came to an end, to the King-Emperor's great regret, relations between the British monarchy and the British Empire were fundamentally transformed. Less well known, but no less important, were the changes that took place, during the same period, in the relations between the British aristocracy and the British Empire. At a time when the future for landed estates in Britain – and, more especially, Ireland – seemed increasingly uncertain, many of the greatest grandees sold off some of their properties and bought land in the colonies or shares in imperial companies.[1] Younger sons and more distant sprigs of nobility sought jobs in imperial administration, in the far-flung realm of the Anglican community, at the colonial bar, or on the colonial bench. More adventurous patricians – some with disreputable pasts to live down, others genuinely eager to make a new start overseas – became 'gentlemen emigrants', and set out to establish new lives for themselves in Canada, South Africa, Australia, Kenya and Rhodesia. Many a needy notable staved off his creditors by taking a comfortable, lucrative and honorific proconsular post in India or the great dominions: as A.J.P. Taylor once remarked, 'going out and governing New South Wales' became the British aristocracy's 'abiding consolation'.[2]

It was not just that the British aristocracy benefitted from the expansion of the British Empire: it was also that the very process of expansion lead to contact with indigenous aristocracies, both old and new. In Malta, the British recognised the claims of the island's nobility, which dated back to the eleventh century. In India, the ruling chiefs were carefully cultivated after the Mutiny, and became an important element in the structure and ceremonial of the Raj.[3] The essence of the system of 'indirect rule', as evolved by Sir Frederick Lugard in Nigeria, was that the British governed through the established native chiefs, as they later did in much of tropical Africa, in Malaya, and in the League of Nations mandates in the Middle East. The appearance of *Burke's Genealogical and Heraldic History of the*

Colonial Gentry in the 1890s suggested that there were many in the Empire who wished to evolve their own aristocracy on the British model.[4] The ennoblement of such imperial figures as Lords Strathcona, Mount Stephen, Althostan, Beaverbrook, de Villiers, Sinha, Morris, Forrest and Rutherford brought some of the most energetic and influential colonials into the Upper House itself. The most ardent imperialists, and resourceful House of Lords reformers, urged that premiers and proconsuls from the Empire and ruling chiefs from India should be made peers, so that they could take part in truly imperial deliberations in the upper house.[5]

Ever since Sir Ronald Syme first drew attention to it in the case of the Roman Empire, the relationships between the aristocracy of the metropolis, and the aristocracies of the periphery, have rightly been recognised as integral to our understanding of any patrician order and any imperial system. National elites from the mother country venture abroad. Colonial elites from abroad return to the mother country.[6] Yet in the case of the British aristocracy and Empire, this link between *nobilitas* and *imperium* has received remarkably little attention – at least during the modern period. This essay sheds some light on some of these little-studied connections by exploring the life, work and reputation of Gerald, first and last Baron Strickland of Sizergh in the county of Westmorland, and sixth Count della Catena in the nobility of Malta, who was born in 1861 and died in 1940, and whose life almost exactly spans this particular era in the history of the British aristocracy and the British Empire.[7]

I

Although he was a Maltese count long before he became a British peer, Gerald Strickland was inordinately proud of his English forebears. They traced their lineage back some twenty-five generations, they had occupied distinguished offices in church and state across the centuries, and they had held the same lands at Sizergh in Westmorland for the best part of seven hundred years.[8] Though lacking a hereditary title, they could boast a pedigree more ancient and more illustrious than most members of the House of Lords, and in the course of his own lifetime four different accounts of the Stricklands' family history were produced, three of which were commissioned by Gerald Strickland himself.[9] The last and most comprehensive, written by his son-in-law, Henry Hornyold, was privately printed in 1928, and coincided – no doubt deliberately – with Strickland's ennoblement. 'A line of honourable ancestry', Hornyold noted rather portentously in the preface, 'is rightly the subject of legitimate pride, and should cause, not an undue or petty vanity, but a desire to maintain the honourable standard of position and conduct which the annals of one's race exhibit.'[10] That pride, and that desire, were the mainsprings of Gerald Strickland's varied, eventful and controversial public career.

The Stricklands were a north-country family whose connection with Sizergh dated from 1239, when Sir William de Strickland married Elizabeth Deincourt, thereby acquiring the lands in Westmorland to which she was heiress. Across the next ten generations, the family prospered, with a succession of Sir Thomas and Sir Walter Stricklands. They built a pele tower at Sizergh and, after the border skirmishes subsided, they domesticated it and added Elizabethan extensions renowed for their woodwork and chimney pieces.[11] They served their kings in battle, leading their soldiers in Wales and Scotland, France and Ireland, and one Sir Thomas Strickland bore the banner of St George at the Battle of Agincourt. They hedged their bets adroitly during the Wars of the Roses, intermarried with other prominent north-country families, augmented their estates in Westmorland and acquired additional lands in Yorkshire, and regularly represented their county in parliament from the thirteenth century onwards. By the reign of Elizabeth, they were established as one of the foremost families in the region, and even the fact that they remained loyal to their Catholic faith did not seem to harm their prospects, as long as they were prepared outwardly to conform to the new Anglican religion.

During the seventeenth century, however, the family entered a period of financial and political decline, from which it was never fully to recover. As Catholics and royalists, the Stricklands were zealous supporters of the House of Stuart, two of them joined the forces of Charles I, and they suffered fines, compositions and sequestrations in the aftermath of the Civil War. But this in no sense lessened their royal and religious ardour, with further unhappy consequences. In 1677, Sir Thomas Strickland was expelled from the House of Commons for being a Catholic, thereby bringing to an end the family's long parliamentary associations; and in 1688, when James II was dethroned in the Glorious Revolution, Sir Thomas and his wife accompanied the king and his court into exile, which meant that Sizergh was unoccupied for the next eleven years. Eventually the Stricklands returned, but it was to a much diminished and sadly neglected inheritance. For most of the eighteenth century the family lived in quiet seclusion, out of sheer financial necessity. Only in 1807 did the prospects briefly brighten, when Charles Strickland married the heiress Cecelia Towneley, who brought with her estates at Standish and Borwick in Lancashire, and set about restoring and rebuilding the castle.

But this revival in the family fortunes was of brief duration. The Standish estates passed to the senior branch of the family, that line died out in 1920, and the property was sold soon after. The Borwick and Sizergh estates were eventually inherited by Walter Charles Strickland, but he also proved incapable of maintaining his inheritance. Borwick was sold in 1854; the lands which remained were heavily mortgaged; and there is no mention of their diminished holdings in John Bateman's survey of great landowners. By the end of the century a family which had once been the equal of the

Lowthers seemed in a state of almost terminal decay. During the 1890s, the magnificent Elizabethan panelling and furnishings of the Inlaid Chamber were sold to the Victoria and Albert Museum.[12] At the same time the family paintings, by Lely and Romney, were sent to auction, as were their unique collection of Stuart portraits, which had been presented to the Stricklands in recognition of their fidelity to that dynasty.[13] To make matters worse, Walter Charles Strickland did not get on with his son, Roger, whose death in 1938 was, in any case, to bring that branch of the family to an end in the male line. Accordingly, in 1896, and to the surprise and dismay of his close relatives, Walter Charles Strickland settled what was left of the Sizergh estates on his fourth cousin, Gerald, the thus-far absent subject of this essay.

Gerald Strickland was a distant relative in more senses than one. His forebears were descended from a junior branch of the family and, like many such sprigs of gentility, had travelled far in search of income and adventure. His grand-father, Jerrald Strickland (1782–1844) became a captain in the East India Company, and served with the young Arthur Wellesley at the Battle of Seringapatam. Jerrald's fourth son, another Walter Strickland (1824–67), went into the Royal Navy, and retired to Malta with the rank of commander. There, in 1858, he met and married Louisa Bonici, who was heiress in her issue to her uncle, Sir Nicholas Sceberras Bologna, fifth Count della Catena, who was descended from one of Malta's oldest families, and whose title had been created by the Grand Master Don Manuel Pinto de Fonseca in 1745. Gerald Strickland was the eldest son of this mixed marriage, and was born, very appropriately in the light of his outlook and his career, on 24 May 1861, which was also Queen Victoria's birthday, and later became Empire Day. His father died when he was only six, and his maternal great uncle when he was fourteen. Thereupon, Gerald Strickland became sixth Count della Catena, but this inheritance was contested by other members of Sir Nicholas's family, and it was not until 1882 that the British Privy Council finally confirmed Strickland in his Maltese title.

His roots therefore lay in two countries, one thousand five hundred miles apart, whose history had come together only when the British expelled the French from Malta during the Napoleonic Wars. Thereafter, they governed the island as a crown colony, but during Strickland's lifetime there were to be several attempts at instituting limited self-government, none of them entirely successful. There was constant bickering between those who favoured British language and culture and those who favoured Italian, and Maltese politics were notoriously acrimonious and vituperative. Strickland was a child of this small island world, and a tireless protagonist in the cause of some measure of Maltese self-government; but he was also a child of the British Empire, always saw Malta in this broader imperial framework, and was convinced that imperial and Maltese interests were identical. His wish was to make the Maltese 'as English as possible', and in the course of his career he went to extreme lengths in pursuit of this passionately held belief.[14] For he had grown up in the era of high imperialism – of the Diamond Jubilee, the Boer War, Joseph Chamberlain and Admiral Fisher – and his pride in his family was equalled only by his pride in the British Empire.

Strickland's education undoubtedly increased his attachment to Britain and its dominions. He attended Oscott School, Birmingham, went on a round-the-world tour in 1883, and in the following year went up to Trinity College, Cambridge, to read law. He was President of the University Carlton Club, and the first Roman Catholic to be President of the Union. He visited Sizergh, where his grandfather had been born, and to which he soon acquired a great attachment, and conceived the ambition of 'entering into English noble society', to the dismay of his mother, who wished him to marry into the Maltese aristocracy.[15] Trinity was the ideal base from which to mount such an assault, and it soon proved to be successful. In 1890, he married Lady Edeline Sackville, daughter of the seventh Earl de la Warr, thereby establishing himself at the very heart of the British aristocracy. The de la Warrs were descended from the Dukes of Dorset, and the sisters of the seventh Earl had married into the Salisbury, Derby and Bedford families. These were powerful connections, and in his later years Strickland and his wife frequently exploited them in furthering his official career.

Strickland wanted more than connections with the British aristocracy: he sought a home base in the country as well; and his marriage to Lady Edeline, who never had much taste for travel, made that need more urgent. As Walter Charles Strickland clearly realised, this combination of personal ambition and family pride made Gerald the obvious candidate to rescue the ailing Sizergh estate in 1896, though even for a Maltese nobleman this was a costly additional burden to assume. In order to guarantee the mortgages on the property, the whole of his marriage settlement was committed, and he was obliged to raise a further loan of £8000 from Coutts'. The estate seems to have generated little rental, and Strickland was often hard pressed to meet the mortgage payments.[16] These were commonplace circumstances for many a late-nineteenth-century landowner, and in coming to terms with them, Strickland adopted appropriately commonplace solutions. He exploited his connections to obtain an succession of imperial appointments which guaranteed him an assured income, without which he could not have kept Sizergh in the family.[17]

In the course of his round-the-world tour he had already established contact with the two senior figures at the Colonial office, Sir Henry Holland, the Secretary of State, and Sir Robert Herbert, the Permanent Secretary. This was partly on account of his strongly-held imperialist sentiments, and partly because, even at that early age, he seems to have

decided that a career in the British Colonial Service was what he wanted.
While still an undergraduate, he became prominent in the public debates
about the reform of the Malta constitution, and he himself was partly
responsible for the new arrangements which came into being in 1887,
which allowed some degree of representative government in the colony.[18]
In the same year, he was Malta's delegate at the first colonial conference
held in London, and soon after was elected to the island's Council of
Government. But he quickly withdrew from politics, threw in his lot with
the imperial administration, and became Assistant Colonial Secretary.
Then, in 1889, he was promoted to Chief Secretary, an appointment which
he held until 1902. In obtaining these jobs when scarcely out of university,
there can be no doubt that his patrician and offical connections had been
of the greatest use.

   As Chief Secretary, Strickland was directly responsible to the Governor
of Malta for the civil administration of the colony and, as he later recalled,
he 'lost no time in pushing, and carrying with a rapidity that was considered
hasty, reforms that had been retarded for years'.[19] He was entrusted by
the British Government with negotiations at the Vatican, the outcome of
which was that Pope Leo XIII accepted the British right of veto over
nominations to the bishoprics of Malta. He helped to found the Royal
Malta Militia, and organised and chaired a committee which successfully
stamped out a severe epidemic of cholera. He increased the number of
schools, and reorganised both the police and the civil service. He promoted
the installation of electric lighting, and took over and expanded the
languishing Malta Railway. He improved the drainage and sanitation
of the island, and greatly extended the breakwater in Valetta Harbour,
so it offered safer and more extensive accommodation to the British
Mediterranean Fleet. In recognition of these services, he was made a
Commander of the Order of St Michael and St George in 1889, and
promoted to Knight Commander in 1897, when still not yet forty. These
were doubly appropriate honours: when originally founded, in 1818, the
Order had been designed to commemorate the British annexation of Malta,
and to reward its inhabitants; and from 1868 onwards it had been given out
to those British subjects working overseas for the Foreign Office or the
Colonial Service.[20]

   By then the Chief Secretaryship was beginning to turn sour. Strickland's
overwhelming aim was to strengthen the ties between Britain and Malta,
and to check what he regarded as the increasingly insidious influence of
the Italians. In this policy he had the support of the British Colonial
Secretary, Joseph Chamberlain, but he was so tactless and overbearing in
his behaviour that he incurred the hostility of the Maltese clergy, and the
animosity of the Maltese nationalists. In 1899, a reform was introduced
which allowed the law courts to use English when a non-Maltese litigant
requested it, and notice was given that by 1914, English would be sub-

stituted for Italian in all legal proceedings. This was followed soon after by a second reform, which secured to parents the right of choice of English as an alternative language in schools. The result was fierce local opposition, and a major political crisis. Chamblerlain's policy was regarded as offensively imperialist and high-handed in nationalist circles, and there was widespread public agitation and unrest.[21] Strickland was pilloried as the supine collaborator of the Colonial Office; there were threats on his life and demands for his removal. Eventually, Chamberlain backed down on reforming the courts (but not on reforming the schools); the Malta Constitution which Strickland had himself helped to draft was suspended; and his own appointment as Chief Secretary was abruptly terminated.

Thus, in the spring of 1902, the first phase of his official career came to an end, amidst turmoil, controversy and disappointment, in very much the same way that the second and third phases of his career were also to do. In part, this was a matter of temperament. At all the stages of his public life, Strickland was too aggressive, too intemperate, too belligerent, too quarrelsome. He fell out with successive Governors of Malta over trivial matters; and even with his masters in Whitehall relations were often strained. 'You should moderate your tone to Colonial Officialism', one well-wisher once remarked, 'or it will be impossible for them, much as they want to, to enlist you in officialism itself.'[22] It was also a matter of background, circumstance and situation. In Malta, Strickland was regarded by the Nationalists and the Catholics as a turncoat who had sold out to the British Empire and the Colonial Office, but in Britain, despite his connections, he was never completely accepted – because he was Maltese, and because he was Catholic. These contradictions he never satisfactorily resolved. The great aim of his life was to do so by promoting Anglo-Maltese amity, within a greater British Empire. But there were few who shared these views, he lacked the political weight to make them prevail, and already the trend of the times was against him.

II

Although much dismayed by the eventual circumstances of his departure, Strickland had been hoping to leave Malta for several years, and by the late 1890s he had become both restless and unhappy. Neither his professional prospects nor his family circumstances seemed as propitious as he would have wished. Because of his mixed parentage, he could not expect to rise any higher in the imperial administration in Malta, and he wanted a wider field in which to exercise his powers. By 1894, Lord de la Warr was lobbying on his behalf for the Governorship of Cyprus or Newfoundland, and once Strickland had acquired Sizergh his importuning became even more intense. He became more than ever preoccupied by his forebears, his wife wrote a history of the family, and he sought in vain for a Strickland earldom or a baronetcy in abeyance, to which he might succeed. He was no more successful in his requests from the Colonial Office for a special pension or a posting to Whitehall. The death of his two young sons, in 1893 and in 1902, meant that his branch of the family was also destined to become extinct in the male line; and between 1899 and 1908, he had to defend his claim to his Maltese estates which was being contested by his younger brother, Paul.[23]

The uproar in Malta over the language reforms of 1899–1902 meant that the Colonial Office finally accepted that Strickland must be found another job, and began to look for a suitable posting to which he might be moved. It was recognised that his transfer must be in the form of a promotion, so as to show the administration's continued confidence, and this meant that he had to be given a junior governorship – easier said than done. He was offered Fiji, but declined it because it was too far away. Instead, he asked for Cyprus, but this was regarded as too senior a post. Eventually, and with great difficulty, a vacancy was created in the Leeward Islands, by moving the incumbent governor, Sir Henry Moore Jackson, to Fiji. Strickland was strongly pressed to take this 'post of greater importance and higher salary than that which you at present hold'. It was worth £2000 a year, the climate was good, and it was within reasonable distance of Britain. Indeed, it was made fairly plain to him that if he refused this offer, nothing else appropriate could – or would – be found. Accordingly, he accepted it, and with a lengthy letter of commendation from the Governor of Malta to the Colonial Office about his years and work as Chief Secretary safely on file, he left the Mediterranean to begin his proconsular career.[24]

Despite these formal signs of official approval, Strickland was under no illusions that he had been offered a very junior post as a way of getting him out of Malta without losing face. He had, however, no choice but to accept it, since it would be another ten years before he qualified for his Colonial Office pension, and with the expenses of Sizergh being what they were, he could not afford to forgo it. Accordingly, he was determined to make a success of the Leeward Islands, in the hope of securing a more substantial governorship in the not too distant future. He took strict control of finance and spending, was especially concerned about defence, and regularly visited the outer islands which came within his jurisdiction. He saw the Leewards as one of the 'undeveloped estates' of the British Empire, about which his hero, Joseph Chamberlain, had recently waxed so eloquently and optimistically, and he was determined to do his best to improve them. To this end, he supported the provision of central crushing factories for the sugar-cane industry, and he encouraged the reintroduction of cotton, on the grounds that the islands must have at least two industries to be economically viable.[25]

Although the governorship provided ample scope for Strickland's reforming instincts and authoritarian methods, he was far from happy there.

He thought government house 'a glorified shanty, without sanitary arrangements', and Lady Strickland, whose health was beginning to fail, hated being so far from Britain, and found the lack of anything approximating to 'society' deeply dispiriting. When home on leave in 1903, Strickland asked Chamberlain for a transfer to Cyprus, but was told firmly he could not be promoted so soon. He was much disappointed: 'I know I must go on working to keep Sizergh in the family at least a few years more.'[26] Sir Robert Herbert, though now retired, intervened on Strickland's behalf, but advised him to settle for Jamaica or an Australian state governorship, rather than expect Cyprus. At the same time, Lady Strickland urged her most illustrious relatives, the Dukes of Bedford and of Rutland, to lobby for her husband. How influential this orchestrated importuning was it is impossible to say. But in July 1904, after spending little more than twelve months actually in the Leewards, Strickland was duly appointed Governor of Tasmania.

He arrived in October of that year, to take up the lowliest state governorship in the recently-confederated Australian Commonwealth, only to learn that the state legislature had just reduced his salary from £3500 to £2750, which robbed the job of much of its financial attractiveness. Nevertheless, and despite the fact that Tasmania was half a world away from Malta and Sizergh, the position was a distinct improvement. The local society was very much better, and there were plenty of visitors from England. The governor's residence, with its seventeen servants, was 'magnificent', and the climate was 'delightful'. He and his wife (to the extent that her failing health permitted) kept up suitably viceregal state. Despite occasional rumours that as a former Crown Colony governor he was too authoritarian a proconsul, Strickland generally resisted the temptation to interfere in politics, and relations with the state government and opposition were usually cordial. He admired and got on well with the Governor-General, Lord Northcote, the most tactful, conscientious and successful of the early proconsuls, and he had 'much leisure time', which initially he seems to have enjoyed.[27]

The major issue during his term of office was the continuing uncertainty about state-federal relationships in the aftermath of confederation, especially as it affected the nature and prospects of state government – and state governors. On the one hand, Strickland wished to maintain the position of state governors against the state parliaments, which were eager to diminish the standing, salaries and splendour of their local notables, now that there was also a Commonwealth Governor-General. On the other, he was anxious to defend states' rights against the centralising tendencies of the federal government, and state governors against the viceregal pretensions of the Governor-General. This centralising trend filled him, as an imperialist, with especial – and somewhat exaggerated – alarm. He feared it was the first step down a slippery slope leading to unification, nationalism, socialism, republicanism and the dissolution of the Empire. This was fantasy: but it gradually became an obsessive pre-occupation during his time as an Australian state governor, to such an extent that it eventually unbalanced his judgement, and helps to explain why his proconsular career ended in the way it did.

As in the Leeward Islands, Strickland was soon turning his attention to his next career move. He toyed with the idea of entering British politics, getting himself elected as an MP for a Westmorland constituency, and even of reaching the Cabinet. Alternatively, he continued to hope that he might be called to London, to be Under Secretary at the Colonial Office. When on long leave in England during the summer of 1908, he asked the Colonial Secretary for the Governorship of Victoria, the Cape of Good Hope, or New Zealand. But his connections were less good than they had been, both in the Colonial Office and in government. Joseph Chamberlain had resigned in 1903, and Sir Robert Herbert died two years later. The Liberal landslide of 1906 meant that his wife's titled relatives could no longer lobby as effectively as they had done before. Moreover, the continued illness of Lady Strickland, who was by this time suffering from an undiagnosed disease of the spine which resulted in creeping paralysis, only further harmed his prospects. Under these circumstances, Strickland was probably lucky to be promoted to the better-paid (worth £4000 a year) and higher-ranking Governorship of Western Australia early in 1909.

Unfortunately, Strickland's elevation occurred very soon after the replacement of Lord Northcote by Lord Dudley as Governor-General of the Commonwealth. Strickland thought Dudley was careless, raffish and ostentatious, and anxious to aggrandise his office still further at the expense of state governors. There was much truth in this, with the result that Strickland's relations with Dudley were as bad as those with his predecessor had generally been good.[28] Strickland was nothing if not belligerent, and his disagreements with Dudley soon became public knowledge. In particular, he became obsessed with the question of who should hold what was called the 'dormant commission', when the Governor-General was away. For reasons that were neither clear nor cogent, Strickland became convinced that he should hold it rather than, as was customarily the case, the Governors of Victoria or New South Wales, who occupied the two oldest and most senior positions. The result was disagreeable all round. He rowed with his fellow governors; he rowed with Lord Dudley; and he rowed with Lord Crewe, the Colonial Secretary.

Strickland was widely advised to stop pressing his claims, on the grounds that it was prejudicing his future career in the Colonial Service. But he still hoped for better things: Jamaica, New Zealand, Madras or Bombay. In 1910, he emphatically refused Fiji again, for this was clearly an appointment far less grand than any he had in mind. Relations with Dudley were so bad that he even thought of resigning, but Dudley's replacement by the

1. The Installation Banquet of the Knights of St Patrick in the Great Hall, Dublin Castle, 1783. This new order of chivalry was one means whereby the Irish nobility was incorporated into a new, authentically British elite.

2. Viscount Castlereagh, later third Marquess of Londonderry, painted, bemedalled and beribboned in his Hussar uniform, by Sir Thomas Lawrence.

3. The Hon. Shute Barrington, by Sir Thomas Lawrence. Bishop, successively, of Llandaff, Salisbury and Durham, sits 'vain, proud, be-robed and well-preserved'.

4. The future first Earl Granville: 'a jaunty, handsome, self-confident youth: the very embodiment of a swagger portrait', by Sir Thomas Lawrence.

7. Eaton Hall, Cheshire: rebuilt to designs by Alfred Waterhouse, as an appropriately stupendo dwelling for Britain's richest family. But even th Grosvenors had to borrow to pay the bills.

8. Carlton Towers. Lord Beaumont's decision entrust its rebuilding to E.W. Pugin and Franci Bentley during the 1870s left him with a debt o £275,000 by the end of the decade.

5. The second Duke of Buckingham and Chandos was the most indebted aristocrat of his generation, and went spectacularly bankrupt in 1848 with encumbrances in excess of £1.5 million.

6. The fourth and last Marquess of Hastings, known as the 'King of Punters', went rapidly to his ruin and death following the notorious Derby of 1867.

· HOME FROM THE DERBY!

RDIFF DOCKS.

9. Cardiff Docks. Created by the
Marquesses of Bute as the outlet for
their Glamorgan coal, they absorbed
huge sums in investment, and paid a
very low return.

10. Sir Edward Grey: landowner, bird-
watcher and Foreign Secretary, he was
also chairman of the North Eastern
Railway from 1904–5, and much
appreciated the salary which he briefly
enjoyed.

11. G.J. Churchward, whose ancestors had been squires of Stoke Gabriel in south Devon, was Superintendent of Locomotives for the Great Western Railway from 1902–21.

12. 'Claud Hamilton', built in 1900, and named after the chairman of the Great Eastern Railway, Lord Claude Hamilton, who was the second son of the first Duke of Abercorn.

13. 'Viscount Churchill', named in 1924 after the chairman of the Great Western Railway, who found himself 'perplexed and ill-at-ease' during the strike-ridden inter-war period.

14. The second Lord Montagu of Beaulieu, who trained as a railway engineer, and later became a tireless and influential propagandist in support of the motor car and the aeroplane.

15. Sir Nigel Gresley was the bearer of one of the oldest names in the country, and was also Chief Locomotive Engineer of the London and North Easte Railway during the 1920s and 1930s.

16. The Hon. C.S. Rolls driving one of his own cars in 1906. Rolls was a brilliant salesman, who exploited his aristocratic connections in selling high-class cars to high-class people.

. Lord Brabazon, a patrician pioneer of motoring and aviation, who was also briefly Minister of Aircraft Production
. Churchill's wartime government.

. The 'Flying' Duchess of Bedford took to the air
cause she was stone deaf, and because the change in
nospheric pressure alleviated the buzzing in her ears.

19. The Hon. Mrs Victor Bruce: one of the most
adventurous drivers and aviators of her generation.
'Speed', she once observed, 'has always fascinated me
since my first pony bolted.'

Kedleston, Derbyshire: Lord Curzon's favourite home, which he lovingly restored, and whose architectural history he personally researched and wrote.

Bodiam Castle, Sussex. This superb medieval fortress was bought by Lord Curzon in 1916; he restored it and bequeathed it to the National Trust on his death in 1925.

Montacute House, Somerset. Curzon rented this magnificent mansion during the later part of his career and, thanks to the wealth of his second wife, entertained there in lavish style.

Tattershall Castle, Lincolnshire. Curzon saved this decayed fifteenth-century fortress-lodging, restored the tower, and left it to the National Trust on his death in 1925.

24. Lord Curzon as Viceroy, wearing the robes of a Knight Grand Commander of the Order of the Star of India, of which he was *ex-officio* Grand Master.

25. Lord Curzon at the Delhi Durbar, January 1903: the Raj at its apogee, and the ultimate ceremonial ego-trip, revealingly described by some critics as the 'Curzonation'.

26. Curzon as Chancellor of Oxford University: 'To see Lord Curzon, in his magnificent robes, leading the procession of Doctors into the Sheldonian Theatre, was in itself a liberal education.'

27. Remembrance Day, 11 November 1920. The new Cenotaph has just been unveiled by King George V, and the coffin of the Unknown Warrior awaits its final journey down Whitehall to Westminster Abbey.

THE GREAT SILENCE AT THE CENOTAPH.

28. Sizergh Castle, Westmorland, was settled on Gerald Strickland in 1896. Thanks to the wealth of his second wife, he did much to restore it during the inter-war years.

29. Lord Strickland: part British landowner, part Maltese nobleman, and a passionate imperialist, who vainly strived to bring Britain and Malta closer together.

30. The Inlaid Chamber at Sizergh Castle. During the 1890s, when the Stricklands were hard-pressed for money, its magnificent Elizabethan panelling was sold to the Victoria and Albert Museum.

31. Blenheim Palace, Oxfordshire: the huge house where Winston Churchill claimed he 'took two important decisions, to be born and to marry, and I never regretted either.'

32. Lord Randolph Churchill: widely regarded as being wayward, unstable and irresponsible – characteristics which many censorious contemporaries also discerned in his son, Winston.

33. Lady Randolph Churchill: a beautiful spendthrift, whose first husband was rumoured to have died of syphilis, and who married twice more, to the dismay and amusement of her friends.

34. Randolph Churchill: rude, spoiled, unstable, headstrong, irresponsible and argumentative, his behaviour caused his father, Winston, much embarrassment during the 1930s.

35. The fourth Marquess of Salisbury, respectability and decency personified, much disapproved of Churchill's raffish friends, especially the hard-drinking and loose-living Lord Birkenhead.

36. The seventh Duke of Devonshire: the man generally supposed to have restored his family finances actually made them even more precarious because of his over-investment in Barrow-in-Furness.

37. Eastbourne: the Grand Parade in its Edwardian heyday. The town was then known as the 'Empress of Watering Places', and much of its cachet derived from the Devonshire connection.

38. Christmas at Chatsworth between the Wars. Harold Macmillan (back row, second from the left) later recalled that the scale and style of living had to be experienced to be believed.

39. Barrow-in-Furness, the town. The serried streets, terraced houses and factory chimneys were a world away from the ducal grandeur of Chatsworth, Hardwick, Lismore Castle and Bolton Abbey.

). The iron and steel works, Barrow-in-Furness. The seventh Duke of Devonshire invested heavily in this ndertaking, but in the long run, it was a most unsuccessful enterprise.

41. Letheringsett Hall, Norfolk: the country seat of the Cozens-Hardys, and an appropriately modest house for a family as much involved in business as in landownership.

42. The first Lord Cozens-Hardy. As a barrister, county M.P., high court judge, and Master of the Rolls, he brought his Norfolk family prominence on the wider national stage.

43. Archibald Cozens-Hardy speaking at the dinner held in Norwich in September 1937 to mark his retirement after forty years as the editor of the Eastern Daily Press.

44. Glavenside, Letheringsett, Norfolk: the house owned by Sydney Cozens-Hardy and his son Basil remains in the family. But it is now shared with paying visitors.

45. Knole, Kent. Vita Sackville-West's ancestral home, which she was not allowed to inherit on account of her gender, and to which she remained obsessionally attached all her life.

46. Tea party at Knole. Despite the Sackvilles' precarious finances, Knole was one of the great houses of the early twentieth-century, and was vividly evoked by Vita Sackville-West in *The Edwardians*.

47. The Marquess of Dufferin and Ava was Harold Nicolson's favourite uncle. After a distinguished diplomatic and proconsular career, his old age was ruined by financial scandal and family tragedy.

48. Lord Carnock: Harold Nicolson's father reached the very top of the diplomatic service, something which his son lacked the determination (and the deferential wife) to do.

49. Sissinghurst Castle, Kent, was bought by Vita Sackville-West in 1930. In many ways it was for her a Knole-substitute, where she lived an increasingly reclusive life until her death in 1962.

50. Vita Sackville-West and Harold Nicolson: two very proud and (in her case) possessive patricians, who disliked the fact that Britain was now being run by people of an inferior social class.

more relaxed Lord Denman, who arrived in July 1911, meant that matters immediately improved.[29] Nevertheless, with his wife in failing health, Strickland feared that his prospects were not good. He came to believe that there had been prejudice against him in the Colonial Service, because he was a Catholic and a half-breed, and he feared that the powerfully-entrenched Orange sentiments in many parts of the country would prevent him from obtaining further promotion in Australia. In this, he was mistaken, for in late 1912 he was appointed Governor of New South Wales (worth £5000 a year) in succession to Lord Chelmsford, and in the following year he was made a Knight Grand Cross of the Order of St Michael and St George.[30] His life-long ambition of achieving a first-class governorship had finally been realised.

But after a grand arrival in Sydney in March 1913, it did not prove a successful term of office. Scarcely a year after Strickland arrived, a new Governor-General was appointed: Sir Ronald Munro Ferguson, a former MP and maverick Liberal Imperialist, who was effectively being 'dumped' by Asquith's government.[31] Since Strickland was a hard-line Conservative, there were bound to be disagreements. To make matters worse, Munro Ferguson made it plain that he regarded state governors as distinctly inferior beings, and he clearly resented Strickland's seniority and attitude. Inevitably, there were renewed arguments about the 'dormant commission'. There was trouble over the official residence at Sydney, which had once been the state governor's, but which the Governor-General now claimed for himself. There were arguments about salutes, precedence, levees and entertainments, and quarrels about the channels of communication between state governors and London: should they be direct, or go via the Governor-General? In all this, Strickland believed he was acting dutifully as the senior governor, upholding the rights of the states and dignity of his office. But others saw him as an interfering and embittered nuisance: indeed, Munro Ferguson occasionally expressed doubts to the Colonial Secretary about Strickland's sanity.[32]

Strickland had been greatly disappointed not to have been offered the Australian Governor-Generalship himself, and was further discouraged when it was made plain to him that there was no prospect of a peerage. Moreover, his ailing wife wanted to go home, he would soon be eligible for a pension, and retirement seemed an increasingly appealing prospect. He was bored with the endless superficialities of social life, regretted the fact that he could do nothing active in politics, and was increasingly at odds with the Governor-General, the Colonial Office, and the Liberal administration in Britain. In all likelihood, therefore, Strickland would have retired at the end of his term as Governor of New South Wales. However, a sudden political row, which blew up in the autumn of 1916, meant that he left the Colonial Service more abruptly than might otherwise have been expected, amidst controversy as public and as acrimonious as that which had accompanied his departure from the Chief Secretaryship of Malta, fifteen years before.[33]

The origins of this crisis lay in the disintegration of the Australian Labour Party in the aftermath of the national debate over wartime conscription. In New South Wales, Labour was the ruling party, and Strickland got on well with the Prime Minister, William Arthur Holman.[34] But by the autumn of 1916, in the aftermath of the conscription controversy, Holman was losing control of his own supporters in the State House, and to make matters more complex, an election was due in October of that year, as the three-year span of the State parliament was coming to an end. As Labour's support for Holman dwindled, he proposed to form a National Government, appropriate for the wartime emergency, which would depend on the support of what had previously been the opposition. Having put together such a coalition, Holman gave notice that he intended to prolong the life of parliament by special legislation, so as to avoid the divisions and controversies of the impending general election.

As the king's representative, Strickland regarded these proposals as unacceptable, on the grounds that Holman no longer enjoyed the support of the New South Wales Labour Party, without which he would never have become state prime minister in the first place. Accordingly, he made it plain that he would not sign any Prolongation Bill, and he called on the Ministry to resign. As Governor, he believed he was not bound to accept Ministerial advice, and that he still had the discretionary power to exercise his own judgement about parliamentary dissolution. Moreover, he was adamant that the people of New South Wales must be allowed to express their opinions on the matter via the ballot box. There can be no doubt that, technically speaking, his conduct was correct. However, as subsequent crises centring on the granting or witholding of dissolutions were to show, the way in which the rules were followed or applied was at least as important as the rules themselves; and there can be no doubt that on this occasion, as so often in his official career, Strickland acted tactlessly, even going so far as to leak to the local press his minute calling on the ministry to resign.

The outcome was predictable, and not long delayed. Forced to chose between the Governor and the Premier, the imperial authorities in London backed Holman. The Colonial Secretary instructed Strickland to sign the Prolongation Bill which, despite his earlier protestations to the contrary, he now had no alternative but to do. Meanwhile, the state premier insisted on Strickland's recall to London, a request which the Colonial Office was only to happy to grant. Accordingly, in April 1917, Strickland left Australia, ostensibly on six months' leave of absence from the Colonial Service, in fact in disgrace. Later in the year, when it was anounced that Sir Walter Davidson, the Governor of Newfoundland, would be replacing him in New South Wales, The Times pronounced a damning but perceptive verdict on Strickland's proconsular career:

Few positions in the imperial service are more delicate than those held by the representatives of the Crown in the self-governing Dominions. Unfailing tact, a keen sense of proportion, savoire faire, and power of adapting means to ends, are among the qualities indispensable to the public servants appointed to them. It cannot be said that during Sir Gerald Strickland's tenure of the Governorship of New South Wales, he exhibited these qualities in the necessary degree.[35]

Inevitably, a controversy ensued in the correspondence columns, and the rights and wrongs of Strickland's behaviour were debated once again. He received explicit defence from Professor Arthur Berriedale Keith, a former Colonial Office mandarin turned academic, who was also a friend of Strickland's and an expert on constitutional questions concerning the Empire; and there was more guarded support from Sir Charles Wade, Holman's predecessor as state premier. Both of them pointed out that, legally speaking, Strickland had been perfectly correct to do what he had done, and Keith later insisted that Strickland had enjoyed 'a career of marked distinction'.[36] But it was to no avail, since the real issue was personality rather than procedure, and on that issue his position had become untenable. When he visited the Colonial Office in November 1917, and asked for the Governorship of Ceylon, Strickland 'received a cold and indifferent reception' at the hands of Walter Long, the new Colonial Secretary.[37] It was the end of his proconsular service, and it was the end of the second phase of his career.

III

The circumstances of Strickland's recall from New South Wales, and his enforced retirement from the Colonial Service in 1917, left him bitter, and the death of his wife in the following year only added to his unhappiness. He was by now in receipt of a Colonial Office pension, but there were still the expenses of Sizergh, and he had five daughters to look after and marry off. Like many landowners, he joined the post-war rush to sell, putting the manor of Sedbergh on the market, which had been in the family since Sir Thomas Strickland bought it between 1598 and 1601. Although he was a widower of fifty-seven, with thirty years of public service behind him, and with estates in England and Malta which required his attention after so long an absence overseas, he immediately set about establishing a new career, in Maltese politics, in British politics, and as an Anglo-Maltese intermediary. In many ways, it was the most remarkable and original phase of his public life – but it also ran true to form, being the usual amalgam of success and disappointment, acrimonious controversy and ultimate defeat.

Strickland's first move was to enter Malta politics, where he joined the campaign for the restoration of self-government in the aftermath of the First World War. The result was the so-called 'Milner-Amery Constitution', promulgated in 1921, a complex and ultimately unworkable scheme, which established a Senate and an elected Assembly, and which granted responsible government in local affairs, while reserving all imperial matters to the governor.[38] The first elections to the Assembly were held in October 1921, and in order to contest them, Strickland founded the Constitutional Party. Its platform was predictable: support for the British imperial connection, and unwavering hostility to the pro-Italian sentiments of the Nationalists. Strickland was duly elected to the Assembly, but his party was in a minority, and for the first six years the Nationalists were in control of the government. Strickland's opposition was vehement, even by the standards of Maltese politics. He denounced their efforts to strengthen ties with Mussolini's Italy, and he turned against the Maltese priests, regarding them as unpatriotic and influential collaborators in the Nationalists' cause. Eventually, in 1927, Strickland and his allies obtained a majority in the Assembly, and the former Chief Secretary became Head of Government, which effectively meant he was now Malta's Prime Minister, a change of identity 'without parallel in the history of the Empire'.[39]

This was only one aspect of Strickland's new political life. Ever since he had taken possession of Sizergh, friends had urged him to stand for a local British constituency, in the traditional manner of a great landowner, and as his own forebears had done from the thirteenth to the seventeenth centuries. He had always refused before, but at the 1924 general election he suddenly decided to stand as Conservative candidate for Lancaster, a marginal constituency in which the Tory majority of 10,000 in 1922 had been overturned by a Liberal majority of 5500 in the following year. Despite the fact that his seat at Sizergh was close by, Strickland was regarded in the district as an absentee landlord, in residence only for the summer months. However, he was backed by the Earl of Derby, whose support was important in any inter-war Lancashire election, and he fought a predictably pugnacious campaign, blending with his strong imperialist views a vigorous denunciation of socialism and communism. He polled 15,243 votes, against 11,085 cast for the Liberal candidate, and 5572 for Labour.[40] As a result, Strickland was now an elected member of two legislatures which were separated by the land mass of Continental Europe, and for the next few years he shuttled back and forth between them.

In 1926 the circumstances of his life changed again, when he married for a second time, and it is difficult to believe that he did not so at least in part for the money. His new wife was Margaret Hulton, daughter of a north-country press magnate, Edward Hulton, who during the last quarter of the nineteenth century was founder and proprietor of several newspapers, among them the *Manchester Evening Chronicle* and the *Daily Dispatch*. She was exceptionally rich in her own right, and when she died left an estate in England in excess of £2 million. She was a great supporter of her husband's activities in both Britain and Malta and, as he somewhat heartlessly explained to one of his daughters, 'she is prepared to spend money like water to keep both political pots boiling'.[41] No doubt much to his relief, she was also prepared to spend on the upkeep and refurbishment of Sizergh. Long-overdue restoration and improvements were undertaken, the gardens were extended and the lake enlarged, and some of the pictures which had been sold during the 1890s were re-purchased. At the same time, Lady Strickland also acquired a palatial London house in Holland Park, where the entertainments were very grand indeed.

This transformation in his fortunes and his circumstances should have provided the ideal base from which Strickland could have launched his Commons career; but it did not work out like that. On the one hand, his long absences in the Mediterranean meant that he was a disappointing constituency representative. To their dismay, the electors of Lancaster soon discovered that they had returned 'the member from Malta'.[42] On the other hand, his performances in the Commons were not designed to win him many friends, either. His main concern was to raise issues concerning Malta with Leopold Amery, the Colonial Secretary and a close friend, but he did so with a tactless and pugnacious persistency which earned him the repeated rebuke of the Speaker, on the grounds that he was wrongly raising essentially domestic questions in the imperial legislature, and criticising the conduct of Colonial Service officials who had no right of reply. As Clement Attlee later recalled, Strickland 'showed great ingenuity in introducing the political controversies of Malta into every possible subject brought before the House'.[43] By 1926, there were demands in Lancaster that he stand down at once as their MP, or at least give notice that he would do so at the next election; and there were demands in the Commons that he should confine himself to non-Maltese subjects. Either way, he was widely regarded as 'a Maltese intruder'.[44]

Nevertheless, in England, Strickland's career soon moved towards the culmination which he had long sought. In the spring of 1927 he agreed to stand down as Lancaster's MP at the next election, and in the new year's honours of 1928 he finally obtained the long-sought-after peerage.[45] Perhaps it was in recognition of his family's lengthy service, across the centuries, as north-country MPs. Perhaps it was in belated acknowledgement of his years as a proconsul. Perhaps it was thought a fitting accolade for a Maltese nobleman who was also the island's Premier. Perhaps it was to console him for the disappointment of giving up as Lancaster's MP, and for failing to obtain the Lord Lieutenancy of Westmorland on the death of Lord Hothfield. Whatever the reason, Strickland himself thought his peerage long overdue, and commissioned his son-in-law, Henry Hornyold, who had married his eldest daughter Mary in 1920, to compile the authoritative version of his family's history, which culminated in so many ways in himself: Gerald, Baron Strickland of Sizergh, the man who had rescued the family estates, and adorned and enriched the family record with achievements to rival the 'past glories' of his most illustrious warrior-ancestors.[46]

Only one sadness marred this earthly apotheosis: there was no son and heir to inherit the title. Gerald was thus, to his deep and abiding disappointment, both the first and the last Baron Strickland, and the unbroken male succession to Sizergh was doomed to come to an end. But his eldest daughter, the Hon. Mary Strickland, played a suitably patrician part in the life of the county, serving as Chairman and President of the Westmorland Women Unionists during the 1930s. Moreover, her husband was descended from a Worcestershire family which could trace its ancestry back to the thirteenth century,[47] and was a local antiquarian of note, compiling, in addition to the history of the Stricklands, an account of Lancashire MPs from 1290 to 1550.[48] Like the Stricklands, the Hornyolds were Catholics: indeed, the Pope had bestowed the Dukedom of Gandolfi on Henry's uncle Thomas during the late nineteenth century. In 1931, so as to avoid death duties, Strickland conveyed the Sizergh estate jointly to Mary and Henry, and in the following year Henry Hornyold assumed by royal licence the additional name and arms of Strickland.[49] He became a Justice of the Peace for the country, and was High Sheriff of Westmorland in 1937, Coronation year. They thus provided an active Strickland presence in the county which had long been lacking, and for the rest of his life Lord Strickland spent part of his time in England with them at the castle.

From 1927, when he became Head of the Government, Strickland's main concern was naturally with affairs in Malta. Here again, the new Lady Strickland's largesse was of great help in promoting her husband's Constitutional Party and the pro-British and anti-Italian causes for which it stood. She soon established herself as the grande dame of the island, travelling around in state in her Rolls-Royce. She gave £100,000 to endow St Edward's College, an English-language Catholic high school, to which she contributed a further £5000 a year.[50] She put up £340,000 for the construction of a luxury hotel, a development which Strickland had long hoped to undertake, but which was only completed just before the outbreak of the Second World War. And she poured thousands of pounds into the creation of an English-language press, in particular *The Times of Malta* and *The Sunday Times of Malta*, which from 1935 were edited and controlled by Strickland's unmarried daughter the Hon. Mabel, who also played a considerable part in the affairs of her father's Constitutional Party of which she was assistant secretary.[51]

As Maltese Prime Minister, Strickland's policy was to combine a vigorous programme of public works with unyielding support of the Anglo-Maltese connection in the face of Italian Fascism and Maltese Nationalism, but almost from the outset, his administration ran into trouble.[52] Although he possessed a majority in the Assembly, Strickland was in a minority in the Senate, where his measures, and his budgets, were regularly defeated.

Although insisting that he was still a loyal son of the Catholic Church, Strickland blamed the ecclesiastical senators, who held the balance of power, in words that were intemperate even by his standards. He denounced them for playing politics, and accused the island's Catholic priesthood of being agents of Italian expansion. The Archbishop of Malta and Bishop of Gozo responded by issuing a joint pastoral letter, proclaiming it a grave and mortal sin for any one to vote for Strickland or his party in the elections of 1930. As a result of this latter-day collision between church and state, the island was soon in an uproar extreme even by Malta's standards, and there was an attempt on Strickland's life. The British temporarily broke off diplomatic relations with the Vatican, suspended the Maltese constitution, and set up a Royal Commission, one of its terms of reference being 'to consider the general fitness of the Maltese people for self-government'.[53]

On three separate occasions, Strickland defended his conduct in the British House of Lords.[54] He reaffirmed his view that the Catholic church had no right to interfere in the political process, and he painted an alarmist picture of Italy's expansionist aims, which were, he insisted, now aided and abetted by the Vatican, which was by this time enjoying harmonious relations with the Fascist regime. Despite their initial support, the British government was reluctant to jeopardise Anglo-Italian relations in defence of what they increasingly came to regard as Strickland's fantasies about an Italian conspiracy to annex Malta. The Foreign Office criticised his 'foolish behaviour' and his 'clumsy handling of the situation'. Lord Passfield, the Foreign Secretary, clashed with Strickland on more than one occasion in the House of Lords. In the Commons, the Labour MP John Oldfield noted that wherever in the Empire Strickland had served, there had sooner or later been trouble.[55] Although Strickland still remained technically Prime Minister, the Governor of Malta resumed the administration of the island and disregarded his recommendations. Eventually, in 1932, the constitution was restored, and Strickland belatedly apologised to the Catholic hierachy; but it was insufficient to prevent his defeat by the Nationalists in the postponed general election held later that year.[56]

Once again, Strickland's career had come to an abrupt halt, amidst crisis and controversy. This time there was to be no comeback, no reprieve, and his closing years were spent in argumentative anti-climax. 'I do wish', one friend wrote to him, 'something could induce you to be less bitter and disappointed.' But Strickland was scarcely the man, and the 1930s were scarcely the decade, for that. In 1933, the Malta constitution was suspended again, and Strickland spent the next years vainly campaigning in the House of Lords for its restoration with all the tactless tenacity at his command.[57] His speeches grew longer and more confused, but were no less belligerent. He spoke sometimes as a supporter of the National Government, sometimes from the opposition benches. He interrupted, spoke out of turn, gave great offence. Even their noble lordships' patience was often sorely tried.[58] His hostility to Italy remained undiminished, but his constant urging that Malta's defences needed improving fell on deaf ears, not least because the Government was anxious to stay on good terms with Mussolini.[59] His campaign for the award of life peerages to colonial premiers was no more successful. He was himself hardly the best advertisement for such a scheme, and no British government in the 1930s was going to take up the treacherous question of second-chamber reform.[60]

In 1938, Strickland tried unsuccessfully to persuade Malcolm MacDonald, the Colonial Secretary, to revise his peerage patent so that one of his nephews might inherit his title. In February of the following year a new constitution was eventually proclaimed for Malta, but with very limited representative provisions. The Constitutional Party won six out of the ten seats, and as the 'Leader of the Elected Majority', Strickland returned to office for the last time. But hostilities with Germany commenced shortly after, and on 10 June 1940 Italy declared war on France and Britain. The bombs which soon rained down on the island showed that his anxieties about Malta's defences, and Italy's acquisitiveness, had been well and wisely entertained. But Strickland did not survive long to enjoy this terrible vindication. He died in August 1940, just one year after the seven-hundredth anniversary of his family's possession of Sizergh, and a few months before the great siege of Malta began. He was buried in the family vault in Mdina Cathedral; there was a requiem mass in London at Westminster Cathedral, attended by Lord Lloyd, the Colonial Secretary; there was a memorial service at Kendal; and the Prime Minister of Australia, Robert Menzies, sent a telegram of sympathy.[61]

Even by the standards of his most travelled and versatile patrician contemporaries, Strickland's was an extraordinary career. In one guise, he was the scion of an ancient British landed family, who brought to his name achievements and honours that were alike fresh and unprecedented. In another, he was a Maltese grandee, who obtained supreme office in his own island, and successfully stormed the exclusive bastions of British high society. Either way, he raised his family's name – whether Strickland or della Catena – to a level it had not attained before, which was precisely what he had set out to do. He was the Governor of four British colonies, and the Chief Secretary and Prime Minister of a fifth. He was an elected representative in two legislatures. He married once into the British peerage and once into the British plutocracy. He acquired a Maltese title by inheritance, and a British title by ennoblement. At different times, he was a Maltese count, an Earl's son-in-law, a Westmorland landowner, an imperial procounsul, and a British peer. It was a bewildering array of different identities to have assumed in one lifetime.

Yet Strickland could never conceal from himself that his career had been a failure, and in that assessment he was undoubtedly correct. In 1902, 1917 and again in 1932, he left office under a cloud. In British politics, he achieved almost nothing; he ended his career as a colonial governor in disgrace; and in Malta his accomplishments were more controversial than constructive. To some extent, his own character was to blame. As Viscount FitzAlan of Derwent pointed out in the Lords in 1930, Strickland had 'not been famed either for judgement or tact in dealing with people. It has often been said of him that if on occasion he has done the right thing, he has been certain to do it in the wrong way.' He was not only 'bereft of all sense of proportion': he was also lacking 'the slightest vestige of any sense of humour'.[62] He was too ambitious, too intolerant, too vindictive. He was terrifying in his rage, but ridiculous in his self-importance. Not for nothing was he known in the Colonial Service as 'Count Delicatessen'. His son-in-law, Henry Hornyold, put it down to his 'Maltese blood'. Whatever the reason, there can be no doubt that Strickland was his own worst enemy, with an unerring capacity for losing the support of the British authorities whose Empire it was his dearest wish to safeguard.[63]

There were also deeper explanations for his failure. He never really knew where he belonged, and he spent his life in the service of an ideal which was rapidly becoming out of date. In Britain, he was too much of the outsider, too singlemindedly the champion of Malta. In Malta, he was too much of the imperialist, too singlemindedly the champion of Britain. 'It has', he once observed, 'been my lot in life to endeavour to bring closer together the people in the fortress of Malta in co-ordination with my Westmorland traditions.'[64] But while he managed this in his own life and person, he was never able to translate it into a more public imperial accomplishment. The vision of a united empire, with a single federal constitution, and with dominion representation in the British House of Lords, which he had derived and developed from the teachings and example of Joseph Chamberlain, was already out of date by the First World War. And the aristocratic world of the 1880s, to which he had so ardently aspired to belong, and in which he sought to establish an honoured and assured niche for the Strickland name, was no less 'dwindling' and redundant by the Second.[65] By 1940 he had outlived not only his time, but also his place – wherever that was.

IV

As if to emphasise the unique nature of the Anglo-Maltese conjunction he had brought about in his own life and work, Lord Strickland's inheritance was effectively divided on his death between the British and Maltese branches of his family.[66] Mr and the Hon. Mrs Henry Hornyold-Strickland continued to reside at Sizergh Castle, and to play their part in the life of Westmorland. He was a conscientious Lord Lieutenant of the County from 1957 to 1965, and she was actively involved with the Women's Voluntary

Service, the British Legion, the County Council, and Conservative Party politics, both local and national. She died in 1970; he in 1975. Their eldest son, Lt.-Cdr. Thomas Hornyold-Strickland, had become seventh Count della Catena on his grandfather's death, the title passing directly to him via his mother. He served in the Second World War, married into a Silesian family as ancient as his own, and followed his parents in residence at Sizergh, where he lives to this day.[67]

In Malta, Strickland's mantle was initially taken up by his nephew Roger, who succeeded his uncle as leader of the Constitutional Party, only to dissolve it in 1945, when he refused to contest the island's elections.[68] But the main bearer of the family standard was Strickland's redoubtable daughter Mabel. She remained editor and chief proprietor of *The Times of Malta*, and continued to produce daily issues even when the wartime siege was at its height. After the dissolution of her father's Constitutional Party, she became the founder and leader of the Progressive Constitutional Party, and was elected to the legislative assembly in 1950 and 1962. She was a staunch supporter of continuing ties with Britain, urging that there should be Maltese represenatives in the House of Lords; a determined opponent of Dom Mintoff, the Labour leader; and until her death in 1988 was widely regarded as the most influential women in Malta, believing – according to her opponents – in the 'divine right' of her family to rule the island.[69]

Despite these continuities, it is the changes since Lord Strickland's death which stand out most markedly. At Sizergh, Mr and Mrs Hornyold-Strickland endured the inevitable deprivations of war, and in 1950, like other landed families, they gave their castle to the National Trust, together with the contents and 1500 acres. 'Owing to the increasing pressure of taxation', *The Times* explained, 'they feel that the chances of the family's being able to retain possession in generations to come as it has done for the last seven hundred years are increasingly remote.'[70] And while the Hon. Mabel Strickland kept up the family interest in politics and papers in Malta, she fought a losing battle against the post-war demands for independence, leading little more than a 'ghost party', consisting of herself, her relatives, and her employees in publishing. Self-government was granted in 1947, revoked in 1959, and restored in 1962. In 1964, Malta became independent within the Commonwealth, in 1974 it became a republic, and in 1979 the British base was closed and the British alliance was ended. The Mintoff governments of the 1970s preferred to cultivate friendships with China and Libya than with Britain, and passed legislation designed to strike at the Strickland business interests.[71]

Neither in Westmorland nor in Malta are the Stricklands the force they were in the first and last lord's day. In part, this can be explained by accidents of succession and quirks of personality; but there have also been broader forces at work. Since Lord Strickland's death in 1940, the connections between the British aristocracy and the British Empire have unravelled around the world. The overseas opportunities which sustained so many needy patricians, Strickland included, soon disappeared. The independence of India swept away the whole paraphernalia of the Raj. South Africa had already appointed a non-British Governor-General in 1937, and the long lines of aristocratic proconsuls in Canada, Australia and New Zealand came to an end in 1957, 1965 and 1967 respectively. 'Going out and governing New South Wales' is no longer an option (even for Prince Charles). In Kenya and Rhodesia, some 'gentlemen emigrants' lingered on, led by the Duke of Portland and the Duke of Montrose, vainly trying to prevent the end of Empire. They failed, and in the newly-emerging post-colonial nations they had no place. Today, some aristocrats still own land, and companies, in what was once the British Empire: but the close ties of an earlier era have gone for ever.[72]

On the other side, the indigenous and aspiring aristocracies of the empire have also been correspondingly weakened. The ruling chiefs of India were one of the casualties of partition and independence; the practice of giving peerages to rich or important colonials soon dwindled; and the idea of ennobling dominion Prime Ministers never came to much. There were hereditary peerages for R.B. Bennett of Canada in 1941, for Stanley Bruce of Australia in 1947, for Sir Bernard Freyberg of New Zealand in 1951, for Godfrey Martin Huggins of Rhodesia in 1955, and for Lord Thompson of Fleet of Canada in 1964; and life peerages for Richard Casey (Australia) and Charles Elworthy (New Zealand). But hereditary titles had never been popular in the Dominions, Lord Thompson had to take British citizenship to get his British peerage, and since then both Canada and Australia have evolved their own system of honours.[73] The imperial peerage has followed the Empire into oblivion. During the nineteenth century the British boasted the greatest *nobilitas* and the greatest *imperium* in the world. During the twentieth, they declined and fell together. As the career of Lord Strickland suggests, it is more than mere coincidence that their historical trajectories have been so similar.

6

Winston Churchill as
an Aristocratic Adventurer

IN HIS EARLY TWENTIES Winston Churchill was briefly the heir to one dukedom, and over half a century later, on his retirement from public life, he declined his sovereign's offer of another.[1] This double connection with the highest rank in the British peerage may not have been his greatest claim to fame, but it certainly makes him unique among British Prime Ministers, and it forcibly reminds us that Churchill himself was in C.P. Snow's words, 'the last aristocrat to rule – not just preside over, rule – this country'. It was at Blenheim Palace that he took the two most important decisions of his life – 'to be born, and to marry, and I never regretted either'. It was to Blenheim that he went with Clementine for the first part of their honeymoon, and it was to Blenheim, which he always treated as his second home, that he regularly returned during the course of his subsequent career. Throughout his life, he regarded the Duke of Marlborough as the head of his family, and revered him as the bearer of the greatest name in the land.[2] And it was in Bladon churchyard, within sight of his great ancestral palace, that he chose to be buried, alongside his father, Lord Randolph Churchill, and Jennie, his mother.

Not surprisingly, Churchill's attitudes were as aristocratic as his pedigree. His arrogance, his self-confidence, his sublime indifference to consequences, his total lack of interest in the thoughts and feelings of others: all this was regarded – and regretted – by observers as emphatic sign of his upper-class origins. He considered servants and secretaries, gardeners and gamekeepers, horses and hounds, to be integral parts of the natural order of things. He had no understanding of the minds or mores of the middle classes, and it cannot be coincidence that so many of his political adversaries came from that social background: Joseph and Neville Chamberlain, Bonar Law, Stanley Baldwin and Clement Attlee.[3] He knew virtually nothing of the lives of the ordinary men and women who made up the majority of Britain's population. He never went into a shop, or travelled on a bus, and on the one occasion when he journeyed on the underground, he got on the Circle Line and went helplessly round and round on it until, several hours later, a friend rescued him from the ordeal. Even as late as 1951, he still believed that most people in Britain lived in 'cottage homes': a phrase which revealingly mingles his paternal benevolence with his aristocratic ignorance.[4]

In retrospect, Churchill liked to present himself as a deprived and disadvantaged child, further handicapped by a minimal education, who achieved renown in the world by his own unaided efforts. But while there can be no doubting his ambition and his application, it is also clear that in the early stages of his career, he shamelessly exploited his aristocratic connections with singleminded purpose and success. As a soldier hungry for action and glory, he secured postings to the Indian frontier and the Sudan, thanks not merely to his own tireless lobbying, but also to that of his mother, who, he later recalled, furthered his plans and guarded his interests 'with all her influence and boundless energy'.[5] By the same means, he obtained the best prices for his reporting of the Boer War, and the most generous advances for his early books. When he began his political career as a Conservative candidate, his cousin the Duke of Marlborough helped to pay his election expenses.[6] When he crossed the floor of the Commons, he was invited to contest Manchester North-West thanks to the intervention of his uncle, Lord Tweedmouth, who happened to be a senior figure in the Liberal Party. In some senses, young Winston may have been a self-made man; but he was also, by birth and connection, a member of Britain's charmed, inner circle, and he early on learned how to pull its strings to his own advantage.

Yet there was another side to Churchill's patrician persona which deserves much fuller exploration than it has so far received. At the outset of his career, he certainly benefitted from the patronage and support of his noble connections. But in the much longer perspective of his ninety-year lifetime, the aristocracy was a declining force in British politics, in British society, and in British history, and Churchill himself was very much an aristocrat of his time. Like many late-nineteenth-century patricians, his immediate family background was impoverished, unstable, and tainted by scandal, and some of his distant relatives were even more accident prone or disreputable. As with many well-born men of his generation, his own finances were exceptionally precarious, and he was often in debt and beholden to those much richer than himself. Like other impoverished aristocrats, he was driven to writing for the newspapers, and to producing pious works of family history. And in his inconsistent opinions, his uncertain party loyalty, his disillusion with democracy, and his admiration for authoritarian forms of government, Churchill was behaving like many disoriented notables, who had lost their bearings in the unfriendly and unfamiliar world of twentieth-century mass politics.

When placed against this broader historical background of widespread aristocratic decline, Churchill emerges as a much more palpable product of his class and his time than is often realised.[7] And as far as his political career before 1940 was concerned, this was on balance a hindrance to him rather than a help. His blue blood may have been of use at the outset, but thereafter it increasingly became a liability. For it was not just that Churchill was widely distrusted as a man of unstable temperament, unsound judgement, and rhetorical (and also alcoholic) excess. Nor even that his record in public life – Tonypandy, Antwerp, the Dardanelles, Chanak, Russia, the General Strike, India – was uniquely controversial. It was also that for most of his career, there hung around him an unsavoury air of disreputability and unseemliness, as a particularly wayward, rootless and anachronistic product of a decaying and increasingly discredited aristocratic order. Before 1940, it was not easy for him to be taken seriously as the man of destiny he believed himself to be, when so many people in the know regarded him as little better than an ungentlemanly, almost déclassé, adventurer.

I

Although he took the greatest pride in the ducal blood that pulsed through his veins, Churchill's family and forebears were hardly those which any politician, eager to establish an unimpeachable public reputation, would freely have chosen. For there were skeletons a-plenty rattling in the Marlborough family cupboard. The first duke may have been a 'heaven-born general', but he was also a man of dubious political and personal morality. Indeed, many Victorians, brought up on Macaulay, regarded him as disreputable and untrustworthy: he had betrayed James II and conspired against William III, and he had pursued power and wealth with unscrupulous and single-minded ardour.[8] Since then, the Marlboroughs had been either unhappy or undistinguished or both. Many of them had been unstable, depressive and bad-tempered. The third, fourth and fifth dukes were profligate even by the standards of the late-eighteenth and early-nineteenth centuries, and none of them had played a significant part in the affairs of their time. Indeed, Gladstone's harsh words of 1882 probably expressed the generally-held late-Victorian view: 'There never was a Churchill from John of Marlborough down that had either morals or principles.'[9] And for the next fifty eight years, that remained the conventional wisdom on the subject.

By the last quarter of the nineteenth century, therefore, the Marlboroughs seemed to be heading rapidly and almost self-destructively downhill. In marked contrast to his predecessors, Churchill's grandfather, the seventh duke, who inherited the title in 1857, was a pious and high-minded Victorian nobleman, and his wife was the formidable Lady Frances Anne, daughter of the third Lord Londonderry. But by mid-nineteenth-century ducal standards the Marlboroughs were far from rich, and the accumulated extravagances of his predecessors meant that the seventh duke inherited the estates in parlous condition. As a result, he was reluctantly compelled to disperse much of the patrimony he would have wished to safeguard. In 1862, he sold the family estates in Wiltshire and Shropshire, and twelve years later he parted with his Buckinghamshire holdings to Baron Ferdinand de Rothschild for £220,000. Heirlooms went the same way as ancestral acres: in 1875, the Marlborough gems were auctioned for thirty-five thousand guineas, and in the early 1880s, the magnificent Sunderland Library was disposed of for £56,581, after the necessary special legislation had been obtained from Parliament.[10]

This process of dispersal was continued by the eighth duke, Churchill's uncle, who succeeded in 1883, and soon parted with most of the magnificent collection of Blenheim Old Masters, for £350,000. There the resemblance between father and son ended, for the eighth duke was one of the most disreputable men ever to have debased the highest rank in the British peerage. As a youth he was expelled from Eton, and soon acquired a well-deserved reputation for being rude, erratic, profligate, irresponsible and lacking in self-control. In 1876, his affair with the already-married Lady Aylesford became a public scandal; the Prince of Wales branded him 'the greatest blaggard alive'; and in 1881 he fathered by her an illegitimate child.[11] Two years later, his first wife divorced him, and the new duke's social disgrace was complete. In 1886, he figured prominently in the sensational divorce case featuring Lady Colin Campbell, his one-time mistress, and shortly after he married a rich American, Lilian Hammersley, which enabled him to install electric light and central heating at Blenheim. Appropriately enough, the eighth duke's politics were as wayward as his libido. During the early 1880s, he was successively a Liberal, an Extreme Radical and a Conservative, and he produced a series of equally confused articles, calling for the reform of the Lords and of the land laws, and the preservation of 'a class of hereditarily trained statesmen connected with the land'. He died, as he had lived, in the tradition of a Gothic villain, being discovered in his laboratory at Blenheim 'with a terrible expression on his face'.[12]

This was the unhappy state of affairs that 'Sunny' Marlborough, Churchill's cousin, sought to remedy during his long tenure as ninth duke, from 1892 to 1934; but he met with only very limited success. In politics, his career fizzled out: he held minor office under Salisbury and Balfour from 1899 to 1905, voted against the Parliament Bill in 1911, and by the inter-war years had become a paranoid and anti-semitic reactionary.[13] In matrimony, he fared no better. His first marriage, to Consuelo Vanderbilt, was blatantly arranged for the money; they separated in 1906 and divorced in 1920. His second wife, Gladys Deacon, was a Bohemian adventuress, who had previously been his mistress. But marriage soured their relationship, and they separated in 1931.[14] In financial terms, the Vanderbilt millions enabled the duke to restore the gardens and terraces at Blenheim, but by the end of his life he was on the brink of selling the family archives to Yale University, and he died virtually insolvent. And in social terms, the Marlboroughs remained unacceptable. The breakdown of the Duke's two marriages was widely publicised, as was his admission into the Roman Catholic Church. Neither King Edward VII nor King George V would receive him at court, nor would they accept from him the annual gift of the Blenheim flag. Most duchesses refused to recognise his second wife, and in Oxford county and episcopal society the duke himself was regarded with scarcely-concealed disdain.[15]

In the course of his short and tragic life, Churchill's father, Lord Randolph, was even more notorious. From his days as an Oxford under-graduate, he had shown an unhealthy delight in gambling, in drinking, and in over-spending. His marriage to another American, Jennie Jerome, was accompanied by unseemly wrangles over money; by the early 1880s, he was heavily in debt and in thrall to money-lenders and company promoters; and at the end of his life, he owed the Rothschilds nearly £70,000. Like so many Churchills, only more so, his temperament was erratic and uncontrollable, and it seems almost certain that he contracted syphilis, which led to the general paralysis which slowly and humiliatingly killed him.[16] In society, the Churchills were publicly ostracised between 1876 and 1884, after Lord Randolph had impulsively taken his elder brother's part in the row with the Prince of Wales over the Aylesford scandal. In politics, he was widely regarded as an unstable and unprincipled adventurer, whose vituperative style earned the condemnation of both Gladstone and Salisbury. His abrupt resignation as Chancellor of the Exchequer in January 1887 merely confirmed the widely held view that he was an unscrupulous menace, so unbalanced as to be almost insane. When, at the end of his maiden speech in the Commons, young Winston described his father as 'a certain splendid memory', many MPs must have found it difficult to recognise the very different Lord Randolph they themselves had known.[17]

Churchill's mother was no less unrespectable. Although renowned for her beauty, and much admired for her public loyalty to Lord Randolph during his last pitiful years, she was as spendthrift, wayward and irrespon-sible as her husband. Their marriage soon became one of convenience only, it was widely known that she was having many affairs (especially with Count Charles Kinsky), and in 1886–7 there were frequent rumours that they were on the brink of divorce. After Lord Randolph's death she showed no inclination to moderate her ways, and in 1898 was obliged to raise a loan of £17,000 to clear her debts. Her response to this financial crisis was a commonplace one for aristocratic ladies in her condition. She briefly edited a magazine, the *Anglo-Saxon Review* (it made no money), and she wrote her reminiscences: but on her own admission, they were 'interesting chiefly in what is left unsaid'.[18] In 1900, after a long affair, she married George Cornwallis-West. But he was twenty years younger than she was, scarcely older than Winston himself. In society, the union was widely condemned; it soon broke down; and it ended in divorce thirteen years later. Undaunted, she married her third husband, Montagu Porch, who was also twenty years her junior. Once again, her behaviour was generally regarded with derision, incredulity and astonishment.[19]

By contrast, Churchill's wife, Clementine Hozier, whom he married in 1908, was high-minded, and endowed with much sounder judgement of men and events than her husband. Far from being the wealthy heiress whose fortune might have helped Churchill's political career, however, Clementine had spent her early life in genteel poverty. Her father, Henry Hozier – who was probably not her father at all – was an unsavoury and unattractive character, who had divorced her mother, Blanche, and left the family pitifully short of money. As the daughter of the Earl of Airlie, Blanche was herself descended from one of the more impoverished of Scotland's great families. Indeed, the household was so poor that Clementine could scarcely afford to take part in the expensive pageant of London high society, and before she met and married Winston she earned money by giving French lessons at 2s 6d an hour. To make matters worse, Blanche Hozier was not only an adulteress, but also an incorrigible gambler, and this latter trait was inherited by Clementine's sister, Nellie, and her brother, William. In 1921, after having resolved to give up gambling altogether, Bill Hozier commited suicide in a cheap Paris hotel.[20] Nor was this the first such scandal that Clementine had to live down: before she was betrothed to Winston, she had already been twice engaged, and in 1909, when Lord Percy, heir to the Duke of Northumberland, was found dead in Paris, it was whispered that he had been a former lover of Clementine's, and that he had been murdered on Churchill's instructions.[21]

The person who was rumoured – quite without foundation – to have carried out this astonishing deed was Churchill's younger brother Jack (who was in fact inoffensive and self-effacing, and took no part in public affairs). Winston remained close to him all his life but, as this story suggests, Jack became the subject of gossip that did his elder brother's reputation no good. In appearance, and in temperament, they were markedly unalike, and it was widely (but mistakenly) believed that Jack and Winston were only half-brothers, and that the fifth Earl of Roden was in fact Jack's father. After all, it was generally known that Lady Randolph had many affairs in the course of her first marriage, and her husband abstained from sexual relations with her once syphilis had been diagnosed.[22] In an attempt to make some much-needed money, Jack took up a career as a stockbroker. But in the early twentieth century, this was still thought by many to be an unsuitable career for a gentleman, and in 1907 Jack had to postpone his marriage to Lady Gwendeline Bertie, because her mother, the Countess of

Abingdon, thought his financial resources inadequate. Nor was this the last time that Jack's profession got him into trouble. When Churchill became Chancellor of the Exchequer, it was mildly awkward that his brother dealt in stocks and shares, and during the Second World War he was criticised for housing Jack in 10 Downing Street after his own London home had been bombed, and for keeping him as a permanent member of his Prime Ministerial entourage.[23]

But this was as nothing compared with the embarrassement that Churchill had been caused, during the 1930s, by his three children, Randolph, Diana and Sarah. They were ill-disciplined, rowed with their parents, and all became heavy drinkers. In 1932, Diana married John Bailey, son of Sir Abe Bailey, a South African mining magnate and friend of her father's. Both her parents were opposed to the marriage, and it ended in divorce three years later. In 1935, Diana married Duncan Sandys, but they, too, were later divorced, and in 1963, she committed suicide. Her younger sister Sarah sought a career in the theatre, and in 1935 became a chorus girl in one of C.B. Cochrane's reviews. While on the stage, she fell in love with Vic Oliver, a twice-divorced, Austrian-born comedian, who was seventeen years older than she was. Her parents were determined to prevent her marriage to this 'itinerant vagabond', but Sarah ran off to join Oliver in New York, and they were duly married on Christmas Day 1936.[24] On both sides of the Atlantic, the publicity was extensive and adverse, and did Churchill no good in political circles. In the autumn of 1938, when the Camrose press was campaigning for his return to the Cabinet, *Truth* wickedly suggested that if Vic Oliver was also made a minister, the comedy turn would then be complete. It was a jibe that Churchill neither forgave nor forgot.[25]

But even Diana and Sarah seemed almost angelic compared to their rude, spoiled, unstable, headstrong, irresponsible and argumentative brother, Randolph. He dropped out of Oxford University, took to drinking and gambling, got into debt, and became notorious as the most dangerous and boorish party guest in London. For a time, he was much attracted by the ideas of Oswald Mosley and the New Party, and later wrote a newspaper column in which he championed his father's views on India with a tactless fervour that can only have been counter-productive. But it was Randolph's active political interventions which did Winston the greatest damage in the eyes of the Tory leadership and the National Government.[26] Early in 1935, he stood at the Wavertree by-election as an unofficial Conservative candidate, on a Diehard platform. It was a sensational campaign, in which Randolph was attacked as a dissipated Mosleyite, and the result was to split the Tory vote and hand over a safe seat to Labour. A month later, he supported a second unofficial and ill-chosen Conservative candidate at Toxteth East: Richard Findlay, a former member of the British Union of Fascists. In January 1936, Randolph himself stood – again unsuccessfully – in a much-publicised by-election at Ross and Cromarty, against Malcolm MacDonald, who was not only a member of the National Government, but also the son of the former Prime Minister Ramsay MacDonald.[27]

Despite their dynastic delinquencies, Churchill's fierce loyalty to his immediate family was one of his most endearing qualities. Like most patricians he sought, when able, to further his relatives' interests with the same zeal that they had earlier shown in promoting his own. Indeed, both Lady Violet Bonham Carter and Sir John Colville believed that Churchill's besetting sin was the appropriately aristocratic one of nepotism.[28] When only a junior Conservative MP, he unsuccessfully tried to persuade the Colonial Secretary, Joseph Chamberlain, to appoint the ninth Duke of Marlborough Governor-General of Australia; and in 1915 he waged a persistent campaign to ensure that, despite his separation from Consuelo, the Duke should be appointed Lord Lieutenant of Oxfordshire.[29] Although he deeply disapproved of Randolph 'leading the life of a selfish exploiter, borrowing and spending every shilling you can lay your hands upon', he did his utmost to help him. One friend, Professor Lindemann, procured a place at Christ Church, Oxford, while two more, Lord Beaverbrook and Brendan Bracken, found him jobs in journalism. In 1933, Churchill paid off £1600 of his son's debts, and later went to speak on his behalf at Wavertree (though not at Ross and Cromarty).[30]

But it cannot have helped Churchill's reputation that so many members of his immediate family were so often in the newspapers for such unedifying reasons. In every generation, among his closest relatives, there were too many debts, too much gambling, too much drinking. Even by the relatively lax standards of the Edwardian era or the inter-war years, there was an above-average amount of infidelity, divorce, erratic behaviour, sexual scandal, social ostracism and court disfavour. Thus described, the Marlboroughs were a textbook case of a declining and degenerate ducal dynasty: Lord Randolph might have stepped straight from the pages of Trollope's *The Way We Live Now*, the ninth duke was a character of almost Proustian pitifulness, and the headline-stealing antics of Diana, Sarah and Randolph might have been taken from a novel by Evelyn Waugh – with whom, appropriately enough, Randolph enjoyed a life-long love-hate relationship. This only reinforced the prevailing view that *all* the Churchills were unstable, unsound and untrustworthy: utterly devoid, as Gladstone had damningly observed, of either morals or principles.

Surrounded as he was by such unsavoury relatives, it is easy to see why many contemporaries concluded that Churchill himself was equally disreputable and unreliable. In 1885, the fifteenth Earl of Derby had dismissed Lord Randolph as 'thoroughly untrustworthy: scarcely a gentleman and probably more or less mad'. Thirty years later, Derby's nephew described Lord Randolph's son in very similar words: 'he is absolutely untrustworthy, as was his father before him'. He was not the first – or the last – man in public life to make such damning and damaging comparisons. When summing up Churchill's performance in his first ministerial job, at the Colonial Office, the Permanent Secretary observed that he was 'most tiresome to deal with, and will, I fear, give trouble – as his father did'.[31] Of course, with the passage of time, there were fewer who could remember Churchill's father – but by the 1930s, everyone knew about Churchill's son. Once again, the similarities between Winston and Randolph II seemed disconcertingly close. As Sam Hoare put it in 1934: 'I do not know which is the more offensive or mischevious, Winston or his son. Rumour, however, goes that they fight like cats with each other, and chiefly agree in the prodigious amount of champagne that each of them drinks each night.'[32]

II

Churchill's sense of clan loyalty extended well beyond his immediate relatives, to encompass those more distantly located on the twigs and branches of his broadly spreading family tree. One of Lord Randolph's sisters was Lady Cornelia Spencer-Churchill, who always took the greatest interest in Winston's career, 'not only for your dear father's sake, but also for you'. In 1868, she had married Ivor Guest, scion of the great dynasty of South Wales iron-masters. Guest was an incorrigible snob and social climber, whose ambitions were widely lampooned during the 1870s in the pages of *Truth* and *Vanity Fair*, so much so that he was widely known as 'the paying Guest'.[33] He was created Baron Wimborne in 1880 by Disraeli, but turned against the Tories in the 1900s. The ostensible reason was his loyalty to Free Trade, but a more likely explanation was rumoured to be his annoyance that his request for promotion to an earldom had been refused. In January 1910 he tried to get one of his sons, Freddie, elected for the local constituency of East Dorset in the Liberal interest. But, as was often the case when a landed family changed sides, it was claimed that the Guests exerted undue influence on their tenants, intimidating some and bribing others, and on petition the election was disallowed.[34]

Lord Wimborne's eldest son, another Ivor Guest, was thus Churchill's first cousin. Like his father, he was a shameless importuner: Asquith thought him 'very unpopular', and the general feeling about him in social and political circles was well expressed in the damning couplet: 'One must suppose that God knew best / When he created Ivor Guest.'[35] In 1900, he had been elected Conservative MP for Plymouth, but in 1906 he followed his father and his cousin into the Liberal Party. Actively helped by his 'friend and ally' Churchill, he sought promotion in the peerage and preferment in government. Asquith was distinctly unenthused, but in 1910 he gave Guest a peerage in his own right as Lord Ashby St Ledgers (his father was still at that time alive), and made him Paymaster-General. This did not satisfy him and, with Churchill's help, he continued to press his claims. Eventually, he accepted the Viceroyalty of Ireland in 1915, but he was not a success there, resigned three years later, consoled himself with a viscountcy, and took no further part in public life. Clementine Churchill never approved of him, and even Margot Asquith thought him 'just a fairly frank bounder'.[36]

Ivor Guest's younger brother, Freddie, was still more suspect. Like so many members of his family, he was a snob, a playboy and a lightweight (in 1919 he suggested that the best solution to any possible working-class unrest was to drug their tea), and he had a 'passion for begging and pushing'. He, too, left the Tories for the Liberals, but failed to get elected in 1906. Churchill thereupon appointed him one of his private secretaries, and in 1910 he became MP for the family constituency of East Dorset at the second attempt. Thanks to his cousin's efforts, minor government office soon came his way, but it was only in 1917 that he became a significant (and shadowy) political figure, when he was appointed Liberal Coalition Whip.[37] For the next five years, Guest was responsible for raising money for Lloyd George's personal campaign fund. As a result he was closely involved in the sale of honours, and he probably set up Maundy Gregory in the touting business. During the dying months of the Coalition, he succeeded his cousin as Secretary of State for Air, but he held no office thereafter. He was completely cynical about honours, probably knew more embarrassing secrets than any other man in public life, and was regarded by Viscount Gladstone as Lloyd George's 'evil genius'. Even his *Times* obituary hinted that Freddie Guest was not a nice man to know.[38]

Through his Marlborough grandfather's marriage to Lady Frances Anne, Churchill was also related to the Londonderry family. This was never so easy a connection as with the two Guest brothers. Between 1910 and 1914, the sixth Marquess took great exception to Churchill's championing of Irish Home Rule, and for most of the inter-war years Churchill and the seventh Marquess were not on the best of terms.[39] On at least two occasions, Churchill certainly put himself out for his relative: in 1919 when, as the newly-appointed Secretary of State for Air, he gave him a junior job as Parliamentary Under-Secretary; and in 1928, when he successfully urged Baldwin to bring him into the Cabinet as First Commissioner of Works and Public Buildings. For much of the 1920s, however, Londonderry devoted himself to Ulster politics, a decision which Churchill thought unwise, and they did not see eye to eye over the General Strike. During the 1930s, they drifted still further apart. Churchill was a vehement critic of Londonderry while he was Secretary of State for Air, from 1931 to 1935; he disapproved of Lady Londonderry's much-publicised friendship with Ramsay MacDonald; and he found his kinsman's

admiration of Adolph Hitler incomprehensible. Not surprisingly, he steadfastly refused to give Londonderry any job in his wartime coalition or
caretaker Conservative administration of 1945.[40]

The final Marlborough connection, which was also much publicised
during the inter-war years, was with a cadet branch, descended from the
second son of the fourth duke: the Churchills of Wychwood. The first
Viscount Churchill, who had inherited the estates in 1886, sold off most
of the ancestral acres and heirlooms soon after, and spent his life as a
professional courtier and businessman, eventually becoming Lord-in-
Waiting to King Edward VII, and chairman of the Great Western
Railway.[41] He achieved notoriety because of his long-standing and much-
publicised quarrel with his wife, which effectively ruined what was left of
the family's riches and reputation. Shortly before the First World War, she
took up spiritualism and theosophy, under the influence of a medium
named Kathleen Ellis. Lord Churchill thereupon separated from his wife,
and pronounced her insane. She fled to North Africa, along with her son,
and Churchill tried unsuccessfully to recapture them at gunpoint. (He
eventually divorced her in a Scottish court in 1927.) During the First
World War, Lady Churchill returned to Paris, set up house with Kathleen
Ellis, and forced her son to marry her friend. Having already broken with
his father, the son now broke with his mother, ran away to America,
smoked opium, went on the stage, and was (falsely) accused of stealing the
Wimborne jewels.[42]

In addition to these more distant Marlborough relations, Churchill was
also connected to another group of patrician families through his mother,
Lady Randolph. Her eldest sister Clare married Moreton Frewen, the
younger son of a Sussex squire, who inherited an Irish estate in the 1890s.
But the man who was thus Winston's uncle mismanaged his affairs so
hopelessly, and so publicly, that he was nicknamed 'Mortal Ruin'. He spent
his portion of £16,000 on a cattle ranch in Wyoming, but by 1887 had
lost his entire investment. Thereafter, he was involved in a variety of
preposterous schemes: to make axle grease for locomotives, to produce ice
artificially, to extract gold from refuse-ore, to separate lead from zinc, and
to cut down timber in Kenya.[43] (He was also responsible for correcting the
proofs of Churchill's first book, and made a terrible job of it.) All these
enterprises lost him borrowed money, and he was regularly on the brink of
bankruptcy. His elder brother's Sussex estate was mortgaged and the timber
cut down; his own Irish property was laden with debt; and he even
persuaded his children to mortgage their life interests as soon as they came
of age. When his daughter Clare married in 1910, it was from a house
borrowed for the occasion; so bad was her father's reputation that her
wedding dress had to be paid for in advance and in cash; and some of his
many creditors gatecrashed the reception. At his death in 1924 he left less
than £50. As Kipling put it, 'he lived in every sense except what is called
common sense'.[44]

Lady Randolph's other sister, Leonie, married Sir John Leslie, a worthy and dutiful Irish baronet, whose family owned land in County Monaghan. Their eldest son, John Randolph, was thus Winston's cousin. In one guise, he was passionately attached to the ascendancy, and wrote a series of books lovingly recalling the lost world of his childhood. He sincerely mourned the end of the old paternalism, the demise of the great Irish estates under the Land Acts, and the suicide of European civilisation as a result of the First World War. He bitterly regretted the corrosion of high society by Jewish adventurers, and the corrupting power of the press.[45] Yet even as he lamented the passing of his patrician heritage, he also deliberately rejected it. He 'deeply affronted the Anglo-Irish Ascendancy into which he had been born', by renouncing his right of succession to the family estates, by embracing Roman Catholicism, and by using Shane, the Irish form of his name. Even more to his relatives' dismay, he took up the cause of Irish Nationalism and, thanks to Churchill's intercession, was introduced to John Redmond. In January 1910, he contested Londonderry City as an Irish Nationalist, standing against the heir to the ducal house of Abercorn, and in 1916, he urged that the British government should not execute those who had taken part in the Easter Rising. He was, in short, an authentically maverick patrician.[46]

Lady Randolph's remarkable matrimonial career brought two more tainted notables into Churchill's family orbit. One of them was her second husband, George Cornwallis-West. He was the heir to Ruthin Castle in Denbighshire, one of the oldest estates on the Welsh borders. By the late nineteenth century it was sadly decayed, and his parents were very short of money. Under these circumstances, marrying the spendthrift Lady Randolph was an extremely imprudent move, and by 1906 Cornwallis-West's finances were so precarious that Churchill was obliged to come to his step-father's assistance.[47] In order to make some urgently-needed money, he mortgaged his reversionary interest in the Ruthin estates, and – against the characteristically shrewd advice of Sir Ernest Cassel – set up a small issuing house in the City. Then everything went wrong. In 1914 he divorced Lady Randolph and married Mrs Patrick Campbell. In 1916 his business collapsed and he was declared bankrupt. And in 1920 he had to sell the family estates, to which he had succeeded three years before, to discharge his debts. Meanwhile, his marriage to Mrs Pat had broken down, he found it impossible to obtain a job in the inter-war years, and he was obliged to eke out a living writing reminiscences, novels and biographies. Mrs Campbell refused to grant him a divorce, and it was only on her death in 1940 that he was able to marry again. Shortly afterwards, he contracted Parkinson's Disease, and he committed suicide in 1951.[48]

Through his step-father's sister, Constance Cornwallis-West, Churchill's family ties were strengthened with another flawed and fallen grandee: Bend Or, second Duke of Westminster.[49] The Marlboroughs and the Grosvenors were already twice connected, via the Guests, and in 1901 Constance became the first of Bend Or's wives. The Cornwallis-Wests hoped thereby to repair their own family fortunes, but the marriage was not a success. The son and heir the Duchess bore her husband died in 1909, and thereafter the couple went their separate ways. In 1919 they were divorced, amidst much adverse publicity, and three more marriages brought Bend Or neither happiness nor repose. He was obliged to resign the Lord Lieutenancy of Cheshire because of his matrimonial irregularities, and neither King George V nor King George VI would have anything to do with him. This social ostracism only intensified his restless paranoia. He hated democracy, disliked Jews, voted against the Parliament Bill in 1910, and favoured a negotiated peace with Hitler.[50] On his death in 1953, Henry Channon composed a damning epitaph: 'he was restless, spoilt, irritable . . . ; his life was an empty failure . . . ; he did few kindnesses, leaves no monument'. Churchill had always felt rather differently, and issued a statement from 10 Downing Street, looking back 'affectionately and thankfully over half a century of unbroken friendship'.[51]

Clementine's aristocratic relatives were at least as unrespectable as those of her mother-in-law. Her sister, Nellie, who gambled and was generally considered rather 'fast', married Bertram Romilly, whose forbears were of illustrious lineage, but not rich. (Indeed, for a time in the 1920s, Nellie was obliged to keep a hat shop to help make ends meet.) There were two children of their marriage, Esmond and Giles, who were thus Winston's nephews, and they regularly visited Chartwell during the inter-war years. In 1934, Esmond became newsworthy in a sensational manner, by running away from Wellington College. He declared himself a Communist, and began to produce a subversive periodical entitled *Out of Bounds*. Inevitably, the press had a field day, publishing sensational stories under such unfortunate but predictable headlines as 'Winston's Red Nephew'. To make matters worse, Esmond possessed both a Churchillian countenance and a Churchillian temperament, and it was widely rumoured that he was in fact Winston's illegitimate son. For the rest of the decade, he remained constantly in the news. In 1936, he went to Spain, and fought on the side of the pro-Republican forces. In the following year, in an even greater blaze of publicity, he eloped with his cousin, Jessica Mitford.[52]

This was not the only connection between Clementine Churchill and the Mitfords. Her aunt, Clementina Ogilvy, had married Bertram Mitford, first Baron Redesdale. (Indeed, it was whispered in some quarters that Bertram was in fact Clementine's father.[53]) As a result, the Mitford children were frequent visitors to Chartwell, and Randolph showed a more than fleeting interest in Diana. By the 1930s the family was in serious financial trouble, and four of the daughters were regularly hitting the headlines: Nancy embraced socialism, and began writing novels; Jessica preferred communism and ran away with Esmond Romilly; Unity became a whole-hearted supporter of Hitler; and Diana, having divorced Bryan Guinness, married Sir Oswald Mosley.[54] Once again, Churchill suffered because of these distant but definite connections. In the late 1930s, both the English and the German press made much of the fact that Winston and Unity were relatives. And it was more than mildly embarrassing to the new wartime Prime Minister that two of the first people to be interned under the Defence of the Realm Regulations in 1940 were Sir Oswald and Lady Mosley. (It was even rumoured that the same fate had befallen Lord Londonderry.)[55]

Of course, these were not the only relatives on Churchill's extended aristocratic family tree. Some were worthy public men, like his uncle, Lord Tweedmouth, who was Lord President of the Council in Asquith's administration (though he did go insane and had to resign). Others lived lives of unostentatious decency, like his aunt, Lady Anne Spencer-Churchill, who married the seventh Duke of Roxburghe, and was Mistress of the Robes to Queen Victoria. But these were not the relations who hit the headlines, or who became the subject of malicious gossip and rumour. By contrast, and by definition, those who did were invariably good copy, and, as with his more immediate relatives, these disreputable family connections can only have done Churchill harm in the eyes of the politicians and the public. In November 1915 Moreton Frewen wrote to every member of Asquith's Cabinet, urging that Churchill should not be allowed to resign in the aftermath of the Dardanelles (his letter was ignored). In September 1939, by which time he was working as a journalist, Esmond Romilly urged that his uncle be made Prime Minister. It is difficult to believe this did his cause much help.[56]

At the very least, Churchill's vigorous loyalty to his more distant kinsmen was regarded by his fellow politicians as 'tiresome' and 'inconsiderate'.[57] He was too persistent and too unsubtle an intriguer, and some of his efforts were clearly counter-productive. More damningly, the fact that he took great trouble to promote the political careers of such suspect patrician lightweights as the Guest brothers or Lord Londonderry can only have reinforced the widely-held view that his behaviour was nepotistic, and his judgement was suspect. And it is difficult to imagine what he must have been thinking of when, at the Westminster by-election of 1924, he took with him on his campaign what Robert Rhodes James tactfully describes as 'a somewhat variegated assemblage of allies', including such déclassés and mavericks as Moreton Frewen, Freddie Guest, Shane Leslie and the Duke of Marlborough.[58] Such ostentatiously flaunted associations, even if based on the admirable view that blood was thicker than water, were exceptionally ill-advised.

III

Viewed from this essential dynastic perspective, Churchill's reputation may best be described as genealogically precarious, and it is in this unsavoury familial context of widespread degeneracy and disreputability that his own finances, friends, and way of life must be set and understood. As the elder son of a younger son, Churchill's inherited wealth was likely to be insubstantial, but because of his father's profligacy it was virtually non-existent. At his death, Lord Randolph's assets almost exactly matched his liabilities, and Winston himself was left to subsist as best he could on an allowance of £500 a year. To make matters worse, his mother was a spendthrift, with no real understanding of the value of money, his marriage to Clementine brought him no financial advantage (quite the reverse), and from his earliest years in the army Churchill believed that he had a right to the most comfortable and indulgent style of life. As a result, his own finances, while never as desparate as those of Moreton Frewen or George Cornwallis-West, were for most of his life decidedly uncertain. From the 1890s until the Second World War, he seems almost never to have been out of debt. Even (indeed especially) for a man of Churchill's aristocratic self-confidence, this was a precarious base from which to launch what soon became a flamboyant and controversial political career.

It was Churchill's proud boast on New Year's Day 1901 that in less than two years he had made £10,000 by his own unaided efforts, from his journalism, his lectures and his books.[59] In this he was quite correct, and to that extent his claim to be a self-made man was entirely justified. By then, his need for capital (and income) had for some time been self-evident. As a cadet at Sandhurst he had been continually short of money, and soon got into debt, and he experienced the greatest difficulty in finding the £650 necessary for equipping himself for the Fourth Hussars in 1895. The Dowager Duchess Lily gave him a charger worth £200, and he borrowed the rest of the money from the bank. Two years later, in India, his combined allowance and income amounted to only £800 a year, he was obliged to resort to local and unscrupulous money lenders, and some of his cheques were dishonoured (a much more serious offence against the gentlemanly code of conduct then than now). Meanwhile, his mother spent and squandered, as if there would be no tomorrow. 'We are,' Churchill remonstrated with her in 1898, 'both you and I, equally thought-less, spendthrift and extravagant. . . . We are damned poor.'[60]

Nor did his turn-of-the-century success as an author, journalist and lecturer improve his financial condition for long. In 1899, when he resigned his commission, he lost his only regular income. Two years later he voluntarily made over to his mother the £500-a-year allowance due from his father's estate.[61] Once he was launched into the costly world of early twentieth-century politics, Churchill's financial position became even more precarious. At that time, MPs received no remuneration, and were further expected to contribute to their own election expenses. Churchill was helped out by the Duke of Marlborough (who also provided him with lodgings in London), and subsequently by the Wimbornes. By 1906, his capital was much diminished. Like his father, he needed an official salary (indeed, there were some who accused him of crossing the floor for this very reason). Like his father, again, he soon sought the society and support of rich financiers, in particular Lord Randolph's old friend, Sir Ernest Cassel. It was not just that Churchill put the management of his £10,000 in Cassel's capable hands; it was also that Cassel found Jack Churchill a job as a stockbroker, and even put some directorships in the way of George Cornwallis-West.[62]

Inevitably, Churchill's marriage to the impecunious Clementine, his rapidly growing family, and his meteoric promotion in government, only increased his financial burdens. By 1910 his official salary was a welcome £2500, but his outgoings were much more than that. Like his father, he was obliged to rely on the largesse of others. Sir Ernest Cassel paid for the furnishings of Churchill's drawing-room 'as an act of spontaneous friendship', and Mrs Keppel (who was, after all, well placed to know) once suggested to Clementine that she could best help her husband's career by taking a rich and well-placed lover. In 1913 it was rumoured that Churchill had speculated in Marconi shares, and by the outbreak of war he was obliged to admit that 'our finances are in a condition which requires serious and prompt attention. . . . Money seems to flow away.'[63] Indeed, at one point the position was so bleak that Clementine was forced to sell a necklace to pay the household expenses. By the time Churchill departed for active service on the Western Front, the loss of his official salary, combined with his accumulated debts, meant he was effectively dependent on the 'unlimited credit' of Sir Ernest Cassel. Had her husband been killed in the trenches, Clementine would have been left with less than £1000 a year.[64]

Although Cassel was both a financial genius and a genuine friend, Churchill's dependence on him did not enhance his own political reputation. For Cassel was widely disliked and distrusted as a 'cosmopolitan financier', whose loyalty was neither to party nor to nation, but only to profits. As a German, a Jew, a millionaire, and a friend of King Edward VII, he seemed a classic example of the unscrupulous and unpatriotic plutocrat who was disfiguring public life, an irresponsible wire-puller who had poor politicians in his pocket. In 1902, Lord Salisbury had refused the King's request that Cassel should be made a peer, and during the First World War he was the subject of much hostile criticism on account of his alien origins.[65] In 1922, Lord Alfred Douglas stated publicly that Churchill was Cassel's creature: that 'this ambitious and brilliant man, short of money and eager for power', had given a deliberately false account of the Battle of Jutland, in exchange for a large sum of money. Douglas was prosecuted for criminal libel, convicted, and sent to prison. But in the course of the trial it emerged that Cassel had indeed paid for Churchill's drawing-room – a gift which, in the climate of the times, he had probably been unwise to accept. Although Churchill won his case, gossip about his unsound financial affairs was never fully silenced.[66]

At almost exactly the same time, Churchill acquired Chartwell Manor, the house which, after Blenheim, he loved the most in all his life. In theory, it was paid for by an unexpected legacy he had received in 1922 from the settlement of his Londonderry grandmother, Frances Anne, combined with an early advance for *The World Crisis*. But from the very beginning its upkeep was a drain on Churchill's meagre resources. To the initial cost of £5000 was soon added £15,000-worth of improvements.[67] There was an indoor and outdoor staff of eighteen to maintain; and there were costly and unsuccessful attempts to rear cattle, sheep, pigs and hens. By 1926, even Churchill admitted the need to economise: the livestock was sold off, spending was curtailed, and there was even talk of letting the house. But extravagance kept breaking out, and Churchill stubbornly refused to moderate his expensive way of life. Servants, he breezily insisted, were there to save trouble, and should be hired and fired with ease.[68] Not surprisingly, Clementine took a less serene view, and her worst forebodings were realised when, in the crash of 1929, Churchill lost most of his American investments.

Throughout the 1930s, Churchill's finances were in a truly parlous condition. Chartwell continued to absorb money like a sponge, and this, combined with the expenses associated with his children (in particular their education and the payment of their debts) meant that by 1931 his overdraft stood at £9500. Seven years later a renewed slump on Wall Street left him owing his brokers £18,000. Stringent economy measures were again introduced, but his creditors were so pressing that Churchill felt compelled to put Chartwell on the market, and even thought of quitting public life altogether. Eventually, his house and his career were saved by the generosity of Sir Henry Strakosch, an Austrian-born financier and South African mining magnate, who took responsibility for all his debts, and guaranteed to pay the interest on them.[69] *Pace* David Irving, this does not mean that Churchill was the creature of an international conspiracy of Jewish money-lenders. Indeed, the exact details of Strakosch's intervention remained secret for many years. But it was widely known that Churchill did not seem able to manage his own finances, and at the time when he was seeking to rouse parliament and the nation to the Nazi threat this must have been a political liability, as well as a grave personal anxiety.

In the same way, Churchill's obvious – and understandable – delight in living well at some one else's expense did not do him any good in the more straitlaced political circles. During the 1900s, he regularly holidayed with Sir Ernest Cassel: in Spain, on Nile cruises, and at his villa in Switzerland. He also enjoyed the equally lavish hospitality of Baron de Forest, both in London and at his estate in Austria. And one of the great attractions for Churchill of being First Lord of the Admiralty, and later Chancellor of the

Exchequer, was that the job carried with it an official residence in London. As First Lord he also had at his disposal the Admiralty yacht, *Enchantress*, which he used as a floating hotel, to entertain officially, to reciprocate the hospitality of his plutocratic friends, and to cosset his family.[70] It cost Churchill 'nothing or next to nothing', and fact that such high living was paid for by the state was the subject of much adverse comment at the time. 'How many lobsters have been eaten?' inquired Leo Maxse in the *National Review*. 'How many magnums of champagne have been drunk? To say nothing of other delicacies comprising a democratic diet.' Churchill was impervious to such criticisms of his subsidised high living. Indeed, for much of the First World War, he was provided with the use of a Rolls Royce by his friend the second Duke of Westminster.[71]

During the inter-war years, he remained a shameless cadger and incorrigible scrounger. When he visited the United States, in 1929 and again in 1931, he invariably travelled in private rail cars, provided by such rich friends as the financier Bernard Baruch and the steel magnate Charles Schwab. In California he was accommodated by William Randolph Hearst at San Simeon, and when he and Randolph put up at the Biltmore Hotel in Los Angeles their suite was paid for by James Rathwell Page, appropriately described by Churchill as 'a hearty banker'.[72] In France, Winston and Clementine regularly stayed at the houses of the Duke of Westminster and Consuelo Balsan, the former Duchess of Marlborough, who had subsequently married a rich Frenchman. Churchill, though not his wife, also loved the French Riviera, and frequently wrote and painted while staying at the villas of Lord Beaverbrook, Lord Rothermere, and Maxine Elliott, the American socialite. Subsidised yachting also remained a favourite pastime. As devotees of Noel Coward will know, the Duke of Westminster owned two magnificent vessels, on which the Churchills frequently cruised. Walter Guinness, Lord Moyne, was equally hospitable: in 1934 the Churchills were taken on an extended cruise of the eastern Mediterranean in his yacht, the *Rosaura*, and in the following year Clementine again sailed with Moyne on a six-month journey to the Dutch East Indies.[73]

As these names suggest, Churchill's friends were almost invariably drawn from the raffish worlds of high politics and high finance. His close collaboration with Lloyd George lasted from 1906 until 1922: first as his ally in radical, peer-bashing reform, then as his colleague in a coalition widely regarded as the most corrupt and irresponsible government of the twentieth century. Either way, this did not endear Churchill to the moralising politicians who dominated British public life from 1922 to 1939. The fact that Churchill had defended Lloyd George at the time of the Marconi Scandal was not soon forgotten. It was rumoured that the reason why Lloyd George had braved Tory wrath in bringing Churchill back into the government in 1917 as Minister of Munitions was that he was 'able to blackmail the Prime Minister'. There is no evidence that Churchill was ever involved personally in the sale of honours; but Freddie Guest was, after all, his cousin, and Churchill himself was a regular attender at the Derby dinners arranged by Maundy Gregory at the Ambassadors Club during the 1920s.[74]

Nor did Churchill's much-advertised and much-celebrated admiration for Lord Birkenhead exactly enhance his reputation as a man of probity and good judgement. They first met in 1906, soon after F.E. Smith (as Birkenhead then was) had made his brilliant maiden speech in the Commons. Together they founded the Other Club, they served in the Lloyd George Coalition from 1917 to 1922, and Churchill never ceased to regard him as his greatest and most gifted friend. Although he was a brilliant barrister, Birkenhead was a drunk, a gambler and a spendthrift, who shamelessly pursued the glittering prizes of life, and treated anyone who got in his way with an unforgivable (and unforgettable) combination of rudeness and ruthlessness. He was a close friend of Maundy Gregory, by whom it was rumoured he was being blackmailed, and he was forced to leave politics in 1928 because his creditors would not wait. Lord Balcarres described him as a man with 'the spirit and sometimes the ethics of a freebooter'. Lord Salisbury was even more censorious: 'I do not imagine', he once observed, 'that he has got many political principles. Poor fellow, he will probably drink himself to death.' And so, in the end, he did.[75]

Lord Beaverbrook possessed greater staying power, and his friendship with Churchill lasted from before the First World War until the end of their days. For most of his life, Beaverbrook was regarded – with good reason – as an unscrupulous adventurer, and a mischief-maker. He was a self-made Canadian businessman, who arrived in England in 1910, and in quick succession became an MP, a knight, a baronet and a peer. Asquith was not alone in believing that Beaverbrook's Canadian business record was 'of the shadiest', and his rapid accumulation of honours provoked 'a howl of indignation and disgust' in his home country.[76] In 1916 he acquired the *Daily Express*, and by the inter-war years he was one of the most powerful press barons in the land. In addition to Churchill, his close friends included Lloyd George, Bonar Law and Birkenhead, and all of them benefitted from his hospitality or financial assistance. The result was that Beaverbrook seemed to wield influence which was both sinister and irresponsible: propelling Law to the conservative leadership in 1911; bringing down the Asquith government in December 1916; and destroying the Lloyd George Coalition in 1922. By then, indeed, he was widely regarded as the embodiment of all the evil forces which threatened to corrupt British public life.[77]

Very much the same was said of Brendan Bracken, who first met Churchill in 1923, and became, by the 1930s, his most stalwart public and parliamentary friend.[78] Bracken was a mysterious Irish hustler, a whole

generation younger than Churchill or Beaverbrook, who established himself as the dominant figure in financial journalism in the inter-war years,
and became MP for Paddington in 1929. His devotion to Churchill was
total: he helped to place his articles in newspapers, and it was thanks to his
initiative that Henry Strakosch came to Churchill's financial rescue in 1938.
This was however another friendship which did Churchill's public standing
considerable harm. Bracken was generally regarded as being a brash, pushy,
meretricious, over-familiar and disrespectfull opportunist; and it was widely
believed (even in the Churchill family itself) that he was Winston's
illigitimate child. With characteristic indifference, Churchill himself
was amused and slightly flattered by such rumours, but Clementine was
understandably enraged at these aspersions on her husband's integrity, and
damningly dismissed Bracken as a 'red-haired freak'.[79]

   Although, as a life-long Liberal, Clementine retained a sneaking admiration for Lloyd George, she greatly disapproved of Birkenhead,
Beaverbrook and Bracken, whom she labelled the 'three terrible Bs'. She
knew that in their roistering, buccaneering company Churchill drank and
gambled to excess. She feared that they brought out all that was worst in
her husband: his irresponsibility, his belligerence and his waywardness. She
was convinced that his widely-known delight in the friendship of three
such piratical adventurers only damaged his public standing.[80] After all, no
one could accuse Churchill of having chosen his disreputable relatives: that
was a matter over which by definition he had no control. But in selecting
his friends, he showed personal preferences for men equally unsavoury.
The least that could be said was that he had been impelled by temperament, by fallible judgement, and by financial necessity to seek wealthy,
untrustworthy and unreliable associates which a more careful and more
prudent politician would have taken pains to avoid. More damagingly, it
bore out the truth of Brendan Bracken's remark, that Churchill too easily
gathered charlatans around him – of whom many believed Bracken himself
to be one.[81]

   These unwise and much-publicised friendships, combined with the
broader family background of ducal degeneracy, help to explain why it was
so easy for critics to disparage Churchill's conduct and character for so
much of his career. Moreover, his own behaviour and way of life only
seemed to confirm this hostile view. From the day he escaped from prison
in the Boer War, there were regular rumours that he had broken his parole,
which repeated libel actions never fully laid to rest. At different times, it
was put about that his brother was not his brother, and that he had fathered
two illigitimate children. Like his father, and his own children, he ate,
drank, gambled and spent to excess. He showed no respect for religious
belief or spiritual values, and his conversation was often Rabelaisian.
His finances were known to be unsound, and there were rumours and
accusations that he was the client of rich and dangerous men. In 1940, for

instance, the Aga Kahn claimed that 'for years' Churchill had been in the pay of the Jews and Lord Beaverbrook.[82] At the very least, it seemed as though Churchill had inherited more than his fair share of Marlborough delinquency and instability.

The whispering and the accusations went further than that, for it was even suggested that Churchill's wayward and erratic behaviour was evidence that his father's syphilis had been congenital. In 1925, Frank Harris published his memoirs, which gave a gruesome and fanciful account of Lord Randolph's terminal insanity. The book was banned in England; but copies certainly made their way into the country, and can only have fed the fires of rumour.[83] All this, combined with Churchill's known liking for alcohol, and his increased consumption in his ten years out of office, made it easy for the official Conservative leadership to launch a whispering campaign against his character and capabilities during the 1930s. Of course, this was a maliciously exaggerated picture, but it must have done Churchill untold damage. For there was ample material available from which to paint it; and the image stuck. In the spring of 1940, when Churchill became Prime Minister, one of the greatest concerns in official circles, in Whitehall, and in Washington, was that he would not be up to the job because he was a drunk.[84]

IV

Unlike many needy notables of the time, Churchill did not get into debt because he would not (or could not) earn a living, but because the very substantial sums which he did pull in were never enough for his indulgent needs. By 1900, he had already resolved that he would support himself by his pen, and 54 years later he could proudly claim that was the only means by which he had ever earned his living. Even for a full-time writer, Churchill's output would have been remarkable. For a man whose main career was politics and government, it was quite extraordinary. By 1914, he had already published four books based on his early adventures, a two-volume biography of his father, several political pamphlets, a collection of his speeches, and one novel. Between the wars, he produced *The World Crisis* in six volumes, his life of Marlborough in four, his own autobiography, and four more books of occasional essays and speeches. They paid astonishingly well. From Macmillan, Churchill received an advance of £8000 for his life of Lord Randolph. For his biography of Marlborough, Walter Harrap paid £10,000, and Charles Scribner another £5000 for the American rights. And Cassell's initial advance for his *History of the English-Speaking Peoples* was £20,000.[85]

Like so much of his life before 1940, Churchill's literary output needs to be set in the broader context of aristocratic activity and decline. From the 1880s to the 1930s there was a marked increase in the number of notables who were publishing books about themselves and their families.[86] Some, like Lord Willoughby de Broke, Lady Londonderry, the Duke of Portland and Lady Fingall, wrote autobiographies which nostalgically recalled the vanished world of their youth. Some published extended editions of family correspondence, like the Earl of Ilchester on the Foxes and Holland House, and Nancy Mitford on the Stanleys of Alderley. Some produced books about dynasties and mansions: Vita Sackville-West on Knole and the Sackvilles, and Lord Lansdowne on Glanerought and the Petty-Fitzmaurices. Some wrote multi-volume biographies of their relatives: Lord Crewe on Lord Resebery, Lady Blanche Dugdale on A.J. Balfour, and Lady Gwendolen Cecil on Lord Salisbury. However varied the quality of these works (they were memorably parodied by Nancy Mitford in the opening pages of *The Pursuit of Love*), they all shared one unstated assumption: in their pious celebration of family greatness, they implicitly recognised that the unchallenged dominion of the traditional governing classes was now becoming a thing of the past.

Much of Churchill's formidable output was clearly derived from these readily available models of aristocratic literary endeavour. His one explicit venture into autobiography, *My Early Life*, was a classic piece of patrician reminiscence, in more senses than one. Its agreeably self-deprecating tone, its wit and its warmth, its pace and its zest, mark it out from most run-of-the-mill productions. But in most respects, it was a recognisable example of the genre: a nostalgic re-creation of a vanished youthful world, in which a series of predictable episodes and experiences were recounted.[87] There were early recollections – of life in the big house, of parents and relatives, of nannies and servants. There were descriptions of school days – of teachers (good and bad), of lessons (mostly unsuccessful) and of games (where the results were rather better). There was an account of entry into Sandhurst, of training for the army, and of the first commission. There were adventures in plenty – war service in Cuba, India, the Sudan and South Africa. There was the beginning of a political career: the early attempts at public speaking, the first battles at the hustings, the successful election to parliament, and the maiden speech.

Churchill's biography of Lord Randolph also followed a standard format: the two-volume life, suffused by a powerful sense of family piety and ancestral veneration. It was dedicated to the ninth Duke of Marlborough 'in all faithful friendship', and opens with a magniloquent description of Blenheim and its park, so *fortissimo* and *noblimente* as to be almost overwhelming in its rhetorical luxurance.[88] Like most aristocratic productions of that type, too much space was given over to the extended printing of original letters and documents, so that in many places the author did little more than provide a commentary on the correspondence. As was also customary, Churchill admiringly and uncritically depicted his father as a public paragon. The many private and temperamental shortcomings were ignored, the evidence was carefully adjusted where needs be, the political triumphs were appropriately celebrated, and the eventual failure was transformed into something akin to a Greek tragedy. Except that in this case, Churchill insisted, it was Lord Randolph's virtues which proved his undoing, for he was too consistent for his own good. Having been rejected by the Tories, Winston clearly implied, his father should have gone over to the Liberals. But that was something he was too high-minded to do.[89]

By thus depicting Lord Randolph as a far-sighted, unswerving, high-principled statesman, Churchill was determined to refute the unflattering image of his father – as a déclassé opportunist and inconsistent adventurer – which still prevailed in political and social circles in the 1900s, only ten years after his death. (How far he succeeded in this is not at all clear: most reviews were favourable, but those who had known Lord Randolph were privately less convinced.) Yet there was more to this exercise in sanitised rehabilitation than the dictates of family piety, strong though that motive undoubtedly was. In his early years in politics, Churchill constantly sought to attract attention by modelling himself on Lord Randolph. But while he wanted to be thought of as embodying his father's virtues, many had reached the parallel conclusion, that he possessed all his father's faults. It was thus of supreme importance for him to project in his biography an image of Lord Randolph that was wholesome and admirable, an imaginative portrayal of 'the best side' of his father which was also deliberately designed to serve Churchill's more immediate political needs. For by arguing that Lord Randolph's supreme tragedy was that he did not join the Liberals, having fallen out with the Tories, Winston provided a carefully worked out defence of his own recent political conduct in crossing the floor.[90]

In his much-larger-scale biography of the first Duke of Marlborough, the theme of family piety was even stronger. Churchill undertook the work as 'a duty', and the ninth Duke kept the Blenheim archive closed until he and his research assistants could work on it. Once again large parts of the resulting volumes consisted of massive extracts from original documents, sometimes ill-digested, and often unnecessarily lengthy. Once again, Churchill conceived this work as an enterprise in advocacy and atonement.[91] For his aim was to destroy the 'odious portrait' which 'a long succession of the most famous writers in the English language' had painted. Instead of Macaulay's unscrupulous adventurer, who changed sides, who loved power, and who loved money, Churchill used all his rhetorical skills to depict Marlborough as a patriotic hero, a 'virtuous and benevolent being', a victorious and magnanimous warrior, and a European statesman of the first rank who was loved by his soldiers, trusted by his allies, and respected even by his enemies. In thus pointing the contrast between 'the glory and importance of his deeds, and the small regard of his countrymen for his memory', Churchill hoped to win for his hero 'a more just and more generous judgement from his fellow countrymen'.[92]

As with his biography of Lord Randolph, Churchill's life of Marlborough was a two-way dialogue with his forebears: but very much on his own terms. It was timely to remind the world of the past glories of his family, in a decade, the 1930s, when they seemed distinctly faded. Once again, the charges levelled at the great duke – his opportunism, his unreliability, his love of money, his craving for power – had often been levelled, not only at Lord Randolph, but at Winston, too. As Henry Steele Commager has rightly pointed out, Churchill's 'vindication of Marlborough from neglect and contumely was, in a sense, a vindication of himself'.[93] And just as the biography of Lord Randolph had legitimated Churchill's change of political party in the 1900s, so his life of Marlborough, depicting the embattled hero surrounded by snarling and sniping politicians, provided ancestral validation for his beleaguered stand against appeasement in the 1930s. The historical parallels were very close, and for Churchill were very real. But not every one was persuaded. In October 1938, he delivered one of his most powerful speeches, against the Munich agreement, yet the *Daily Express* contemptuously dismissed it as 'an alarmist oration by a man whose mind is soaked in the conquests of Marlborough'.[94]

Churchill's autobiography and works of ancestral piety belonged to a recognisable genre of contemporary aristocratic writing, and the same was true of his journalism. For the revolution in newspaper production during the last quarter of the nineteenth century coincided with the decline in aristocratic incomes as a consequence of the agricultural depression, and in this changed financial climate many straitened notables took to writing for the press. Some were entirely serious, like Lord Montagu of Beaulieu, proprietor of *Car Illustrated,* and later motoring correspondent for *The Times.*[95] Some were less respectable, like the Countess of Warwick, or Churchill's mother, who wrote a series of articles for *Pearsons Magazine* during the First World War on such inconsequential subjects as 'The Girl of Today', 'Friendship' and 'Extravagance' (she certainly knew something about that). Some, trading on their good connections, became gossip columnists, like Lords Castlerosse and Donegall (and also, during the 1930s, Randolph Churchill, who maintained a long-running and much-publicised feud with Castlerosse.) These déclassés were greatly disapproved of by high-minded grandees like Lord Crawford, who saw in them the ultimate sign of aristocratic degeneracy. In more senses than one, writing for the papers had become a common patrician pastime.[96]

From the 1890s until the 1930s, Churchill was closely involved in this journalistic world. Initially, as a soldier of fortune, he wrote for the press as a war correspondent. By the 1920s his work was appearing regularly in British newspapers, and was widely syndicated in the United States and continental Europe. Much of Churchill's inter-war journalism was of a very high quality: in particular his reviews of biographies and his essays on political affairs, some of which were later republished as *Great Con-*

temporaries and *Thoughts and Adventures*. Not surprisingly, his pen was sought after by most of the great proprietors, including Hearst, Beaverbrook, Rothermere and Camrose, and they all paid him handsomely. In 1930 he signed a ten-year contract with *Colliers*, and undertook to produce six articles annually for £2000. In 1931, the *Daily Mail* agreed to pay him £7800 if he wrote a weekly article for twelve months, and he earned another £2400 from the *Sunday Pictorial* for twelve essays on 'British personalities'.[97] Together with the advances on his books, it was these lucrative newspaper contracts which provided Churchill with his main source of income. Like many an impoverished aristocrat, he was driven to write for the papers by sheer financial necessity.

Inevitably, this meant that many of the four hundred-odd articles that he churned out during the 1930s were little more than pot-boilers. For American readers, he dashed off pieces on 'Depression', 'Iced water', and 'Corn on the cob'. For his British audience, he wrote on 'Premiers on the sick list', 'How we carry liquor', 'I was astonished by Morocco', and 'Have you a hobby?' In 1931 he was run over in New York, and promptly described his misadventures in two articles for the *Daily Mail*, which earned him £600. In the following year he agreed to retell 'Twelve great stories of the world', for the *Chicago Tribune* and the *News of the World*. They were largely prepared by Eddie Marsh and included *Don Quixote*, *Uncle Tom's Cabin*, and *Ben Hur*.[98] In the same vein, he later summarised *War and Peace* for the *New York News* for $1000. On occasions, Churchill was so hard pressed for time and for money that he even re-cycled his own work. *My Early Life* was published in 1930. Five years later, Churchill produced twelve pieces for the *News of the World*, entitled 'My Life'. And in 1937–8 he cobbled together ten more essays on 'My life and times', for the *Sunday Chronicle*.[99]

This steady outpouring of journalistic ephemera cannot have enhanced Churchill's reputation. Although recognising that it was financially necessary, Clementine constantly regretted that he wrote for the papers, and was convinced that 'unworthy or unsuitable contracts for "pot-boiling" newspaper and magazine articles' trivialised his standing in the public eye.[100] (It certainly did so in the cases of Lord Birkenhead, Lloyd George and Ramsay Macdonald, the other politicians who regularly appeared in the press.) There can be no doubt that his financial dependence on the press barons – those inter-war harlots, who craved power without responsibility, and were heartily despised by all decent folk – only reinforced the view that Churchill was beholden to the most unsavoury and mischievous elements in public life. It can hardly have seemed coincidence that Rothermere contributed to Randolph's election expenses at Wavertree, or that Beaverbrook and Churchill were in alliance at the time of the Abdication.[101] There is no reason to think that any of the press barons directly influenced Churchill's political views, but his independence and integrity must have seemed compromised by his close association with these disreputable men.

Like so much else about him, Churchill's literary endeavours – whether his journalistic pot-boilers or his multi-volume excursions into family piety – were a larger-than-life version of a commonplace aristocratic practice. But for all the money which they realised, there was also a price to be paid. As an historian and biographer, it is not at all clear that Churchill succeeded in his self-appointed role as guardian of the family flame. Theodore Roosevelt dismissed his book on his father as 'a clever, tactful, and rather cheap and vulgar life of that clever, tactful, and rather cheap and vulgar egoist'. And Churchill's attempt to rehabilitate Marlborough by traducing Macaulay provoked a magisterial rebuke from G.M. Trevelyan.[102] Even more unfortunately, he was compelled to spend so much time on his books and his journalism that he spent less time on public affairs than was wise. During the 1930s, Churchill hardly ever attended the Commons except to make a speech, and this certainly did his reputation harm, and diminished his political appeal and effectiveness. Indeed, by the very end of the decade, he was so hard pressed for his publisher's final advance of £7500 that he continued to work on his *History of the English-Speaking Peoples* through-out his time as First Lord of the Admiralty, even when the Norwegian campaign was at its height.[103]

V

The last aspect of Churchill's ambiguous aristocratic inheritance that must be considered is its impact on his political activity and his political outlook. As Sir John Plumb has explained, Churchill's view of the world, and of his own place within it, was essentially conditioned by a strong but crude attitude towards the past: the Whig interpretation of history which the British upper classes had evolved to explain (and justify) themselves and their pre-eminence, a myth in which Churchill believed with all the unquestioning certainty of a religious creed.[104] To him, British history was the saga of the nation's gradual, providential rise to greatness, guided by the firm but benevolent hand of an enlightened ruling aristocracy. Limited monarchy, parliamentary government, liberty and property, expanding overseas dominion: this was the picture of the British Empire, the British constitution and British society which Churchill absorbed during those formative years at the close of the nineteenth century. How, in the light of this essentially aristocratic outlook, did he react to the first forty years of the twentieth century, when events increasingly conspired to question, rather than to affirm, this serene patrician view?

If his biography of his father was to be believed, it was an easy and natural step from Tory Democracy, as preached by Lord Randolph, to a broader belief in Liberal social reforms, and from 1908 to 1911 Churchill zealously devoted himself to this cause. All his efforts on behalf of the poor – regulating wages and conditions in the mines and the sweated trades, and setting up labour exchanges and unemployment insurance – were essentially authoritarian and paternnalistic in their benevolence. As Lord Crawford later remarked, the whole tenor of Churchill's mind was 'anti-radical'.[105] For all his 'discovery of the poor', his social vision remained fundamentally aristocratic: of a benign but hierarchical society, in which the natural order was strengthened, not subverted, by social reform. As Lady Violet Bonham Carter observed, 'Lloyd George was saturated with class consciousness; but Winston accepted class distinction without a thought.' Or, as C.F.G. Masterman put it, 'He desired in England a state of things where a benign upper class dispensed benefits to an industrious, *bien pensant*, and grateful working class.' In 1942 Herbert Morrison made precisely the same point, describing Churchill as 'the old, benevolent, Tory squire, who does all he can for the people – provided they are good, obedient people, and loyally recognise his position, and theirs'.[106]

Having left the Tories for the Liberals between 1904 and 1906, Churchill was widely believed to have committed the ultimate act of class disloyalty, of social apostasy. His performance during the debates over the People's Budget and the House of Lords crisis did nothing to dispel this view, for his language was almost as violent as that of Lloyd George himself. 'The upkeep of aristocracy', he observed, in a memorable retort to Lord Curzon, 'has been the hard work of all civilisations.' He dismissed the House of Lords as 'an institution absolutely foreign to the spirit of the age and the whole movement of society', which was 'one sided, hereditary, unpurged, unrepresentative, irresponsible, absentee'. Indeed, in his most extreme moments, he seemed prepared to contemplate the total abolition of the House of Lords, and even the break-up of the system of great estates.[107] Yet this was a man who weekended at Blenheim and worked to advance the careers of his titled relatives! To many Liberals, it merely betokened a lack of sincere commitment; to many Conservatives, it was the predictably squalid action of Lord Randolph's appropriately opportunist son. Either way, Churchill never seems to have realised that, by agitating the language of class war so vigorously, he was in danger of destabilising that very paternal and aristocratic society which at heart he so loved and so unthinkingly accepted.[108]

By the inter-war years, this realisation had finally struck home, and Churchill became 'deeply disturbed by the collapse of settled values and ancient institutions'. Much of his writing in this period was suffused by the commonplace patrician nostalgia for the lost eden of great estates, great families, and 'the old, spacious country-house life'.[109] In *The World Crisis* he lavished some of his most fulsome rhetoric on the 'old world', which in its sunset had been fair to see, with its majestic 'princes and potentates', its secure ruling classes, and its splendid social pageantry. His later accounts, of the fall of the Romanoffs, the dethronement of the Habsburgs, and the ruin of the Hohenzollerns, were no less grandiloquent.[110] In *My Early Life* there was another lyrical lament for the vanished supremacies of the old nobility, in whose houses he had spent so much of his youth. The same theme was played out, with more eleborate variations, in the second chapter of the first volume of *Marlborough*. For over two hundred years, Churchill contended, it was a 'small and serious ruling class', consisting of 'several thousand families', which had produced the great captains and great states-men who had been responsible for Britain's rise to world power. That was all now gone and 'our aristocracy', he lamented, 'has largely passed from life into history'.[111]

This regret at the departed glories of the old regime received its fullest articulation on the death of 'Sunny' Marlborough in 1934.[112] Churchill wrote a moving tribute in *The Times*, the theme of which was that the Duke had lived out his sad life in admirable but vain defiance of the trends of twentieth-century history. On his accession to the dukedom, Churchill argued, 'the old world still existed', and 'in the glittering and it seemed stable framework of aristocratic society, he had a place where few were his equals and none his betters'. But in the years which followed, he went on, 'the organism of English society underwent a complete revolution'; politics became 'more vehement and democratic'; 'successive crashes of taxation descended upon the old world'. The great governing families 'lost their authority and control'; were 'almost entirely relieved of their political responsibilities'; and were 'to a very large extent stripped of their property, and in many cases driven from their homes'. Inevitably, this regrettable process 'cast a depressing shadow upon the Duke of Marlborough's life'. He was 'always conscious that he belonged to a system which had been destroyed, to a society which had passed away', and understandably, this 'saddened and chilled him'.

This was, perhaps, an excessively apocalyptic view of the decline and fall of Churchill's own caste, the British aristocracy, though on the basis of his family experience it is easy to see why he felt and wrote as he did. Among his more distant relatives, the Churchills of Wychwood, the Cornwallis-Wests, the Frewens and the Leslies had all parted with their family houses and ancestral estates. Despite their Vanderbilt money, and the restoration of Blenheim, the Marlboroughs remained financially impoverished and socially unrespectable. Even Churchill's still super-rich kinsmen – the Wimbornes, the Westminsters and the Londonderrys – were no longer the territorial potentates or the political forces they once had been. For Churchill, this was a wholly regrettable development, and 'the disappear-ance of the aristocracy from the stage' was a trend which he rightly believed the Second World War further intensified. Like his ducal cousin, Churchill regarded the social structure that had existed in his youth as the best of all possible worlds. He did not welcome aristocratic eclipse, but he could not prevent it. As Harold Laski perceptively noted in 1942, 'the premises of Mr Churchill's thinking are set by the old world that is dying'.[113]

The other side of this lament for past glories was a growing dis-enchantment with parliamentary government as it had evolved during the twentieth century. By the inter-war years, Churchill was, like many disaffected and disoriented patricians, deeply alienated from the democratic process. He much regretted the granting of universal adult franchise in 1918, which he saw as the cause of all subsequent constitutional ills. The 'elegant, glittering, imposing trappings' had 'faded from British parlia-mentary life', and had been replaced by 'the caucus, the wire-puller and the soap box'. The great statesmen of his youth – Balfour, Rosebery, Morley, Asquith – had been followed by a new breed of insignificant pygmies: 'little men', vainly trying to cope with 'great events'.[114] 'Real political democ-racy', as it had existed before 1914, had been superseded by a mass electorate, ignorant and volatile in its opinions, and easily swayed by an irresponsible press. Under these circumstances, it was not surprising that the Socialists had made such regrettable headway, that the prestige of Parliament had markedly declined, that general elections produced violently fluctuating results, and that universal suffrage seemed totally discredited.[115]

More to the point, Churchill believed that parliamentary government, thus decayed, could no longer deal with the seemingly intractible com-plexities of contemporary issues. As far as the handling of economic problems was concerned, Churchill set out his own proposals in his Romanes Lecture, delivered at Oxford University in June 1930. Since the Commons and the Lords were incapable of dealing effectively with such questions, the solution was to entrust them to a new economic sub-parliament, 'free altogether from party exigiencies, and composed of persons possessing special qualifications in economic matters'.[116] And as to the other tasks of government, the only hope was to improve the quality and standing of parliament by abandoning 'complete democracy'. In a series of newspaper articles, published during the early 1930s, Churchill developed this theme in more detail. The franchise should be moved away from one man one vote, back towards the traditional system which had been weighted in favour of the 'more responsible elements', by giving plural votes to householders and heads of families. Voting should be made compulsory, there should be proportional representation for great cities, and there should be a 'reformed and strengthened second chamber'.[117] (This from the man who had once hailed the Parliament Act as 'territory reconquered by the masses from the classes'.)

During the 1920s and 1930s, Churchill was thus gradually developing into a reactionary class warrior, and came to share the widespread belief of disenchanted aristocrats that everything was going wrong, and that all change was change for the worse. From 1917 to 1922, he waged an impassioned but ineffectual campaign against the 'foul baboonery' of Bolshevism though, as Lloyd George wickedly but perceptively observed, one of the reasons for such obsessional hostility was that Churchill's 'ducal blood revolted against the wholesale liquidation of Grand Dukes'.[118] At the time of the General Strike, Churchill further alienated working-class opinion, by publicly assuming such a belligerent posture against the trades unions, and by articulating it with such apparent enjoyment in the pages of the *British Gazette*. In his equally alarmist opposition to reform of the Indian government – where he was supported by such diehard grandees as Lord Salisbury and the Duke of Westminster – he once again placed himself in determined opposition to progress and democracy. By the mid 1930s, therefore, Churchill had become almost a parody of the paranoid aristocrat: intransigent, embittered, apocalyptic, 'a reactionary of the deepest dye', 'the chief exponent of the class war', and wholly without sympathy for the 'foreign and fallacious creeds of socialism'.[119]

An even more ominous sign of Churchill's alienation from democracy was his growing interest in and admiration of authoritarian forms of government, especially the Fascist dictatorship.[120] In 1926, he visited Italy, and immediately conceived a great admiration for the Duce's 'gentle and simple bearing'. In articles for British newspapers, Churchill praised Mussolini as a man of firmness, honour and destiny who, after a period of Bolshevik-inspired anarchy, was busy restoring Italy to her former greatness. For a time, indeed, a picture of the Duce was displayed at Chartwell, and on his return to the Commons Churchill was greeted with cries of 'Mussolini' by some MPs. In 1933 Churchill was still describing him in the press as 'the greatest lawgiver among men'. Four years later, he felt no doubt about 'the enduring position in world history which Mussolini will hold', as a result of the 'amazing qualities of courage, comprehension, self-control, and perseverance which he exemplifies'. Not surprisingly, given his trenchant criticisms of parliamentary democracy, Churchill was widely suspected, on both the left and the right, of wishing to become the British Duce: 'the potential Mussolini of a wave of reaction'.[121]

There was certainly some domestic political evidence in support of this view. Ever since his time at the Admiralty, there were those who believed that 'at heart' Churchill was 'dictatorial' in his outlook.[122] In the early 1930s, he hankered after an alliance with Oswald Mosley, whose youth and ebullience he much admired, and whose vision of a corporate state closely resembled that sketched out by Churchill in his Romanes Lecture. At about the same time, the pitifully déclassé Duke of Manchester published his autobiography, in which he expressed great admiration for Mussolini and urged in his concluding chapter that Britain needed a new leader, who would put an end to the pointless talking of parliament, and run the country with authoritarian benevolence as an aristocrat ran his landed estate. One of his candidates for that position was the seventeenth Earl of Derby. The other was Winston Churchill. In the same year, 1932, Harold Nicolson published a novel, *Public Faces*, which was set in the near future, and presumed that the country would by then be run by a Churchill-Mosley Coalition.[123] Nor should it be forgotten that during the Second World War Churchill did indeed wield more absolute power than any Prime Minister before or since, and that even friends like Beaverbrook admitted that, in some moods, he had in him 'the stuff of which tyrants are made'.[124]

In his political opinions, the authoritarian Churchill of the 1930s had clearly travelled a long way from the Tory Democrat and the Liberal reformer of the 1900s. Since then, he had been a Lloyd George Coalitionist, a Baldwinite Conservative, and a Diehard reactionary. As Lord Beaverbrook once opined, he had held 'every view on every question'.[125] But such erratic behaviour was far from being unusual between the 1880s and the 1930s, as many aristocrats found themselves adrift in the new hostile world of democratic politics, and boxed the political compass in essentially the same way. Some families split apart, like the Bedfords, the Trevelyans and the Mitfords, as one branch went to the right, others to the left. Some individuals moved with bewildering speed across the political spectrum: Whigs like Viscount Halifax became conservatives and then Diehards; the Buxton brothers moved from the Liberal Party to Labour; and Mosley went from Conservative to Labour to the British Union of Fascists. Here again, Churchill's apparently rootless behaviour was more typical of the declining aristocracy than is usually recognised.[126]

VI

Shortly after his illustrious cousin's death in 1965, Sir Shane Leslie predicted that the end of the twentieth century would have to be reached before Winston Churchill's astonishing career could be seen in its proper historical perspective.[127] With rather less than a decade to go, the wisdom of Leslie's prophecy seems to have been well borne out. That Churchill will occupy a conspicuous place in the history of his times seems certain – but until the pattern of that history has itself emerged more distinctly, the true nature of his own place within it is bound to remain unclear. Nevertheless, when any final reckoning is made, the fact that Churchill was an aristocrat, and the fact that for most of his life the aristocracy to which he belonged was in decline, will need to be given their due weight.[128] Of course, there is a great deal that this will *not* explain about a personality so protean, so remarkable, so long-lived, so variously gifted, so internationally influential, and so much larger than life. But it will certainly help us to see him, and to understand him, as an historically credible figure to a greater degree than has hitherto been possible. Only by putting the Churchillian colossus in such a context can some of his true contours be discerned.

By viewing Churchill as the product of a declining aristocratic order, we can much better understand the doubts, the dislike and the distrust which he engendered for so much of his long political career. For it was not just that he was widely believed to be uncertain in judgement, and unreliable in his political conduct. It was also that there was something about him more generally which was not entirely respectable. Labour politicians like Attlee and Bevin felt this; so did middle-class moralists like Reith, Baldwin and Neville Chamberlain. Although he was an aristocrat by birth, Churchill was widely believed to be not really a gentleman at all. On the contrary, he was often described as a highly gifted, but undeniable, 'cad'.[129] Beyond any doubt, some of the more imaginative whispers – that he had broken his parole during the Boer War, that he was the creature of an international Jewish conspiracy, that he had fathered illegitimate children – were without factual foundation. But in the generally unseemly context of his family background and his own way of life, it is easy to see why such rumours adhered to him so tenaciously, and the political consequences of this in the years before 1939 should not be underestimated.

The aristocracy to which Churchill belonged, by connection and by inclination, was not that exemplified by such high-minded Christian gentlemen as Viscount Grey of Fallodon, Lord Halifax, or Sir Alec Douglas-Home, who stood for 'respectability' and 'spiritual values'.[130] Nor was it the restful, intimate world of squirearchical estates, decaying manor houses, agricultural politics and village cricket.[131] In terms of its characters and its orientation, Churchill's version (and vision) of aristocracy was romantic, raffish, restless, déclassé, metropolitan, plutocratic. Genealogically, financially, and socially, he was on the edge. To be sure, he was not a 'typical' aristocrat: but in the course of his own lifetime, the aristocracy changed, adapted, dispersed and declined so much that it would be difficult to suggest anyone who was. Nevertheless, in terms of his ancestors, his family, his friends, and his own way of life, he belonged to a recognisable (and highly suspect) stratum of aristocracy, which put Churchill at a distinct disadvantage for much of his political career.

All this makes it easier to appreciate why his advent to power in the spring of 1940 was greeted with such widespread doubt and dismay, as a man variously described as a 'cad', a 'half-breed', a 'dictator', a 'rogue elephant', the 'greatest adventurer in modern political history', took charge of Britain's affairs.[132] It also enables us to understand the truly miraculous transformation in Churchill's reputation which the events of 1940–5 eventually brought about. The aristocratic anachronism became the embodiment of the bulldog breed. The drinker, the gambler, the spendthrift became a national 'character'. The impoverished patrician became, thanks to the sensational sales of his war memoirs and his *History of the English-Speaking Peoples*, financially secure. The incorrigible scrounger off family and friends became the deserving recipient of gifts, legacies, prizes and honours from a grateful world. The pot-boiling journalist and self-justifying family biographer became the Nobel Prizewinner for Literature. The belligerent class warrior, the man once likened to Mussolini, became the champion of freedom and liberty. The reactionary authoritarian became the saviour of his country. The ungentlemanly cad became the greatest Englishman of his time.

In an appropriately Churchillian manner, these antitheses are, no doubt, too crude. Before 1940, even his enemies grudgingly recognised that Churchill's larger-than-life faults were matched by at least some corresponding virtues; and after 1945, disagreeable rumours about his family, his friends and his finances continued to circulate (or be suppressed).[133] But they also contain an essential and little-regarded truth. For the transformation in Churchill's image wrought by the Second World War should not obscure the very different, and much more damaging, reputation which he had acquired during the forty years which had gone before. And we cannot understand that earlier, more flawed, and more suspect Churchillian incarnation, unless we see him in the broader context of the declining aristocracy of which he was a product, and to which he never doubled for a moment that he belonged.

PART THREE

THE DYNASTIC PERSPECTIVE

7

The Landowner as Millionaire

The Finances of the Dukes of Devonshire

Who were the wealthiest landowners in the United Kingdom between the Battle of Waterloo and the Battle of Britain? Many names were suggested by contemporaries. In 1819 the American Minister David Rush recorded that the 'four greatest incomes in the kingdom' belonged to the Duke of Northumberland, Earl Grosvenor, the Marquess of Stafford, and the Earl of Bridgewater, each of whom was reputed to possess 'one hundred thousand pounds, clear of everything'.[1] Forty years later, another foreign observer, the Frenchman H.A. Taine, visited the House of Lords where

the principal peers present were pointed out to me, and named, with details of their enormous fortunes: the largest amount to £300,000 a year. The Duke of Bedford has £220,000 a year from land; the Duke of Richmond has 300,000 acres in a single holding. The Marquess of Westminster, landlord of a whole London quarter, will have an income of £1,000,000 a year when the present long leases run out.[2]

Shortly afterwards, A.C. Ewald added some extra noble names:

In point of wealth, the House of Lords exhibits a standard which cannot be equalled in any other country. Take the Dukes of Northumberland, Devonshire, Sutherland and Buccleuch, the Marquesses of Westminster and Bute, and Earls of Derby, Lonsdale, Dudley and Leicester, and Baron Overstone, and where (in the matter of wealth) will you find their equals collectively?[3]

Early in the twentieth century, T.H.S. Escott recorded these comments made by a friend about the Dukes of Northumberland and Cleveland:

These . . . are the persons who make the fortunes of the great private West End banks; they take pride in keeping a standing balance for which they never receive six pence; but whose interest would make a hole in the national debt.[4]

More precisely, all these peers – with the exception of Lords Leicester and Overstone[5] – possessed broad acres in the early 1880s with a gross annual value in excess of £60,000 a year, according to John Bateman's famous survey of great landowners.[6] Indeed, on the basis of the data he provided, there were forty patrician families which came into this opulently comfortable category. From this total should be removed the Calthorpes, Haldons, Ramsdens, and St Aubyns, whose incomes were artificially inflated by mistakenly crediting them with the entire rentals of their urban estates, when in fact they received only the ground rents.[7] Of the remaining 36 wealthy dynasties, 24 also threw up individuals who left more than one million pounds between 1808 and 1949.[8] Beyond any doubt, these were the richest aristocrats in Britain, and perhaps in the world: augmenting their wealth throughout the nineteenth century, maintaining it well into the twentieth, and often surviving as major social and political influences until the Second World War.

Three significant omissions from John Bateman's list must certainly be repaired in order to arrive at a comprehensive roll-call of the richest British landowners: the Cadogans, the Portmans and the Westminsters, each of whom owned exceptionally valuable parts of London.[9] As a result, the sixth Earl Cadogan's estate was valued in 1933 at two million pounds, that left by the seventh Viscount Portman fifteen years later was just under four and a half millions, and the Westminsters surpassed them both. Described as early as 1865 as 'the wealthiest family in Europe', the second Duke was reputed to be enjoying an income of £1000 a day by the early 1900s.[10] But because Bateman excluded the revenues that the great ground landlords drew from their metropolitan acres, none of these families appears in his survey as very wealthy.[11] And the Westminsters do not even make the list of landed millionaires before the Second World War. The first duke, reputed to be worth fourteen millions in 1894, left a personal estate of only £947,000 on his death, while the second duke, who did not die until 1953, left a fortune in excess of ten million pounds.[12]

The relative position of these forty-odd super-rich landed families changed in two significant ways during the course of the nineteenth and twentieth centuries. On the one hand, as Walter Bagehot noted in 1866, their wealth might still be growing, but it was less Himalayan than before, as an increasing number of bankers and businessmen made fortunes of unprecedented size.[13] Yet, while their grip on the monopoly of great wealth weakened, they actually increased their lead over their fellow, but relatively poorer, landowners. The accumulation of estates by advantageous marriage, inheritance, or purchase, and the burgeoning incomes which many drew from mineral royalties, docks, and urban estates, put them on a pedestal far – and increasingly – beyond the reach of the squire and the middling aristocrat. As Professor Burn once noted: 'the Duke of Omnium and the small squire were half a world apart', and this was as true of their incomes as of their politics.[14] Indeed, the late-nineteenth-century agricultural depression served only to widen the gap still further, as the super-rich, already buttressed by alternative sources of revenue, became – in a relative sense – even richer.[15]

Accordingly, these 'commercial potentates' were a distinct sub-group, both of all millionaires and of landowners in general.[16] Sharing some of the characteristics of each, they cannot be completely classed with either. Unlike millionaire businessmen, who might buy their way into land, they could boast generations of inherited and accumulated broad-acred wealth. Compared with their poorer landowning cousins, the extent and diversity of their incomes were on an unrivalled scale. The basis of their wealth, and thus the reasons for their survival, might be listed as follows: exceptionally wide acres in England, Wales Scotland or Ireland; the lucrative exploitation of the non-agricultural resources of their estates; the increase, decrease or maintenance of extensive, but not ruinous, debts; resilience to falling rental income brought about by the agricultural depression; and a capacity to restructure their finances on a more 'rational' basis during the closing years of the nineteenth century and the early decades of the twentieth.[17] Of course, there were exceptions: the Ellesmeres' and the Grosvenors' acres were relatively narrow, and the Northumberlands, Sutherlands and Dudleys were in debt only for very short periods.[18] But even allowing for individual differences, this seems an appropriate catalogue of their collective characteristics as landed millionaires. The purpose of this essay is to examine the finances of one great, rich, powerful family of whom all these statements were true – yet not quite the whole story: the Dukes of Devonshire.[19]

I

On 21 May 1811 William Spencer Cavendish, Marquess of Hartington and heir to the fifth Duke of Devonshire, came of age, and the event was celebrated with all the magnificence associated with the highest echelons of the aristocracy.[20] 'The expense is not to be considered, even in hundreds of pounds', noted the Chatsworth agents, and the ensuing festivities, at Chatsworth itself, at Staveley, Shottle, Buxton, Hardwick and Lismore, amply bore this out.[21] Only seven months later, however, rejoicing changed to mourning, and then to rejoicing again, as the Marquess succeeded his prematurely-deceased father as the sixth Duke of Devonshire. He thus became the owner of everything that rank and fortune could give, and as a result 'he had always the world at his feet'.[22] Indeed, the glittering and spacious inheritance into which the sixth duke entered had been growing almost every generation since the days of Bess of Hardwick.[23] As a result the Duke could boast four great country houses: Chatsworth itself, nearby Hardwick Hall, Bolton Abbey in Yorkshire and Lismore Castle in Ireland. In addition, there were three London palaces: Chiswick House, Burlington House and Devonshire House. All this was supported by land in Ireland and eight English counties, yielding a current income of £70,000 a year in 1813–15.[24] As his biographer later noted, the sixth Duke was 'an only son, of illustrious descent, and heir to an immense fortune: none could excell, and few could rival him, in position'.[25]

This golden inheritance was tarnished in two ways. To begin with, the Duke inherited his estates heavily mortgaged. Indeed, as early as 1790 encumbrances had stood at £310,298, of which £170,000 had been spent on the purchase of land since 1773, and £63,000 had gone on the construction of the crescent at Buxton.[26] The high living of the fifth Duke, his wife, and his mistresses, only increased such burdens. In 1804 Duchess Georgiana admitted to gambling debts of £36,000.[27] But as her husband discovered on her death, she had not revealed all: two years later, her total indebtedness came to £109,135.[28] Accordingly, by 1814 the aggregate sum secured on the Devonshire estates came to £593,000 which, with interest payments at 5 per cent, was absorbing over £29,000 or 41 per cent of the Duke's annual income. If to this figure are added annuities and jointures in excess of £15,000 annually, then some 60 per cent of the sixth Duke's income was not available for his own use.[29]

Moreover, there was no legal constraint to prevent him from increasing his already-substantial encumbrances still further. In the short period between his own coming-of-age and his father's death there had been no time to re-settle the estates jointly so as to keep them tied up under the terms of a strict settlement.[30] Because he succeeded so young, the sixth Duke inherited his properties in fee simple, and thus owned them outright as the freeholder, as his three successors were also to do. In understanding the Devonshires' nineteenth- and early-twentieth-century financial history this fact must be born constantly in mind. While many super-rich landed families, like the Bedfords and the Grosvenors, deliberately kept some of their property out of settlement, so as to give themselves essential room for financial manoeuvre, the Devonshires were unusual in that, following this accident of family history, four successive generations enjoyed absolute possession of all their estates.[31] Put another – and more ominous – way this meant that as a result, they had total freedom: to buy, to sell – and to mortgage. The only limits to increasing indebtedness were the amounts which could actually be raised using their lands as security, and the restraint or irresponsibility of the successive ducal freeholders.

The scope for borrowing was thus considerable, and the sixth Duke – who in this as in much else took after his spendthrift mother Georgiana – reaped full advantage of it. He had little interest in figures, and even less sense of financial responsibility.[32] Deaf and unmarried, he was a lonely man, and the two closest friendships of his life, with Joseph Paxton and Jeffry Wyatville, served only to encourage his innate tendency towards extravagance. His love of building, of travel, of collecting, and of display amounted almost to mania.[33] Not surprisingly, historians have seen him as a prince among profligate patricians, as the quintessence of early-nineteenth-century indulgence and financial irresponsibility. They are right to do so, and the evidence to be presented here gives no cause for quarrelling with that interpretation.[34]

From 1818, when he asked Jeffry Wyatville to design a new wing at Chatsworth, there was no end to the Duke's building. The ensuing work there lasted twenty years; there followed extensive alterations at Devonshire House and Bolton Abbey in the 1840s; and finally, from 1849 until 1858, the year of his death, there was large-scale construction at Lismore Castle.[35] The Duke's love of building was matched by his relish for horticulture, and this was greatly encouraged by Paxton, who became head gardener at Chatsworth in 1826. Paxton gradually increased his friendship with, and hold over, the Duke, so that by the 1840s he was as dominant a figure in managing the Duke's finances as was his auditor. The results of this collaboration were to be seen in the arboretum, in the expeditions to Canada, Mexico and India to collect exotics, in the rebuilding of Edensor village between 1838 and 1842, and in the construction of the Great Conservatory between 1836 and 1840.[36] If to this are added the Duke's embassy to Russia in 1826 for the coronation of the Emperor Nicholas I, and the purchases of books designed to give Chatsworth 'the first library in England', then it can be seen that he did indeed live according to the pattern of his coming-of-age celebration: 'the expense is not to be considered'.[37]

All this activity made Chatsworth 'the most splendid, and at the same time the most enjoyable place that one could imagine', and the festivities held there, culminating in the visit of Queen Victoria, Prince Albert and the Duke of Wellington in 1843, exhausted the superlatives of contemporaries.[38] But such extravagance had to be paid for, and a current income of between £80,000 and £100,000 – to which the sixth Duke's had grown by the 1820s and 1830s – was quite inadequate. Interest payments and annuities were gobbling up over 50 per cent of it by the 1830s, and household expenses at Chatsworth alone amounted to £36,000 a year. If there had been no additional outlay it might have been possible to make ends meet; but as the sixth Duke got into his spending stride, such a prospect vanished. Between 1812, his first full year of possession, and 1815, he overspent on current account to the extent of £270,000, and between 1817 and 1829 the deficit averaged £16,400 a year. In the same period, £54,753 was lavished on furniture at Chatsworth and Devonshire House, and £147,681 on the new building at Chatsworth. Between 1830 and 1842 a further £38,075 was spent on furniture and £155,107 on Chatsworth, bringing the costs of rebuilding there to more than £300,000. To this should be added the alterations at Devonshire House and Bolton Abbey; £50,000 laid out on a collection of coins subsequently resold at Christies for a mere £7057 in 1844; and £26,000 spent on the embassy to Russia.[39]

Not surprisingly, anxious solicitors and worried advisers begged the Duke to stop. 'All that you want', observed one in 1819, 'is the power of self-restraint.' But it was never discovered.[40] Encumbrances soared, topping £700,000 by 1830.[41] Such extravagance could not be financed by borrowing alone: assets had to be liquidated as well. In 1813 the Nottingham estates were sold for £229,727; two years later Burlington House was disposed of to the Duke's uncle, Lord George Cavendish, subsequently Earl of Burlington, for £70,000; and in 1824 the Wetherby estate in Yorkshire was put under the hammer for £160,000.[42] Indeed, by 1830 it was even suggested that the Irish estates might be sold. Well might Charles Greville write in 1835 of 'the Dukes of Bedford and Devonshire of the present day, who appear to have lost their senses, and to be ready to peril all their great possessions to gratify the passion of the moment'.[43]

The late 1830s and early 1840s saw extravagance reach its peak, with the visit of Queen Victoria, the last phase of the extensions to Chatsworth, and the building of the Emperor Fountain and the Great Conservatory. The result was that by 1844 indebtedness was only just short of one million pounds, with interest and annuity payments at £54,000 taking over 55 per cent of current income, a situation nearly as bad as that which the sixth Duke had inherited; and that despite the reduction of interest charges to 4 per cent over the years 1824–8.[44] Even Paxton, when he saw the consolidated accounts which had been compiled by his auditor and solicitor, William Currey, was taken aback. 'I have been the cause of Your Grace spending a great deal of money', he wrote in concerned apology; 'had I been at all aware of your real position, I certainly never should have done so.' It was now realised that further assets must be sold. The Irish estates were again suggested, but ultimately the choice fell on lands at Londesborough and Baldersley in Yorkshire.[45] Together they fetched £575,000, which was immediately applied to the reduction of debt, and this, along with further falls in interest rates and a decline in annuity payments, reduced fixed outgoings to £28,000 by the early 1850s, or 30 per cent of current income. Paxton was ecstatic at a deal which he thought had been triumphantly concluded.[46] But the Duke's heir, the second Earl of Burlington, viewed the whole affair in a more sceptical light:

Currey has been talking to me about the duke's plan for getting rid of his debt: on the whole I cannot disapprove of the large sales he proposes to make, though I cannot help regretting the extravagance which has rendered them necessary.[47]

Thereafter, the position further improved, as the Duke's spending finally lessened. Wyatville died in 1840, and Paxton, too, was less active at Chatsworth in the 1850s, becoming increasingly preoccupied with the Great Exhibition and his duties as a Member of Parliament. The Duke suffered a stroke in 1854, which inevitably diminished his zestful extravagance. Income, too, began to increase, in part from the revenue of the

Grassington lead mines, which reached £20,000 a year net by 1854, and in part from the Duke's investments in railway shares, turnpikes, and other securities totalling £56,000.[48] As a result, 1848 was the last year for which records exist of expenditure exceeding income (by £20,000) and of plaintive cries from William Currey that 'It is absolutely necessary that all extraordinary expenditures should be carefully avoided, and that ordinary expenditure should be of a fixed and certain amount.'[49] By 1849 the long-hoped-for surplus at last materialised, and it continued throughout the early 1850s, despite new building projects at Lismore. In 1854 it reached £12,000, enabling Currey to present a triumphant report, 'more satisfactory than any account which I have previously submitted to you'.[50] But this was, of course, all relative. A decade's belated economy was scarcely sufficient to eradicate the effects of thirty years' unbridled ducal extravagance.

II

No previous successor to the title found the family estates in such a condition of unexampled splendour and severe indebtedness as did William Cavendish, who became seventh Duke in 1858. Nor was this his only inheritance. Since the death of his grandfather in 1834 he had already been second Earl of Burlington, possessed in his own right and in fee simple of extensive estates in Lancashire and Sussex, each with its own big house, Holker Hall and Compton Place respectively. Moreover, since the 1840s, he had begun to interest himself in their development, investing in the Furness Railway at Barrow and in sea walls, roads and speculative building at Eastbourne.[51] These two estates had originally been settled on the seventh Duke's grandfather by the fourth Duke, but thanks to two accidents of family history (whereby William inherited directly not only from his grandfather's property but also the estates of the sixth Duke) they were now reunited with the main family holdings. But as the acres were enlarged, so the encumbrances were correspondingly increased, for the Burlington estates had their own share of debt – some £250,000 – as a result of the extensive purchases of land made by the seventh Duke's grandfather. This meant that the total mortgage debt on the seventh Duke's consolidated estates stood at just under one million pounds.[52]

What type of man was the seventh Duke? Second Wrangler and First Smiths Prizeman at Trinity College, Cambridge, Chairman of the Royal Commission on Scientific Instruction and the Advancement of Science, sometime Chancellor of London and Cambridge Universities, President of the Royal Agricultural Society and of the Iron and Steel Institute, he was, by any yardstick, 'one of the finest flowers of the Victorian nobility'.[53] As the commentary to his *Vanity Fair* caricature put it in 1874: 'Had he not been a duke, he would have been a rare professor of mathematics.'[54] In his youth he had been a radical supporter of the Great Reform Bill. In middle age he largely withdrew from politics, leaving the field to his three sons. In later life he came to differ from Gladstone over Home Rule. He found the responsibilities of his great position burdensome, and for all his intellectual brilliance he was a lonely man, never recovering from the death of his beloved wife Blanche in 1840, when he was still only 32. Thereafter he lived as a recluse, steering as clear of the sixth Duke and Paxton as was possible without straining family links, and avoiding the frenetic whirl of high society even after he inherited the dukedom.[55]

The contrast with his immediate predecessor could not have been more marked. Just as one epitomised the Regency world of self-indulgence, so the other was the archetypal mid-Victorian, and it has understandably been assumed that it was the seventh Duke who rescued the Devonshire estates from their embarrassed condition. 'On entering into position of the ducal estates', observed one early authority, 'he found them heavily encumbered, and devoted himself to relieving them of their burdens.'[56] Others noted 'his careful personal management', his 'capable hands', his 'wise and far-seeing' policies, and claimed that his estates 'could hardly have been better managed'.[57] Moreover, from the time of Prof. David Spring's seminal article historians have consistently repeated this view, citing the seventh Duke as the classic instance of mid-Victorian recovery following earlier extravagances – thanks to careful management, reduction of debt, and imaginative exploitation of non-agricultural resources.[58] How far is this favourable interpretation actually valid?

Beyond any doubt, the seventh Duke wasted no time in grasping the full extent of the problems he had inherited. As he recorded in his diary, the general picture was indeed sombre:

The income is large, but by far the greater part of it is absorbed by the payment of interest, annuities, and the expense of Chatsworth, leaving but comparatively insignificant surplus, and much of this will at present be required for legacy and succession duties. This is a worse condition of matters than I had expected, although from knowing the duke's ignorance of business, I did not expect to find them very flourishing.[59]

He reached one decision immediately: general economies had to be made, which meant that any remaining connection with Paxton must be severed. 'Reductions on an immense scale are obviously required', he noted, 'and Paxton is not the man to undo much of what has been his own creation.' Realising that the writing was on the wall, Paxton gracefully withdrew, leaving the Duke to dismiss many unnecessary employees on the Chatsworth estate.[60]

While economies might stop the incurring of new debt, they would make little inroad into his heavy accumulated encumbrances. The only means of reducing them substantially was to follow the sixth Duke's example and sell off agricultural land. For any excessively indebted patricians, this was a standard ploy. Indeed, in the late 1840s, when worried by the size of the Burlington debt, the future seventh Duke had thought of selling the Sussex estates to achieve a similar objective.[61] This time, as he contemplated his greater acres and his greater debts, he considered disposing of his Irish estates.[62] His professional advisers did not support this policy, and so he wrote to the seventh Duke of Bedford, another member of the super-rich landowners' club, who had recently retrieved his inheritance from debt, 'mentioned to him my project of selling in Ireland', and asked for his thoughts.[63] Initially, Bedford seemed 'rather to approve' the scheme, but wrote later 'dissuading extensive sales', partly on the grounds that such an act of territorial reduction would diminish the social and political standing of the House of Cavendish, and partly because 'a large estate, with such a rental as yours, is soon brought round to an improved condition, as I have found in my own case'.

Still unconvinced, Devonshire replied by explaining his financial position to Bedford more fully. He pointed out that while his gross revenue was in the region of £200,000 a year, he was left with only £115,000 net after the deduction of costs of estate administration and maintenance. Of that much-reduced amount, some £60,000 a year went on interest payments, annuities and other fixed charges, and a further £20,000 from his Grassington mines had to be regarded as uncertain. Thus his disposable income was at best only £55,000 and at worst a mere £40,000. While this was adequate for ordinary expenditure, it was insufficient for such extra items as the legacy and succession duties levied on the estate of the sixth Duke, or the 'large election expenses' that 'from time to time' he expected to incur in north Derbyshire, north Lancashire, and east Sussex. 'My impression on the whole', the seventh Duke concluded, 'is that my position is at present very insecure.' Bedford wrote again, stressing the relative insignificance of purely financial considerations when compared with the question of the family's social and political standing. At the same time Benjamin and William Currey bombarded the Duke with evidence to show how the Irish remittances could be substantially increased. Confronted by such arguments and figures, his resolve began to weaken, so that by June the Duke had 'nearly made up my mind not to sell the bulk of the property this year'. Soon afterwards he must have reached a definite decision, for throughout his tenure of the title no substantial sales of land for purpose of debt-reduction ever took place.[64]

With no land sales and a limited policy of retrenchment, it was inevitable that little progress was made in the reduction of the ducal debt. By 1864 only £60,000 had been paid off – an almost trivial sum in the context of one million pounds. Yet, only five years later, Lord Granville described the seventh Duke's credit to Gladstone as 'being very nearly as good as that of the state', a far cry from the days of Georgiana and the sixth Duke.[65] How had this sudden transformation been effected? In part it resulted from the Duke's public standing as a prudent, sober, moderate man, for in the popular imagination his estates were indistinguishable from his own reputation. More important was the unprecedented rise in current income, which ballooned from £120,000 a year in the late 1850s to a peak of £310,000 in 1874. With total indebtedness remaining relatively static until the late 1860s, and the service charges on subsequent new mortgages increasing less rapidly than income, the amount of current income apportioned to servicing the debt fell from 40 per cent in 1861 to a mere 16 per cent by 1874, the lowest figure thus far recorded.

How had this spectacular financial recovery come about? Thanks to the prosperity of Mid-Victorian agriculture, income from estate rentals had increased considerably, from £94,000 in 1863 to £141,000 eleven years later. This was completely eclipsed, however, by the prodigious growth in dividend income from a mere £14,000 in 1863 to £169,000 by 1874, in which year it represented over half of the total current income. As will be seen from the details of the Devonshires' investment portfolio, it was not from the development of Eastbourne, the revival of Buxton, or the outlay on Irish railways that the Duke's dividends were preponderantly derived. The income from all these sources was completely dwarfed by that which he received from his massive investment in the town of Barrow-in-Furness. In 1873, over 80 per cent of all Devonshire investments were concentrated there, and some 90 per cent of dividend income came from that source. Taken together, his rentals and his dividends brought him an income in 1874 in excess of £300,000, probably the largest current revenue of any aristocratic millionaire at that time.

The rise of Barrow, directed by Hannay, Schneider, Ramsden and the Curreys, and with the seventh Duke himself hovering in the background, has already been amply described elsewhere, and is a story which need not be re-told here.[66] Suffice it to say that the building of the Furness Railway in the late 1840s, and the subsequent discovery of the largest single accumulation of iron-ore in Britain to date at Park-Vale, converted Barrow from a small Lancashire village of 150 inhabitants in 1846 to a bustling industrial town with more than 40,000 people by 1874.[67] For much of this time the Furness Railway's dividends were larger than those of any other major British railway company, and the Haematite Steel Company regularly paid dividends in excess of 15 per cent. Confidence soared and entries like 'very prosperous' and 'busy and prosperous' appeared with monotonous regularity in the Duke's diary throughout the 1860s and early 1870s. In such a euphoric atmosphere, the future seemed limitless, and the present was a marvellous time in which to be involved in Barrow.[68] 'The affairs of the company are so flourishing that business only occupied a quarter of an hour', he recorded after the annual general meeting of the Haematite Company in 1871.[69]

What did the seventh Duke do with all this money? Clearly, it did not go on extravagance and profligacy. The Duke himself lived the simplest of lives, and the two sums of £25,338 and £40,776 which he made over to his eldest son, the Marquess of Hartington, in 1877 and 1881, were relatively trivial items. Nor did it go on house-building: only £38,000 was so spent, on the rebuilding of Holker Hall in 1873–9 after a fire.[70] Nor did much go on high politics; the largest expenditure was £16,000 in 1868, an election year, and again a relatively small item. Nor was it swallowed up in agricultural improvement: for while the seventh Duke had a well-deserved reputation as an improving landlord, all such expenditure was financed out of current income. Nor was it spent on developing Buxton or Eastbourne: the first was too small an enterprise, and the second was deliberately designed to be self-financing. During the first decade of the ninety-nine year building lease, the lessee was given the unusual option of purchasing the freehold, and it was with the money thus acquired that expenditure on roads, sewers and seawalls was funded.[71]

As the tables in Appendix C make plain, the Duke's entire dividend income was ploughed back into Barrow in the form of additional investment.[72] But even this was not enough to satisfy Barrow's insatiable demand for funds, and as a result the seventh Duke was obliged to borrow still further to provide extra finances to supplement these substantial re-cycled sums.[73] Accordingly, new mortgages were obtained from insurance companies such as the Scottish Widows', the Equitable and the Union, or from relatives, friends and clients of the Curreys.[74] By this means the seventh Duke's total indebtedness was pushed up to a new peak of £1,200,000 in 1874. Since the income from dividends was expanding even more rapidly than were the charges of this increasing debt, it was not regarded with any undue alarm. Early in 1875, however, William Currey sounded a note of warning to his ducal employer:

I think the time has arrived when the question of meeting the further requirements of capital expenditure at Barrow must be considered. The requirements are becoming so large that it will be impossible for the companies to rely upon Your Grace as has been too much the case hitherto.[75]

His suggestion was that the Furness Railway should be sold to a major company such as the Midland Railway or the London and North Western, and that the money thus obtained should be used to finance the next round of investment in the other Barrow companies, thus freeing the Duke from further responsibility; but the scheme did not materialise.

Currey's warning had been more perceptive than he knew, for in the very same year the whole Barrow venture began to turn suddenly, unexpectedly and ominously sour. On the brink of diversification, but not safely beyond, the town was badly hit by the fall in the demand for iron and steel, and the even greater slump in prices, which occurred in the mid-1870s.[76] Dividends from the Furness Railway and the Steel Company collapsed almost as spectacularly as they had risen, the latter from £115,000 in 1874 to £1298 ten years later.[77] While the established companies faltered, the newly-formed shipping, shipbuilding and jute undertakings all struggled for their very existence. The buoyant and optimistic entries in the seventh Duke's diary were replaced by a cloud of gloom and despondency. 'We are not doing at all well at Barrow', he noted in 1879, 'and matters there are likely to give us a good deal of anxiety.'[78] 'The prospects of the steelworks do not improve', he wrote later in the same year, 'and there is no probability of our having any dividend this year.'[79] A local boom in the early 1880s brought some temporary relief, but thereafter the graph of dividend income once more slopes ominously downhill. 'The state of both companies', he noted after meetings of the shipbuilding and jute managers, 'is as bad as usual. . . . The state of things is becoming more anxious, and I fear a collapse cannot be much longer averted. In fact there seems a great risk of Barrow and all its works becoming an utter and complete failure.'[80]

It was not only his reduced income which gave the seventh Duke fully justified cause for alarm. As the Barrow companies threatened to collapse, the only possible source of further capital was Devonshire himself. 'It will clearly be necessary for me to find a great deal of money to prevent a smash', he noted in March 1877.[81] So it was; and so he did. In 1874–6, he poured no less than £300,000 into the ailing shipbuilding company, but to little purpose. In 1878 all the shares were written down in value from £25 to £10, and Devonshire was obliged to find another £270,000. In this manner the company staggered along until 1887, when a new syndicate took it over, converted it from constructing merchant ships to men-of-war, and renamed it the Naval Construction and Armaments Company.[82] The Flax and Jute Company, founded in 1874, fared no better. In 1876 Devonshire was obliged to contribute £150,000, followed by a further £87,000 in 1882.[83] By the mid-1880s, therefore, the seventh Duke's personal investments in Barrow amounted to more than two million pounds – a colossal, uncertain and excessive commitment. As Professor Pollard has noted: 'there can be no doubt that in the fifteen years following 1874 the resources of the great estates of the house of Devonshire were diverted to shorting up Barrow's crumbling industrial enterprises'.[84]

With reduced dividend income to plough back, indebtedness necessarily increased, soaring to nearly two millions by 1888, double the figure it had been on his succession thirty years before. Once more the Curreys begged the Duke 'to adopt a policy whereby, by a realisation of securities, Your Grace's indebtedness might be reduced'.[85] The advice was not heeded, even though it was sound. To make matters worse the Duke's income was being squeezed on all sides during the 1880s. It was not just that dividends were reduced to £25,000 a year, and continued to fall, while the cost of servicing the huge debt had risen from £40,000 a year in the mid-1860s to

£80,000. It was also that at the same time revenue from the agricultural estates declined from £140,000 to £106,000, with rent rebates of from 10 per cent to 30 per cent being given throughout the Duke's properties. 'Agricultural affairs have a gloomy appearance', he noted in May 1885, in one of a series of entries on that subject which rivalled those on Barrow in their despondency.[86] Far from Barrow cushioning the Devonshires against this depression, its collapse served only to make matters worse.[87] The result was that by the late 1880s current income was only £20,000 greater than it had been in the late 1850s and early 1860s, whereas outgoings had risen by £40,000 a year. Thus may be explained the paradox, noted by F.A. Currey in 1887, of a surplus of only £12,067, which was certainly 'not large having regard to the magnitude of the total income'.[88]

On every side the seventh Duke thus saw little but gloom in what should have been his serene sunset years: falling land values, reduced rentals, shares written down, declining dividend income, and increased encumbrances. In 1890, the Scottish Widows' Insurance Company, to whom he owed £80,000 secured on his Irish estates, took fright at having so much of its funds lent out on what had become such dubious security, and required repayment at the rate of £10,000 a year.[89] 'My private affairs', the Duke had noted five years before, on his seventy-seventh birthday, 'seem drifting into a very unsatisfactory condition.' In the following year he was even more despondent: 'I am beginning to think large reductions of estate expenditure will soon be necessary as my income is fast falling to a very unpleasant extent.' Again in 1888 he recorded that 'the position of my affairs' was 'far from comfortable, owing to the general depression which has largely reduced my income in all its sources'.[90] For a man supposed to have been the saviour of his family finances, his last years were very seriously troubled, and the legacy which he bequeathed to his successor was particularly burdensome.

III

Unaware of these facts, most historians have assumed that the eighth Duke, who succeeded his father in 1891, played a passive role in the Devonshires' financial history. Here, for instance, is Bickley's account of his stewardship:

He loved his lands, but the fact that his father's life overlapped with his by so many years relieved him, during the greater part of his career, of his responsibilities of the management of his broad acres. When at last his property came to him from the capable hands of the seventh duke, it was in a very different condition from that to which it had been reduced by the sixth duke's lavishness.[91]

Accordingly, so the argument runs, the eighth duke was free to *enjoy* his estates. Moreover, this lack of energetic interest in his financial affairs seemed consistent with the conventional interpretation of him as an idle and lethargic politician, and squared with what was known of his social life.[92] He fraternised and shot with the Prince of Wales, both before and after he became king. Lord Rosebery described him as the 'most magnificent of hosts'. Gladstone, less enthusiastically, felt he had 'a worldly standard much affected by the Newmarket kind of life'.[93] Just as the sixth Duke was a Regency figure in his time, and the seventh Duke was an archetypal mid-Victorian, so the eighth Duke's temperament places him appropriately in the naughty 'nineties and the early Edwardian era.

But in the same way that as recent research has undermined the view of the eighth Duke as an idle and slow-witted politician, by depicting him instead as an exceptionally shrewd, skilled and ambitious operator, so the argument advanced here compels a different interpretation of his performance as landlord and man of business.[94] For the record shows that it was he, rather than his illustrious predecessor, who successfully rehabilitated and restored the family finances. His grasp of the situation which he had inherited, and the decisiveness with which he took steps to deal with it, mark him out as a major figure in his own right, under whose tenure of the title new lines of financial policy were evolved which remained operative, and were further developed, in the years until the Second World War. By 1894 his late father's affairs had been sorted out and the new Duke was overwhelmed to discover so large a debt. 'It vexed me to see you so worried and bothered about affairs', his sister wrote to him after a meeting at which the sale of Devonshire House had been discussed. Urging him to reconsider, she recommended the sale of lands in Derbyshire and Ireland.[95] Her suggestion brought him little comfort. 'I am sorry to say', he wrote back, 'that financial prospects do not improve on examination.' He went on to explain why:

I do not think they were ever so bad, even in the time of the old duke. . . . An immense amount of capital, in the shape of coal and iron royalties, has been used up and sunk in unproductive Barrow investments, and there is now no surplus income over the fixed charges except that from such dividends as remain, and are liable to still further reductions. I can't say that at present I see anything to be done except to shut up Chatsworth and Hardwick, and make large reductions there.[96]

As he investigated the accounts more deeply, his anxiety only increased. 'Money cannot be shorter anywhere than it is here', he noted – a not unreasonable comment, given that estate revenue had plummeted to £65,000 in 1892–3, that dividend income was sliding to a mere £15,000 in 1896, and that more than half his current income was going to service the debt.[97] To make matters worse, the year in which the eighth Duke first came to terms with his troubles was also the year in which the Chancellor of the Exchequer, Sir William Harcourt, introduced death duties. At the rate of 10 per cent on estates over one million pounds, they were hardly in themselves crippling, but to a landowner as encumbered as the eighth

Duke, they represented a severe additional burden; so much so that he wrote to Harcourt, pointing out the difficulties that his successor at Chatsworth would face with heavy mortgages and a depleted income in meeting such demands.[98] But Harcourt was unsympathetic.[99] How unsuspectingly apposite, under these circumstances, was the *Punch* cartoon on death duties, which pictured a worried and concerned Duke of Westminster saying to the Duke of Devonshire: 'We may consider ourselves lucky if we can keep a tomb over our heads.'[100]

The eighth Duke's immediate response was to blame his solicitors and financial advisors for mismanaging his father's affairs. 'I begin to think that the Curreys are enough to ruin anybody', he told his sister.[101] As the evidence shows, this was hardly just as regards their handling of Barrow matters. Assuredly, Benjamin Currey had prodded the reluctant Earl of Burlington in the late 1840s, but his successors had constantly urged the seventh Duke to lessen his financial involvement in the town's business in the 1870s and 1880s.[102] More plausibly, the eighth Duke suspected that the Eastbourne building estate had been mismanaged, so in 1894 he called in Price Waterhouse to check the accounts and an expert surveyor to give a critical appraisal of management policy. Their conclusions supported his suspicions, and provoked the Curreys to produce a hand-written report of 125 pages in which they defended their conduct and tried to refute the charges which had been levelled against them.[103] It is noteworthy, however, that between 1895 and 1908 expenditure on that estate was abruptly reduced to a mere £7000 a year, only half what it had been during the years 1880-94.[104]

While the eighth Duke and his advisers disagreed on the Eastbourne estate, they were unanimous in wishing to extricate themselves from the stricken Barrow enterprises. Here was one new line of policy vigorously and immediately implemented. Control of the Steel Company was surrendered to east-coast interests; the jute works were sold in 1894-6 for £10,000; and in 1903 the Steamship Company was closed down, Devonshire receiving a mere £1146, 'His Grace's share of the assets divisible on the winding up of the company'.[105] The Naval Construction and Armaments Company continued to languish, so much so that it was decided 'to go in for armour as a last throw in a gamble'.[106] Accordingly, it was sold in 1896-7 to Vickers, the Duke himself receiving £125,000 for the freehold and £300,000 worth of debenture shares in the new company.[107] In the eighth Duke's lifetime extensive holdings in the Steel Company were maintained, amounting to some £370,000 in 1900, on which no dividend was paid.[108] These, too, were gradually liquidated, so that by 1930 the ninth Duke possessed only a token holding of 180 ordinary and 67 preference shares. Only in the Furness Railway did the Devonshires retain overall control, and this vanished in 1923 when the company was absorbed by the newly-formed London, Midland and Scottish Railway.[109]

The second strand of the eighth Duke's policy was – predictably – to reduce the debt. The seventh Duke had intended to, but had failed. The eighth Duke was determined to, and succeeded. By 1899 total indebtedness had been diminished to the level it had been at in 1858, and had been consolidated in two large mortgages, one of £550,000 to the Equitable in 1894, the other to the Scottish Widows' for £400,000 in 1897.[110] By the time the eighth Duke died in 1908 it had been further brought down to less than half a million, with interest charges (a mere £20,000) taking only 15 per cent of current income, a lower proportion than for any previous period in the nineteenth century. This was an achievement as substantial as it was timely. Between 1911 and 1916 the need to find some £540,000 to pay duties on the eighth Duke's estate temporarily increased the debt again by £200,000, so that it was back to £600,000 in 1915.[111] But after the First World War the reduction continued, so that by 1933 the last remnants of the two outstanding mortgages were paid off. With debts, as with Barrow investments, the eighth Duke's policy had been successfully completed by his successor.

How was this reduction accomplished? Clearly, there were no large profits from Barrow which could have been used. Only by embracing the policy which the seventh Duke considered then rejected, of selling off land to an unprecedented extent, did the eighth Duke and his successor make so large a hole in the encumbrances. To be sure, while paying off a million pounds' worth of debt up to 1899, the eighth Duke had received £213,000 from life assurance companies in respect of the seventh Duke. But he had also sold off land worth £790,000, most of it in Ireland and Derbyshire, those very places where his sister had recommended that sales should be made. By 1914, when a further half-a-million pounds of debt had been paid off, land sales had realised another £660,000, again mainly in Ireland and Derbyshire.[112] These were the obvious places to sell: in Ireland, because the Land Purchase Acts made selling possible and attractive, and because the days of the traditional ascendancy were clearly numbered; in Derbyshire, because the family's holdings were so massive that they could be substantially lessened but still remain extensive.

These sales, along with money obtained by selling out in those Barrow ventures where the shares were not worthless, gave the eighth Duke a surplus on capital account, the proceeds of which were reinvested, not in land, but in a wide range of British, colonial and U.S. government bonds, and railway shares overseas. These diverse dividends contributed 30 per cent or more to the eighth and ninth Dukes' current income in the years before the First World War, and in the immediate post-war years the Devonshires' involvement with the stock market increased still further.[113] Between 1919 and 1922 they joined the general scramble to sell, parting with estates worth £640,000, mostly in Somerset, Derbyshire and Sussex, and they also sold Devonshire House itself for £750,000.[114] Some of the money was used to reduce debt still further, but most of it was invested in an even wider range of equities than had been bought before the First World War. The result was a startling transformation. In the final phase of the Devonshires' financial history for which detailed records are available, over two-thirds of their current income was drawn from dividends. Put the other way, by the mid-1920s they had ceased to obtain most of their revenue from agricultural rents. Instead, they had become rentiers, maintaining a style of life that was still landed in its mode of *expenditure*, but increasingly plutocratic in its sources of *income*.

Of course the Devonshires had drawn over half of their current income from dividends once before – in the 1870s during the great Barrow boom, and the early 1880s, when the second and smaller Barrow upswing had coincided with falling agricultural revenue. But these were only brief episodes, and the income thus obtained arose from the long-standing aristocratic policy of exploiting non-agricultural estate resources. In the 1920s, by contrast, the dividend income was, relatively speaking, much larger, and resulted from a fundamentally changed policy of selling land and investing proceeds in a wide range of companies around the globe which had no connection whatsoever with the Devonshire estates. This was a new financial world, the practices and presuppositions of which would have been alien to the seventh Duke's way of thinking; but its results were in many ways satisfactory, for it gave the ninth Duke a current income comparable to that enjoyed by his predecessors. At £110,000 a year in the early 1920s, it was as large as the eighth Duke had known, as great as the seventh Duke's before the Barrow venture was begun, and more than the sixth Duke's. Even if there was now supertax to pay, interest payments on the debt had all but vanished.[115]

Thus, despite both this radically changed asset structure and the furore over death duties on the eighth Duke's estate (which had obliged his successor to sell off his stud farm and some Chatsworth heirlooms, and temporarily let Compton Place), the Devonshires managed to live out the 1920s and 1930s in a manner which apparently belied both the changes and the challenges of the preceding half-century.[116] The ninth Duke was Governor-General of Canada from 1916 to 1921: indeed it was precisely during this long period of absence from the country that the fundamental re-ordering of his financial affairs took place. He was Colonial Secretary in the government of Bonar Law, while his successor held minor ministerial office under Chamberlain and Churchill, and was reputedly offered the Viceroyalty of India in 1943. Just as King Edward VII accompanied the eighth Duke to Compton Place, so King George V convalesced there in 1936. The semi-feudal regime at Chatsworth continued largely intact, and the constant moves from one great house to another went on very much as before.[117] When the ninth Duke died in 1938 his funeral was still decidedly traditional in character. Outwardly, little had changed since the days of the seventh Duke; financially – and politically – there had been a revolution during the intervening years.

Yet despite this resourceful and audacious display of financial adjustment, there must have been times during the 1940s and 1950s when it looked as though the game was up. Inevitably, the Second World War brought with it increased taxation and austerity, and the Devonshires moved out of Chatsworth, which was occupied by the girls of Penrhos College. 'I must say', observed Harold Nicolson, after lunching with the recently-succeeded tenth Duke in September 1939, 'I do admire a man like that, who must realise that all his grandeur is gone for ever, not showing the slightest sign of gloom or apprehension.'[118] The next decade was to bring gloom and apprehension in morbid abundance. The tenth Duke's heir, the Marquess of Hartington, was killed in action in the last stages of the Second World War, and the tenth Duke himself died suddenly in 1952: had he lived a mere four months longer, the £2.5 million duties that were levied on his estate would have been avoided. 'What dread score', inquired Henry Channon, 'has destiny to pay off against the Devonshires? Is this the end of Chatsworth? And of Hardwick?'[119]

The answer was both yes and no. Beyond any doubt, this was an even greater challenge to the family fortune than had been presented by the indulgent profligacy of the sixth Duke or the dutiful expenditure of the seventh. Inevitably, there were further massive sales of land, especially in Derbyshire, and Hardwick Hall and its contents were given to the Treasury in part payment of death duties. Works of art were also sold, including paintings by Rembrandt, Holbein and Rubens. The final payment of duty was not made until 1967, and it was not until 1974 that the family finances had fully recovered.[120] Meanwhile, the eleventh Duke and his Duchess returned to Chatsworth in 1959, which they had carefully restored, opened to the public, and turned into one of the greatest stately homes in the country. At the same time, the Duke held minor office in the administration of his uncle by marriage, Harold Macmillan. Today he plays no part in politics, and his acreage and his houses are much diminished by comparison with the seventh Duke's day. He is not optimistic about the future of very great estates, but thanks to the rise in land values and art prices, he is probably the richest Duke of Devonshire there has ever been, and his pessimism may yet turn out to be premature.[121]

IV

It is now appropriate to return to the general reflections with which this essay opened, and to pose explicitly the questions implicitly stated there. First: how far does this account suggest that some modification of the popularly held views of the Devonshires' finances is in order? Second: what light does the experience of this individual family throw on the condition of super-rich landlords in general?

Like many other nineteenth-century aristocratic millionaires, the

Devonshires' acres were broad, their income large, and their involvement in non-agricultural ventures extensive. None of the evidence presented here alters the conventional picture of the activities or consequences of the sixth Duke. Nor, as regards his character or reputation, has any revision been made of the seventh Duke; but there is much concerning his steward-ship of the family finances that cannot be reconciled with the traditional interpretation. Far from restoring them, as he intended, he undermined them further. While the Barrow venture began well, it ended disastrously, and his other non-agricultural schemes were on too small a scale to outweigh so great a failure. Unable to eradicate debt out of a desire for economy, he ended by enlarging it out of sense of duty. Motivated by the loftiest of feelings, the seventh Duke encumbered his family estates to a greater extent than his two spendthrift predecessors put together. Sobriety and responsibility ultimately proved to be more costly than dissipation and self-indulgence.

Instead of being a turning point, therefore, the seventh Duke may most usefully be seen as the last in a line of Cavendishes going back to the first Duke and before. They may have been temperamentally dissimilar, and they spent their money in different ways – some on houses, some on high living, some on politics, some on commercial and industrial developments. But they all shared the same basic presuppositions about the high and enduring status of land itself, of the landed aristocracy, and of landed incomes, and it was on this basis that they all spent, whether out of sheer exuberance and self-indulgence or from a sense of duty and responsibility.

For the Devonshires, as for many other landed families both super-rich and less wealthy, the pivotal decades were not so much the early Victorian years but the period of and after the agricultural depression, which saw an end to those activities and presuppositions which had characterised landed society from the time of the Glorious Revolution onwards. More than many other landed millionaires, the Devonshires entered the last decade of the nineteenth century with their prime non-agricultural venture an embarrassing, expensive and worrying failure, with indebtedness larger than ever, and with current income disconcertingly reduced on all fronts. Yet, in extricating themselves from this gloomy predicament, the eighth Duke, his successors and advisers displayed resourcefulness and flexibility of a high order. If this family, so burdened and encumbered in the late nineteenth century, could adapt and survive with such conspicuous success in the first decades of the twentieth, then how much more true must that have been of those superpowers less disadvantaged – the Bedfords, the Westminsters, the Dudleys, the Sutherlands and the Butes? In outlining the fluctuating fortunes of the Devonshires, this essay may thus have thrown more general light on that curious hybrid, part businessman and part landowner: the aristocratic millionaire.[122]

8

Landowners, Lawyers and Litterateurs

The Cozens-Hardys of Letheringsett

ALTHOUGH NEVER DISTINGUISHED for its large number of great estates, the county of Norfolk may justly be regarded as one of the most aristocratic in the land.[1] England's premier duke draws his title from the shire, and England's premier baronet resides in the county at Raveningham. The great houses of Blickling, Felbrigg, Raynham, Houghton and Holkham are vivid reminders of the wealth, power and prestige once enjoyed – and in some cases still enjoyed – by Norfolk's traditional territorial elite. The leading part taken by Sir Robert Walpole, by 'Turnip' Townshend and by Coke of Holkham in the agriculural revolution is aptly commemorated in the phrase 'Norfolk husbandry'. The last squire of Felbrigg, Robert Wyndham Ketton-Cremer, was the foremost Norfolk historian of his day, and a generous benefactor of the University of East Anglia. From 1949 to 1978, the Lord Lieutenant of the county was Sir Edmund Bacon, whose lifelong involvement in local affairs is commemorated in a memorial window in Norwich Cathedral. And in 1990, the Marquess of Cholmondeley left the largest estate ever proved in the British Isles, worth more than £118 million.[2]

One reason for this continued aristocratic survival is that the Industrial Revolution largely passed Norfolk by: there were no mineral resources beneath its fertile soil, no sprawling Victorian cities blighted the landscape, and factory towns were virtually unknown. Even the industries in Norwich were 'very small beer compared with those in some of the Northern and Midland towns'.[3] Inevitably, in a county dominated by agriculture, there was much commercial and industrial activity associated with it: in particular banking, brewing, insurance and food processing. This, in turn, lead to the rise of a group of mercantile families – the Hoares, the Buxtons, the Barclays, the Gurneys, the Bignolds and the Colmans – who might best be described as 'gentlemanly capitalists'.[4] They possessed a strong sense of dynastic identity, and frequently inter-married. They tended (though there were exceptions) to be Liberal in politics and nonconformist in religion. They bought landed estates, but continued to draw a significant proportion of their incomes from their businesses. They enjoyed the amenities of country life, and many became keen naturalists, but they worked hard for their livings.[5] They were equally at ease with the citizens of Norwich and with the landowners of the county. They were neither traditionally aristocratic nor conventionally middle class, but were somewhere in between. The Cozens-Hardys of Letheringsett were just such a family.

I

Letheringsett village lies two miles to the west of Holt, where the main road to King's Lynn crosses the valley of the River Glaven. Nearby, the Hall, the church, a brewery and a water mill, comprise 'a single visual group of enchanting compactness'. In 1781, William Hardy acquired the brewery, and fifty acres of land, for £1600. It was well situated, close to a large market town; there were two sea ports nearby at Cley and Blakeney; there was waterpower immediately available from the river; and there was no local competition. William Hardy was a self-made man, born in Yorkshire in 1732, who moved to Norfolk and established himself first as a farmer, and then as a brewer. He was a radical in politics, and he consistently supported the Cokes, whose great estate was nearby at Holkham. William Hardy, by contrast, bought his modest acres at Letheringsett as an adjunct to his brewery, rather than because he cherished any territorial ambitions. Yet it was from this inauspicuious beginning that a dynasty developed which played a major role in the affairs of the county of Norfolk and the city of Norwich for the best part of the next two hundred years.[6]

In 1797 the sixty-five-year-old William Hardy handed over the control of his thriving business to his twenty-seven-year-old son, also called William Hardy.[7] William Hardy II shared his father's radical political views and his nonconformist beliefs, and was one of the few dissenters of his time to be made a county magistrate. He was also a forceful, vigorous and innovative entrepreneur, in whose charge the family business continued to profit.[8] He installed the latest machinery, put up new buildings in 1814 and 1823, and rebuilt the malthouse after a fire in 1827. He designed and constructed three bridges over the Glaven, one of which, built of cast iron in 1818, still carries the traffic from Holt to King's Lynn. In 1813, he financed the construction of the first Methodist chapel in Holt, and in 1837 he provided funds for a second. On his death five years later, a tablet was placed in this 'new' chapel as 'an enduring record of the zeal with which he supported the cause of Wesleyan Methodism, amidst the obloquy, the reproach and the persecution, which attended its introduction into the neighbourhood'.

This was not his only memorial: another such tablet commemorated William Hardy II in Letheringsett parish church, aptly reflecting the position he established during his lifetime as the village squire. Neither he, nor any of his descendants, ever held the patronage of the living. But in the forty years after 1802, he ploughed the profits from his brewery into the purchase of land, gradually piecing together an estate of more than a thousand acres which extended continuously from Letheringsett to Cley, on the coast. At the same time, he began the systematic afforestation of the Glaven valley, and claimed he had planted 300,000 trees in three years. The result was a compact estate, as well managed as the brewery, which was greatly admired by William Cobbett when he visited it on his rural rides in 1821. 'The fields, the stables, the yards, the buildings, the cattle,' he observed, 'all showed the greatest judgement and industry.' 'There was', he concluded, 'really nothing that the most critical observer could say was out of order.' This opinion was corroborated two years later, when the Rev. W. Stones, who was probably a Methodist minister, composed a lengthy, effusive and banal poem about Letheringsett, rather fancifully entitled *The Garden of Norfolk*.

Having created an estate and a park, William Hardy II set about building himself a modest country mansion, by extending an old farmhouse near the parish church, which had been one of his original purchases in 1802.[9] Towards the end of that decade, he deflected the nearby main road, so as to provide more space and more privacy, and he constructed a new south wing, with dining-room, drawing-room, and bedrooms above. The south front was screened by a giant portico, built to his own design, which was one of the first in England to use Doric columns ('pillars, massive, high and fluted, too', according to Stones). Their spacing was irregular, and their number was uneven; but despite this blatant solecism, there is a primitive strength and utilitarian boldness about the scheme which aptly reflected Hardy's forceful and innovative personality.[10] In 1832 he added a new east wing, again in the Greek style, which included a grand staircase and a library, and cost less than two thousand pounds. Apart from minor extensions in the 1840s and the 1930s, Letheringsett Hall has remained unaltered since. It was William Hardy II's creation, and as such it symbolised the family's modest arrival in the lower echelons of Norfolk landed society. As the commemorative tablet in the parish church recalls: 'over his grave wept a the whole neighbourhood, and each man felt that he had lost a friend'.[11]

Like most such upwardly mobile men, William Hardy II was clearly buying and building with posterity in mind. But there were no surviving children of his marriage, and so he was obliged to leave his business and his estate to a more distant relative. Accordingly, on his death in 1842, he bequeathed everything to his nephew, William Hardy Cozens, who had been born in 1806.[12] He was the only son of Mary Anne Hardy, the sister of William Hardy II, and her husband, Jeremiah Cozens of Sprowston. Like William Hardy I, Jeremiah Cozens was a self-made farmer, who had gradually put together an estate of five hundred acres at Sprowston, on the outskirts of Norwich.[13] Although Mary Anne Hardy was Jeremiah Cozens' second wife, the children of his first marriage pre-deceased him, with the result that William Hardy Cozens came into both the Hardy properties of his uncle and the Cozens properties of his father. On the death of William Hardy II, he inherited the Letheringsett estate, on condition that he add Cozens to his name, thereby becoming William Hardy Cozens-Hardy. On the death of Jeremiah Cozens, in 1849, he inherited the Sprowston acres as well. These consolidated holdings he was to enjoy – and to augment – for the best part of half a century, so that by the early 1880s the Cozens-Hardy estates in Norfolk amounted to 2929 acres, worth £3764 a year.[14]

As his uncle's chosen heir, William Hardy Cozens-Hardy trained as a solicitor, and qualified in 1829. He handled legal business in Letheringsett until he inherited the estate, and thereby established a connection between his family and the law which was to be consolidated and extended in later generations.[15] Like his Hardy and Cozens forebears, he was a radical in politics, and remained a firm supporter of Gladstone, despite Home Rule. As an old man he proudly drove his carriage more than twenty miles to vote for Joseph Arch at the three general elections which he contested in Norfolk in the 1880s. He was also a fervent believer in the cause of religious freedom and equality. He took an active part in the mid-century Wesleyan reform movement, and soon found himself at odds with the more con- servative Wesleyan Conference. In 1849 he joined the Free Methodists, and was turned out of the 'new' Holt chapel, which his uncle had built, and of which he himself was a trustee. There followed a much-publicised dispute, which resulted in a Chancery lawsuit being brought against him by the Wesleyan Conference. Cozens-Hardy successfully defended himself, but the affair left much bitterness. He never returned to the 'new' chapel in Holt, preferring instead to establish his breakaway congregation in its own, more elaborate place of worship, on Obelisk plain.[16]

Despite his robust involvement in political and religious controversy, William Hardy Cozens-Hardy was widely regarded as a model squire who devoted his life, and much of his income, to public works in Letheringsett and Holt. He was a close friend of Johnson Jex, the Letheringsett black- smith and inventor, whose life he commemorated in a public lecture.[17] In 1843 he became a magistrate, and for many years was proud to be the only nonconformist Justice of the Peace. He served for half a century, and for 25 years he was Chairman of the Holt bench. In 1851, he built the local British School, and he was a member of the Holt School Board from the outset. He was the moving spirit in the foundation of the Holt Literary Society, and was the founder and President of the Reepham Provident Society. He was Chairman of the local Board of Guardians for fifty years, and was a warm friend of the Sunday School movement, regularly throwing open his gardens to visitors. On his death in 1895 a town meeting at Holt unanimously passed a resolution of condolence, shops were closed on the day of the funeral, and he was mourned throughout the district as 'an English Christian gentleman', 'a man of rare purity of purpose and nobility of character'.[18]

In 1830, William Hardy Cozens-Hardy had married Sarah Theobald. Her father was a textile manufacturer in Norwich, but she easily adjusted to the environment of a country village, and was closely involved in the religious and philanthropic life of the parish. When William and Sarah celebrated their diamond wedding anniversary in 1890, they received a congratulatory telegram from Mr and Mrs Gladstone, and an illuminated address from their seven surviving children, their twenty-six grandchildren, and their five great-grandchildren.[19] Even by Victorian standards, this was a large family, and five of their children became particularly distinguished. Their eldest son, Clement William, inherited the estates. Their second son, Herbert, became a barrister and Member of Parliament, and was eventually made a judge and a peer. Their third son, Theobald, was another public-spirited country gentleman. Their fourth son, Sydney, was a solicitor who became one of the most important men in Norwich. Their eldest daughter, Caroline, married Jeremiah Colman, the mustard king and Liberal MP for the City of Norwich. This was a formidable family to have sired, and between them this younger generation of Cozens-Hardys straddled the public life of Norwich and Norfolk in unprecedentedly influential ways.

It was also a very large family, and even with the revenue from the brewery to boost his rentals William Hardy Cozens-Hardy clearly found so many children a heavy charge on his resources.[20] Their coming of age coincided with the agricultural depression, which hit Norfolk very hard. Rentals declined by anything from twenty to seventy per cent, and small estates the size of Letheringsett were especially vulnerable. The Joneses of Cranmer were forced to let their house, and become 'a family of exiles', living 'poor' and 'rootless' abroad. The Rolfe estate at Heacham was so heavily encumbered that in 1899 Eustace Rolfe was obliged to sell it. The Felbrigg estate of the Kettons deteriorated badly between 1872 and 1924.[21] The documentation is regrettablty limited, but from the provisions of William Hardy Cozens-Hardy's will it seems clear that the Letheringsett estate finances were also very tight at this time. The brewery was sold, after more than a hundred years in the family. Some of the land at Cley was realised to pay legacies. Most of the Sprowston estate was auctioned off in lots for building development. Instead of taking up residence at Letheringsett, the new squire, Clement William Cozens-Hardy, let the house, and continued to reside at Cley Hall, where he had been living since 1855, shortly after he came of age.[22]

For the senior branch of the family, this represented a distinct contraction in financial resources, and Clement William Cozens-Hardy seems to have lacked the vigour and the stamina of his father. He grew barley, bred sheep, and delighted in country pursuits. He chaired the local Board of

Guardians and the Cley School Board. He was one of the original members of Norfolk County Council, and was much concerned with elementary education and the provision of allotments. He was a strong Liberal, who shared the Secretaryship of the North Norfolk Constituency Association with C.L. Buxton. It was an unostentatiously useful life, but compared with his father he lived it in a minor key.[23] The same could be said of his only son, Arthur Wrigley Cozens-Hardy, who succeeded him in 1906. He, too, preferred to live at Cley, where he enjoyed country pursuits, and took his place on the bench and the Board of Guardians. Appropriately enough, he died of a stroke while out shooting, 'a true sportsman and an ideal English gentleman'.[24] But with his death, in 1925, the senior branch of the Cozens-Hardy family came to an abrupt end in the male line. How did this happen?

The answer, as for so many landed families, was simple, terrible, and unexpected: the First World War. Arthur Wrigley Cozens-Hardy fathered one son and two daughters. The boy, Raven Cozens-Hardy, was born in 1886, and was by all accounts a person of singular charm, modesty and goodness who, like his father and grandfather, was devoted to country life and country sports. After Oxford University, he joined a firm of London stockbrokers, Foster and Braithwaite (another sign, incidentally, that the family finances were not all they might be). In the autumn of 1914, he was amongst the first to volunteer, and soon obtained his commission in the Norfolks. Three years later, Lieutenant Raven Cozens-Hardy was killed leading his platoon over the top at Polderhoek.[25] There was a memorial service at Cley parish church, and his bereaved mother put together a book, entitled *A Beloved Memory*, which contained all the letters of condolence which she received. Many were written in the conventional phraseology of the time, describing how Raven 'played the game of life straight to the end, and was a shining example of all that is best in manhood'. Another, more sensitive (or perhaps more insensitive?) to what it all meant, noted that 'had he been spared, what a wonderful squire he would have made'.[26]

But that was not to be; and who was there to take his place? 'I think we all felt', wrote Raven's kinsman and contemporary Basil Cozens-Hardy, 'that our goodly family traditions would be so safe in his hands when, in years to come, he would assume the headship of the clan.'[27] But not only was Raven dead: he had no wife, no children, no brothers. Like many a bereaved landowner, Arthur Wrigley Cozens-Hardy was obliged to reconsider how to dispose of his estates. In the end, he divided them between his two daughters. The elder, Gladys Lily, married her cousin, Edward Herbert Cozens-Hardy, and in 1918, scarcely a year after his son's death, Arthur Wrigley Cozens-Hardy sold the bulk of the Letheringsett estate to him. The younger daughter, Helen Maguire, married Kenneth Knott, and on her father's death she inherited the Cley Hall estate, large parts of which were sold off after 1945.[28] The family holdings, scarcely three generations in accumulation, were already being dispersed.

II

The vigour and longevity that had characterised William Hardy Cozens-Hardy were inherited more by his younger sons than by his heir. Indeed, his second boy, Herbert, who was born in 1838, achieved a reputation which extended well beyond the confines of Norfolk.[29] He followed his father into the law, but as a barrister rather than a solicitor, and he graduated from University College, London, in 1858. Four years later, he was called to the Bar at Lincoln's Inn, and thanks to his excellent Liberal and nonconformist connections he rapidly built up a flourishing and lucrative practice as a Chancery junior. After twenty busy years, he took silk in 1882, and was constantly employed in heavy cases in the Chancery division, especially those which went to appeal, one of the most famous being the protracted suit which arose out of the failure of Harvey & Hudson's Bank at Norwich. He was never an outstanding advocate, but he was hard working, level-headed and fair-minded. He was devoid of stateliness and pomposity, was courteous and straightforward in all his dealings, and was very much liked. All this was recognised in his election to the chairmanship of the General Council of the Bar.

In 1885, Herbert Cozens-Hardy went into politics, and was adopted as the prospective Liberal candidate for North Norfolk, one of the new constituencies created in the aftermath of the Third Reform Act, which had enfranchised the agricultural labourers. Some of the local landlords, such as Lord Hastings, were strongly Conservative. Others, like Lord Leicester and Lord Suffield, were more lax. And some, like the young Robert Ketton of Felbrigg, were devoted Liberals. The towns of Aylsham, Cromer and Wells generally reckoned to be Conservative, but in an overwhelmingly rural division it was clear that the decision would effectively be made by the agricultural labourers.[30] As a Liberal and a nonconformist, whose family came from the neighbouring constituency, Cozens-Hardy was an obvious choice. Moreover, his elder brother, Clement William, was Secretary of the North Norfolk Liberal Association, and his younger brother, Sydney (of whom more later), was election agent. The organisation was good, great trouble was taken to ensure that the agricultural labourers knew how and where to vote, and in three weeks of energetic campaigning Cozens-Hardy addressed more than twenty-five meetings. He opposed jingoism and high taxes, and he supported religious toleration, the reform of local government, and changes in the land laws. On this platform he defeated Samuel Hoare, his Conservative opponent, by 5028 votes to 3342, a comfortable majority of 1686.[31]

Thereafter, the Conservatives put up a succession of serious locally-connected candidates, but Cozens-Hardy proved to be 'utterly unseatable'. There was some anxiety at the general election of 1886, because he had abstained from voting for Gladstone's Home Rule Bill, and many Liberal supporters were reported to be 'vexed' by this. As a result, he was obliged to confront the Constituency Association, at a special meeting chaired by Sir Thomas Fowell Buxton, and to explain and justify his conduct. It was, he insisted, to the ill-thought-out details of Gladstone's scheme, rather than to Home Rule itself, that he objected. So great a matter, he went on, could not be settled by hurried and poorly-drafted legislation.[32] He was given a rousing reception, and thereafter his position was, indeed, unassailable. He was strongly supported by the resident Gurneys and Buxtons, by the *Eastern Daily Press*, and by Joseph Arch, who was himself standing in a neighbouring constituency, and who went out of his way to urge the agricultural labourers to vote for Cozens-Hardy. They clearly did so, albeit in reduced numbers, and he defeated his opponent, the Hon. Ailwyn Fellowes, by the reduced but still comfortable majority of 760 votes.[33]

In concluding that 'the seat is the possession of the present occupant so long as he shall please to seek the suffrage of the constituency', the *Eastern Daily Press* did not err. For the 1892 election the Conservatives chose another local candidate, John Cator, but his chances were slim. By then, Cozens-Hardy had proved himself 'a thoroughly consistent Liberal and a hard-working Member of the House of Commons'. His name was 'a household word in this part of Norfolk', and was bound to 'ensure him hearty support'. And so, indeed, it did, as Cozens-Hardy romped home with an increased majority of 1283.[34] Even in the more difficult times of 1895, his hold on the seat could not be shaken. As befitted the scion of a local landowning family, he was much concerned by the depressed state of agriculture, but was opposed to any form of protection. The constituency organisation remained excellent, and on polling day, the Buxtons and J.J. Colman sent their carriages to get the voters out. His Tory opponent, Sir Kenneth Kemp, succeeded in reducing his majority to 508, but in a bad election year for the Party the *Eastern Daily Press* 'rejoiced to know that Mr Cozens-Hardy has once more secured a victory for the cause of Liberalism in North Norfolk'.[35]

Although recognised by friend and foe alike as 'a singularly upright and disinterested character', Cozens-Hardy was never prominent in the House of Commons, and seems to have cherished no political ambitions beyond representing Norfolk at Westminster.[36] Thus described, he was a classic example of the country gentleman in politics, even though that breed was well in retreat by then, both at Westminster and in Norfolk. As a busy lawyer, with a large and lucrative practice, the amount of time he could give to parliamentary business was, inevitably, limited. Appropriately enough, his infrequent interventions in Commons debates were confined to the two subjects he knew most about: the law, and Norfolk affairs. He spoke on bankruptcy, tithes and copyholds, the winding-up of companies, married women's property, and the law relating to trustees. He asked questions about allotments in Norfolk, the reform of the Norwich town charities, the danger to the crab and lobster fisheries of North Norfolk from the lack of regulation, and the refusal of the Cromer Church School to grant admission to girls unless they were wearing pinafores.[37] He also helped to carry what his *Times* obituarist described as 'a very useful act, known by his name, on the law of Mortmain'.

It was clear that if preferment was to come his way it would be judicial rather than political, though at a time of Conservative hegemony Herbert Cozens-Hardy's nonconformist Liberalism was clearly a drawback. But in 1899 Lord Chancellor Halsbury, who was not ordinarily predisposed towards political opponents, raised him to the bench in the Chancery division, when he received the customary knighthood.[38] As a judge, he showed the same industry and care that had marked his work at the bar, and in 1901 he became a Lord Justice of Appeal and was sworn into the Privy Council. Six years later, by which time the Liberals were back in power, he became Master of the Rolls, and thus head of the Court of Appeal. Predictably, he performed his duties with dignity, efficiency and application. Appeals under the recently-passed Workmen's Compensation Act were especially numerous, and Cozens-Hardy dealt with them well, though unversed in this branch of the law. His familiarity with equity law and practice made him a strong president of the court when Chancery appeals were being heard. The peak of his career was reached in 1914, when he was given a peerage, and became the first Baron Cozens-Hardy of Letheringsett in the County of Norfolk.

Despite the fact that he was never a truly outstanding lawyer or judge (his *Times* obituarist observed that 'a layman would have been puzzled to understand his success'), Cozens-Hardy was undoubtedly the most famous member of his family, the only one to rate an entry in the *Dictionary of National Biography*. Drawing strength and support from his local connections, he had successfully projected the family on to the national stage. Yet his roots in Norfolk remained deep and important. When Clement Cozens-Hardy inherited the estates in 1895, but continued to live at Cley, he allowed Herbert to rent Letheringsett Hall as his holiday home.[39] While in residence he served as chairman of the Norfolk Quarter Sessions, and he built a village hall at Letheringsett at his own expense. When ill-health forced him to retire in 1918, it was to Letheringsett that he returned, and it was at Letheringsett that he died, two years later, leaving £123,228, a substantial sum in those days. His metropolitan and national prominence were reflected in the fact that he was buried at Kensal Green Cemetery in London. But the local press coverage was extensive and appreciative, there was a memorial service in Letheringsett church, and soon afterwards a commemorative tablet was placed there.[40]

For a time, it looked as though the family's new-found position of national prominence might be continued and consolidated by the first lord's eldest son, William Hepburn Cozens-Hardy. He was born in 1868, and was educated at New College, Oxford, where he was a prominent member of the (advanced Liberal) Russell Club and President of the Union.[41] He followed what had by now become a family tradition by going into the law, was called to the bar in 1893, took silk in 1912, and became a Bencher of Lincoln's Inn in 1916. In 1907, he became secretary to his father as Master of the Rolls, and he held that position until Lord Cozens-Hardy retired in 1918. In part because of his own charm, intelligence and forcefulness, and in part because of his father's position, William Cozens-Hardy established close connections with some of the foremost members of the Liberal Governments of 1905–14, especially Lloyd George and Rufus Isaacs, later Lord Reading. He also acquired extensive business interests in Europe, which he loved to visit, being a keen motorist and an excellent linguist. In 1919, he co-authored a report on the commercial prospects of modern Morocco for the Bank of British West Africa.[42]

On the outbreak of the First World War, he organised a more efficient system of voluntary recruiting in Norfolk, then offered his services to the Admiralty, and obtained a commission in the Royal Naval Volunteer Reserve. He was immediately attached to the Naval Intelligence Division, under Admiral Sir Reginald Hall, and seems to have done useful and important – though controversial – work.[43] He helped establish a War Trade Intelligence Department and a Central Intelligence Bureau for the Ministry of Blockade. He was credited with devising a plan for supplying food to the retreating Serbian army during the winter of 1915–16, which saved it from total destruction. Early in 1917 he recruited the original staff of the Admiralty Historical Section, and drew up the scheme for the series of *Peace Handbooks*, which were produced to assist the British delegation at the Versailles conference. But his relations with his subordinates, especially George Prothero, were far from happy, and within scarcely a year he was moved to other work, and the Historical Section was transferred to the Foreign Office. In the summer of 1918 he paid his visit to Morocco (his financial report owed much to the format of the *Peace Handbooks*), and on his return he sought a position on Lord Reading's impending mission to the USA, or on Lloyd George's staff at the Versailles conference.[44]

Nothing came of these proposals, and so Cozens-Hardy decided to follow his father into the House of Commons for a Norfolk constituency. He took up residence in Gunthorpe Hall, became a county JP, and in November 1918 was adopted as the Coalition Liberal candidate for South Norfolk. He ran with the support of the Conservatives, and was nominated by Geoffrey Fowell Buxton and Russell Colman. He campaigned on a conventional Coalition programme: support of Lloyd George and a harsh peace with Germany, and jobs and houses for the returning soldiers, all topped off with expressions of concern about agriculture, and repeated references to his own Norfolk roots. His only opponent was George Edwards, the Labour Candidate and Secretary of the Norfolk Agricultural Labourers' Union, and after a good-humoured campaign, Cozens-Hardy defeated him by more than five thousand votes.[45] Like his father, he rarely spoke in the Commons, and within less than two years he succeeded to the title, and entered the House of Lords. There was talk that he might go out to India (his daughter was married to Frederick Bailey, a member of the Indian Political Service), either as Chief Justice of Bengal or as a provincial governor, but nothing came of either idea.[46]

In any case, Cozens-Hardy's promising public career was cut short before it ever really took off. In May 1924 he was killed when his car overturned at Buchhor, near Starnberg, in upper Bavaria, some twenty miles from Munich. The funeral and interment were at Gunthorpe, and a second memorial tablet was placed on the south wall of Letheringsett church.[47] Since the second lord's daughter was his only child, the title, so recently acquired, could not pass directly on. Within six years Raven Cozens-Hardy, the heir to the family estates, and William Cozens-Hardy, the heir to the family peerage, had both been killed. The man who should have been leader of the family clan, and the man who might have followed him, were both dead. But the descendants of William Hardy Cozens-Hardy were numerous. It is time to introduce Caroline, his eldest daughter, and Theobald, his third son. Their appearance leads us away from Letheringsett, the land and the brewery, and brings us to the Colman connection, to Norwich, and – perhaps unexpectedly – to newspapers.

III

Caroline Cozens-Hardy was born in 1831, and was the eldest of the nine children of William Hardy Cozens-Hardy and his wife, Sarah. She was a woman of strong character, radical political views, great intellectual curiosity, and deep religious convictions. She was also devoted to the countryside around Letheringsett, and possessed a powerful sense of family loyalty.[48] In 1856 she married Jeremiah James Colman, thereby linking the Cozens-Hardys with what was soon to become the greatest mercantile dynasty in Norwich. One forebear, Jeremiah Colman, had founded the family mustard firm, while another, also named Jeremiah, served as Mayor of Norwich in 1846–7. It was under Jeremiah James that the family and the firm established their pre-eminent position in the city. He moved the business to Carrow, on the outskirts of Norwich, and by the end of the nineteenth century it was employing more than two thousand workers. He became a member of the town council, served as Sheriff (1862–3) and as Mayor (1867–8), and from 1871 to 1895 was Liberal MP. He spoke rarely in parliament, but his close connections with the senior members of the party, his high-minded philanthropy and his religious zeal meant he was a formidable figure in Liberal counsels. In 1893 he refused a baronetcy from Gladstone, but accepted the honorary freedom of Norwich, when Liberals and Conservatives alike paid tribute to his 'eminent public services to the city, [his] unostentatious generosity, and [his] estimable private life'.[49]

Compared to the Cozens-Hardys, the Colmans were richer, more vigorous, more plutocratic, and more in the public eye. But Caroline made the transition from Letheringsett to Norwich, and from land to business, with relative ease. She took a leading part in the paternalist administration of the Carrow works, superintending the day and Sunday schools, the Home for Girls, the medical staff and the kitchens. Along with her husband, she became a regular attender at the Princes Street Congregational Church, where Sydney Cozens-Hardy also worshipped. Yet she remained in touch with Letheringsett ('the old and ever dear home'), and was particularly close to her brother Herbert, who became a trustee of the Carrow pension scheme.[50] She also brought up six children. The eldest surviving son was Russell James Colman, who became a partner in the family company and followed his father as Sheriff (1893) and Mayor (1901–2) of Norwich. In addition, he was Lord Lieutenant of Norfolk from 1929 to 1944, and chairman of the County Council from 1925 to 1941. Equally remarkable were his two unmarried sisters, Ethel and Florence, who were both involved in the Carrow works, and in civic and county philanthropy. In 1923 Ethel was the first woman Lord Mayor of the City, and Florence served as her Lady Mayoress.[51]

One of Jeremiah James Colman's most important political contributions was the extensive financial support he gave to the Liberal press. From the early 1870s, he had been the driving force behind a syndicate of Norwich businessmen, who owned what eventually became the Norfolk News Company. Its purpose was to diseminate throughout the region the Liberal principles of 'civil, religious and commercial freedom', and after an uncertain start its most important newspaper soon became the *Eastern Daily Press*. Later, in the 1880s, Colman collaborated with John Brunner, another Liberal plutocrat, to buy the London *Star* from T.P.O'Connor, so as to establish it as an advanced evening paper for the metropolis. Finally, in 1892, he put up the money for the halfpenny *Morning Leader*, begun as a daily companion to the Liberal evening *Star*. By the mid 1890s, Colman was in direct control of all three newspapers: he was chairman of the Norfolk News Company; he had installed his son-in-law, James Stuart, as chairman of the *Star*; and he made his Norwich partner, Frederick Wilson, the managing director of the *Morning Leader*.[52]

It was this accumulation of proprietorial power by their most illustrious in-law which facilitated the entry of two members of the younger generation of Cozens-Hardys into the newspaper world, at the very time when popular journalism was on the brink of its first great expansion. The connecting link was Theobald, the third son of William Hardy Cozens-Hardy. On his father's death, he inherited Oak Lodge, the only part of the Sprowston estate which did not go under the hammer, and he spent his life quietly as a suburban country gentleman, devoting himself to public works in a high-minded and selfless way. He was a JP for Norfolk, a member of his local Board of Guardians for more than forty years, and one of the first aldermen of the County Council. He was a generous benefactor to local charities, and was an active President of the East Norfolk Liberal Association. Unlike his brothers Herbert and Sydney, he seems never to have worked for a living; but his regularity of attendance at meetings of the County Council and the Board of Guardians was legendary, as was his mastery of the business, and it was rumoured that he had never in his life read a novel, entered a theatre, or played cards.[53] By the time he died in 1910, his two sons were both established as successful journalists on the Colman papers.

The first, and more important, was Archibald Cozens-Hardy, who went directly from school to join the *Eastern Daily Press* in 1888, and two years later joined the London *Star*, which was then edited by H.W. Massingham. In 1897, when not yet thirty, he was brought back to Norwich as the third editor of the *Eastern Daily Press*, a position which he continued to occupy for the next forty years, thus becoming the longest-serving editor of any major British newspaper. (At the same time, Russell Colman, Archibald's cousin, followed his father as chairman of the board of Norfolk News from 1899 to 1945.) During the 1900s, he moved the paper from its antiquated accommodation in Museum Street to new printing works in Exchange Street, equipped with the very latest machinery; he changed the layout, expanded the coverage, and introduced photographs; he opened branch offices throughout the region; and he utilised the motor-car to ensure that the paper reached the remotest districts. A short-lived challenge from a rival Conservative newspaper, the *Eastern Morning Gazette*, was easily beaten off; by 1914, the *EDP* was established as the foremost paper in the county; and in the following year, Archibald was elected president of the Newspaper Society.[54]

During the war years, he had to deal with the problems arising from the shortages of staff and supplies, and in the 1930s he struggled hard to sustain the quality and coverage of the paper, despite the fall in advertising revenues consequent upon the slump.[55] He fended off a take-over bid from Lord Rothermere in 1928, and shortly afterwards the Norfolk News Company was reorganised, when he himself joined the board, the first employee ever to do so. The 1930s witnessed a succession of political crises at home and abroad, accompanied by the Silver Jubilee and death of George V, the abdication of Edward VIII, and the Coronation of George VI. For a newspaper editor, these were demanding and stirring times. 'I took up my appointment', he observed at the farewell dinner in his honour, 'a few days before the Diamond Jubilee of Queen Victoria. I retired a few weeks after the Coronation of her great-grandson. What an eventful chapter of English history has been recorded in the newspapers during these forty years.' He forbore from adding that during that period the circulation of the *EDP* had increased five-fold.[56]

Like most members of his family, Archibald Cozens-Hardy was a staunch Liberal, and so experienced no difficulty in maintaining the traditional outlook of the paper from the Boer War to 1914. Indeed, he followed his father as president of the East Norfolk Liberal Association, and played a major part in recruiting acceptable candidates for the constituency. But by the inter-war years he had come to recognise that the party of Gladstone and Asquith was dead, and in the 1930s he followed the example set by Sir John Simon, and became a supporter of the National Government 'without reservation'.[57] 'This is', he wrote in 1934, 'a Liberal National paper' – in favour of the government's policy towards India, and strongly commited to the policy of appeasement, because 'a European War must be averted at all costs'. One result of this change in the political spectrum was that he became a friend of Sir Samuel Hoare, 'a Norfolk man of whom every Norfolk man is proud'.[58] In an earlier generation, Sam Hoare's father had fought Archibald Cozens-Hardy's uncle Herbert for the possession of North Norfolk at the general election of 1885; but now they found themselves in close political harmony, and in 1937, when he was Home Secretary in the National Government, Hoare went down to Norwich and made a touching and teasing speech at Cozens-Hardy's retirement dinner.[59]

Yet Archibald was too high-minded, too public-spirited, and too judicial (that word was often used to describe him), to regard his paper as a partisan vehicle of political propaganda. He abhorred sensationalism, was more interested in news than in comment, and left the writing of leading articles to others. His constant aim was to 'give fair play to all three parties', and it was generally recognised that he did so. When appointing new journalists, he always insisted on 'accuracy, promptness and impartiality', and failure to observe these rules invariably earned a withering editorial rebuke.[60] Cozens-Hardy drove his staff hard: but he drove himself even harder. He worked ten hours a day, six days a week, was never ill, and took only three weeks' holiday a year. In addition to editing the *Eastern Daily Press*, he was manager and secretary of the Norfolk News Company, and he also exercised general editorial control over the evening and weekly papers. On his retirement as editor, he continued as a director of Norfolk News until his death. As in any Colman enterprise, the management style was – in both senses – strictly paternal: the staff were called 'company servants', there was a strong ethos of family loyalty, and long-serving employees were appropriately rewarded.[61]

This long-borne burden of punishing work would have exhausted any ordinary man; but Archibald Cozens-Hardy simultaneously carved out a

second, and no less demanding, career in public service and county administration. As a young man, he had been present at the first meeting of
Norfolk County Council in 1889; in 1915 he was himself elected as
member for Sprowston; and he later became an alderman. Every Saturday,
having finished his work at the Norfolk News Company, he went round
to the Shirehall to begin his next round of labours. From 1923 until 1948
he was chairman of the Finance Committee, during which time he presented 26 budgets and missed only one meeting. His budget speeches were
models of clarity and lucidity, and were regarded as one of the highlights
of the county council year: not for nothing was he known as Norfolk's
'Chancellor of the Exchequer'.[62] This was not the only hat he wore in
county administration. In 1924, he helped to found the Norfolk library
system, and for seventeen years he was chairman of the Library Committee.
Indeed, by the end of his time at the Shirehall, there was scarcely a
committee on which he had not sat – or had not chaired. He retired from
the County Council in 1955 after an unbroken contribution of forty years,
his span of public service exactly matching his time as editor of the *Eastern
Daily Press*.[63]

Beyond doubt, Archibald Cozens-Hardy was a man of remarkable
energy and stamina, and was rightly described in his eightieth year as 'one
of the best-known, albeit one of the most modest, public figures in the
county'.[64] According to his own exacting standards, he was selfless, high-
minded, public-spirited and incorruptible. Yet he was also the greatest
beneficiary in his family of the Colman connection, which stood him in
good stead at the Norfolk News Company and on the County Council,
since his cousin Russell Colman was for much of the time the chairman of
both organisations. Not surprisingly, then, his funeral in 1957 was one
of the great public occasions of post-war Norfolk life. The Bishop of
Norwich preached the sermon; the Colmans and Cozens-Hardys turned
out in force; the directors and employees of the Norfolk News Company
paid their last respects; the Lord Lieutenant of Norfolk and the chairman of
the County Council were both present; and the Lord Mayor, the Sheriff
and the town clerk of Norwich sent their representatives. Perhaps among
the mourners there were some who recalled Sam Hoare's speech in 1937:
Archibald Cozens-Hardy, he had then observed, was 'first and foremost . . .
a Norfolk man'.[65]

By contrast, his younger brother, Henry ('Harry') Theobald Cozens-
Hardy began his career at the *Eastern Daily Press* in 1890, then exchanged
places with Archibald at the *Star* in 1897, both moves, as he later freely
admitted, being the result of the benevolent intervention of Jeremiah James
Colman.[66] Thereafter, he lived the bachelor life of a man about town, and
covered such momentous events as the San Francisco earthquake, the
Titanic disaster and the General Strike. The fruits of his experience were
garnered in permanent form in his book, *The Glorious Years*, which was

sub-titled, 'Random recollections of prominent persons in parliament, in literature, and on and off the platform, on the playing fields and in the pulpit, the prize ring and the press, recaptured in London, Paris and New York between 1897 and 1952.' It was an apt summary, of a book – and a career – which seem oddly frivolous compared with Archibald's varied, energetic and public-spirited endeavours. 'My brother Harry', he once remarked, perhaps a touch censoriously, '. . . enjoys London life more than I should do.'[67]

IV

The first and second Lords Cozens-Hardy moved between Norfolk and London. Archibald Cozens-Hardy, more modestly, but also more effectively, straddled Norfolk and Norwich. And this connection between county and city was further consolidated by Sydney Cozens-Hardy and his son, Basil. Sydney was the youngest child of William Hardy Cozens-Hardy of Letheringsett, and was born in 1850. It was originally intended that he should become the manager of the local brewery, but he preferred to follow what had by this time become the family tradition, and go into the law. He trained as a solicitor, first in Norwich, then in London, spent six months in his elder brother's chambers, and qualified in 1873. He was never attracted by London, and decided that Norwich, where he had 'the advantage of a name', was the place where he would establish himself. He settled at Bracondale, near the Colman mustard works at Carrow, and stayed in close touch with his much-loved sister Caroline. In 1877, he moved into splendid offices in Opie Street, financed by a loan from his brother Herbert, and designed by Edward Boardman, a relative by marriage. He rapidly acquired important clients in the city and the county, and in 1892 went into partnership with Frank Jewson, scion of another of the city's great and governing families. It was from this solid professional base that he launched himself into the public and political life of the region.[68]

Much of Sydney Cozens-Hardy's work was done in Norwich itself, beginning in 1875, when at the age of only twenty-three he became clerk to the Norwich School Board, which effectively made him responsible for superintending the provision of elementary education in the city, and he held the appointment until the Board was abolished in 1903. Shortly before that, in 1900–1, he served as Sheriff of the City, and was thus called on to fulfill various ceremonial duties in connection with the death of Queen Victoria and the accession of King Edward VII. Nine years later there was strong pressure on him to become the city's first Lord Mayor but, being in receipt of a pension from the Council as compensation for the loss of his job as clerk to the School Board, he was deemed to be ineligible. In the same year, 1909, he became a JP for the City, and in 1918 he was appointed solicitor to the Norwich Union Insurance Company.[69] Not surprisingly, he once observed that he had drafted more minutes of meetings than any other man in Norwich, and most of them were in connection with two very important city charities.

In 1880, when still barely thirty, he was appointed clerk of what was known as the Norwich Municipal Charities (General List), the chairman of which was his brother-in-law, Jeremiah James Colman.[70] This family influence no doubt helped, but since the Charity was responsible for providing alms and education for the poor, Cozens-Hardy's experience on the School Board also made him the obvious choice. Throughout the 1880s, the NMC was involved in a long-running battle with the Charity Commissioners, who sought to alter the terms under which it was administered, by diverting its funds from the children of the deserving poor to the middle classes. Cozens-Hardy was in the thick of the fight to prevent this, and gave detailed evidence to the Select Committee on the Endowed Schools Act in 1886, of which his elder brother Herbert was a sympathetic member.[71] Eventually, in 1892, new terms were agreed, reaffirming the principle that the money should be distributed to those in need, but also widening the terms under which such disbursements could be made. In 1910, the NMC was absorbed into what became known as the Norwich Consolidated Charities, and Cozens-Hardy continued as clerk until 1934, thus serving uninterruptedly for 54 years.[72]

During the 1880s another important city charity was also in turmoil: the Norwich Town Close Estate. It owned one hundred acres of land to the south of the city, between the Ipswich and the Newmarket Roads, which was gradually being developed from the 1850s as a fashionable, exclusive, high-class residential suburb. Between 1882 and 1892 there was a protracted legal battle between the Corporation and the freemen of Norwich, as to who owned it, who administered it, and who should benefit from its revenues. This was eventually resolved in favour of the freemen, but only on condition that the administration was placed in the hands of independent trustees, most of whom were also on the board of the Municipal Charities.[73] Once again, Sydney Cozens-Hardy became the clerk, responsible for administering a disposable income which rose from £650 in 1914 to £2000 in 1928. Instead of being given exclusively to deserving freemen, as had been the case before 1892, a large portion of it was now distributed to their children, once again for educational purposes. This job, also, Sydney held until 1934, and when he retired he wrote a brief history of Norwich Charities: A Retrospect, 1880–1934.[74]

Like most members of his family, Sydney Cozens-Hardy was a staunch and active Liberal, and he worked hard, in Norwich and in North Norfolk, to ensure the return of candidates (who in both cases were his close relations).[75] In 1880 he was the agent for Jeremiah James Colman in Norwich, and successfully ran a campaign which was remarkably uncorrupt by the standards of Norwich elections. After he ceased to be clerk to the School Board, he became active in city politics once more, serving as president of the Norwich Liberal Association, and playing a major part in the selection of candidates. During the intervening years, he turned his attention to the new constituency of North Norfolk, which his elder brother Herbert represented from 1885 to 1899. He was not only joint secretary of the Liberal Association, but also unpaid election agent, and the unshakeable hold which Herbert soon exerted on the seat owed much to Sydney's indefatigable organising efforts.[76] He continued to serve as secretary of the Liberal Association until the end of the First World War, and in 1909–10, when a new candidate had to be chosen, was responsible for healing the rift between two rival factions. It was even suggested that he might put his own name forward, and the position would probably have been his for the taking: but he steadfastly refused to do so.

Throughout his life, religious endeavour was at least as important to Sydney as his Liberal activism, and here again he worked in both the city and the county.[77] He had been brought up at Letheringsett in a pious nonconformist atmosphere; he never smoked or drank alcohol; prayers were held at his home every morning; and the Sabbath was strictly observed. He taught Sunday school at the Carrow works for many years, he supported the building of nonconformist churches in Norwich, he was Chairman of the Norfolk Congregational Union in 1902, he was treasurer and secretary of the Norfolk Protestant Dissenters' Society for forty four years, and he was an ardent temperance worker all his life. Although brought up as a member of the Holt Methodist Chapel, he attended Princes' Street Congregational Church after he had taken up residence in Norwich, and became a pillar of the community. He was a Deacon for 64 years, treasurer for 45, and played a major part in supporting and choosing new ministers. In 1875, he had resolved to give a tenth of his income each year to charities, and he kept that resolve all his life – later increasing the amount to fifteen per cent.

Like his nephew Archibald, Sydney Cozens-Hardy was an indefatigable worker in both the city and the county. His professional ambitions, and the Colman connection, drew him to Norwich; but his brother's political career, and the lure of Letheringsett, drew him back to the country. The Colman house at Bracondale, which he rented for 60 years without a written tenancy agreement, was the base for his operations in Norwich. In 1901 he moved into the Mill House at Letheringsett, which he re-named Glavenside, after the river which ran through the garden. The house was extended, to designs by Thomas Boardman, and with the help of his wife Jessie he created one of the loveliest small gardens in the county, complete with bowling green, boathouse and ornamental lake. One especial source of pleasure was that his elder brother, Herbert, was now often in residence at the Hall nearby.[78] From 1910 to 1936, Sydney was chairman of the Letheringsett Parish Council, and he regularly opened the garden at Glavenside to organised visits from the Carrow works. His health was never robust, but in 1932 he celebrated his Golden Wedding, and in the following year his Diamond Jubilee as a Norwich solicitor, both events being amply covered by Archibald in the *Eastern Daily Press*. He continued to work almost to the end of his life, and in July 1940, at the age of ninety, contributed an article entitled 'From Crimean to Boer War: Recollections from 1856 to 1905'. He died two years later.[79]

To a remarkable degree, Sydney's city-and-county career was replicated in that of his eldest son, Basil Cozens-Hardy, who inherited Glavenside on his father's death, and divided his time between Letheringsett and a house in Albemarle Road, Norwich.[80] He served articles with Sydney, qualified as a solicitor in 1911, joined the family firm in the same year, and eventually became senior partner. As an Oxford undergraduate, he had been a noted sportsman, but he lost his right leg on active service in the First World War. This never prevented him from cycling to work, and he displayed throughout his life the same prodigious energy as his father, many of whose duties he came to assume. In 1934, Basil succeeded Sydney as clerk to the Norwich Consolidated Charities, and to the Norwich Town Close Estate Charity, holding both jobs for nearly thirty years. He was the Sunday school superintendent at Princes Street Chapel, sat briefly as a Liberal on the City Council between 1920 and 1925, and followed his father as Sheriff in 1936, when he had to announce the death of King George V and the accession of King Edward VIII. He was also a Deputy Lieutenant for the County, a director of the Norwich Union Insurance Society, and was an active supporter of the Norfolk Territorial Force Association.[81]

The only area of endeavour where Basil did not follow his father, after his brief spell on the city council, was into party politics. Instead, he devoted his spare time to local history. In 1919 he joined the Norfolk and Norwich Archaeological Society, and within three years had been elected excursion chairman. In 1928 he became general secretary, in 1947 treasurer, and in 1956 vice-president. He was involved in every aspect of the Society's work, and in forty years, scarcely missed a meeting. But, as one who 'disliked the platform and prominence which office gives', he resolutely refused to let himself be elected president, and instead was made the Society's first honorary life fellow.[82] In 1922 he had been the moving spirit behind the establishment of the Norfolk Archaeological Trust, and in the same year he joined the Church Advisory Committee set up by the Bishop. In 1924 he had begun to supervise the national scheduling of the county's ancient monuments, and it was largely thanks to his zeal that more were scheduled for Norfolk than any other county. In 1929 he helped to found the Norfolk Record Society, of which he was chairman from 1933 to 1973. In recognition of this work, he was elected a Fellow of the Society of Antiquaries in 1931.[83]

These were only the administrative aspects of his passion for the past. Throughout his long life he poured out a succession of articles, pamphlets and edited books, all of them concerned with the history of the county and the city.[84] Some were works of family piety, like the edited version of the diary of Mary Hardy, the wife of William Hardy I. Some were about places which he knew well, like Letheringsett, Cley, the Holt Road and the Glaven Valley. Some reflected his own professional background, such as the work on sixteenth-century Norwich Consistory Court Depositions, and his essay on Norfolk lawyers. Some were about the history of Norfolk nonconformity, especially during the Civil War years, as in his studies of churches and chapels in Guestwick, Yarmouth and Norwich. Some were based on the Blickling Manuscripts, deposited by Lord Lothian at the Norfolk Record Office, including his edited edition of the Norfolk Lieutenancy Journal. Most of them were concerned with printing documents, or evoking the history of a building or a place. There was no conceptual framework beyond the history, archaeology and topography of Norfolk – but the resulting thirty articles and seven books would put an averagely active academic historian to shame.

While Archibald Cozens-Hardy led the citizens of Norwich and the people of Norfolk through the present in the columns of the *Eastern Daily Press*, his cousin Basil was an equally sure-footed guide to the past in the journals of county history. As a local historian and Norfolk antiquarian, he yielded pride of place in his generation to Robert Wyndham Ketton-Cremer of Felbrigg; but in Basil's case this work was all accomplished in the few idle moments of a prodigiously busy life. Like his father, Sydney, and like his cousin, Archibald, he was a man of remarkable stamina and longevity. Well into his eighties, he still appeared regularly at the offices of Cozens-Hardy and Jewson in Opie Street, and continued to pour out articles for the Norfolk Archaeological Society. As he observed on his ninetieth birthday, 'I never spend an idle hour.'[85] By then, he had turned his attention to writing the history of his family, in which he himself had played so significant a part. Regrettably, he died before he had completed it. It is now time to draw this version of that history to a close, by returning to the Letheringsett estate, and to the Cozens-Hardy peerage, and by taking up that story where it had been left off, in the early 1920s.

v

The first Lord Cozens-Hardy produced two sons and two daughters. We have already met the first son, William Hepburn, who inherited the title in 1920, and who died in a car crash four years later. The second son, Edward Herbert Cozens-Hardy, was born in 1873, and set out to make his own career as an electrical engineer, thus following in the footsteps of such mechanically-minded aristocrats as the Hon C.S. Rolls and Lord Montagu of Beaulieu. After Rugby School, he served his apprenticeship with the Brush Electrical Engineering Company of Loughborough, and in 1898 he went into partnership with Mervyn O'Gorman. They set themselves up as consulting electrical engineers in Victoria Street, London, and one of their most important commissions was to superintend the installation of electrical equipment for the Norfolk News Company when it moved offices in 1902. Four years later Edward married his cousin, Gladys Lily, elder daughter of Arthur Wrigley Cozens-Hardy. In 1918, scarcely a year after the death of Raven Cozens-Hardy at the front, Edward bought the Letheringsett estate from Raven's father, Arthur Wrigley.[86] Then, six years later, on the unexpected death of his elder brother, Edward became the third Lord Cozens-Hardy. Quite by chance, the family estate and the family title had been brought together, and a new head of the clan had thus emerged.

As such, Edward was the first Lord Cozens-Hardy actually to own the Letheringsett estate; but it was no longer the patrimony his forebears had known. The five hundred acres at Sprowston had been sold in 1896, and the Cley Hall property eventually passed to Gladys Lily's sister, Helen Maguire. By the early 1920s, the Letheringsett estate amounted to scarcely one thousand acres, and the farms and cottages were yielding less than £1000 a year, while total expenditure on the estate, the mansion and the interest on mortgages was almost four times as much. As agricultural prices plummetted after the brief post-war boom, rentals were reduced during the early 1930s by fifty per cent. For much of the 1920s, Letheringsett Hall was let, its annual rental of £525 providing a much-needed boost to the estate's income.[87] As a display of family piety, the purchase of Letheringsett by the future third Lord Cozens-Hardy was easily understandable, but he was able to keep the estate going during the inter-war years only because he enjoyed a considerable private income as a successful businessman. This, in turn, was the result of another unusual marriage: that of his younger sister, Hope Cozens-Hardy, to Austin Pilkington, in 1903.

The Pilkingtons, who manufactured glass at St Helens, Lancashire, were a dynasty remarkably like the Colmans: self-made, nonconformist, paternalistic, very clannish, and exceptionally public-spirited. (Only in politics did the two families differ: William Pilkington had refused a baronetcy from Lord Salisbury in the same decade that Jeremiah James Colman had turned down a similar offer from Gladstone.) Austin Pilkington was a director of the family firm, but in 1907 he contracted tuberculosis, and two years later he was sent to North America to recuperate. The vacancy temporarily created on the board was filled by his Cozens-Hardy brother-in-law.[88] As such, the appointment may best be described as nepotism tempered by merit: Edward knew nothing about glass-making, but he had already been employed by Pilkingtons to advise on the electrification of their Cowley Hill factory, and he now settled down to a full-time career in the family business. By the 1920s, when his brother-in-law Austin returned as chairman, he was much involved in development on the manufacturing side, and he also travelled extensively in Europe, Russia, America and Australia, conducting delicate negotiations with other companies, with potential customers, and with subsidiary undertakings.

It was during the 1930s that the third Lord Cozens-Hardy made his greatest impact on the company. The generation to which Austin Pilkington belonged lacked the vigour and stamina of their predecessors, and in 1931 both Austin and his brother Cecil resigned. The 1920s had been a disappointing decade for the company, and this, combined with the world depression, had led to a sudden fall in profits, and a drastic reduction in dividends.[89] At the same time, it was widely believed that the structure of management, which was essentially unchanged since the late nineteenth century, was in urgent need of reform. As the senior family director, it fell to Cozens-Hardy to grapple with these problems. He created a new executive committee, to be responsible for the day to day running of the company, which consisted only of active directors, each of whom were charged with particular tasks. Cozens-Hardy not only chaired the executive committee from 1931 to 1939: he also took charge of the key departments concerning costs and finance. As a result, he became much the most powerful figure in the company, and the improved performance of Pilkingtons during the 1930s owed much to his efforts. In 1939 he retired as an executive director, but he remained on the board for the rest of his life.[90]

From the broader standpoint of the Cozens-Hardys' family history, it was this Pilkington connection which made it possible for the third lord to keep and maintain the Letheringsett estate. In 1920 Pilkingtons directors were paid £2500 a year; in 1925 the amount was raised to £4500. Moreover, these sums were free of income tax (though not of surtax), and there were additional bonuses, as well as dividends from shares in the company, all of which were still in the hands of the family. During the early 1930s Cozens-Hardy was diverting nearly £3000 a year from his Pilkington earnings to the Letheringsett estate: only by this means could the accounts be balanced.[91] This was clearly a strain on his resources: in 1922 he had been forced to sell 3000 Pilkington shares so as to reduce his own overdraft, and in the late 1940s the Letheringsett estate account was heavily overdrawn. Despite his lengthy and important services to Pilkingtons, he never became a particularly wealthy man. In 1950 he made over the majority of the Letheringsett estate to his son, retaining only the house and 55 acres.[92] When he died in 1956, he left a decidedly meagre sum: £58,000 gross, much less than either Archibald (£78,732) or Basil (£226,622).

For the thirty years that he worked at Pilkingtons, the third Lord Cozens-Hardy was a full-time businessman, the very antithesis of those titled, 'guinea-pig' directors who sat on company boards but played no part in company affairs. And so, for thirty years, he was also a full-time resident of St Helens – a smoky industrial town, with a damp, bronchitic and rheumatic climate. He had little leisure, and little freedom, and this inevitably meant he was an absentee from Letheringsett. Like many an impoverished inter-war landowner, the only way he could hang on to his estate was by going into business, which meant cutting himself off from the very thing he wished to preserve.[93] Insofar as a family presence was maintained in the village, it was through Sydney and Basil at Glavenside. Meanwhile, in what spare time he had, the third lord played the kind of part in the affairs of Lancashire that his forebears had played in the affairs of Norfolk. He was a JP and a Deputy Lieutenant, chairman of Huyton College and a member of the Council of Liverpool University, and extensively involved in the administration of local voluntary hospitals, serving for ten years as the first chairman of the Merseyside Hospital Council.[94]

Only on his retirement from business in 1939 did the third lord return to Letheringsett, take up full-time residence in the Hall, and re-establish himself in the life of the village and the county. He became a JP for Norfolk, and followed his father and his grandfather on to the Holt bench, of which he was for a time vice-chairman. He became a governor of Gresham's School, and chairman of the Letheringsett Parish Council. In 1950, the year he made over most of the estate to his son so as to avoid death duties, he retired from the bench, resigned from the Liberal Party, and joined the Conservatives (though since he took no active part in politics, this scarcely mattered). On his death, six years later, a memorial service was held at St Helens' Parish Church. But the funeral was held at Letheringsett, and the Pilkingtons and the Cozens-Hardys were there in force. The Bishop of Norwich described the third lord as a man who took 'a keen interest in all that concerned the social and personal needs of the people among whom he lived'. A memorial tablet was placed alongside those of his two predecessors in Letheringsett church, and his widow continued to live in the Hall, sustained by a Pilkington pension, until her death in 1975 at the age of ninety.[95]

The third lord's only son was Herbert Arthur Cozens-Hardy, known as Peter, who was born in 1907, the year before his father became a director of Pilkingtons. After Winchester and Worcester College, Oxford, he, too, set out on a business career. He spent three years as a trainee at Colmans in Norwich, and in 1932 joined Pilkingtons. His father had been put on the board immediately, but Peter was subjected to five years' heavy probationary training before he became an executive director.[96] He took a close interest in welfare and personnel matters, and during the Second World War organised the firm's civil defence, but he was never as significant a figure in the affairs of the company as his father had been. The new generation of Pilkingtons were more vigorous and innovative than their inter-war predecessors, especially Lord (Harry) Pilkington and Sir Alastair Pilkington. From 1947 to 1965 the chairman of the executive committee was Douglas Phelps, who had married the fourth lord's sister, Helen Rosemary Cozens-Hardy. As Pilkington's expanded into a multi-national, public company, under such dynamic leadership, Peter Cozens-Hardy was too self-effacing to be highly profiled in its affairs. He continued as an executive director until 1967, and retired from the Board in 1971.[97]

Like his father, the fourth lord took up residence near the Pilkington works, and devoted his leisure hours to public work in Lancashire. He was a JP and Deputy Lieutenant for the County. He was chairman of the Prescot Magistrates and of the Lancashire Magistrates Court Committee, president of the Lancashire Royal Agricultural Society, chairman of the Huyton College School Committee, a life governor of Liverpool College, and a lay member of the Liverpool Cathedral Finance Committee. He was also a member of the executive committee of the Order of St John. But unlike his father, Peter Cozens-Hardy never returned to Letheringsett, or established himself in the life of Norfolk. He outlived his mother by only three months, and died in Lancashire. The *Eastern Daily Press* gave his death (and his life) scarcely a mention, and his funeral at Letheringsett was much less of a Norfolk or a family occasion than those of Archibald, Basil or his own father.[98] Only with his memorial tablet in Letheringsett Church did the fourth Lord Cozens-Hardy truly come home.

VI

Clearly, there is a limit to the generalisations that can be supported or undermined on the basis of one family's history – even when the family possessed, as the Cozens-Hardys most certainly did, a powerful sense of dynastic pride and collective identity, which was further reinforced by the importance of, and by the opportunities which resulted from, the Colman connection. 'There are no friendships', Caroline Colman once wrote to one of her brothers, 'so deep and true and lasting as one's own immediate circle, one's own kith and kin'; and that was a view which, across the generations, most of her relatives seem to have shared.[99] Hence the close collaboration at election time between brothers, sisters, cousins and in-laws, not just in the 1880s when Herbert Cozens-Hardy stood for Parliament, but on into the 1930s, when Ethel Colman lent her car, which 'helped to swell the majority' of Mary Cozens-Hardy (the sister of Archibald and Harry), who was elected to the county council. Hence the many commemorative biographies, filled with letters and exhortatory conclusions, which were produced with such pietistic frequency; and hence Archibald Cozens-Hardy's reply to Basil, who had proposed bringing some of his children to see the offices of the *Eastern Daily Press* in

January 1935: 'we shall be glad to show the rising generation round our works'.[100]

Nevertheless, there are many broader historical themes which the history of the Cozens-Hardys richly illuminates: the close links between the brewing industry and the land; the purchase and consolidation of a country estate by a radical, dissenting and upwardly mobile entrepreneur;[101] the subsequent shifts from Liberalism to Conservatism, from nonconformity to established religion, and from party politics at Westminster to non-partisan public service in the county; the urgent need, from the late nineteenth century, to find alternative sources of non-agricultural income; and the eventual decline and dispersal of the family estate. There is also much to be learned about some of the more obscure corners of modern British history: the interdependency of landownership and the law; the varied activities of younger sons and more distant relatives; the ease with which patricians might move into business or industry of a certain type; and the strong connections that might exist between the country and the town, agriculture and industry, the rural and the urban elites.[102] No doubt Norwich and Norfolk were very different from Birmingham and Warwickshire, and the degree of inter-penetration in East Anglia may have been unusually high. But it is certainly a subject deserving of more extensive investigation than it has hitherto received.

Be that as it may, the urban patriciate of Norwich and the rural elite of Norfolk are no longer as influentially interlinked as they were in the heyday of the Cozens-Hardys. Norfolk may still be in some ways an aristocratic county, but Basil Cozens-Hardy lived long enough to lament the demise of many of its greater and lesser houses, and its invasion by 'petrol pumps and stucco'.[103] The Buxtons, the Gurneys, the Hoares and the Colmans survive, but they do not dominate the public and political life of the city or the county in the way they once did. The growing complexity of county administration, and demands for more openness in government, mean it is not now possible for anyone to emulate the remarkable dual career of Archibald Cozens-Hardy. And the massive proliferation of legal work means that no one today could be both a solicitor and an antiquarian in the way that Basil Cozens-Hardy was. The small, local, closely-knit world, in which a few liberal, disinterested and public-spirited men could do many things, is no longer what it was.

Nor are the Cozens-Hardys the force they once were, either in the city or the county. The fourth lord was the last of the line, and after only three generations the title is now extinct. Cozens-Hardy and Jewson continue as one of Norwich's most esteemed firms of solicitors: but since Basil's death no member of the founding family has been involved with its affairs. (The son who he hoped might follow him was killed in the Second World War.) Letheringsett Hall still stands, but it is no longer occupied by the family, and on the death of the fourth baron it became a nursing home. Glavenside is still lived in by one of Basil's descendants, but it is now a guest house, offering bed and breakfast.[104] As for the Letheringsett estate: the fourth lord left it to his nephew, John Edward Vandeleur Phelps, and when he came of age he sold it outright.[105] In Norwich and Norfolk, London and Lancashire, a family that made history and recorded history has now very largely ceased to do either. All that remain are the monuments in Letheringsett Church, and John Betjeman's fanciful but evocative poem:

> Oh Lord Cozens-Hardy
>   Your mausoleum is cold,
> The dry brown grass is brittle
>   And frozen hard the mould
> And where those Grecian columns rise
>   So white among the dark
> Of yew trees and of hollies in
>   That corner of the park
> By Norfolk oaks surrounded
>   Whose branches seem to talk,
> I know, Lord Cozens-Hardy,
>   I would not like to walk.
>
> And even in the summer,
>   On a bright East Anglian day
> When round your Doric portico
>   Your children's children play
> There's something in the stillness
>   And our waiting eyes are drawn
> From the butler and the footman
>   Bringing tea out on the lawn,
> From the little silver spirit lamp
>   That burns so blue and still,
> To the half-seen mausoleum
>   In the oak trees on the hill.
>
> But when, Lord Cozens-Hardy,
>   November, stars are bright,
> And the King's Head Inn at Letheringsett
>   Is shutting for the night,
> The villagers have told me
>   That they do not like to pass
> Near your curious mausoleum
>   Moon-shadowed on the grass
> For fear of seeing walking
>   In the season of All Souls
> That first Lord Cozens-Hardy
>   The Master of the Rolls.[106]

9

Portrait of More Than a Marriage

Harold Nicolson and Vita Sackville-West Revisited

HAROLD NICOLSON and Vita Sackville-West were two very remarkable people; but that is no reason for regarding them as having been more remarkable than they actually were. Yet since their deaths – she in 1962, he in 1968 – they have received an excessive amount of deferential attention and ahistorical celebration, especially from the 'bedint' bourgeoisie, the very class of people that they themselves most despised. They have been more biographied than many of their greater contemporaries.[1] Their diaries and letters have been published and re-published at indulgent length.[2] Their private lives have been described and televised in excessive and sometimes prurient detail.[3] Their books – especially hers – have been analysed in defiance of contemporary critical opinion that she had a 'pen of brass' and that he was incorrigibly 'superficial'.[4] Their garden at Sissinghurst has been incorporated into that cult of snobbish nostalgia and conservation-ist escapism by which so much of post-war Britain has been blinded and blighted.[5] The result, as one reviewer recently complained, is that 'Vita and Harold' have come to offer 'voyeuristic frissons for bourgeois have-nots', frissons which turn out to be little more than 'the surrogate erotics of a history of upper-class possessiveness and possessions'.[6]

This may be putting things a little harshly. But it cannot be denied that while the mass of published material conveys (and all too often merely repeats) a great deal of fascinating personal information, it provides little by way of accompanying comment, critical analysis, or historical context. Indeed, the very fact that the couple are so often referred to as 'Vita and Harold' is indicative of the cosy immunity which they seem to enjoy, and of the specious familiarity with which they are widely regarded. To some degree, this also reflects the important part played in guarding and fashion-ing their posthumous reputations by their son, Nigel Nicolson: as the inheritor of Sissinghurst Castle and of his parents' papers, as the friend and patron of their biographers, as the editor of their letters and of his father's diaries, and as the chronicler of their marriage. Since the mid 1960s, he has combined the roles of loyal champion, tireless publicist, fastidious editor and revelatory apologist with consumate skill and remarkable success. Despite, or perhaps because of, Britain's economic decline, the Sissinghurst industry has blossomed and bloomed under his hand.

But no son, however well-intentioned, can realistically expect to view his parents square-on. By definition, he knows too much about them in some ways, yet sees too little in others. He is too near to get them in a broader perspective, too emotionally involved to regard them with the detachment necessary for the reaching of an even-handed or authoritative verdict. In the case of Nicolson's mother and father, it is high time that alternative patterns of interpretation were developed, not so much to contradict his views, but rather to complement them by exploring other ways in which his parents might be assessed and understood. Nostalgic voyeurism, filial piety and biographical celebration have dominated the Sissinghurst scene for too long. There is an urgent need to look at its creators and its habitués afresh and anew. How, then, do these two people look, when examined in a less enthralled and more searching light, not as close acquaintances (whether real or imagined) but as historical personalities, not as 'Harold and Vita' but as Nicolson and Sackville-West?

I

The essential starting-point in such an overdue re-appraisal is to stress that they were both aristocrats, possessed of an abiding sense of their superior status and privileged position.[7] They were born (he in 1886, she in 1892) into a world where the traditional patrician certainties were already beginning to dissolve, but where the hierarchical ordering of society was still largely taken for granted. It was certainly taken for granted by both of them. Nicolson once observed that 'the process of decontamination from class superiority' was 'a fine thing'[8] – but it was a process which neither he nor his wife ever showed any desire to experience. Throughout her life, Sackville-West 'hated' the proletariat and was far from enthused about the middle classes, while Nicolson's concern with the manners and minutiae of social distinctions bordered on the obsessional.[9] But their lives, their writings, and their snobbish attitudes need to be understood in the context of their forebears and their families – partly because, as with all aristocrats, their ancestors mattered a great deal to them; and partly because, although both patricians, they came from very different sectors of that large and varied class. Either way, the dynastic perspective is crucial,[10] but it should be a perspective provided by the forebears who went earlier, rather than by the son who came afterwards.

Of the two, Sackville-West was significantly the more nobly born. Her family was very ancient and had once been very grand, and she herself wrote its history soon after the First World War.[11] The Sackvilles' ancestors were recorded in the Domesday survey, and rose from relative obscurity through royal and state service to become one of the greatest dynasties of early modern England. The real founder of the family's fame and fortune was Thomas Sackville, who was created Baron Buckhurst (1567) and Earl of Dorset (1604), was Lord High Treasurer of England, and was granted the reversion of the manor of Knole near Sevenoaks in Kent by his cousin Queen Elizabeth. As a result, he acquired a magnificent house, which had been built for Thomas Bourchier, Archbishop of Canterbury, between 1456 and 1486, and had been further enlarged by Henry VIII, who had appropriated it from Thomas Cranmer, and from whom it eventually descended to the Queen. In turn, Thomas Sackville further re-modelled Knole between 1603 and 1608, making it one of the most magnificent prodigy houses in the kingdom – more a village than a mansion, and reputedly containing three hundred and sixty-five rooms, fifty-two stair cases, and seven courtyards, covering four acres.[12]

During the first half of the seventeenth century the family's fortunes went into decline. The third Earl of Dorset was a notorious spendthrift, and his successors suffered for their support of Charles I during the Civil War. Knole's original furnishings and pictures were seized, and for a time the house was occupied by the Parliamentarians.[13] Later in the century, the Sackvilles' circumstances markedly improved. Marriages to two heiresses brought in new lands and new money, and the sixth Earl of Dorset, who was additionally created Baron Cranfield and Earl of Middlesex, was Lord Chamberlain to King William III from 1689 to 1697. Thanks to the perquisites which he enjoyed by virtue of his courtly office, he was able to fill Knole with its matchless collection of furniture, pictures, tapestries, carpets and silver, much of which remains there to this day. In recognition of the Sackvilles' grandeur no less than of their Whiggery, his son, the seventh Earl, was created Duke of Dorset in 1720 – an appropriately splendid title to match his splendid residence. Had this upward trajectory continued, the Sackvilles might have remained one of the greatest families in the land, on a par with the Dukes of Devonshire, Norfolk or Bedford.

Then they were hit – as were many landowning families – by the demographic crisis of the eighteenth century.[14] The dukedom passed, with increasing uncertainty, from son to nephew to son to cousin, and on the death of the fifth duke in 1843 all the proud titles which had been acquired and accumulated across the generations became extinct. Eventually, the Knole estates devolved on Elizabeth Sackville, daughter of the third duke and sister of the fourth, who in 1813 had married John West, fifth Earl de la Warr. In 1843, she combined her own name with that of her husband as Sackville-West, and in 1864, the year in which she inherited the Sackville estates, she was made a peeress in her own right, as Baroness Buckhurst. Two of her sons, Charles and Reginald, became sixth and seventh Earls de la Warr, and inherited the estates that went with those titles. A younger son, Mortimer Sackville-West, who had spent most of his life as a minor courtier, succeeded to what remained of the Knole estates on the death of his mother in 1870, and as a consolation prize he was created Lord Sackville six years later. This restored a title to the occupant of Knole, and included a special remainder so that, if the new peer failed to produce a male heir, the barony could pass to his younger brothers.

This was a prudent provision since, although he married twice, Mortimer sired no son, and on his death in 1888 he was succeeded by his younger brother, Lionel. By this time, the inheritance was much diminished: there were eight thousand acres yielding £11,250, hardly a princely income with which to keep up such a princely palace as Knole.[15] Lionel Sackville-West had followed a standard career pattern for a younger son, and entered the diplomatic service in 1847. He never married, but fathered five illegitimate children by Josepha Duran, a Spanish dancer with whom he lived intermittently for more than twenty years, and who was known as Pepita. In 1881, he became Minister to Washington, but was recalled in disgrace seven years later, having foolishly expressed his preferences about the presidential election of 1888 which subsequently found their way into a national newspaper.[16] As the newly-inherited second Lord Sackville, he retired to Knole, where he died unmarried in 1908. He was succeeded by his nephew, another Lionel, who was the son of the second baron's youngest brother. 'Young' Lionel, now the third Baron Sackville, had married Josephine Victoria in 1890, who was herself one of the illegitimate children of 'old' Lionel, second Lord Sackville, and Pepita.[17] The Hon. Victoria Mary Sackville-West was born at Knole, and was their first and only child.

By contrast, the Nicolsons were distinctly less grand, and were Scots-Irish rather than English. Harold Nicolson knew that he came from a 'landless tribe', and all his life yearned to feel like 'the son of some hereditary soil'. But he was proud of the 'Scotch and Ulster blood in my veins', and once admitted that 'deep in me is a dislike of the English'.[18] His forebears originated on the Isle of Skye, moved to Edinburgh in the sixteenth century, and established themselves as solicitors. In 1637, Thomas Nicolson of Carnock in Stirling, son of John Nicolson of Edinburgh, obtained a baronetcy, and in the late seventeenth century, the Nicolson title, and the family lands at Carnock, were merged with the Barony and estates of Napier. By the time George Nicolson inherited as sixth baronet in 1699, however, the lands and the Barony had been separated from his title, and he was obliged to earn his living in military service. So, in turn, were the ninth baronet, who soldiered in America, India, Ireland and Mauritius, and also his son, the tenth baronet, who ended his days as an Admiral. As such, the Nicolsons belonged to a readily identifiable sub-group of titled but impoverished families: they were Celtic notables successfully joining a greater Britain, poor patricians working for the British state.[19]

By the late nineteenth century, this meant that as the Sackvilles were going down in terms of worldly achievement, the Nicolsons were going up, and the high point was reached with the career of Harold Nicolson's father, Arthur, who became eleventh baronet in 1899. Like his forebears, Sir Arthur Nicolson had to work for a living, but instead of the armed forces, he preferred the foreign service, which he entered in 1870.[20] After junior postings at Constantinople, Tehran, Bulgaria, Morocco and Madrid, he became Ambassador at St Petersburg, and played a major part in negotiating the Anglo-Russian Alliance in 1907. Three years later he returned to London as Permanent Secretary at the Foreign Office, where he remained a determined Russophile and was no less resolute in his hostility to Germany, and where he increasingly found himself out of sympathy with the domestic policies of the Liberal Government.[21] After war broke out, his influence was much diminished, and he retired in 1916, when he was created Baron Carnock, aptly recognising the Scottish estate once held by his ancestors. In 1882, he had married Catherine, daughter of Archibald Rowan Hamilton, who owned nearly four thousand acres and Killyleagh Castle in County Down (hence his opposition to the Irish policies of the Liberal Government between 1912 and 1914).[22] Harold George Nicolson, who was born in Tehran, was their third son.

Although both patrician, these two families were clearly not on an equal social or financial footing. Despite their limited means and realtively recent title, the Sackville-Wests were authentic territorial aristocracy, whereas by comparison the Nicolsons were 'impecunious high civil servants', drawn from the ranks of the service nobility. Appropriately enough, after she came out on the upper-class marriage market in 1909, Victoria Sackville-West was pursued by men with backgrounds similar to her own: Lord Lascelles, son of the Earl of Harewood, who eventually married the daughter of King George V; and Lord Granby, heir to the Duke of Rutland, and brother of Lady Diana Cooper. When she began to show greater enthusiasm for Harold Nicolson, her parents were predictably put out.[23] Lord Sackville was 'disappointed she is not making a great match with a great title', while Lady Sackville thought Nicolson's parents 'both very ugly and very small and unsmart looking'. Throughout their marriage, which had taken place at Knole in 1913, Sackville-West never concealed her dislike of her husband's relatives, or her disapproval of his diplomatic profession. For his part, Nicolson knew that she regarded him as her social inferior, and their two sons, Benedict and Nigel, saw themselves as Sackvilles first, and Nicolsons a long way second.[24]

Nevertheless, their two families did share one common characteristic: neither Nicolson nor Sackville-West could boast any close relatives of real distinction. Her father, the third Lord Sackville, who held the title from 1908 to 1928, was 'a quiet, conscientious country gentleman': Vice-Chairman of the Kent County Council, Chairman of the Kent Territorial

Army Association, a Deputy Lieutenant and Justice of the Peace. His brother Charles, who became fourth Lord Sackville, was a professional soldier who served in India, in South Africa and in the First World War; was Lieutenant-Governor of Guernsey from 1924 until 1929; and then retired to Knole.[25] On his death in 1962 the title passed to his son, Eddy, who thus became fifth Lord Sackville. In a minor sort of way, he had been a music critic, a novelist, a man of letters and a BBC radio producer. But he was self-centred, ineffectual, delicate, neurotic, lonely and melancholy, and never fully came to terms with his homosexuality; he was immortalised by Nancy Mitford in her novels as 'Uncle Davey'; he spent his last years in reactionary exile in Ireland; and he held the title only briefly. 'No [Sackville]-West', he once remarked, 'ever did anything great, and I am a typical representative of that family.'[26]

On the Nicolson side, the cast of coronetted characters was no more distinguished. The first Lord Carnock lingered on until 1928, but he was broken in health by the time he left the Foreign Office. His widow survived until 1951, increasingly ill at ease in a world she could no longer understand, and disappointed in her sons. Their eldest boy, Frederick Archibald Nicolson, followed family tradition, went into the army, and served in the First World War. He then became a barrister, wrote two volumes of regimental history, and was a chairman of committees in the House of Lords. But he never married, his career fizzled out, he took to drink, and he died in 1952 a lonely, miserable, embittered failure.[27] The title then devolved on the second son, Erskine Arthur Nicolson, who went into the Navy, saw service in the First World War, rose to the rank of Captain, and retired in 1924. Thereafter, he lived the life of a classic backwoods peer: he settled down in Devon, listed his recreation in *Who's Who* as hunting, and died in 1982. Some more words of Eddy, fifth Lord Sackville, will bear quotation: 'I have come to the conclusion that all the old families of England are degenerating.' There was ample evidence among the twentieth-century Nicolsons and Sackville-Wests to corroborate this view.[28]

In both cases, the most famous (and notorious) members of their families were more distantly related. On Sackville-West's side, the most important connection was with the de la Warrs, the family into which Lady Elizabeth Sackville had married in 1813. Two of her daughters married exceptionally well, one to the ninth Duke of Bedford, the other to the second Marquess of Salisbury (father of the prime minister), and then to the fifteenth Earl of Derby (son of the prime minister). One of her grandsons, Gilbert, became eighth Earl de la Warr on the death of his father, Reginald, in 1896, but his tenure of the title was unhappy, marred by scandal, and ultimately tragic. In search of easy and much-needed money, he allowed himself to be bribed by the speculator E.T. Hooley, and became the guinea pig director of several of his motor and bicycle companies. The idea was that de la Warr's aristocratic name would encourage credulous investors (which it did), and when the companies with which he was connected went bankrupt in 1898, he was subjected to much public censure.[29] To make matters worse, his marriage to the daughter of Earl Brassey ended in divorce in 1902. He fought in South Africa, and died while on active service in the First World War.

His son, who followed him as ninth Earl de la Warr, was a very different sort. He seems to have rehabilitated the family finances successfully, and after serving in the Navy during the First World War took up a career in public life. To many people's surprise, he started out as a supporter of the Labour Party, held minor office in 1924 and 1929, then followed Ramsay MacDonald into the National Government, where he was given Parliamentary Secretaryships at Agriculture, Education and the Colonies. From 1937 to 1940, he was Lord Privy Seal and then President of the Board of Education. There was no job for him in Churchill's wartime coalition, but he reappeared in the Conservative Government of 1951–5 as Postmaster-General. For more than thirty years, de la Warr was thus in and out of office: he was a great survivor, who changed party with disconcerting ease.[30] He was especially highly profiled during the 1930s, and more than once put himself out for Sackville-West's husband. It was largely thanks to him that Nicolson was invited to contest West Leicester as a National Labour Candidate in 1935, and that he was made a member of the parliamentary delegation inquiring into education in British East Africa two years later.[31] Although he was Sackville-West's kinsman, he was also Nicolson's closest connection with the corridors of power.

On Nicolson's side, the most important family connections came through his mother's Anglo-Irish relatives. Catherine Rowan Hamilton's eldest sister, Hariot, had married Frederick Temple Hamilton-Temple-Blackwood, fifth Baron Dufferin and Clandeboye in the Irish peerage, and another substantial landowner in County Down. After serving as Chancellor of the Duchy of Lancaster and Paymaster-General in Gladstone's first Cabinet, Dufferin went on to enjoy a glittering career overseas.[32] As a proconsul, he filled the two most exalted positions available under the crown: Governor-General of Canada and Viceroy of India. As a diplomat, he was Ambassador to Russia, Turkey, Italy and France. He was promoted from a British barony, via an earldom, to the Marquessate of Dufferin and Ava, and he was loaded with more orders of knighthood than the first Baron Carnock. He was, in addition, Vice-Admiral of Ulster, Lieutenant of County Down, Chancellor of the Royal University of Ireland, and Lord Warden of the Cinque Ports. He was far more eminent than any contemporary from the Sackville clan, and during the modern period, was the most distinguished figure produced by either family – though whether this distinction was achieved by merit and endeavour or by charm and luck is, perhaps, debatable.

In any case, everything then went sadly and spectacularly wrong, not only for Dufferin, but also for his descendants. As an Irish landowner, he was indebted, and far from rich, and had been selling off his estate to his tenantry from the 1870s. After he retired from public life in 1896, he needed to earn more money and became involved with Whittaker Wright, another speculator very much in the Hooley mould. Although knowing nothing of business, Dufferin agreed to become chairman of one of Wright's companies, the London and Globe. In 1901 it, too, went bankrupt, and Dufferin not only lost money, but was severely criticised in the press for allowing himself to become chairman of a company whose complex and unsound finances he simply did not understand.[33] To make matters worse, his eldest son, Lord Ava, was killed during the Boer War, and this combination of public censure and family tragedy undoubtedly hastened his own death in 1902. Thereafter, the reaper scarcely let up. Another of Dufferin's sons died in action in 1917; the second Marquess expired of pneumonia in 1918; the third Marquess did not survive a plane crash in 1930; and the fourth marquess was killed on active service in Burma in 1945.[34] When the fifth Marquess died in 1988, the titles accumulated by his illustrious forebear became extinct. All that remains is the original Irish Barony of Dufferin and Clandeboye, which is now held by a retired chemical engineer who lives in Australia.

As with all aristocrats, it is impossible to understand Nicolson and Sackville-West unless they are set within the appropriate familial context and, for all the differences between their dynasties, they had much in common. Both came from extended families of great titles and great houses, of state service and high achievement. Not surprisingly, they looked down on most of the rest of the world as 'bedint': a Sackville word, appropriated by Nicolson, meaning lower or middle class, vulgar or undistinguished.[35] Yet for both families there was also a darker side. During the late nineteenth and early twentieth centuries, three careers had crashed spectacularly into ruin: a Dufferin, a de la Warr, and a Sackville. Albeit in different ways, both the Nicolson and the Sackville-West finances were unsound. The general lack of distinction in both families only echoed a broader national trend: the marginalisation and decline of the traditional titled and territorial classes. 'It is', Harold Nicolson observed in 1943, 'no doubt a tragic and bewildering experience to discover that the elite into which one was born, and to which one was educated . . . seems . . . to be losing its authority.'[36] How, in the light of their own family backgrounds and of the inescapable evidence of aristocratic decay which they provided, did Nicolson and Sackville-West live their own lives?

II

The formative influences on Harold Nicolson's life and outlook were the legations and embassies in which his father and his 'Uncle Dufferin' lived and worked, and the great houses of his mother's Ulster relatives –

Clandeboye, Killyleagh, Shanganagh – which provided him with the closest he ever came to that 'hereditary soil' he so craved.[37] He was a child of diplomacy and of aristocracy, and knew nothing of the cities or slums or suburbs of late-nineteenth and early-twentieth-century Britain. Instead, he remembered the royal courts of Bulgaria, Spain and Russia, and the great receptions held at the British Embassy in Paris. He recalled the garden parties and horse shows given and attended by the Anglo-Irish landowners, and the downstairs world of 'rows of fire buckets with crowns upon them, and the sense of many servants cleaning plate'. As he later noted, only half in jest, 'I was extremely snobbish when I was young.' He claimed that he admired peers in accordance with the elevation of their rank, thought baronets rather inferior, and mere knights the lowest form of titled life.[38] Not surprisingly, given the proconsular and diplomatic accomplishments of his father and his uncle, his own youthful ambitions soon turned towards the ambassadorial and the viceregal.

Before the First World War diplomacy was still preponderantly a small, close-knit, aristocratic and hereditary profession, much favoured by patricians of limited resources but good connections.[39] It was impossible to take the entrance examination without a nomination from a senior figure in the Foreign Office, but given his father's position this did not present Nicolson with any difficulty. After Wellington and Balliol, he duly went overseas to learn the requisite foreign languages, and in 1909 he passed the entrance examination with very high marks. His early years were spent in Madrid and Constantinople, and during the war he was exempted from military service. He served in the British delegation to the Versailles peace conference, played a part in the establishment of the League of Nations, worked in the Foreign Office during the early 1920s, accompanied Lord Curzon to Locarno, and was then posted abroad to Tehran and Berlin. The best evocation of this life and milieu is to be found in Nicolson's early novel *Sweet Waters* (1921) and his 'imaginative sketches', *Some People* (1927), which contain thinly-disguised portraits of the men and women he knew, and show just how narrow were the social circles he moved in: public-school contemporaries, Oxford friends, assorted European aristocrats, ambassadors, diplomatic underlings, butlers, governesses, and the like.

As Nicolson later remarked, 'in our own Foreign Service . . . the man of letters has always been regarded with bewildered, although quite friendly, disdain', and like many other young diplomats he spent his spare time writing.[40] His first book was a study of the French poet and degenerate, *Paul Verlaine* (1920), but thereafter he turned his attention to English writers, all of whom boasted, as he himself did, aristocratic connections. There was *Tennyson* (1923), whose father was a disinherited landowner, who himself spoke with the authentic voice of Victorian squierarchy, who found himself increasingly ill at ease in the modern democratic world, who refused a baronetcy but accepted a peerage, and who set himself up as a country gentleman at Farringford and Aldworth. There was *Byron* (1924), who unexpectedly inherited a title and an estate at Newstead, who was very much aware that he belonged to the aristocracy and was a friend of the fourth Duke of Dorset, but whose rebellious behaviour meant he was scarcely a gentleman at all. Then there was *Swinburne* (1926), whose father, like Nicolson's grandfather, was an Admiral, whose family was a long-established dynasty of Northumberland baronets, and who took great pride in his ancestry. Together, these books enabled Nicolson to establish a certain literary reputation, which emboldened him to resign from the Foreign Service late in 1929.

Nevertheless, he remained much attacted to his 'dear old profession', 'so calm, so quiet, so distinguished'. He thought of returning to it more than once during the 1930s, continued to daydream about being an ambassador, and on many subjects his views were invariably those of the pre-1914 patrician-diplomat that at heart he always remained.[41] He believed in what came to be denounced as the 'old diplomacy': the conduct of relations between states by an expert, cosmopolitan and self-contained ruling group, negotiating confidently and confidentially behind closed doors. He favoured the maintenance of the balance of power by unostentatious statesmanship rather than vulgar public relations. He was convinced that diplomacy should be left to the diplomats, that the politicians should keep out of it, and that the increased influence of the sensationalist press and of ignorant and capricious public opinion was altogether bad. He shuddered at the idea of diplomatic business being dragged into the parliamentary arena, or made the stuff of partisan propaganda at general elections. In his eyes diplomacy was an exclusive and fastidious profession, and he had no time for 'democratic diplomacy', or 'diplomacy by conference', both of which became so popular during the inter-war years.[42]

These were not the only ways in which Nicolson's views reflected his background, his upbringing, and the outlook of his profession. Like most aristocrats and most diplomats, he 'loathed the dark races', and although he disliked anti-semitism he also disliked Jews. He wanted them kept out of the Foreign Service, had very few Jewish friends, and there are disparaging references to them scattered throughout his diaries and correspondence.[43] He thought that 'every American is more or less as vulgar as any other American', and that the whole nation was 'incurably suburban'. He regretted the Industrial Revolution, which he felt had blighted the English countryside and ruined the nation's cities, and he wished that the machine had never been invented. He did not like, and did not understand, big business or commerce or finance, and thought it was no part of the diplomat's function to get involved with them. 'I regard bankers and banking as rather low-class fellows', he once observed. 'They regard officials as stupid and corrupt.' He was clearly unhappy that during his lifetime 'our mercantile class' had become 'the governing class'.[44] Like most diplomats and aristocrats, he regretted that Britain was now being run by a political class that he generally regarded as socially inferior.

Having resigned from the Foreign Office, Nicolson was obliged to establish a second career. He had no money, and there was no diplomatic pension. As with many poor patricians, he was compelled to earn, and he now took up writing full time. Since he needed a regular income, it was to journalism that he first turned, editing the Londoner's Diary for Lord Beaverbrook's *Evening Standard* at a salary of £3000 a year; and he also started broadcasting on the BBC.[45] But while the money was good, he disapproved of Beaverbrook, regarded the work as intolerably superficial, and hated the milieu. He thought journalists 'bedints', found Fleet Street 'culturally degrading', and feared he had become a 'radio comedian'.[46] He soon withdrew from his contract with Beaverbrook, but (although he never again went near popular journalism) he was forced to turn to the more serious newspapers out of sheer financial necessity. In 1932 he began regular reviewing for the *New Statesman*, later switched to the *Daily Telegraph*, and finally moved to *The Observer*. In 1934, he started writing regularly for *Figaro*, and four years later began a column for *The Spectator*, which eventually became known as 'Marginal Comment'. This was a heavy labour of hack work: but Nicolson needed the money, and his journalistic earnings provided his only regular income for most of the rest of his life.

Journalism was, however, only one part of his writing career. During the next fifteen years he also poured out books at an astonishing rate, something he was able to do only by writing about subjects and people he already knew first hand, and by setting down quite unreflectively the views and prejudices which were the commonplaces of his class and his profession. He began with a diplomatic trilogy covering the years 1870 to 1924, which had witnessed the convulsive and regretted transition from the old diplomacy to the new. His biography of *Lord Carnock* (1930) was a case-study in the virtues of the old diplomacy; it showed how much his father had owed to the patronage of his brother-in-law, Lord Dufferin, early in his career; and it treated the negotiation of the Anglo-Russian Convention of 1907 as a textbook example of diplomatic negotiation at its best. His account of the Versailles Treaty, *Peacemaking, 1919* (1933), drew heavily on his own recollections, vividly evoked the unhealthy and unhappy atmosphere in which the negotiations took place, was critical of both Lloyd George and (especially) Woodrow Wilson, and much regretted the pernicious influence of the press barons and public opinion. His study of *Curzon: The Last Phase* (1934), which again relied on his own memories of the early 1920s, depicted his hero as the last in the long line of aristocratic Foreign Secretaries, and as a patrician out of his depth in a democratic world, who was fatally handicapped by a 'middle class' lack of proportion, and who was obliged to endure the subordination of foreign policy to Prime Ministerial whim.

As a pendant to this trilogy, Nicolson completed a biography of *Dwight Morrow* (1935), the American lawyer, businessman, politician and diplomat. It was, he later admitted, 'the worst book I ever wrote'. He did not understand America, thought Morrow 'a shrewd and selfish little arriviste who drank himself to death', had no sympathy with his work on Wall Street or as a partner in J.P. Morgan, and was clearly ill at ease describing the complexities and crudities of oil diplomacy in Mexico.[47] He then returned to more familiar territory and produced two studies of his Anglo-Irish forebears. His biography of Lord Dufferin, *Helen's Tower* (1937), depicted his favourite uncle as an eighteenth-century Whig born out of his time, who hated the Industrial Revolution and was ill at ease with parliamentary controversy. It drew heavily on Sir Alfred Lyall's official life, and contained vivid personal reminisences of the Paris Embassy and Clandeboye at the turn of the century, but never really explained how Dufferin managed to enjoy the glittering career he did. He then wrote *The Desire to Please* (1943), a life of Hamilton Rowan of Killyleagh, his mother's most famous forebear, who had joined the United Irishmen in 1791 and was successfully prosecuted for sedition in 1794. But although this gave him a chance to set down his boyhood memories of the Anglo-Irish ascendancy, Nicolson was clearly uneasy in dealing with a rebel, found Rowan a suspect, jumbled and wrong-headed character, and was evidently relieved when, in later life, he calmed down and was 'conquered by his duty to his family and his great possessions'.[48]

Nicolson's output as a writer was indeed exceptional: from the 1930s until the early 1960s reviews, essays, lectures, broadcasts, pamphlets and books flowed from his typewriter in extraordinary abundance. Since it was his sole means of livelihood, it was as well that he produced with such facility. But although he never wrote a boring line, he never wrote a profound one, either:[49] as he himself grudgingly recognised, the need to turn out so much so quickly meant that his output was invariably superficial. He could not distinguish, and did not have the time to distinguish, between authorship and journalism. His articles were rarely of lasting value, and his books invariably lacked intellectual bite. There was, he once conceded, no 'inner divination' in his writing, and there was 'a lack of muscle in my mind'. More damaging still, he wrote from a very limited experience and perspective; all his writing was 'class bound and inhibited'. As Edmund Wilson observed, in a famous review of Nicolson's work, he too obviously belonged 'to a definite class, by birth, education, experience, and consequent outlook'. As a result, he could not handle sexual scenes, he could not write about ordinary men and women, and he had no insight into the deeper forces which animated and propelled the historical process. In short, he viewed the world 'through the embassy window'.[50]

Because he knew his books were 'not good enough to justify myself having cut adrift from public service', Nicolson embarked on his third career 'as a sort of alibi from literary failure'.[51] After several false and indecisive starts, he got himself into politics, but of the many activities to which he turned his hand this proved the most humiliating and the least successful. To begin with, he came from a family more attuned to public service than to party bickering, and like most patrician diplomats he had little time for – or understanding of – democracy or public opinion. His knowledge of England was largely confined to its clubs and country houses, and he was completely ignorant of the hopes and fears of the ordinary voter. He knew nothing at first hand about politics, and tended to see it, as aristocrats had always been inclined to do, in terms of family and friendship.[52] He thought of himself as an Asquithian Liberal, but this was hardly a relevant or inspiring label by the early 1930s. He had a vague sense, which was widely shared at the time, especially by disenchanted patricians, that parliamentary democracy was an inadequate mechanism for dealing with the problems of the age. Having refused to stand as a Liberal for Falmouth, he decided to throw in his lot with Oswald Mosley, and in 1931 he joined his recently-formed New Party.[53]

His reasons for doing so were twofold. In the first place, he was drawn to Mosley, a youthful, vigorous, aristocratic friend, and to his wife, Lady Cynthia, who was the daughter of Lord Curzon, whose protegé Nicolson had been, and whose biographer he was soon to become.[54] In addition, he was convinced that a 'serious crisis' was impending, perhaps even a 'proletarian revolt', and that this could only be dealt with by transforming the parliamentary system into 'the Corporate, the Organic State', which Mosley by this time was preaching. In August 1931 Nicolson left the *Evening Standard* to become editor of *Action*, the New Party magazine. Its contributors included Mosley, Nicolson himself, Sackville-West (on gardening), Osbert Sitwell and Christopher Isherwood; its tone was lurid, violent and apocalyptic; and during its short life circulation collapsed from 160,000 to 16,000. Meanwhile, Nicolson had stood as the New Party candidate for the Combined English Universities in the general election of October 1931, and had come bottom of the poll. 'I have', he rightly concluded, 'made a fool of myself in every respect', and when Mosley dissolved the New Party in April 1932, and embraced Fascism, Nicolson parted company with him.[55] But he remained personally friendly, and in his novel *Public Faces* (1932) predicted a Mosley government later in the decade.

To be sure, Nicolson was no Fascist, but the authoritarian overtones of Mosley's movement clearly appealed to him, as they did to other anxiety-ridden patricians. Thereafter, he seemed for a time completely disoriented, unable (again like many of his class) to find his bearings in an alien and bewildering political world. In July 1935, he considered standing for

Maidstone as a Conservative, but Lord Sackville was unable to deliver the nomination.[56] Later in the same year, he was invited to contest West Leicester under the banner of National Labour, as a supporter of Ramsay MacDonald and those members of the Labour Party who had joined the National Government. The nomination had been fixed by Lord de la Warr, who was not only Nicolson's relative by marriage, and holder of a junior ministerial office, but was also responsible for dividing up the parliamentary seats between the different parties who supported the National Government. Predictably, Nicolson hated campaigning in Leicester. It was the sort of town of which he knew nothing, he was appalled by 'the mud baths of ignorance and meanness' he found there, and he 'loathed every moment of this election'.[57] But because he was supported by the Conservatives, he squeezed in past the official Labour Party candidate, and won with a majority of 87.

Sustained by this slim and precarious mandate, Nicolson's parliamentary career lasted ten years; but just as he never reconciled himself to the mass democracy of the Leicester electorate, so he never really found his feet at Westminster. He had unwisely committed himself to a party which scarcely existed in anything but name, but at the same time he was regarded as a traitor to his class. He had been returned as a supporter of the National Government, but soon found himself profoundly disagreeing with them over foreign policy. Although he spoke with real knowledge on international affairs, he lacked the toughness, the ambition and the relish for parliamentary battle. His hostility to Chamberlain's policy of appeasement owed much to his Foreign Office background, and he looked down on the Birmingham-born and -bred Prime Minister for possessing 'the soul of the ironmonger', and 'the mind and manner of a clothes brush'.[58] Most people regarded Nicolson as too lightweight, too superior, and neither Chamberlain nor, later, Churchill ever took him really seriously. The trouble, as he himself admitted, was that he suffered from 'a profound disbelief in myself, coupled with a rather self-indulgent and frivolous preference for remaining an observer'. Like the aristocracy as a whole, he found himself very much 'on the edge of things'.[59]

Despite the rich and varied existence depicted in the first volume of Nicolson's diaries, and despite his oft-repeated claims that he would not have lived his life any other way, the fact was that during the 1930s his career conspicuously failed to gather momentum. He jumped from one profession to another, from one party to another, from private life to public life, with impressive ease, but also with bewildering frequency. No one really knew – and he himself did not know – what the central thread of his life was supposed to be. As Nicolson later said of Lord Berners (who, incidentally, lampooned him rather wickedly as Mr 'Lollipop' Jenkins in *Far From the Madding War* in 1941), so it could also be said of him: 'he might have been happier had he lived in another age . . . his talents were so

dispersed that he failed somehow to get his centre into his middle'.[60] Like
Lord Dufferin, who was the man in his family he most admired and in some
ways most resembled, Nicolson was in many ways an eighteenth-century
Whig, born out of his time; but while charm, luck and good connections
had carried Dufferin to the twin peaks of the diplomatic and proconsular
professions, they were no longer enough in Nicolson's day, unless accompanied by a toughness he himself never possessed.[61] As a result, his sense of
superiority was based on ancestry more than accomplishment, on attitudes
rather than attainment.

III

The same might also be said of Sackville-West, although in her case
the ancestral inheritance was both more powerful and more ambiguous.
Because her grandfathers were brothers, this meant that her parents were
cousins, and so she was herself a Sackville twice over. She grew up as a
lonely only child, in one of the great houses of England, to which she soon
became possessively attached with an 'atavistic passion'. She delved into the
history of Knole and the Sackvilles and wrote novels about her forebears
when still in her teens, and her knowledge was so detailed that she was
often called on to take visitors on conducted tours.[62] Like Nicolson, she
knew nothing of urban or industrial England; but unlike him she acquired
a deep and lasting attachment to the countryside of Kent. Her mother,
despite her illegitimate origins, was one of the great hostesses of her time,
presiding over opulent country-house parties and an elaborate hierarchy of
servants, which Sackville-West was later to recreate in *The Edwardians*.
Very early in her life, she developed a strong 'sense of class', and she
was soon able to tell who was 'bedint' and who was not. Like her
future husband, she absorbed the 'commonplaces of well-bred thought':
'genealogies and family connections, tables of precedence and a familiarity
with country seats, formed almost part of a moral code'.[63]

Yet for all this comfort and privilege, Sackville-West's youth was lived
out against a background of unhappiness, anxiety and insecurity. Until 1908
her grandfather, the second Lord Sackville, lingered on at Knole, lonely,
unmarried, taciturn, disappointed and embittered. Her parents' union did
not last; they both went their separate ways; and even by the lax standards
of the Edwardians, their affairs were indiscreet. The family finances were
far from secure, there were sales of furniture and works of art, and Lady
Sackville even opened a shop in Mayfair.[64] In 1910, there was a sensational
law case, when Lady Sackville's brother, Henry, vainly tried to prove that
he was in fact the legitimate son of the second Lord Sackville, and thus the
rightful inheritor of the peerage, Knole and the family estates. Three years
later, the family was in court again, as Lady Sackville successfully fought off
an action which would have prevented her being a substantial beneficiary

under the will of Sir John Murray Scott, a fabulously wealthy bachelor, who had been one of her close friends. But these two triumphs were dearly bought: the costs of the first case were in excess of £40,000, and during the course of both the hearings a great deal of the family's dirty linen was washed in public.[65]

In Edwardian England, this was widely viewed as unpardonable, and it is difficult to gauge the effect of all this on Sackville-West. Well before the first court case of 1910, she knew that there was a risk that her parents would be dispossessed of Knole, and until the succession was finally settled, the revenues from the estate were put in the hands of the trustees. As far as she herself was concerned, there was worse to come. For at some point – it is not clear exactly when – she learned that, although she was her parents' only child, she would not inherit Knole. Along with the title, the house and estate were entailed to pass through the male line, to her father's brother Charles, and then on to his son Eddy. By virtue of the accident of her gender, Sackville-West was thus a disinherited patrician, denied the house and the 'hereditary soil' which she so adored, and this was to mark her for the rest of her life. It explains her dislike and resentment of her cousin Eddy Sackville-West.[66] It explains her strong sense of possessiveness ('my Knole', 'my Sissinghurst', 'my ancient homes', 'my Kent', 'my name', 'my jewels'). It explains why country houses and inheritance loom so large in her novels. And it explains her search for a substitute Knole, which she eventually found in Sissinghurst.

Although Sackville-West was not an heiress, this did not mean she was poor. She was guaranteed an income of £2400 a year under her marriage settlement, and after the second successfully contested lawsuit her mother became a rich woman in her own right. Lady Sackville inherited £150,000, and also the contents of Sir John Murray Scott's Paris house, which she sold for a further £270,000.[67] Although she was later to be difficult, demanding and in some ways quite unbalanced, she was initially very generous to her daughter and son-in-law, and it was partly as a result of this that Nicolson and Sackville-West were able to set themselves up in some considerable style. There was a London house at Ebury Street, there was Long Barn in Kent, there was a Rolls-Royce; there were furnishings, portraits and tapestries brought over from Knole; there were servants, nannies, gardeners and chauffeurs; and there was a lavish, hectic social life.[68] However rebellious and nonconformist Sackville-West's behaviour was during the course of her widely-known affair with Violet Trefusis, which occurred between 1918 and 1921, it took place against a background of conventional country comforts. And she was enjoying these comforts at a time when the traditional structure of aristocratic landownership was dissolving, and when the unprecedented glut of estate sales in the aftermath of the First World War amounted to a 'revolution in landholding'.[69]

As a country lover, and as the scion of a great house, Sackville-West was much affected by these developments, which profoundly influenced her post-war writings. One of her earliest novels, *The Heir* (1922), tells the story of an Elizabethan manor house, Blackboys, which was modelled on Groombridge Place, on the Kent-Sussex border, and was also a scaled-down version of Knole. After being held in the same family for five hundred years, the house and estate are inherited by a distant relative, Peregrine Chase, who is the manager of a Wolverhampton insurance company. The estate is heavily mortgaged, there are death duties to pay, and the only option seems to be to put everything up for sale. That, at least, is the view of Chase's advisors, and initially he shares it. But gradually he finds himself overwhelmed by the beauty, the magic and the tradition of the house, and by the homely charm and country ways of the tenants. At the eleventh hour, he withdraws the house and the estate from auction, Blackboys is saved, and the story has a happy – and quite fantastically implausible – ending. The 'revolution in landowning' may have been taking place in fact, but *The Heir* successfully and sentimentally denied it in fiction.

At the same time, Sackville-West was completing the study of her own family history, *Knole and the Sackvilles* (1922). Although such books were commonplace by this time, this was no standard dynastic saga. The ordering of the title was itself significant: for it is a study of the house first, and of the family who inhabited it a long way behind. The book opens with a romantic evocation of Knole: 'It has all the quality of peace and permanence; of mellow age; of stateliness and tradition. It is gentle and venerable. . . . It is, above all, an English house. . . . No other country but England could have produced it.'[70] Then comes the history of the Sackvilles – a history which turns out to be one of mediocrity and misery, rather than of fame or achievement. Most of the men, Sackville-West insists, were untalented spendthrifts, or selfish incompetents, who obtained their grand-sounding positions by virtue of their titles rather than their merits. They were 'a race too prodigal, too amorous, too weak, too indolent, and too melancholy': in short, 'a rotten lot, and nearly all stark staring mad'.[71] Indeed, it was her belief that her forebears were rarely worthy of the great house they occupied – a subject she was to address again in *The Edwardians*.

There was another theme to this book, namely the differing qualities of the men and the women in her family's history. While she did not find much to admire among her male ancestors, the same was not true of the women. There was Lady Anne Clifford, heiress to great estates in Cumberland, who married the third Earl of Dorset, refused to allow her own inheritance to be dissipated by such a spendthrift, later married the Earl of Pembroke, and spent her last years as a grand, matriarchal recluse, progressing from one of her northern castles to another.[72] There was Arabella Diana Cope, another heiress and another 'commanding figure', who married the third Duke of Dorset, who exercised 'the real control, under a show of submission', and who, as a long-lived and powerful dowager, kept the family estates together as the male line faltered and failed at the turn of the nineteenth century.[73] And there was Lady Elizabeth Sackville, heiress to Knole, and a peeress in her own right, from whom the Lords Sackville, and thus she herself, were descended. It seems clear that Sackville-West found these dominant, capable, assertive women more impressive than the men, and they may well have provided a model which she herself would have wished to emulate. But there was one big difference, of which she would not fail to have been aware: they possessed or controlled or inherited great prosperties. She herself did not.

By this time, Sackville-West was also working on her poem, *The Land*, which had first been conceived in 1921, and was eventually published five years later. Here she took another look at the rural world, this time not so much aristocratic-nostalgic as conservative-pastoral.[74] Like many people of her class and generation, she believed that the countryside embodied the true, the real, the authentic England. Implicitly, at least, her poem was a riposte to Eliot's *The Waste Land*, which had ushered in the inter-war fashion for angst-ridden, damp-pavement, urban poetics. By contrast, Sackville-West re-asserted the spiritual values and wholesomeness of nature: 'the country habit has me by the heart'. Like *The Heir*, and her history of Knole, *The Land* was another celebration of permanence in an era of change. She 'sang the cycle of my country's year', the enduring rhythm of the seasons, the 'classic monotony' of country life and country living.[75] And she evoked the rural workers, with their archaic dialect and their time-honoured crafts: the yeoman, the thatcher, the shepherd, the tool-maker, the dairyman. Both in its form and in its content, *The Land* was a self-consciously traditional poem, a 'mild continuous epic of the soil', defending what was old and what was true against the ever-encroaching forces of 'modernity' and 'bookish townsmen in their dry retreats'.[76]

Two years later, Sackville-West's father died, and after three days during which she had been mistress of Knole, supervising the funeral arrangements, she yielded the house to her Uncle Charlie, now fourth Lord Sackville, and scarcely set foot in it again for the next thirty years. But she was still bound to Knole by 'some sort of umbilical cord', and that obsessional connection was brilliantly evoked later that year by Virginia Woolf in *Orlando*.[77] Woolf had little time for Sackville-West as a writer, but she was captivated by her aristocratic manner and her family history, and above all by Knole. In *Orlando*, she immortalised Sackville-West's myths and fantasies about herself and about Knole better than Sackville-West could ever have done.[78] By making Orlando androgynous, Woolf not only evoked Sackville-West's lesbian inclinations, but also recognised the powerful women who were an integral part of the Sackville family's history. And she perceptively extended Sackville-West's deep sense of personal loss into the more general lament that the greatest days of England's country houses were over:

The house was no longer hers entirely, she sighed. It belonged to time now; to history; was past the touch and control of the living. Never would beer be spilt here any more . . . , or holes burnt in the carpet. Never two hundred servants come running and brawling down the corridors with warming pans and great branches for the great fireplaces. Never would ale be brewed and candles made and saddles fashioned and stone shaped in the workshops outside the house. Hammers and mallets were silent now. Chairs and beds were empty; tankards of silver and gold were locked in glass cases. The great wings of silence beat up and down the empty house.[79]

Orlando has been described as a love-letter from Virginia Woolf to Sackville-West, giving her back in fiction the house she had been denied in fact. By the same token, The Edwardians (1930), which she began soon after Orlando was published, was a love-letter from Sackville-West to Knole – albeit much more pedestrian. Here she created a novel 'absolutely packed with the aristocracy' which, 'for snobbish reasons', turned out to be 'hugely popular'.[80] The great mansion, Chevron, was a thinly-disguised version of Knole, and the country-house parties, and the rigid below-stairs hierarchy, were based on her own pre-war recollections. But the recreation of the rich, opulent world of her youth was more than an exercise in turn-of-the-century nostalgia. It evoked images of waste, decadence, extravagance and superficiality, which suggested that the owners of Chevron were somehow unworthy of their great inheritance. Like The Land, it celebrated the therapeutic qualities of the countryside, the un-changing cycle of the seasons, and the traditional crafts of country folk, this time employed in a great house. It restored a ducal occupant to Knole, placed a formidable duchess in charge, created a young, well-meaning but ineffectual duke, depicted an aristocracy determined at all costs to avoid scandal, and hinted that the stable world of the country-house community was not going to survive unchanged and unchallenged for much longer.

In the aftermath of The Edwardians, which was hugely successful as a commercial venture, and sold thirty thousand copies in the first six months, Sackville-West turned from novel-writing to house-hunting. Long Barn was in danger of becoming overlooked, and after considerable searchings she settled on Sissinghurst Castle. It was a ruin, the garden was in chaos, and it cost £12,000 to buy and £15,000 to make habitable (much of which was made available by the Sackville trustees). But it was in Kent, and it had once been owned by one of Sackville-West's forbears. As Nicolson explained, these were for her compelling arguments: 'Through its veins pulses the blood of the Sackville dynasty. True it is that it comes through the female line – but then, we are both feminist, and after all, Knole came the same way. It is for you an ancestral mansion.'[81] Together, they rescued it from decay, and began to create the garden for which Sissinghurst became famous. Here, again, their superior attitudes came out. In planning and planting the garden, they exercised complete powers – as all gardeners do – of inclusion and exclusion. Any flowers remotely tainted with the middle class or the suburbs were ruthlessly excluded. Azaleas were unsuitable because they were 'Ascot, Sunningdale sort of plants'; rhododendrons were like 'fat stockbrokers, whom we do not want to have to dinner'; and so on. There were no bedint flowers at Sissinghurst.[82]

The purchase of Sissinghurst inaugurated a new period of creativity for Sackville-West, and once again houses, possession and inheritance were central themes. She wrote a poem about Sissinghurst: a place 'by birthright far from present fashion', where she could escape 'through centuries to another clime', and enjoy the 'timeless spell' of 'assembled fragments of an age gone by'. Her next novel, *All Passion Spent* (1931), was ostensibly set in Hampstead, but it owed nothing to its urban location: indeed, the house, which is again central to the story, might as easily have been in the country. Its occupant is the recently-widowed Lady Slane, whose late husband combined the attributes and achievements of Arthur Balfour, Lord Rosebery and Lord Lansdowne, all of whom had recently died. The book is shot through with episodes and allusions drawn from – or deliberately contrasted with – Sackville-West's experience, family and in-laws. Lady Slane has been Vicereine of India (something Sackville-West, unlike Lady Dufferin, would never have been). She was 'a wonderful help to her husband in his career' (something Sackville-West, unlike Lady Carnock, conspicuously refused to be). And she inherits a great deal of money (as Lady Sackville had done and as Sackville-West was soon to do), which she then shows no interest in hanging on to (unlike Lady Sackville or Sackville-West).

Despite its feminist interludes, *All Passion Spent* is far from being a straightforward expression of its author's opinions. Whereas Lady Slane finds herself by renouncing possessions, Sackville-West found *herself* by retaining and accumulating them, and in the novels which followed, such patrician preoccupations became even more prominent. *Family History* (1932) was a fictional dynastic saga which mimicked the factual account of her forebears she had already produced. The Jarrolds are a two-dimensional, parvenu bourgeois family, rising from the factory floor to a peerage in three generations, about whom Sackville-West wrote with an ignorant lack of conviction. She contrasted them with Miles Vane-Merrick, a patrician Labour MP, whose house is closely modelled on Sissinghurst, and who believes in a traditional feudal hierarchy where everyone knows his place. *The Dark Island* (1934) was set in a house very like St Michael's Mount in Cornwall, which was lived in by Nicolson's sister Gwen and her husband, the future third Lord St Levan. It featured another memorable dowager, Lady le Breton, and explored the ties and the tensions of aristocratic family life, played out against the brooding backdrop of Storn Castle, and the conflicting claims of possessiveness to which it gave rise. Again, it is the house rather than the occupants which dominates the story.

Like Nicolson, Sackville-West could write only of what she knew, and because she had seen even less of the world than he had her range was, correspondingly, even more limited. She could not write convincingly about the suburbs of Dulwich or of Wolverhampton, and her depictions of the working class, whether urban or rural, were little better than cardboard cut-outs. Notwithstanding the fact that it made a great deal of money for its publisher, the Hogarth Press, Virginia Woolf once disparagingly dismissed her fiction as 'sleep-walking, servant girl novels'.[83] But it was those above stairs, rather than below, by whom Sackville-West was preoccupied, and much of her writing about the aristocracy directly reflected her own background and circumstances. Just as she loved Knole more passionately than any human, so she evoked houses more perceptively, vividly and sensually than any individual characters. She had an 'intense sense of the character of places', and her heroes were always in possession of their ancestral homes. She wrote with assurance about money, or the lack of it, about the need to avoid scandal at all costs, and about what it felt like to possess a house or to own broad acres. She made her women more strong-willed than her men, and produced a formidable cavalcade of domineering dowagers and tyrannical matriarchs. And she knew that 'one's resentment of family claims is at least as strong as the bond which secures one to them'.[84]

Having exhausted this fictional vein, Sackville-West returned to her own family history and took up the account where she had left it off in Knole and the Sackvilles, with her double biography of her grandmother Pepita, the Spanish gipsy dancer who had been the second Lord Sackville's lover, and of Pepita's daughter Victoria, who had married the third Lord Sackville and was Sackville-West's mother. In the course of the book (Pepita, 1937), she sought to bring to life the grandmother she had never known (Pepita had died in childbirth in 1871), to exorcise her troubled relationship with her mother, which had become particularly acrimonious during its last years, and to resolve what she believed to be the contradictions between the 'Spanish' and the 'English' sides of her own nature. As in her earlier study, she again drew attention to the vigour and importance of the women in the Sackville family. The two men were passive and withdrawn; but Pepita and Lady Sackville were headstrong, assertive and imperious. Perhaps subconsciously, she was also describing her own marriage, which in this sense, at least, was typically Sackville. Here again, it was she, and not her husband, who was the dominant partner. He had resigned from the diplomatic service to accomodate her, because she could not bear playing the part of an embassy wife.

She also dominated because she held the purse-strings of their marriage. Nicolson's journalism and books paid his own living expenses, but he was occasionally obliged to borrow money from his wife, and it was she who owned Sissinghurst, and who was completely responsible for maintaining and running it. She extended her holdings by purchasing neighbouring farms, delighted in being 'absolute lord' in her 'own domain', and was in complete charge of the estate's finances.[85] Her income came from the Sackville family trusts, from farm rentals, and from the royalties of her novels, and she had also inherited a substantial sum on the death of her mother in 1936. By the mid 1930s the Sissinghurst regime consisted of two secretaries, one cook, one lady's maid, one chauffeur, one valet and three gardeners. This might not have approximated to the Edwardian splendours of Knole, but by inter-war standards it was a substantial and self-sufficient establishment, which Sackville-West found increasingly fulfilling and absorbing. Like Lady Anne Clifford, 'she was too fully occupied in order-ing her small kingdom to pay much attention to the crisis of the larger kingdom without'.[86] And like several Sackvilles before her, she was well on the way to becoming a recluse.

By the late 1930s, one of her catch-phrases, 'another quiet day at Sissinghurst', was something of a family joke; but by now this was her preferred mode of life. She wore breeches and gaiters, cultivated her garden, wrote an essay extolling the beauties of Kent, and started work on a new poem as a companion piece to *The Land*. She 'loathed' the modern world, had no time for politics, and refused to go to Leicester in 1935 to be present with her husband in his electoral campaign. She began contrib-uting a column called Country Notes to the *New Statesman*, where she celebrated nature's power of self-renewal, regretted that the population was becoming 'urban minded' to the point of 'spiritual death', and told of her 'absurd pleasure in owning land' and in saving it from 'any builder-aggressor'.[87] For Virginia Woolf, the woman by whom she had been socially and sexually enthralled at Long Barn and Knole had now become fat, indolent, tomato-cheek'd, and was surrounded by dogs and flowers. 'At heart', Sackville-West was 'nothing but an old Tory squire' with an 'incurably Tory soul'. She flew the Sackville flag from Sissinghurst tower; and when war broke out in 1939, her banner was symbolically pulled down for the duration of the conflict.[88]

IV

Like most members of their class, both Nicolson and Sackville-West saw the Second World War as threatening the stable, hierarchical society in which they believed, and their privileged place within it. When war broke out, Nicolson lamented that 'the world as I know it has only a few more hours to run', and from 1939 to 1945 he was certain that the 'old order', which was essentially his order, had 'collapsed'. Early in 1940, he discerned a 'great and angry tide which is rising against the governing classes', and feared that 'my whole class is being assailed'.[89] His abrupt dismissal by Churchill, after holding junior office at the Ministry of Information, only further increased his gloom. His 'Marginal Comment' columns dwelt on the 'silent revolution' through which the country was passing: 'we assume today', he wrote in November 1941, 'that the levelling process will continue with increased momentum through the war, and that in the end we shall emerge as an almost classless state.' He feared the prospect of 'a Woolworth life hereafter', and dreaded 'the tide of vulgarization' which would inevitably 'sweep in from the west'. He disliked 'the smoke cloud of class rancour', and by 1945 was convinced – quite rightly – that 'class feeling and class resentment are very strong'.[90]

Sackville-West agreed: 'it is', she felt, 'not as if we were fighting to preserve the things we care for. This war, whatever happens, will destroy them.' When the Beveridge Report was published, she was almost apoplectic:

I think it sounds dreadful. The proletariat being encouraged to breed like rabbits because each new little rabbit means eight shillings a week – as though there weren't too many of them already, and not enough work to go round, with two million unemployed before the war – and everyone being given everything for nothing, a complete discouragement to thrift and effort. . . . I don't hold with Sir William Beveridge, and it all makes me feel very pre-1792.[91]

When bombs fell on Knole, she was not only enraged but also hurt:

I mind frightfully, frightfully, frightfully. I always persuade myself that I have finally torn Knole out of my heart, and then the moment anything touches it, every nerve is alive again. I cannot bear to think of Knole wounded, and I not there to look after it, and be wounded with it. Those filthy Germans! Let us level every town in Germany to the ground! I shan't care.

And when it was proposed to run a new local bus service near her land, she was positively beside herself:

Why people have this passion for moving about passes my understanding, but there it is. What a world! It is like drawing up one's own death warrant.

My manifesto: I hate democracy. I hate la populace. I wish education had never been introduced. I don't like tyranny, but I like an intelligent oligarchy. I wish la populace had never been encouraged to emerge from its rightful place. I should like to see them as well fed and well housed as T.T. cows, but no more articulate than that.[92]

Of course, as the owner of Sissinghurst, Sackville-West had much more to lose than Nicolson by way of possessions, and her non-fictional writing reflected her greater stake in the land. In Country Notes in Wartime (1940),

she wrote of nature's consolatory powers, and described the tower at
Sissinghurst, standing 'English, perennial, rustic and alone'. She produced
a pamphlet on *English Country Houses* (1941), which she saw as the product
of centuries of natural growth, an integral part of the national landscape. As
a self-confessed 'Tory squire', she naturally disapproved of the great Whig
palaces at Blenheim, Chatsworth and Bowood, which were too vulgar and
ostentatious. She admired domesticated castles, Tudor manor houses, and
seventeenth-century Palladian, but almost nothing which came after. She
feared that the high taxation and levelling tendencies of the twentieth
century, made worse by the war, would spell the end of the country-house
world. She also composed a handbook on *The Women's Land Army* (1944),
which noted how hard it was for workers from the town to settle down in
the country, described the tasks that the 'land girls' were called upon to
undertake, and revealingly admitted that 'whenever one is dealing with
human beings in the mass, some very odd and unforseen factors emerge'.

With the end of the War in Europe, both Nicolson and Sackville-West
were obliged to face an immediate future no more appealing than the
immediate past. At Leicester, Nicolson stood as an Independent with
Conservative backing, and expressed his strong support for Winston
Churchill. Once again, he hated 'the falsity, the noise, the misrepresenta-
tion, the exhaustion and the strain of the whole thing', and he was swept
aside in the electoral avalanche.[93] Having unsuccessfully sought a peerage
from Attlee as an Independent, he joined the Labour Party in the hope of
improving his prospects of ennoblement. His family were appalled. His
mother thought her son had betrayed his country, while his eldest brother
presumed (erroneously as it turned out) that Nicolson would now resign
from all his clubs.[94] His Conservative friends were dismayed, and there
were renewed accusations that he was a traitor to his class. In February
1948, he fought a by-election at Croydon, but his heart was not in it. He
was obliged to lodge in acute discomfort in a local hotel; the only food
available was fish and chips; and he hated 'canvassing these dumb idiots'.
He lost the election, and thereupon wrote a 'Marginal Comment' in *The
Spectator* in which he poured out all his disdain for politics, for the Labour
Party, for electioneering, and for the people of Croydon.[95] His denunciation of this 'harlequinade' was never forgotten, and his political career
evaporated, along with the hoped-for peerage.

It seems clear that Nicolson had wanted his ennoblement very badly.
Part of the attraction of an hereditary peerage was that it would have
atoned for the sense of 'failure' that he now increasingly felt, and would
have allowed him to get back to Westminster without the need to fight any
more elections.[96] It would also have enabled him to change his name. 'I
am', he noted, 'amused to find in myself a fat grub of snobbishness. I have
always hated the name Nicolson as being a common plebian name.' And,
although she disapproved of his joining the Labour Party, his wife was

equally enthused at the prospect of the peerage. 'It certainly isn't for snobbish reasons', she wrote with a singular lack of conviction, 'although I would like the boys to be Hon. (isn't that odd?)'[97] The fact that Nicolson had resolved to revive the Sackville title of Cranfield would also, presumably, have given her dynastic satisfaction. When he was later given a KCVO for his biography of King George V, they were both disappointed: in part because Sackville-West did not want to be Lady Nicolson (though it does not seem that she would have minded having been Lady Cranfield); in part because it put him in the 'third eleven'; and in part because they both regarded knighthoods as being middle-class, and vulgar.[98]

Insofar as he retained, and she acquired, a public position after the war, it was by joining with other members of their class as the self-appointed cultural guardians of rural values and conservationist endeavours. Sackville-West became a local magistrate and a member of the Society for the Preservation of Rural Kent. She joined the newly-formed Gardens Committee of the National Trust, offered advice on horticultural matters, and later wrote guides to Hidcote Manor Garden and Berkeley Castle, the latter giving her another opportunity to evoke the romance of a venerable house, and explore its influence on the people who inhabited it across the generations. Nicolson was a wartime Governor of the BBC, a Trustee of the National Portrait Gallery, and for many years sat on the Historic Buildings Committee and the Executive Committee of the National Trust. He was dismayed that many great houses could no longer be kept up by their owners, was much involved in the negotiations whereby some were taken over by the Trust, and took every opportunity to speak out on behalf of the organisation. He also regretted that its patrician personnel did not go down well with the post-war Attlee administration. 'We are getting more and more evidence', he noted in 1949, 'that the present government (or rather their supporters) do not like the Trust because it is managed by aristocrats working on a voluntary basis.'[99]

The other side of this was an increased distaste for all those who did not belong to the same superior stratum as himself. 'I believe that our lower classes are for some curious reason congenitally ignorant', he observed in 1946. 'How difficult the proletariat are!', he opined two years later, 'I fear my socialism is purely cerebral. I do not like the masses in the flesh.' As for the Labour Party, he soon came to realise that joining it had been 'the cardinal error of my life'. 'The realities, and above all the personalities, of Labour politics really revolted me.'[100] More and more, his articles in *The Spectator* dwelt on the splendours of the past, and the shortcomings of the present. He wrote of great houses and great hostesses he had known. He lamented the demise of the 'old stratified code of manners'. He described the real and – he claimed – harmless pleasures of being a snob. He defended the complex structure of titles and precedence: 'people of my generation learnt these tricks of the trade automatically, even as they learnt to handle a knife and fork'. And he noted that 'those of us who lived before the First World War . . . have experienced a revolution more rapid and fundamental than any recorded in human history'.[101]

These attitudes also emerged in his later books, where the old themes were re-stated and re-cycled, and where his own increasingly querulous personality intruded more and more. *The Congress of Vienna* (1946) celebrated the success of peacemaking in 1814–15, when there had been no mass electorate or mass media to pay heed to, compared with the later efforts of 1918–19 and 1945–6. His official biography of *King George V* (1952) set the sovereign's reign in the context of the dissolving certainties, international convulsions and 'silent revolutions' of the twentieth century. *The Evolution of Diplomatic Method* (1954) restated the view that the old diplomacy was much superior to the new, especially the new as practised by the Russians and the Americans. *The Age of Reason* (1960) was a last – ostensibly sceptical – look at the stable aristocratic European regimes before the French and Industrial Revolutions destroyed them, and was peppered with disparaging remarks about the 'torment and anger' and 'spiritual restlessness' of the younger generation, and the delinquencies of the inhabitants of Bournemouth.[102] And in *Monarchy* (1962), he described himself as 'a congenital liberal', unhappy at the prospect of a 'Coca Cola world'.

In his less substantial books Nicolson gave himself away more completely. *The English Sense of Humour* (1946) explored its subject in essentially class terms – the higher up the social scale one went, the more sophisticated humour became – while denying that it was actually doing so. *Benjamin Constant* (1949) was a study of the French aristocrat-bohemian (and as such represented a return to the interests of the 1920s), but it was also something of a self-portrait: of a man much influenced by his family and forebears, who never thrust roots deep into his native soil, and who constantly changed political parties to the dismay of his relatives and friends. *Good Behaviour* (1955) celebrated the elites who in the past had practised and perfected manners, lamented their decline in the increasingly uniform post-war world, restated his views on the Industrial Revolution and Americans, and defended snobbery once more. *Saint-Beuve* (1957) was a self-referential study in failure: a man of letters ill at ease in politics, who spent his latter decades churning out weekly essays, reviews and journalistic hack-work. And *Journey to Java* (1957) was an account of Nicolson's first winter cruise, and was full of remarks about the bedintness of Mr Pooter, the Americans' preference for legend over history, and 'that creeping infection of vulgarity that will subdue the world'.

Predictably, as a self-proclaimed 'Tory squire', Sackville-West was even more reactionary in her final years than her husband, at war with the modern world and everything that went with it. The obsession with her ancestral home remained: 'I can't get it out of my system. . . . Nobody really feels Knole as I do.' As 'an instinctive Tory' she disapproved of her husband joining the Labour Party, and did not care to think of him 'being associated with these bedints' (unless, of course, it had brought him a peerage), not least because she did not 'like people who cannot speak the King's English'. By 1948 she was 'clinging more and more to the security and happiness of Sissinghurst and our life – our way of life, as we have made it'.[103] Her last two novels, *The Easter Party* (1953) and *No Signposts in the Sea* (1961), were respectively set in a country house and on a cruise liner, the only realms of the post-war world that she knew at first hand. As in her earlier fiction, it is the mansion, Anstey, which is the dominant force in *The Easter Party*, and its destruction by fire may well symbolise the widespread demolition of country houses which was taking place at that time. In *No Signposts in the Sea*, as in her private letters, Sackville-West inveighed against the ugliness and vulgarity of the modern world, even in far-off and supposedly 'unspoiled' places.[104]

More even than during the inter-war years, the majority of her writing was now about the English countryside. In 1946 she published *The Garden*, a companion piece to *The Land*, which had been conceived during the 1930s but was largely written in wartime. Once again, it explored the themes of stewardship, continuity, decency, 'spiritual values', and nature's yearly cycle. Once again, and this time explicitly, it answered T.S. Eliot, preferring a 'rich and hopeful land' to his 'waste land'. Although ostensibly about 'agriculture's little brother', it set out 'all my beliefs and unbeliefs', in particular her 'dislike of modern life and vulgarity', her 'love of the graces of life and retirement'.[105] She was homesick for 'another and different world', 'daring to find a world in a lost world, a little world, a little perfect world'. In one particularly revealing passage she expressed her love of the land and of her country, and her fears for its modernised, mechanised future:

> Thus do I love my England, though I roam.
> Thus do I love my England: I am hers.
> What could be said more simply? As a lover
> Says of his mistress, I am hers, she mine,
> So do I say of England: I do love her.
> She is my shape; her shape my very shape;.
> Her present is my grief; her past, my past.
> Often I rage, resent her moderate cast,
> Yet she is mine, I hers, without escape.
> The cord of birth annexes me for ever.[106]

A year later, Sackville-West contributed a chapter on 'Outdoor Life' to a symposium edited by Ernest Barker entitled *The Character of England*, and she took the opportunity to let herself go.[107] The 'essential virtue of the English character' was to be found on the land and in the countryside. Relations between squire and yeoman had always been characterised by 'friendliness, convenience and mutual respect'. The country was threatened by prefabricated houses and ribbon development, and by the 'entirely utilitarian and materialistic outlook of the present world'. Country sports survived, binding together the Eton-educated gentleman and the village blacksmith on the cricket ground or the hunting field. So did 'decent' agricultural labourers, who were 'England in a sense that the citizens of our industrial towns are not England'. So did the farmer, who was English, Conservative and stubborn. So did the village shops, though increasingly threatened by the 'co-op and the chain store'. And so − just − did the squire and the landowner, who were virtuous, public-spirited and incorruptible. For many, she lamented, the battle to keep up their houses and estates was going to prove too much. The future was bleak: a 'cheapened, standardised' world, devoid of spiritual distinction.

Much of this was little more than reactionary fantasy, but it came from recognisably the same pen as produced regular gardening articles in *The Observer* between 1946 and 1961. To be sure, they often provided good practical advice, and they were written in a brisk businesslike prose which was much more appealing than the pretentious tone Sackville-West so often adopted in her novels and her poetry. But time and again the Tory squire emerged. She feared that the countryside was being 'vandalised', and regretted the mechanisation of country living. She refused to write about window-boxes and hanging baskets because she knew nothing about town gardening. She thought that 'popular taste' was likely to be 'bad taste', and disliked public gardens, privet hedges, bedding plants, herbaceous borders, bird baths and garden gnomes. She preferred villages and cottage gardens to suburbs or housing estates, the 'old and tried tools' to new modern 'gadgets'.[108] Above all, she hated the fame and popularity which these articles brought her. Meanwhile, she herself became more reclusive than ever, and saw her own garden as 'a series of escapes from the world, giving the impression of cumulative escape'.[109]

After 1945, both Nicolson and Sackville-West became increasingly possessed by the idea of escaping to alternative worlds: hence their joint poetry anthology, aptly entitled *Another World Than This* (1945); hence the cruises that they went on each winter in the last years of their marriage (Sackville-West paid). By then, they knew they belonged to a vanished generation. The great houses and estates of the Anglo-Irish Ascendancy had been sold or destroyed. Shanganagh had become a girls' school, while the romance of Clandeboye had faded long ago.[110] In 1935, Lord Sackville had begun negotiations with the National Trust, and after interminable delays they were finally completed in 1946. 'I hate that beastly National Trust symbol', Sackville-West remarked, predictably. 'Knole should have been mine, mine, mine.' Equally predictably, she was determined that Sissinghurst should not go the same way: 'never, never, never'. But within two years of her death, her son Nigel, to whom she had left it, had made it over to the National Trust.[111] After cremation, her ashes were placed in the Sackville crypt at Wythiam, where her ancestors had been buried since the sixteenth century. Nicolson had originally intended that his remains should join hers there; but he knew he was not a Sackville, and in the end he settled for the non-'hereditary soil' of Sissinghurst parish churchyard.[112]

V

The evidence on which this essay rests is in no sense original, and there is no need for it to have been. It has been culled from the wide range of published material which Nicolson and Sackville-West produced themselves, and which has been written about them since their deaths. But it has been selected and arranged with the aim of offering an overall interpretation which makes them more historically credible as individuals than do many of the books from which it has been derived. Of course, such a truncated treatment leaves a great deal out, especially as regards their private lives. But those aspects have already been thoroughly gone into elsewhere, and in any case, there is much more to people's private lives than the issue of their sexual orientation or the names of those with whom they went to bed. That was certainly the case with Nicolson and Sackville-West. Their ancestry, their family relationships, their inherited prejudices, and their financial resources profoundly influenced the sort of people they became, the nature of the views they held, the kinds of careers they took up, the substance of the things they wrote, the way of life they lived, and the type of marriage they had.

At one level, much of their writing should thus most appropriately be seen as a dialogue – sometimes deliberate, sometimes unawares, sometimes easy, sometimes unhappy – with their own forebears. Like most aristocrats, they were the products and the prisoners of their ancestors to a degree that has been insufficiently appreciated and explored. In many ways, Nicolson was a recognisable product of the late-nineteenth-century Scots-Irish service nobility to which he belonged. As a younger son, his worldly professional ambitions were set by the proconsular and ambassadorial achievements of Lord Carnock and Lord Differin, and to the end of his life he felt disappointed that he had not gone farther along the road towards emulating them. But while he made less of his life than he might have hoped to in the public realm, the influence of his relatives and his forebears pervaded almost everything he wrote in his later career as a journalist, biographer and historian. Thanks to a particularly powerful combination of will, talent and sheer financial necessity, Nicolson successfully inflated his family history, his diplomatic recollections and his personal prejudices into what he believed were central themes of national history. The inevitable result is that, viewed in a longer perspective, the real interest of his writings is not so much what they tell us about the subject, but rather what they tell us about the author.

The same is obviously true of Sackville-West. Viewed in the broader context of her dynastic history, the fact that she could not inherit Knole has been both too little stressed, and too much. It has been too little stressed because, as she herself knew very well (but as writers about her have failed to notice), previous women in her family had inherited or owned or controlled much more property than she ever did. It has also been too much stressed because it underestimates the extent of her accomplishment at Sissinghurst. For there she not only created a substitute Knole, she also established a powerful matriarchal regime inspired by the sort that had existed in her family in earlier generations. Moreover, it was the very kind of *ménage* which she would have been unable to control had she married rich broad-acred grandees like Lord Lascelles or Lord Granby. When deciding to marry the well-connected but landless Nicolson, who never owned a house in his life, and who was much less careful about money than she was, she probably chose better than at that time she knew. 'A crushed life is what I lead', Nicolson once observed, 'similar to that of the hen you ran over the other day.'[113] No wonder Sackville-West's novels and her biographies were so concerned with assertive women: she was one herself.

While we cannot understand Nicolson and Sackville-West without recognising how much they were both 'family bound', we should also note how many of the standard themes of twentieth-century aristocratic decline play themselves out in their own lives.[114] The diplomatic career and outlook, the need to earn through journalism and writing, the changes in political party, the unease with democracy and with parliament, the decision to join Labour, the work on behalf of what we would now call the 'national heritage', the sense of talents wasted, of a career that failed: all these aspects of Nicolson's life are commonplaces of modern aristocratic history. The same was true of Sackville-West. The early anxieties over sexual scandal and financial insecurity, the loss of an ancestral mansion and the search for an alternative, the disagreements with her mother over money and jewels, the romanticisation of country houses and the rural cult of spiritual values, the attempt to make an escapist world of patrician fantasy which would never let her down, the strong matriarchal undercurrent beneath the surface of male ascendancy and manly values:[115] all this, too, is typical of the twentieth-century aristocracy to which Sackville-West belonged, and provided many of the themes, not just for her own writing, but also for the novels of Francis Brett Young, D.H. Lawrence, Aldous Huxley, Evelyn Waugh and P.G. Wodehouse.[116]

There remain the more intractable issues raised by the couple's snobbery and sexuality. As to the first, Nigel Nicolson has admitted that his mother 'attached exaggerated importance to birth and wealth', but has strenuously denied that his father was a snob, while coyly admitting he was undeniably

'superior'. This semantic quibbling misses the essential point.[117] Enough
evidence has been advanced here (and it is only a small selection of the
total) to show that both Nicolson and Sackville-West were deeply hostile
to the twentieth century, and to most of the people who were living in it.
They knew they belonged to the aristocracy of birth (albeit different parts
of it), but they could not conceal from themselves that during the course
of their own lives this came to signify less and less. And they aspired to
belong to the aristocracy of achievement, but both were obliged to admit
that they lacked the outstanding gifts to do so. The bedints were not only
in charge, they were also cleverer, and Nicolson and Sackville-West did
not like that at all. As a result, she took refuge – like many Sackvilles before
her – in country-house reclusiveness, he found consolation in snobbery (or
'superiority'), and they both sought solace and reassurance by telling each
other how marvellous they were, and how wonderful their unusual
relationship was: 'no bourgeois bedint marriage' because they were 'rather
subtle and difficult people'.[118]

As for their sexuality, it seems clear that too much attention has recently
been given to it. Or, rather, that too little historical attention has been
given to it. It cannot be sufficiently emphasised that both Nicolson and
Sackville-West were aristocrats first, and homosexuals a long way second.
As Virginia Woolf had so perceptively spotted, their family histories and
their social position were much more important in determining their sense
of themselves, the lives they lived and the books they wrote, than were
their sexual orientations. They knew that they belonged to dynasties, and
to a class, whose greatest days were over. They both recognised, however reluctantly, that they were marginal people: aristocrats in an era of
democracy, patricians in an age of landed decline. For Sackville-West,
there can be no doubt that her sense of marginality was intensified by her
gender. And for both of them, there can be no doubt that their homosexuality served to put them even further on the edge. But far from providing
the mainspring of their lives, this merely reinforced their basic *class* feeling
that they were not, and could not be, at the centre of events.

Unless we understand that Nicolson and Sackville-West were first and
foremost 'superior' people, that they were profoundly influenced by their
patrician background, and that they were conscious of the fact that in the
course of their lifetimes aristocracy was in decline, we shall not begin to
understand them properly either as people or as writers. Much about them
has been over-explained in terms of their character, temperament and
sexuality, without paying due attention to the broader historical developments of their class as a whole – broader historical developments in which
they themselves were inevitably and inexorably caught up. To be sure, the
balance between personality and circumstance, individual accomplishment
and historical change, is never easy to get right. Biographers (and sons)
strike it one way, historians another, and doubtless there is much to be said

for both approaches. But in the case of 'Harold and Vita', it is clear that they have been too much the objects of a cult of personality, and too little the subjects of serious historical inquiry. Beyond any doubt, Harold Nicolson and Vita Sackville-West were two very remarkable people – but that is no reason for regarding them as having been more remarkable than they actually were.

Beyond the Country House

Iᴛ ᴡᴏᴜʟᴅ ᴄʟᴇᴀʀʟʏ ʙᴇ ᴜɴᴄᴏɴᴠɪɴᴄɪɴɢ to suggest that the rather random accumulation of these essays over the years gives this book a coherently-articulated message beyond that of aristocratic diversity and (I hope) historiographical liveliness. But there is an underlying argument which each of these chapters in some ways illuminates, however obliquely, and it might be helpful to make it more explicit by way of conclusion. There is no better means of doing so than by quoting from one of Mark Girouard's most recent writings. 'I am', he observes, 'depressed by the mixture of snobbery and nostalgia which forms so large an element of the country-house cult of today.'[1] – and so, I must confess, am I. As the twentieth century draws to its close, the image of Britain which is projected abroad (and at home) becomes ever more that of a Ruritanian theme park, a contrived fantasy of hype and heritage and, while the monarchy still occupies the starring part in this deluded pageant of self-indulgent historical backwardness, the cult of the country house follows very close behind.

To be sure, no historian of the modern British aristocracy can be – or should be – entirely indifferent to the claims and charms of our nation's country houses. It is highly unlikely that they are, as their most impassioned defenders assert, Britain's greatest contribution to civilisation. If anything deserves that accolade, it is surely Shakespeare or the railway, neither of them, incidentally, upper-class products. Some country houses are certainly magnificent examples of architecture, contain works of art no less splendid, and are located in parks of exquisite beauty. Some of them allow ample public access, display their contents with style and discernment, and welcome scholars to work in their archives – though increasingly, alas, at a price which many research students cannot afford. Only an individual of Gradgrindian philistinism and insensitivity would seek to denude such places of their contents, to demolish the empty house, to sell off the timber, and to turn the park into a building site. To that extent, we are surely all conservationists now. Or, at least, most of us like to think that we are.

Of course, it is not the intrinsic merit of the buildings, the pictures or the parks which are the points at issue (except in those dubious cases where the most obsessive conservationists claim a greater merit for these things than the facts of the case actually warrant). It is rather, as Girouard rightly remarks, the snobbery and the nostalgia which during the course of the twentieth century have created the cult which now surrounds the country house like a suffocating shroud. The snobbery takes it for granted that the owners of these houses were or are persons of greater merit than the rest of us, simply by virtue of who their parents were – a claim which is contrary to reason, to common sense, and to the historical evidence. The nostalgia presumes that country houses were the setting for a way of life more exquisite, more cultivated and more refined than that which lesser mortals are capable of living – a presumption of which very much the same may be said. But in the hands of the more impassioned members of the heritage lobby, these arguments are mobilised in support of the claim that the traditional owners of country houses should be allowed to continue in occupation of their ancestral mansions and acres, even if they themselves can no longer afford to do so unaided, and that the state should recognise it has an obligation to subsidise and succour them.

It is not my present concern to discuss these rather tendentious claims made on behalf of the surviving aristocracy as the self-appointed, live-in guardians of the 'national heritage'. I have already done so elsewhere.[2] My immediate purpose is to draw attention to the strangeness of this country-house cult, and to suggest that it is a uniquely twentieth-century creation. How odd it is that, in a nation which boasts some of the finest galleries in the world, it is widely believed that works of art should ideally be displayed in the country houses whose walls they were bought to adorn. Why so, when ease of access is greater, and the cost of admission is less, if these pictures are put on public display? We should remember also that from Tudor to Victorian times country houses were bought and sold, built and demolished at will, as architectural fashion changed, and as owners came and went. They were not then regarded as shrines to be venerated, as relics of a vanished golden age which must be preserved untouched and unchanged, at all cost. Instead, they were viewed more dispassionately as machines to be lived in, and they were regularly (and often scathingly) criticised by contemporaries on utilitarian or artistic grounds if they failed to fulfill their functions.

Only since the turn of the century has the worship of the country house become a national obsession. One way it can be traced is in the writings of such novelists as Francis Brett Young, D.H. Lawrence, Evelyn Waugh, P.G. Wodehouse – and Vita Sackville-West. In many of their books, it is the mansion, rather than the inhabitants, which dominates the story, and one of their favourite stylistic devices is to describe the scene when the hero or heroine first comes unsuspectingly upon the house, and to do so in enraptured prose, straining every literary artifice for high-flown effect, something for which there is no precedent in the earlier writings of Hardy, Trollope, Dickens or Jane Austen (who was memorably disparaging about Northanger Abbey). The rise and influence of this romantic, deferential and fictional approach to the country house would well repay serious historical study – as would its down-market incarnation in films and television serials. Even in our own time, the heart-string-tugging saga of a once-great house, whose owners are threatened by death duties, who may be forced to sell, but who are rescued (or not) at the eleventh hour, is virtually guaranteed a large and appreciative prime-time audience.

Somewhere behind these pervasively peddled sentiments, both as promoter and as beneficiary, is to be found the National Trust. That the Trust is in many ways a great British institution cannot be said too often, but it is remarkable how little we actually know about its history and its policies, and as its centenary year approaches it is to be hoped that some light will be shed on both these subjects. Nevertheless, it seems clear that its original purpose was primarily to safeguard outstanding places of natural (*not* man-made) beauty, and to protect commons and bridle-paths from enclosure or private acquisition. Only in the inter-war years was the day-to-day management of the Trust taken over by patricians such as G.M. Trevelyan and Lord Zetland, and only in the aftermath of Lord Lothian's Country House Scheme and the Second World War did it become concerned – indeed, for a time preoccupied – with protecting and preserving the homes of once-rich landowners now fallen upon difficult days. It is hardly surprising that at this time, and under these circumstances, Harold Nicolson and Vita Sackville-West became devoted supporters – a devotion which in her case existed despite her wish that neither Knole nor Sissinghurst should go to the Trust.

From the standpoint of the historian, the particular difficulty with this country-house cult, in both its sentimentalised and its institutionalised forms, is that the people who had once built, owned and occupied such houses rarely receive the notice they deserve, and all too often possess no substantial historical identity whatsoever. At best, they are represented by the (often indifferent) family portraits on the wall, and by a genealogical table coyly printed near the back of the guide book (a practice, I am well aware, that I have followed here). But what is invariably missing is any sense of these people as three-dimensional figures, as members of the national elite of wealth, status and power, who collectively made British history from the time of the Tudors to the late nineteenth century. For most of its existence the British aristocracy was not primarily concerned with building houses, and filling them with works of art, in the hope that at some future date a descendant would show them to an admiring, deferential and entry-fee-paying public eager to view this particular slice of the 'national' heritage. On the contrary, it was concerned with the things that have always preoccupied aristocrats throughout history: getting and spending money, accumulating and wielding power, and revelling in prestige and authority.

It is, of course, no coincidence that the rise of the cult of the country house has taken place in precisely the same century which has witnessed the decline and fall of the aristocracy as a self-conscious, self-confident elite of wealth, power and status. Indeed, in some ways there can be no doubt that the cult of the country house is yet another attempt by what remains of the aristocracy to safeguard its increasingly uncertain and beleaguered future. Even in our own time, however, let alone in the centuries which have gone before, it is wholly misleading to see the aristocracy as country-house owners and custodians first and foremost, and to neglect or to ignore their many other activities – some admirable and important, some far less so – which constitute their substantial, unassailable claim to serious historical study. It is the serious historical study of those other activities which I have sought to practise – and now to advocate – in this book. Enough of snobbery and nostalgia. Good riddance to ignorant and sentimental deference. It is time we got beyond the country house.

APPENDIXES

Aristocratic Indebtedness in the Nineteenth Century

	Earls of Lisburne (£)	Sneyds of Keele Hall (£)	Lords Hatherton (£)	Grahams of Netherby (£)	Earls of Scarbrough (£)	Marquesses of Downshire (£)	Earls Fitzwilliam (£)	Marquesses of Bute (£)
1801–10	29,000	25,000	1,000	n.a.	41,000	n.a.	n.a.	n.a.
1811–20	n.a.	19,000	n.a.	55,000	n.a.	250,000	n.a.	83,000
1821–30	94,000	2,000	n.a.	100,000	n.a.	n.a.	n.a.	n.a.
1831–40	41,000	n.a.	90,000	200,000	n.a.	407,000	n.a.	n.a.
1841–50	68,000	189,000	n.a.	c.200,000	n.a.	n.a.	c.800,000	399,000
1851–60	n.a.	n.a.	n.a.	c.200,000	90,000	480,000	n.a.	271,000
1861–70	n.a.	c.189,000	148,000	c.200,000	120,000	n.a.	n.a.	381,000
1871–80	39,000	n.a.	n.a.	275,000	n.a.	329,000	827,000	c.550,000
1881–90	44,000	c.100,000	159,000	275,000	n.a.	n.a.	n.a.	n.a.
1891–1900	nil	c.134,000	n.a.	275,000	n.a.	n.a.	n.a.	n.a.
Gross annual value of estates in 1883	14,000	18,000	23,000	27,000	32,000	97,000	137,000	151,000

Sources: J.M. Howells, 'The Crosswood Estate, 1547–1947', Ceredigion, III (1956), pp. 78–83; Howell, 'The Crosswood estate: Its Growth and Economic Development, 1683–1899' (M.A. dissertation, University of Wales, 1956), p. 249; R. W. Sturgess, 'The Response of Agriculture in Staffordshire to the Price Changes of the Nineteenth Century' (Ph.D. dissertation, University of Manchester, 1965), p. 132, 237, 272; Sturgess, 'Landownership, Mining and Urban Development in Nineteenth Century Staffordshire', in J.T. Ward & R.G. Wilson (eds.), Land and Industry: The Landed Estate and the Industrial Revolution (1971), pp 188–89,

193–97, 199–200; D. Spring, 'A Great Agricultural Estate: Netherby Under Sir James Graham, 1820–45', *Canadian Historical Review*, XXXIII (1952), p. 76; T. W. Beastall, *A North Country Estate: The Lumleys and Sandersons as Landowners, 1600–1900* (1975), pp. 108–9, 183–4; W. A. Maguire, *The Downshire Estates in Ireland, 1801–1845: The Management of Irish Landed Estates in the Early Nineteenth Century* (1972), pp. 83, 97; D. Spring, 'Earl Fitzwilliam and the Corn Laws', *American Historical Review*, LIX (1954), p. 298; Wentworth Woodhouse MSS, 182, analytical table of debts, 1878; J. Davies, 'Glamorgan and the Bute Estate, 1866–1947' (Ph.D. dissertation, University of Wales, 1969), pp. 136, 304, 371, n182; M. J. Daunton, 'Aristocrat and Traders: The Bute Docks, 1839–1914', *Journal of Transport History*, new ser. III (1975), p. 77; J. Bateman, *The Great Landowners of Great Britain and Ireland*, (4th edn 1883, ed. D. Spring, 1971), pp. 69, 168, 190, 212, 272, 414.

Notes: All figures are rounded to the nearest £1000. Figures given for debt in each decade are *not* an average, but for a single year. In certain instances, the authorities cited give conflicting figures for debt for the same year. In such circumstances, I have always taken the lowest figure available, so that some of the evidence presented here may be an underestimate.

n.a. = not available.

Sneyds: The precise figures for debt end in 1848. Subsequent figures are estimates calculated from interest charges; they are therefore only very approximate, but a reliable guide as to overall trends.

Hathertons: These figures refer only to debts secured on the Teddesley estate. In 1888 the Walsall estate also was encumbered to the extent of £54,000.

Scarbroughs: 1801–10 figure is for 1802; by 1808 the debt was reduced to £31,000. Similarly by 1874–5, it had been reduced to £40,000, and sprang up again at the end of the decade.

Downshires: All figures refer to debt secured on the Irish Estates, and ignore English encumbrances.

Butes: All figures are for English and Welsh Estates, ignoring Scotland. In 1922 outstanding loans came to £1 million.

The Churchills

1. GENEALOGICAL TABLE OF THE DUKES OF
MARLBOROUGH

2. CLEMENTINE HOZIER'S RELATIVES

1. Genealogical table of the Dukes of Marlborough

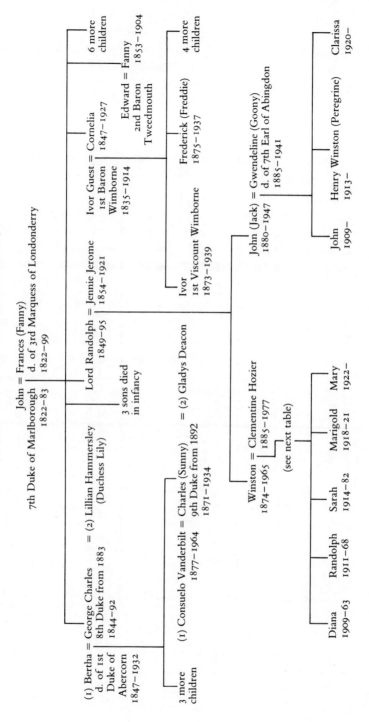

2. Clementine Hozier's relatives

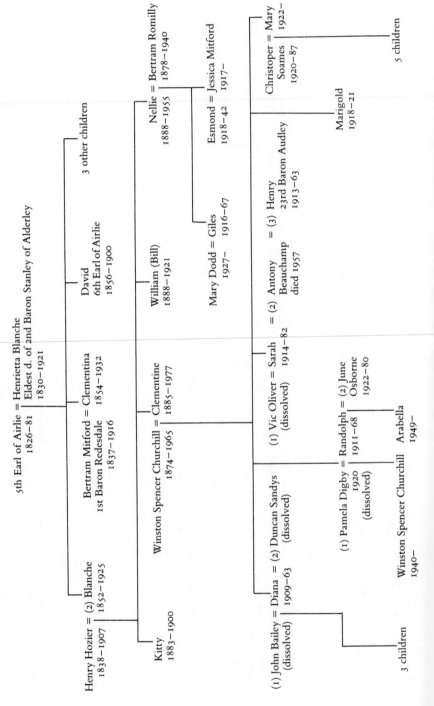

The Devonshires

1. *The Wealthiest Landowners of Great Britain and Ireland, Possessing Land of Gross Annual Value in Excess of £60,000 Per Annum, in 1883*

Landowner	Acreage	Gross annual value (£)	Chief sources of stated revenue
Marquess of Anglesey	29,737	110,598	Minerals
★Duke of Bedford	86,335	141,793	English land
Viscount Boyne	30,205	88,793	Minerals
★Earl Brownlow	58,335	86,426	English land
★Duke of Buccleuch	460,108	217,163	Scottish land
★Marquess of Bute	116,668	151,135	Minerals and Scottish land
Lord Calthorpe	6,470	122,628	Urban land
★Duke of Cleveland	104,194	97,398	English land
★Earl Cowper	37,869	60,392	English land
★Earl of Derby	68,942	163,273	Minerals and urban land
★Duke of Devonshire	198,572	180,750	English and Irish land
Marquess of Downshire	120,189	96,691	Irish land
★Earl of Dudley	25,554	123,176	Minerals
★Earl of Durham	30,471	71,671	Minerals
★Earl of Ellesmere	13,222	71,209	Minerals, canals and railways
★Earl of Fife	249,220	72,563	Scottish land
★Earl Fitzwilliam	115,743	138,801	Minerals and Irish land
Lord Haldon	10,109	109,275	Urban land
Duke of Hamilton	157,743	73,636	Scottish land
★Marquess of Landsdowne	142,916	62,025	Irish land
★Lord Leconfield	109,935	88,112	English and Irish land
★Marquess of Londonderry	50,323	100,118	Minerals and Irish land
Earl of Lonsdale	68,065	71,333	Minerals and English land
★Duke of Newcastle	35,547	74,547	Minerals
Duke of Norfolk	49,886	75,596	Urban land and English land
★Duke of Northumberland	186,397	176,048	Minerals and English land
Earl of Pembroke	44,806	77,720	Urban land and English land
★Lord Penrhyn	49,548	71,018	Welsh land and minerals
★Duke of Portland	183,199	88,350	English and Scottish land
Sir John Ramsden	150,048	181,294	Urban land and Scottish land
Duke of Richmond	286,411	79,683	Scottish land
Duke of Rutland	70,137	97,683	English land
Sir John St. Aubyn	6,555	95,212	Urban land
Earl of Seafield	305,930	78,227	Scottish land
★Duke of Sutherland	1,358,545	141,667	Scottish and English land and minerals
★Lord Tredegar	39,157	60,000	Welsh land
★Sir Richard Wallace	72,307	85,737	Irish land
Baroness Willoughby D'Eresby	132,220	74,006	English and Scottish land
★Lord Windsor	37,454	63,778	Urban land and Welsh land
Earl of Yarborough	56,893	84,649	English land

★ Those landowners asterisked appear also in Table 2

Source: J. Bateman, *The Great Landowners of Great Britain and Ireland* (4th edn, 1883, ed. D. Spring, 1971), passim.

Notes: These figures, both for acreage and as a guide to income, should be treated with extreme caution, since Bateman's data in general exclude mineral as well as metropolitan (i.e. London) values, though he sometimes gave the former separately and sometimes included them while saying he did not. Four examples of misleadingly large valuations are given in the text. At the other extreme, the income of the Duke of Bedford is understated, because the revenue from their London estates is excluded (and is therefore not mentioned in the table). For earlier and more precise figures see: D. Spring, *The English Landed Estate in the Nineteenth Century: Its Administration* (1963), p. 191; D.J. Olsen, *Town Planning in London in the Eighteenth and Nineteenth Century* (1964), pp. 219–22. For a more recent attempt to revise some of Bateman's figures see W.D. Rubinstein, *Men of Property: The Very Wealthy in Britain since the Industrial Revolution* (1981), pp. 194–5.

2. *Wealthiest Landowners Leaving Estates of £1 million and more, 1809–1949*

Family	Individual	Date of Death	Size of estate
Dukes of Bedford	11th Duke	1940	£4,651,000
Earls Brownlow	3rd Earl	1921	£1,644,000
	5th Earl	1927	£1,074,000
Dukes of Buccleuch	4th Duke of Queensberry	1810	'Upper value'
	6th Duke	1914	£1,159,000
	7th Duke	1935	£1,126,000
Marquess of Bute	3rd Marquess	1900	£1,142,000
Dukes of Cleveland	1st Duke	1842	£1,000,000
	4th Duke	1891	£1,449,000
Earls Cowper	7th Earl	1905	£1,327,000
Earls of Derby	15th Earl	1893	£1,936,000
	16th Earl	1908	£1,101,000
	Lord Edward Stanley	1938	£2,210,000
	17 Earl	1948	£3,218,000
Dukes of Devonshire	Henry Cavendish	1801	'Upper value'
	7th Duke	1891	£1,864,000
	8th Duke	1908	£1,165,000
Earls of Dudley	1st Earl	1885	£1,026,000
Earls of Durham	3rd Earl	1928	£1,559,000
	4th Earl	1929	£1,207,000
Earls of Ellesmere	4th Earl	1944	£1,243,000
Dukes of Fife	1st Duke	1912	£1,000,000
Earls Fitzwilliam	6th Earl	1902	£2,882,000
	7th Earl	1943	£1,320,000

2. *Continued*

Family	Individual	Date of Death	Size of estate
Marquesses of Landsdowne	5th Marquess	1927	£1,278,000
	6th Marquess	1936	£1,684,000
	7th Marquess	1944	£1,023,000
Lords Leconfield	3rd Lord	1901	£1,861,000
Marquesses of Londonderry	7th Marquess	1949	£1,022,000
Dukes of Newcastle	7th Duke	1928	£1,407,000
Dukes of Northumberland	7th Duke	1918	£1,108,000
	8th Duke	1930	£2,510,000
	9th Duke	1940	£1,801,000
Lords Penrhyn	3rd Lord	1927	£1,112,000
Dukes of Portland	5th Duke	1879	£1,500,000
Dukes of Sutherland	1st Duke	1833	'Upper value'
	2nd Duke	1861	£1,000,000
	3rd Duke	1892	£1,378,000
	4th Duke	1913	£1,221,000
Lords Tredegar	2nd Viscount	1949	£1,719,000
Wallaces	Sir Richard	1890	£1,226,000
Lords Windsor	2nd Earl of Plymouth	1943	£1,204,000

Source: W.D. Rubinstein, 'British Millionaires, 1809–1949', *Bulletin of the Institute of Historical Research*, XLVII (1974), pp. 206–23.

Notes: Family names are given as in Bateman. Where individual titles differ it is because of inheritance through the female lines (4th Duke of Queensberry), the premature death of an heir (Lord Edward Stanley), or a further step in peerage (2nd Earl of Plymouth). It should be stressed that this is not a list of *all* landowner millionaires, any more than is Table 1. As Rubinstein notes: 'The valuations given in the case of millionaire landowners proved before 1898 refer to their personalty only, and thereafter until 1926 include only their unsettled realty.' Only from 1926 is the value of settled land included. If the list of top wealth-holders from Bateman were extended to cover all with land of gross annual value in excess of £33,000 (which, multiplied by the commonly held formula of thirty-three years' purchase, would be sufficient to give an estate of £1 million) then 161 landowners come in this category. Those appearing in Table 1 were therefore very rich; those coming in Table 2 were super-rich.

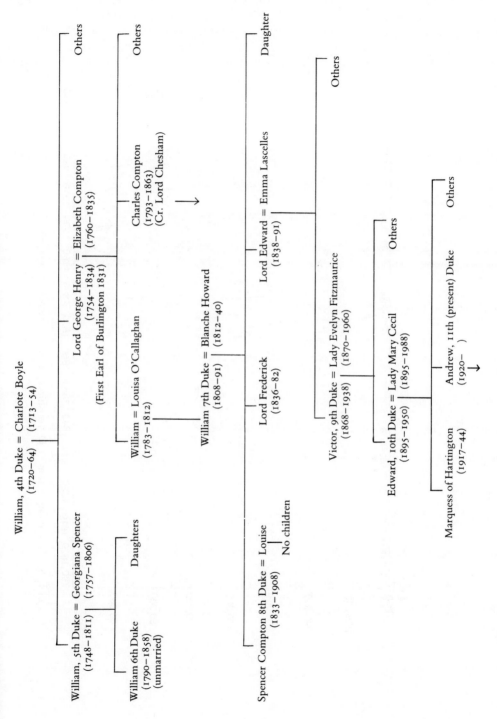

3. Genealogical table of the Dukes of Devonshire

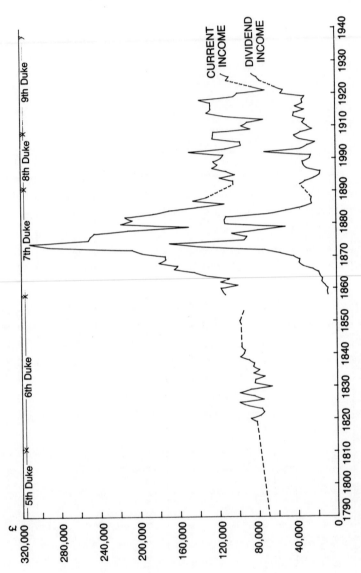

Graph 1. Size and composition of Devonshires' current income, 1790–1926.

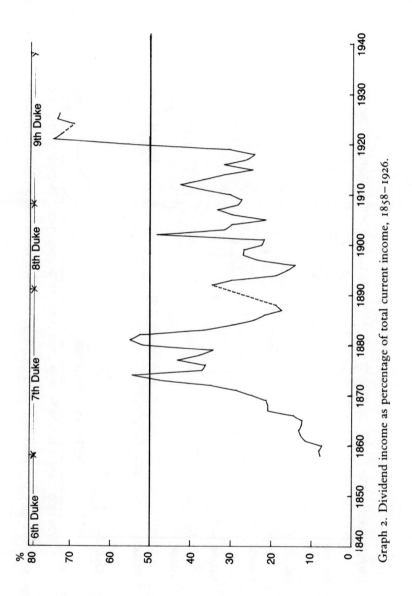

Graph 2. Dividend income as percentage of total current income, 1858–1926.

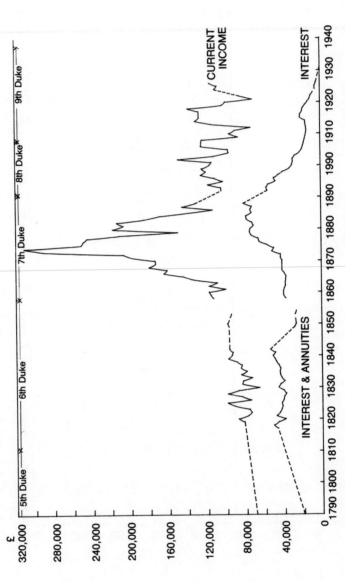

Graph 3. Devonshires' current income, and expenditure on interest and annuities (1790–1854) and interest (1858–1931).

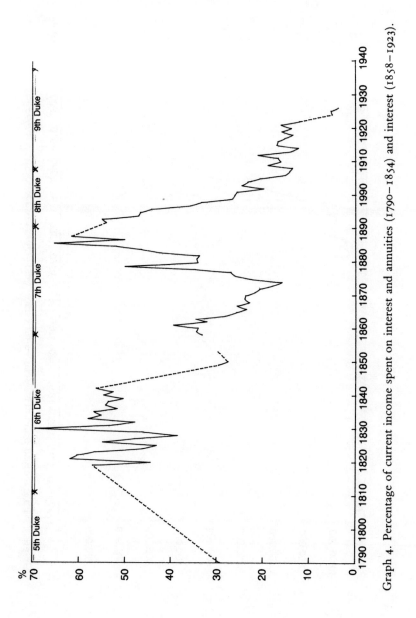

Graph 4. Percentage of current income spent on interest and annuities (1790–1854) and interest (1858–1923).

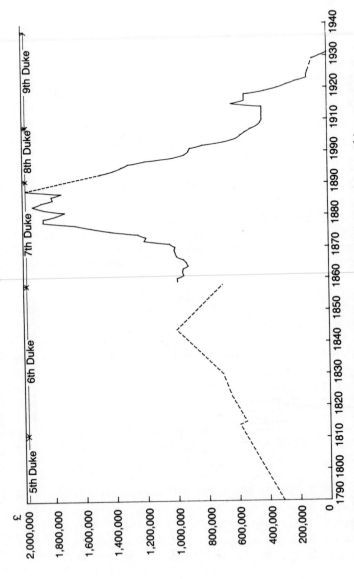

Graph 5. Mortgage and bond debts secured on estates held, Dukes of Devonshire, 1790–1931.

5. The Finances of the Seventh Duke of Devonshire, 1858–91

1. Income and Expenditure on Current Account (£)

	1863	1874	1888
Income			
Net estate rental	94,456	141,716	106,888
Dividends	14,483	169,361	25,084
Miscellaneous	224	233	nil
Total	109,163	311,310	131,972
Expenditure			
Debt interest	38,390	50,102	81,353
Annuities	7,940	5,655	2,645
Insurance	6,791	7,223	7,168
Family allowances	3,900	4,710	6,300
Subscriptions	5,407	15,640	4,135
Legal and admin. fees	3,591	2,954	3,011
Elections	664	10,182	408
Holker rebuilding	nil	9,088	nil
Household	12,867	23,340	17,727
Miscellaneous	2,310	653	736
Surplus to capital a/c	27,303	181,763	8,489
Total	109,163	311,310	131,972

2. Composition of Investments (£)

	1858		1873		1885	
Barrow	102,945	(67.9%)	948,896	(81.8%)	2,144,306	(83.9%)
Buxton	4,748	(3.1%)	23,229	(2.0%)	26,800	(1.0%)
Eastbourne	700	(0.4%)	41,589	(3.5%)	115,235	(4.5%)
Irish railways	nil	(0.0)%	117,810	(10.1%)	202,343	(7.9%)
Other	43,135	(28.6%)	28,919	(2.6%)	67,659	(2.7%)
Total	151,528		1,160,443		2,556,343	

3. Composition of Dividends

(1) year	(2) Total dividend income (£)	(3) Barrow dividend income (£)	(3) as % of (2)
1858	8,987	6,470	71.9
1860	8,945	6,139	68.6
1862	14,991	7,795	51.9
1864	16,894	12,065	71.4
1866	24,016	19,996	83.2
1868	37,656	32,029	85.0
1870	43,202	38,298	88.6
1972	72,236	65,822	91.1
1874	169,361	151,820	89.6
1876	91,005	64,645	71.0
1878	80,113	62,206	77.6
1880	113,139	89,972	79.5
1882	112,541	91,090	80.9
1884	50,951	16,742	32.8
1886	24,974	7,623	30.5
1888	25,084	8,487	33.8

Source: Currey MSS, Account Books, 1858–72, 1873–88.

4. Income and Acreage in 1883

	Acres	Gross annual value
Derbyshire	89,462	89,557
York, W. R.	19,239	16,718
Lancashire	12,681	12,494
Sussex	11,062	14,881
Somerset	3,014	4,918
Lincoln	1,392	2,657
Cumberland	983	1,925
Middlesex	524	3,079
Notts	125	130
Stafford	26	40
Chesire	28	21
Co. Cork	32,550	19,326
Co. Waterford	27,483	15,000
Co. Tipperary	3	4
Total	198,572	180,750

Source: J. Bateman, *The Great Landowners of Great Britain and Ireland* (4th edn, 1883, ed. D. Spring, 1971), p. 130.

The Cozens-Hardys

I. Genealogical Table of the Cozens-Hardys of Letheringsett

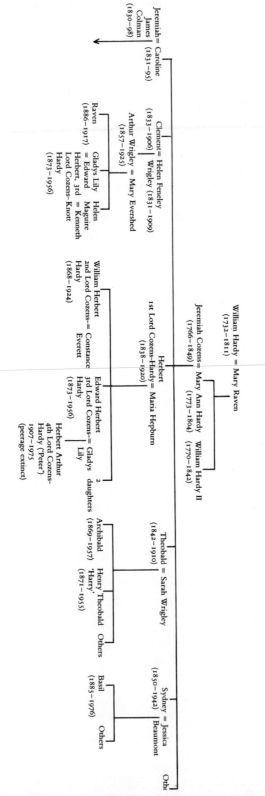

2. Principal Publications of Basil Cozens-Hardy, 1923–1972

'The First Seventy Years of Guestwick Independent Chapel', *Norfolk Archaeology*, XXI (1923), pp. 155–74.

'A Muster Roll and Clergy List in the Hundred of Holt, c1523', *Norfolk Archaeology*, XXII (1926), pp. 45–58.

'The Sepulchral Slab at Blickling Church', *Norfolk Archaeology*, XXII (1926), pp. 79–82.

'Scheduling of the Norfolk Ancient Monuments', *Norfolk Archaeology*, XXII (1926), pp. 221–6.

'A Puritan Moderate: Dr. Thomas Thorougood STB, 1596 to 1669, Rector of Grimston, Little Massingham and Great Cressingham', *Norfolk Archaeology*, XXII (1926), pp. 311–37

A Short History of St. Margaret's Church, Cley-Next-The-Sea (Holt, 1928).

'Cley-Next-The-Sea and its Marshes', *Transactions of the Norfolk and Norwich Naturalists' Society*, XII (1924–9), pp. 354–73.

'An Ecclesiastical Dispute at Westwick, c1450', *Norfolk Archaeology*, XXIII (1929), pp. 51–5.

'A Calendar of Such of the Frere MSS as Relate to the Hundred of Holt', *Norfolk Record Society*, I (1931), pp. 5–40.

'Norfolk Crosses', *Norfolk Archaeology*, XXV (1935), pp. 297–336

'The Maritime Trade of the Port of Blakeney, Norfolk, 1587–1590', *Norfolk Record Society*, VIII (1936), pp. 17–37.

'Presents to the Sheriff of Norfolk, 1600–1603', *Norfolk Archaeology*, XXVI (1938), pp. 52–8.

'Norfolk Coastal Defences in 1588', *Norfolk Archaeology*, XXVI (1938), pp. 310–14.

'Norwich Consistory Court Depositions, 1499–1512 and 1518–1530' [with E.D. Stone], *Norfolk Record Society*, X (1938).

The Mayors of Norwich, 1403–1835: Being Biographical Notes on the Mayors of the Old Corporation [with E.A. Kent] (Norwich, 1938).

'The Norwich Chapelfield Home Estate Since 1545 and Some of Its Owners and Occupiers', *Norfolk Archaeology*, XXVII (1941), pp. 351–84.

'The Early Days of the [Norfolk and Norwich Archaeological] Society', *Norfolk Archaeology*, XXIX (1946), pp. 1–7.

'Chantries of the Duchy of Lancaster in Norfolk, 1548', *Norfolk Archaeology*, XXXIX (1946), pp. 201–10.

The Diary of Silas Neville, 1767–1788 [editor] (Oxford, 1950).

'Old Meeting House, Norwich, and Great Yarmouth Independent Church: Observations on their Origins', *Norfolk Record Society*, XXII (1951), pp. 1–5.

'The Lavile and Curson Families at Letheringsett', *Norfolk Archaeology*, XXX (1952), pp. 338–52.

'Extracts from the Two Earliest Minute Books of the Dean and Chapter of Norwich Cathedral, 1566–1649' [with J.F. Williams], *Norfolk Record Society*, XXIV (1953).

'The Holt Road', *Norfolk Archaeology*, XXXI (1957), pp. 163–77.

The History of Letheringsett in the County of Norfolk, with Extracts from the Diary of Mary Hardy (1773–1809) (Norwich, 1957).

'Some Norfolk Halls', *Norfolk Archaeology*, XXXII (1961), pp. 163–208.

'Norfolk Lieutenancy Journal, 1676–1701', *Norfolk Record Society*, XXX (1961).

'Norfolk Lawyers', *Norfolk Archaeology*, XXXIII (1965), pp. 266–97, 514.

'The Glaven Valley', *Norfolk Archaeology*, XXXIII (1965), pp. 491–523.

'Mary Hardy's Diary', *Norfolk Record Society*, XXXVII (1968).

'The Old Shirehouse at Norwich', *Norfolk Archaeology*, XXXV (1970), pp. 145–8.

'Havens in North Norfolk', *Norfolk Archaeology*, XXXV (1972), pp. 356–63.

'The Countess Versus Methodism Versus Independency', *Transactions of the Congregationalist History Society*, XXI (1972), pp. 74–6.

Genealogical Table of the Nicolsons and the Sackville-Wests

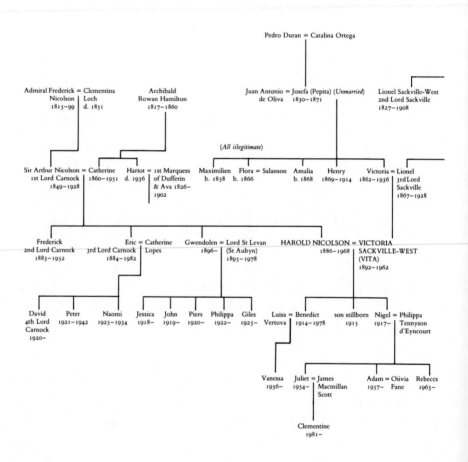

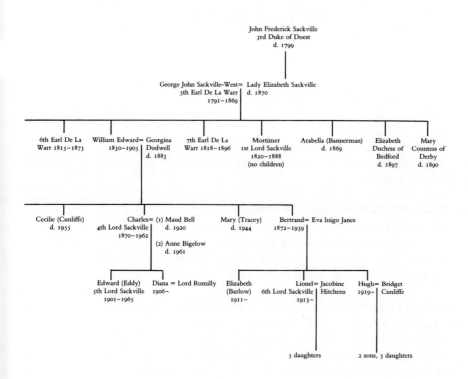

John Frederick Sackville
3rd Duke of Doest
d. 1799

George John Sackville-West= Lady Elizabeth Sackville
5th Earl De La Warr | d. 1870
1791–1869

6th Earl De La | William Edward= Georgina | 7th Earl De La | Mortimer | Arabella (Bannerman) | Elizabeth | Mary
Warr 1815–1873 | 1830–1905 | Dodwell | Warr 1818–1896 | 1st Lord Sackville | d. 1869 | Duchess of | Countess of
| | d. 1883 | | 1820–1888 | | Bedford | Derby
| | | | (no children) | | d. 1897 | d. 1890

Cecilie (Cunliffe) | Charles= (1) Maud Bell | Mary (Tracey) | Bertrand= Eva Inigo Janes
d. 1955 | 4th Lord Sackville | d. 1920 | d. 1944 | 1872–1959
1870–1962	
	(2) Anne Bigelow
	d. 1961

Edward (Eddy) | Diana = Lord Romilly | Elizabeth | Lionel= Jacobine | Hugh= Bridget
5th Lord Sackville | 1906– | (Barlow) | 6th Lord Sackville | Hitchens | 1919– | Cunliffe
1901–1965 | | 1911– | 1913–

5 daughters   2 sons, 3 daughters

A Note on Sources

The following archival collections have been consulted during the preparation of this book:

Bedford MSS (Bedford Estate Office, London)
Cabinet Minutes (Public Record Office, Kew)
Chatsworth MSS (Chatsworth House, Derbyshire)
Cinque Ports MSS (Kent Archives Office, Maidstone)
Currey MSS (Currey and Co., London)
Curzon MSS (India Office Library, London)
Eastern Daily Press MSS (Norfolk Record Office, Norwich)
Hardinge MSS (Cambridge University Library)
Hoare's Bank MSS (Hoare's Bank, London)
Hornor MSS (Norfolk Record Office, Norwich)
Ketton-Cremer MSS (Norfolk Record Office, Norwich)
Local Collection (Norwich City Library)
Radnor MSS (Kent Archives Office, Maidstone)
Reading MSS (India Office Library, London)
Royal Exchange Assurance MSS (Royal Exchange Assurance, London)
Templewood MSS (Cambridge University Library)
Wentworth Woodhouse MSS (Sheffield City Library)

Since the references to each chapter constitute what is, in effect, a running bibliography, I have dispensed with a separate list of further reading. In each chapter, references are given in full with every first citation, and are abbreviated thereafter. The place of publication is the United Kingdom, unless otherwise stated.

Notes

Abbreviations

The following abbreviations have been used throughout the notes:

AC-H	Archibald Cozens-Hardy
AgHR	*Agricultural History Review*
BC-H	Basil Cozens-Hardy
DNB	*Dictionary of National Biography*
EcHR	*Economic History Review*
EDP	*Eastern Daily Press*
HC	House of Commons
HJ	*Historical Journal*
HL	House of Lords
HN	Harold Nicolson
HND	S. Olson (ed.), *Harold Nicolson: Diaries and Letters, 1930–1964* (1980)
HND I–III	N. Nicolson (ed.), *Harold Nicolson: Diaries and Letters*: vol. I, *1930–39* (1966)
	vol. II, *1939–45* (1967)
	vol. III, *1945–62* (1968)
JEH	*Journal of Economic History*
JTH	*Journal of Transport History*
PP	Parliamentary Papers
PRO CAB	Cabinet Minutes
RC	Royal Commission
7DDD	Diary of the Seventh Duke of Devonshire
VS-W	Vita Sackville-West
WSC	Randolph S. Churchill & Martin Gilbert, *Winston S. Churchill* (8 vols., 1966–88)
WSC CV	Companion volumes to the above

Prologue

1. T. Stoppard, *Arcadia* (1993), p. 56.

1. The Making of the British Upper Classes

1. J.C.D. Clark, *English Society, 1688–1832* (1985); A.J. Mayer, *The Persistence of the Old Regime: Europe to the Great War* (1981).

2. For a useful starting point, see R. Porter, 'Georgian Britain: An Ancien Regime?', *British Journal for Eighteenth-Century Studies*, XV (1992), pp. 141–4.

3. See esp.: J.G.A. Pocock, 'British History: A Plea for a New Subject', *Journal of Modern History*, XLVII (1975), pp. 601–21; Pocock, 'The Limits and Divisions of British History: In Search of an Unknown Subject', *American Historical Review*, LXXXVII (1982), pp. 311–36; L. Colley, 'Britishness and Otherness: An Argument', *Journal of British Studies*, XXXI (1992), pp. 309–29.

4. J. Ehrman, *The Younger Pitt: The Reluctant Transition* (1983), pp. 129, 135–9, 143, 150, 170–1; L. Colley, *Britons: Forging the Nation, 1707–1837* (1992), pp. 149–55.

5. N. Gash, 'After Waterloo: British Society and the Legacy of the Napoleonic Wars', *Transactions of the Royal Historical Society*, 5th ser., XXVIII (1978), pp. 152–6; T. Paine, *Rights of Man* (ed. H. Collins, 1969), pp. 96–7, 102–6, 113, 194, 246–50, 277–9; J. Wade, *The Black Book: or Corruption Unmasked* (1820), pp. 93–4, 389–91; G.D.H. & M. Cole (eds.), *The Opinions of William Cobbett* (1944), pp. 11–21, 23–6, 93, 105, 210–11, 241, 281–8.

6. R.R. Palmer, *The Age of Democratic Revolution: A Political History of Europe and America, 1760–1800* (2 vols., 1959–64), vol. I, pp. 286, 308–17, 369; vol. II, pp. 459–64. See also O. Hufton, *Europe: Privilege and Protest, 1730–1789* (1980), pp. 367, 373.

7. The literature on this subject is extensive and expanding. See esp.: C. Clay, 'Marriage, Inheritance and the Rise of Large Estates in England, 1660–1815', *EcHR*, 2nd ser., XXI (1968), pp. 515–17; L. Bonfield, 'Marriage Settlements and the "Rise of Great Estates": The Demographic Aspect', *EcHR*, 2nd ser., XXXII (1979), pp. 486–7; L. & J.C.F. Stone, *An Open Elite?: England, 1540–1880* (1984), pp. 93–124.

8. Coles, *Cobbett*, pp. 26, 61–2, 218.

9. J.V. Beckett, *The Aristocracy in England, 1660–1914* (1986), pp. 96–7; P.R. Roberts, 'The Decline of the Welsh Squires in the Eighteenth Century', *National Library of Wales Journal*, XIII (1963–4), pp. 157–73; R.T. Jenkins & H.M. Ramage, *A History of the Honourable Society of Cymmrodorion* (1951), pp. 16–17; D.W. Howell, 'The Economy of the Landed Estates of Pembrokeshire, c.1680–1830', *Welsh History Review*, III (1967), p. 266; P. Jenkins, *The Making of a Ruling Class: The Glamorgan Gentry, 1640–1790* (1983), pp. xxi–xxvi, 1–42; Jenkins, 'The Demographic Decline of the Landed Gentry in the Eighteenth Century: A South Wales Study', *Welsh History Review*, XI (1982), pp. 31–49; Jenkins, 'The Creation of an "Ancient Gentry": Glamorgan, 1760–1840', *Welsh History Review*, XII (1984), pp. 29–49; P. Roebuck, *Yorkshire Baronets, 1640–1760* (1981), pp. 276–316; C. Shrimpton, 'The Landed Society and Farming Community in Essex in the Late Eighteenth and Early Nineteenth Centuries' (Ph.D. dissertation, Cambridge University, 1965), pp. 49–50.

10. P.C. Otto, 'Daughters of the British Aristocracy: Their Marriages in the Eighteenth and Nineteenth Centuries, with particular reference to the Scottish Peerage' (Ph.D. dissertation, Stanford University, 1974), pp. 387–408; A.P.W. Malcomson, *The Pursuit of the Heiress: Aristocratic Marriage in Ireland, 1750–1820* (1982), passim.

11. *Estates Gazette*, 30 Jan. 1886. The Cowpers also benefitted unexpectedly from the deaths of the male heirs in the families of the wives of the first and second earls, which transformed the family from being moderately wealthy to super rich. See L. Stone, 'Cole Green Park, Hertfordshire', in H. Colvin & J. Harris (eds.), *The Country Seat: Studies in the History of the British Country House* (1970), pp. 78–9.

12. W.A. Maguire, *The Downshire Estates in Ireland, 1801–1845: The Management of Irish Landed Estates in the Early Nineteenth Century* (1972), pp. 1–9; A.P.W. Malcomson, 'The Gentle Leviathan: Arthur Hill, Second Marquess of Downshire, 1753–1801', in P.J. Roebuck (ed.), *Plantation to Partition: Essays in Ulster History in Honour of J.L. McCracken* (1981), pp. 102–7; H.M. Hyde, *The Londonderrys: A Family Chronicle* (1979), pp. 23, 29; J. Davies, *Cardiff and the Marquesses of Bute* (1981), pp. 1–21.

13. J.J. Sack, *The Grenvillites, 1801–29: Party Politics and Factionalism in the Age of Pitt and Liverpool* (1979), pp. 3–8.

14. E. Richards, *The Leviathan of Wealth: The Sutherland Fortune in the Industrial Revolution* (1973), pp. 7–9.

15. J. Roselli, 'An Indian Governor in the Norfolk Marshlands: Lord William Bentinck as Improver, 1809–27', *AgHR*, XIX (1971), p. 47; F.M.L. Thompson, 'Landownership and Economic Growth in England in the Eighteenth Century', in S.J. Woolf & E.L. Jones (eds.), *Agricultural Change and Economic Development: The Historical Problems* (1969), pp. 50–1.

16. H.J. Perkin, *The Origins of Modern English Society, 1780–1880* (1969), pp. 88–9; D. Rapp, 'Social Mobility in the Eighteenth Century: The Whitbreads of Bedfordshire, 1720–1815', *EcHR*, 2nd ser., XXVII (1974), p. 380; E.L. Jones, 'Industrial Capital and Landed Investment: The Arkwrights in Herefordshire, 1809–43', in E.L. Jones & G.E. Mingay (eds.), *Land, Labour and Population in the Industrial Revolution: Essays Presented to J.D. Chambers* (1967), pp. 52–9, 69; T.J. Raybould, *The Economic Emergence of the Black Country: A Study of the Dudley Estate* (1973), p. 113; Jenkins, 'Creation of an "Ancient Gentry" ', p. 36.

17. W.D. Rubinstein, 'The End of "Old Corruption" in Britain, 1780–1860', *Past &*

Present, no. 101 (1983), p. 61, n. 8.

18. J.V. Beckett, 'Landownership and Estate Management', in G.E. Mingay (ed.), *The Agrarian History of England and Wales*, vol. VI, *1750–1850* (1989), pp. 620–5; D. Howell, *Land and People in Nineteenth-Century Wales* (1977), p. 9; M. McCahill, 'The Scottish Peerage and the House of Lords in the Late Eighteenth Century', *Scottish Historical Review*, LI (1972), p. 174; D. Large, 'The Wealth of the Greater Irish Landowners, 1750–1815', *Irish Historical Studies*, XV (1966), pp. 21–9, 46–7; P. Roebuck, 'Rent Movement, Proprietorial Incomes, and Agricultural Development, 1730–1830', in Roebuck, *Plantation to Partition*, p. 90.

19. F.M.L. Thompson, *English Landed Society in the Nineteenth Century* (1963), pp. 122, 220; A.D. Harvey, *Britain in the Early Nineteenth Century* (1978), p. 337.

20. P. Mathias, *The First Industrial Nation: An Economic History of Britain, 1700–1914* (2nd edn, 1983), pp. 47–54, 67; M.E. Turner, *Enclosure in Britain, 1750–1830* (1984), passim.

21. J.D. Chambers & G.E. Mingay, *The Agricultural Revolution, 1750–1880* (1966), pp. 77–84. For one study of a great improver, see J.R. Wordie, *Estate Management in Eighteenth-Century England: The Building of the Leveson-Gower Fortune* (1982), pp. 53–72, 175–205, 214–25, 272–7.

22. Howell, *Land and People*, p. 38; A.H. John, *The Industrial Development of South Wales* (1950), pp. 5, 170–1; A.H. Dodd, *The Industrial Revolution in North Wales* (2nd edn, 1951), pp. 34–45, 60–7.

23. K.H. Connell, 'The Colonization of Waste Land in Ireland, 1780–1845', *EcHR*, 2nd ser., III (1950–1), p. 46; E.R.R. Green, *The Lagan Valley, 1800–50: A Local History of the Industrial Revolution* (1949), pp. 127–33; L.M. Cullen, *An Economic History of Ireland Since 1660* (1972), pp. 82–4, 114; D. McCourt, 'The Decline of Rundale, 1750–1850', in Roebuck, *Plantation to Partition*, pp. 127–34.

24. E. Richards, *A History of the Highland Clearances*, vol. I, *Agrarian Transformation and the Evictions, 1746–1886* (1982), pp. 3–34, 112–219; J.E. Handley, *The Agricultural Revolution in Scotland* (1963), pp. 16–37, 64–94; R.A. Gailey, 'Agrarian Improvement and the Development of Enclosure in the South West Highlands of Scotland', *Scottish Historical Review*, XLII (1963), pp. 105–25; T.M. Devine, 'Social Stability in the Eastern Lowlands of Scotland During the Agricultural Revolution, 1780–1840', in T.M. Devine (ed.), *Lairds and Improvement in the Scotland of the Enclosure* (1978), pp. 59–69.

25. T.J. Raybould, 'Aristocratic Landowners and the Industrial Revolution: The Black Country Experience, c.1760–1840', *Midland History*, IX (1984), pp. 80–4; Raybould, *Dudley Estate*, pp. 35–51.

26. M.W. Flinn, *The History of the British Coal Industry*, vol. II, *1700–1830: The Industrial Revolution* (1983), pp. 36–42; B.F. Duckham, *A History of the Scottish Coal Industry*, vol. I, *1700–1815* (1970), pp. 141–69.

27. For a full list, see D. Spring, 'English Landowners and Nineteenth-Century Industrialism', in J.T. Ward & R.G. Wilson (eds.), *Land and Industry: The Landed Estate and the Industrial Revolution* (1971), p. 32.

28. Flinn, *Industrial Revolution*, pp. 26, 206–11, 326–7; Raybould, *Dudley Estate*, p. 193; Spring, 'Landowners and Nineteenth-Century Industrialism', pp. 33–5.

29. J.R. Ward, *The Finance of Canal Building in Eighteenth-Century England* (1974), pp. 72–6, 157; Raybould, *Dudley Estate*, pp. 53–9.

30. Richards, *Leviathan of Wealth*, p. 39; F.C. Mather, *After the Canal Duke: A Study of the Industrial Estates Administered by the Trustees of the Third Duke of Bridgewater in the Age of Railway Building, 1825–1872* (1970), pp. 27–43, 357–8.

31. Dodd, *Industrial Revolution in North Wales*, pp. 101–7; Cullen, *Economic History of Ireland*, p. 94; Green, *Lagan Valley*, pp. 35–6; V.T.H. & R. Delany, *The Canals of the South of Ireland* (1966), pp. 41, 52–4, 80–3, 155; W.A. McCutcheon, *The Canals of the North of Ireland* (1965), pp. 31, 42, 46, 86, 103.

32. J. Dunlop, *The British Fisheries Society, 1786–1893* (1978), pp. 23–6.

33. D.G. Lockhart, 'Planned Village Development in Scotland and Ireland, 1700–1850', in T.M. Devine & D. Dickson (eds.), *Ireland and Scotland, 1600–1850: Parallels and Contrasts in Economic and Social Development* (1983), pp. 133–42; T.C. Smout, 'The Landowner and the Planned Village in Scotland, 1730–1830', in N.T. Phillipson & R. Mitchison (eds.), *Scotland in the Age of Improvement: Essays in Scottish History in the Eighteenth Century* (1970), pp. 73–106; B.J. Graham & L.J. Proudfoot, 'Landlords, Planning and Urban growth in Eighteenth- and Early Nineteenth-Century Ireland', *Journal of Urban History*, XVIII (1992), pp. 308–29.

34. D. Cannadine, *Lords and Landlords: The Aristocracy and the Towns, 1774–1967* (1980),

pp. 31–2, 414–15; Beckett, 'Landownership and Estate Management', p. 628.

35. For two different views, see J.R. Wordie, 'Introduction', in C.W. Chalklin & J.R. Wordie (eds.), *Town and Countryside: The English Landowner in the National Economy, 1660–1860* (1989), pp. 1–25; Beckett, 'Landownership and Estate Management', pp. 583–7, 601–7.

36. Rubinstein, 'End of "Old Corruption"', pp. 55–86; Colley, *Britons*, pp. 188–9.

37. P.R. Harling, 'The Rise and Fall of "Old Corruption": Economical Reform and British Political Culture, 1779–1846' (Ph.D. dissertation, Princeton University, 1991), pp. 41–5, 80–8, 189–211, 233–8. But cf. J.R. Breihan, 'Economical Reform, 1785–1810' (Ph.D. dissertation, Cambridge University, 1977), pp. 104–40, 155, 160, 256, 270–9.

38. E. Longford, *Wellington: The Years of the Sword* (1969), pp. 267, 291, 363; I. Butler, *The Eldest Brother* (1973), pp. 175, 264–6.

39. Wade, *Black Book*, p. 87; Sack, *Grenvillites*, pp. 35–44; A.D. Harvey, 'The Grenville Party, 1801–1826' (Ph.D. dissertation, Cambridge University, 1972), pp. 270–82.

40. W.D. Rubinstein, *Men of Property: The Very Wealthy in Britain since the Industrial Revolution* (1987), pp. 59–61; Rubinstein, 'The Structure of Wealth-Holding in Britain, 1809–39: a Preliminary Anatomy', *Historical Research*, LXV (1992), p. 78.

41. Richards, *Leviathan of Wealth*, pp. 9–12; Mather, *After the Canal Duke*, pp. 7, 38–9.

42. J. Cannon, *Parliamentary Reform, 1640–1832* (1973), pp. 37–39; Cannon, 'The Isthmus Repaired: The Resurgence of the English Aristocracy, 1660–1760', *Proceedings of the British Academy*, LXVIII (1982), p. 446; J.A. Phillips, 'The Structure of Electoral Politics in Unreformed England', *Journal of British Studies*, XIX (1979), pp. 77–81; B.D. Hayes, 'Politics in Norfolk, 1750–1832' (Ph.D. dissertation, Cambridge University, 1958), pp. 4–14.

43. Harvey, *Britain in the Early Nineteenth Century*, p. 29; A.H. Dodd, *A History of Carnarvonshire, 1284–1900* (1968), pp. 195, 312–17; R.J. Colyer, 'The Gentry and the County in Nineteenth-Century Cardiganshire', *Welsh History Review*, X (1981), pp. 512–13.

44. B. Lenman, *Integration, Enlightenment and Industrialization: Scotland, 1746–1832* (1981), pp. 71–9, 100–9; L. Timperley, 'Landownership in Scotland in the Eighteenth Century' (Ph.D. dissertation, Edinburgh

University, 1977), pp. 42–7, 85; Cannon, *Parliamentary Reform*, p. 28.

45. G.C. Bolton, *The Passing of the Irish Act of Union: A Study in Parliamentary Politics* (1966), pp. 30–2; A.P.W. Malcomson, *John Foster: The Politics of Anglo-Irish Ascendancy* (1978), pp. 197–203; Malcomson, 'Gentle Leviathan', pp. 103–5.

46. E.M. Johnston, *Great Britain and Ireland, 1760–1800* (1963), pp. 252–69; C. Ross (ed.), *Correspondence of Charles, First Marquess Cornwallis* (3 vols., 1859), vol. III, pp. 321–4.

47. Cannon, *Parliamentary Reform*, p. 108.

48. Wade, *Black Book*, p. 389; A.S. Turberville, *The House of Lords in the Age of Reform, 1786–1837* (1958), p. 246; T.H.B. Oldfield, *The Representative History of Great Britain and Ireland* (6 vols., 1816), vol. VI, pp. 295–9; J.J. Sack, 'The House of Lords and Parliamentary Patronage in Great Britain', *HJ*, XXIII (1980), pp. 916–19.

49. Sack, *The Grenvillites*, pp. 20–32; J.M. Robinson, *The Dukes of Norfolk: A Quincentennial History* (1982), pp. 172–3.

50. M. McCahill, *Order and Equipoise: The Peerage and the House of Lords, 1783–1806* (1978), p. 177; B. Bonsall, *Sir James Lowther and the Cumberland and Westmorland Elections, 1754–1775* (1960), pp. 151–2.

51. Harvey, *Britain in the Early Nineteenth Century*, p. 19; G.P. Judd, *Members of Parliament, 1734–1832* (1955), pp. 84–5; R.G. Thorne (ed.), *The House of Commons, 1790–1820*, vol. I, *Introductory Survey* (1986), pp. 282–6.

52. Turberville, *House of Lords*, p. 250; Wade, *Black Book*, p. 445.

53. Coles, *Cobbett*, p. 281.

54. Harvey, *Britain in the Early Nineteenth Century*, p. 19; Turberville, *House of Lords*, p. 256.

55. Thompson, *English Landed Society*, p. 47.

56. P.B. Munsche, *Gentleman and Poachers: The English Game Laws, 1671–1831* (1981), pp. 25–6, 41–7, 133–63.

57. Perkin, *Origins of Modern English Society*, p. 192.

58. Stones, *Open Elite?*, pp. 225–8; T.H. Hollingsworth, 'The Demography of the British Peerage', *Population Studies*, XVIII (1964), supplement, pp. 30–3.

59. Colley, *Britons*, pp. 167–70, 183–7; P. Mansel, 'Monarchy, Uniform and the Rise of the *Frac*', *Past & Present*, no. 96 (1982), pp. 104–23; P. Lucas, 'A Collective Biography of Students and Barristers of Lincoln's Inn, 1680–1804: A Study in the "Aristocratic Resurgence" of the Eighteenth Century', *Journal of Modern History*, XLVI (1974),

pp. 227–61.

60. Sir N. Chester, *The English Administrative System, 1780–1870* (1981), pp. 12–30; E. Halévy, *England in 1815* (1929), pp. 15–18; H. Roseveare, *The Treasury: The Evolution of a British Institution* (1969), pp. 120, 154; Gash, 'After Waterloo', p. 147.

61. M. Lewis, *The Navy in Transition, 1814–1864: A Social History* (1965), p. 22; P.E. Razzell, 'Social Origins of Officers in the Indian and British Home Army', *British Journal of Sociology*, XIV (1963), p. 253; Halévy, *England in 1815*, pp. 45, 93.

62. P. Mansel, *Pillars of Monarchy: An Outline of the Political and Social History of the Royal Guards, 1400–1984* (1984), p. 78; I. Fletcher & R. Poulter, *Gentlemen's Sons: The Guards in the Peninsular and at Waterloo, 1808–15* (1993), passim; Halévy, *England in 1815*, pp. 81–2; Turberville, *House of Lords*, p. 349.

63. One of the reasons why absenteeism in Ireland increased during the late eighteenth century was because more landowners were taking up careers in British politics or in the service of the state. See A.P.W. Malcomson, 'Absenteeism in Eighteenth-Century Ireland', *Irish Economic and Social History*, I (1974), pp. 15–19.

64. Lenman, *Integration, Enlightenment and Industrialization*, p. 82; C.H. Phillips, *The East India Company, 1784–1934* (1961), pp. 35–6; H. Furber, *Henry Dundas, First Viscount Melville, 1742–1811* (1931), p. 31.

65. Lenman, *Integration, Enlightenment and Industrialization*, p. 40; M.E. Chamberlain, *Lord Aberdeen: A Political Biography* (1983), pp. 79–80, 105, 169.

66. R. Mitchison, *Agricultural Sir John: The Life of Sir John Sinclair of Ulbster, 1754–1835* (1962), pp. 226–8; C.A. Bayly, *Imperial Meridian: The British Empire and the World, 1780–1830* (1989), pp, 133–6, 193–216.

67. R.A. Solway, *Prelates and People: Ecclesiastical Social Thought in England, 1783–1852* (1969), pp. 6–8; N. Ravitch, *Sword and Mitre: Government and Episcopate in France and England in the Age of Aristocracy* (1966), pp. 118–32.

68. Turberville, *House of Lords*, pp. 298–9.

69. Jenkins, *Making of a Ruling Class*, pp. 89–90; E. Evans, 'Some Reasons for the Growth of English Rural Anti-Clericalism, c.1750–c.1830', *Past & Present*, no. 66 (1975), pp. 102–7.

70. N.V. Murray, 'The Influence of the French Revolution on the Church of England and Its Rivals, 1789–1802' (D. Phil, dissertation, Oxford University, 1975), pp. 331, 356–9.

71. McCahill, *Order and Equipoise*, p. 164;

Stones, *Open Elite?*, pp. 271–5.

72. McCahill, *Order and Equipoise*, pp. 171–6; Malcomson, *John Foster*, p. 253; J.R. Western, 'The Formation of the Scottish Militia in 1797', *Scottish Historical Review*, XXXIV (1955), pp. 1–18; E. Inglis-Jones, *Peacocks in Paradise* (1950), pp. 114, 193.

73. Cannadine, *Lords and Landlords*, pp. 43, 46; D. Spring, 'Earl Fitzwilliam and the Corn Laws', *American Historical Review*, LIX (1954), pp. 293–6; E.A. Smith, *Whig Principles and Party Politics: Earl Fitzwilliam and the Whig Party, 1748–1833* (1975), pp. 363–7.

74. E. Robinson, 'Matthew Boulton and the Art of Parliamentary Lobbying', *HJ*, VII (1964), pp. 221–4; M. McCahill, 'Peers, Patronage and the Industrial Revolution, 1760–1800', *Journal of British Studies*, XVI (1976), pp. 86, 93–7, 101.

75. M. Girouard, *The Return to Camelot: Chivalry and the English Gentleman* (1981), pp. 56–66; Sir K. Digby, *The Broad Stone of Honour: or, Rules for the Gentleman of England* (1822), p. vii.

76. Stones, *Open Elite?*, pp. 364–74, 384–5; Timperley, 'Landownership in Scotland', pp. 34–6; S. Bluntman, 'English Country Houses, 1780–1815' (M.A. dissertation, London University, 1968), passim.

77. Jenkins, *Making of a Ruling Class*, p. 42; L.P. Curtis, Jr., 'Incumbered Wealth: Landed Indebtedness in Post-Famine Ireland', *American Historical Review*, LXXXV (1980), p. 337; W.A. Maguire, 'A Resident Landlord in His Local Setting: The Second Marquess of Donegall at Ormeau, 1807–1844', *Proceedings of the Royal Irish Academy*, LXXXIII (1983), pp. 377–83; J. Macaulay, *The Gothic Revival, 1745–1845* (1975), pp. 1, 84–109, 163, 194–7, 202, 319; T.R. Slater, 'The Mansion and Policy', in M.L. Parry & T.R. Slater (eds.), *The Making of the Scottish Countryside* (1980), p. 226.

78. Robinson, *Dukes of Norfolk*, p. 177; H. Prince, *Parks in England* (1967), pp. 6–9, 29–56.

79. G. Lindsay & M. Cosh, *Inverary and the Dukes of Argyll* (1973), pp. 229–43; J.P. Neale, *Views of the Seats of Noblemen and Gentlemen in England, Wales, Scotland and Ireland* (6 vols., 1818–23).

80. Thompson, *English Landed Society*, p. 104; F.H.W. Sheppard (ed.), *The Survey of London*, vol. XXX, *The Parish of St James, Westminster*, part I, *South of Piccadilly* (1960), pp. 491–6; Sheppard, *The Survey of London*, vol. XXXII, *The Parish of St James, Westminster*, part II, *North of Piccadilly* (1963), pp.

407–12.

81. Hyde, *Londonderrys*, p. 29; Richards, *Leviathan of Wealth*, p. 16; Sheppard, *The Survey of London*, vol. XL, *The Grosvenor Estate in Mayfair*, part II, *The Buildings* (1980), pp. 242, 264, 277–8.

82. F. Haskell, *Rediscoveries in Art: Some Aspects of Taste, Fashion and Collecting in England and France* (1976), pp. 25–6; G. Redford, *Art Sales* (2 vols., 1888), vol. I, pp. 69–78.

83. Sheppard, *Mayfair*, part II, *The Buildings*, pp. 263–6.

84. M. Clarke & N. Penny (eds.), *The Arrogant Connoisseur: Richard Payne Knight, 1751–1824* (1982), passim; S. Deuchar, *Paintings, Politics and Porter: Samuel Whitbread II (1764–1815) and British Art* (1984), esp. pp. 9–12; M. Greaves, *Regency Patron: Sir George Beaumont* (1966), pp. 56–7, 150; D. Hall, 'The Tabley House Papers', *Walpole Society*, XXXVIII (1960–2), pp. 59–63.

85. Robinson, *Dukes of Norfolk*, p. 181; D. Spring, 'Aristocracy, Social Structure and Religion in the Early Victorian Period', *Victorian Studies*, VI (1962–3), p. 271; St John Gore, 'Three Centuries of Discrimination', *Apollo*, no. 105 (1977), pp. 352–7; J. Kenworthy-Browne, 'The Third Earl of Egremont and Neo-Classical Sculpture', *Apollo*, no. 105 (1977), pp. 367–73; E. Joll, 'Painter and Patron: Turner and the Third Earl of Egremont', *Apollo*, no. 105 (1977), pp. 374–9.

86. L.G. Mitchell, *Charles James Fox and the Disintegration of the Whig Party, 1782–1794* (1971), p. 257.

87. Thompson, *English Landed Society*, p. 104.

88. D. Itzkowitz, *Peculiar Privilege: A Social History of English Fox Hunting, 1753–1885* (1977), pp. 6–49; Thompson, *English Landed Society*, p. 145.

89. R. Carr, *English Fox Hunting: A History* (1976), p. 138; Jenkins, *Making of a Ruling Class*, p. 265; Colyer, 'Nineteenth-Century Cardiganshire', pp. 509–10.

90. Hayes, 'Politics in Norfolk', p. 431; Malcomson, 'Gentle Leviathan', pp. 104, 113; P. Jupp, 'County Down Elections, 1783–1831', *Irish Historical Studies*, XVIII (1972–3), pp. 181–3; Sack, 'House of Lords and Parliamentary Patronage', p. 916; J.R. McQuiston, 'The Lonsdale Connection and its Defender, William Viscount Lowther', *Northern History*, XI (1976 for 1975), p. 174.

91. Malcomson, *John Foster*, pp. 331, 341; J.R. McQuiston, 'Sussex Aristocrats and the County Election of 1820', *English Historical Review*, LXXXVIII (1973), pp. 555–7.

92. Sir I. de la Bere, *The Queen's Orders of Chivalry* (1964), pp. 67, 103, 116, 139, 174–5.

93. Thompson, *English Landed Society*, p. 12; Beckett, *Aristocracy in England*, pp. 30–1; G.C. Richards, 'The Creation of Peers Recommended by the Younger Pitt', *American Historical Review*, XXXIV (1928–9), pp. 47–54.

94. M. McCahill, 'Peerage Creations and the Changing Character of the British Nobility, 1750–1830', *English Historical Review*, XCVI (1981), p. 259; McCahill, *Order and Equipoise*, p. 148.

95. Richards, *Leviathan of Wealth*, p. 7; Hyde, *Londonderrys*, pp. xiv, 6, 29. For another Irish example, see Maguire, *Downshire Estates*, pp. 1–22.

96. Sack, *Grenvillites*, pp. 3–19, 35; Thompson, *English Landed Society*, p. 12; Turberville, *House of Lords*, p. 368.

97. McCahill, 'British Nobility', pp. 269–75.

98. Longford, *Wellington*, pp. 198–9, 267, 291, 302, 347; Ross, *Cornwallis Correspondence*, vol. III, p. 311.

99. Lenman, *Integration, Enlightenment and Industrialization*, pp. 8, 79; Turberville, *House of Lords*, p. 104; McCahill, 'British Nobility', pp. 263–4; McCahill, 'Scottish Peerage and the House of Lords', pp. 172–96.

100. Chamberlain, *Lord Aberdeen*, pp. 91–9, 169; W. St Clair, *Lord Elgin and the Marbles* (1967), pp. 85, 185–6, 223, 261, 270.

101. Ross, *Cornwallis Correspondence*, vol. III, 318–19; R.B. McDowell, *Ireland in the Age of Imperialism and Revolution, 1760–1801* (1979), pp. 681–2.

102. McCahill, 'British Nobility', pp. 265–6, 280; Turberville, *House of Lords*, pp. 106–8, 128. Irish peers were as eager as their Scottish cousins to obtain UK titles. The Duke of Wellington's elder brother inherited an Irish barony, viscountcy and earldom, and himself obtained the order of St Patrick, the Garter and a UK barony. But in 1799 he was given an Irish marquessate, and it was a source of lifelong disappointment to him that it was not a UK title. See Butler, *Eldest Brother*, pp. 26, 42, 94, 211–15, 435, 566–7.

103. McCahill, 'British Nobility', pp. 276–9; Thompson, *English Landed Society*, pp. 12–14.

104. Colley, *Britons*, p. 161.

105. Palmer, *Age of Democratic Revolution*, vol. I, pp. 78–9.

106. Jenkins, 'Creation of an "Ancient Gentry" ',

p. 49.

107. *Morning Post*, 9 Dec. 1813. I am grateful to Prof. Linda Colley for this reference.

108. Quoted in Lord Butler (ed.), *The Conservatives: A History From their Origins to 1965* (1977), p. 114.

109. Girouard, *Return to Camelot*, pp. 43–4, 50; Girouard, *Life in the English Country House: A Social and Architectural History* (1978), p. 242.

110. Flinn, *Industrial Revolution*, p. 327; Jenkins, 'Creation of an "Ancient Gentry" ', p. 47.

111. M. Levy, *Sir Thomas Lawrence, 1769–1830* (1979), esp. pp. 9–19; J. Wilson, 'The Romantics, 1790–1830', in R. Strong et al, *The British Portrait, 1660–1960* (1991), pp. 243–97.

112. K. Garlick, *Sir Thomas Lawrence: A Complete Catalogue of the Oil Paintings* (1989), passim; Garlick, *Sir Thomas Lawrence: Portraits of an Age, 1790–1830* (1993), passim.

113. Colley, *Britons*, pp. 176–7, 188–92.

114. For an argument very similar to that made in this chapter, dealing with Scotland, see R.H. Campbell, 'The Perpetuation of the Landed Interest', in T.M. Devine (ed.), *Conflict and Stability in Scottish Society, 1700–1850* (1990), pp. 122–35. For another study of the 'modernised gentry ethos', see P. Mandler, 'The Making of the New Poor Law *Redivivus*', *Past & Present*, no. 117 (1987), p. 133. For a very suggestive account of the failure of middle-class politicians and middle-class politics in the aftermath of Reform and Repeal, see G.R. Searle, *Entrepreneurial Politics in Mid-Victorian Britain* (1993).

2. Aristocratic Indebtedness in the Nineteenth Century

1. This paragraph is a summary of the arguments developed in the following articles by Prof. Spring: 'The English Landed Estate in the Age of Coal and Iron: 1830–80', *JEH*, XI (1951), pp. 3–24; 'The Earls of Durham and the Great Northern Coalfield, 1830–80', *Canadian Historical Review*, XXXIII (1952), pp. 237–53; 'A Great Agricultural Estate: Netherby under Sir James Graham, 1820–45', *Agricultural History*, XXIX (1955), pp. 73–81; 'Ralph Sneyd: Tory Country Gentleman', *Bulletin of the John Rylands Library*, XXXVIII (1955–6), pp. 535–5; 'English Landownership in the Nineteenth Century: A Critical Note', *EcHR*, 2nd ser., IX (1957), pp. 472–84; 'Aristocracy, Social Structure and Religion in the Early Victorian Period', *Victorian Studies*, VI (1963), pp. 263–80.

2. For this alternative view, see the following articles by F.M.L. Thompson: 'The End of a Great Estate', *EcHR*, 2nd ser., VII (1955), pp. 36–52; 'English Landownership: The Ailesbury Trust, 1832–56', *EcHR*, 2nd ser., XI (1958), pp. 121–32; 'English Great Estates in the Nineteenth Century (1790–1914)', in *Contributions to the First International Conference of Economic History* (Paris, 1960), pp. 385–97. Disposable income is defined as 'gross income minus expenses of estate management, repairs, and housekeeping': Thompson, 'The End of a Great Estate', p. 39.

3. There is no mention of it in F.M.L. Thompson, *English Landed Society in the Nineteenth Century* (1963), and only a brief allusion in D. Spring, *The English Landed Estate in the Nineteenth Century: Its Administration* (1963), p. 39.

4. E. J. Hobsbawm, *Industry and Empire* (1969), pp. 80–1; H.J. Perkin, *The Origins of Modern English Society, 1780–1880* (1969), pp. 183–95.

5. G. Best, *Mid-Victorian Britain, 1851–75* (1971), pp. 242–3; S.G. Checkland, *The Rise of Industrial Society in England, 1815–85* (1964), p. 283; G. Kitson Clark, *The Making of Victorian England* (1962), p. 217. For a similar expression of views, see D.E.D. Beales, *From Castlereagh to Gladstone, 1815–85* (1971 edn), p. 70. For a discussion of the influence of Prof. Spring's arguments see: D. Spring, 'Aristocratic Indebtedness in the Nineteenth Century: A Comment', *EcHR*, 2nd ser., XXX (1980), pp. 564–8; D. Cannadine, 'Aristocratic Indebtedness in the Nineteenth Century: A Re-Statement', *EcHR*, 2nd ser., XXX (1980), pp. 569–73. For a recent summary and discussion, see J.V. Beckett, 'Landownership and Estate Management', in G.E. Mingay (ed.), *The Agrarian History of England and Wales*, vol. VI, *1750–1850* (1989), pp. 634–40.

6. W.L. Burn, *The Age of Equipoise* (1964), p. 307.

7. Thompson, *English Landed Society in the Nineteenth Century*, p. vii.

8. L. Stone, *The Crisis of the Aristocracy, 1558–1641* (1965), pp. 505, 541–3, app. xx–xxii, pp. 777–81.

9. J.V. Beckett, *The Aristocracy in England, 1660–1914* (1986), pp. 295–302.

10. L. Stone, *Family and Fortune; Studies in Aristocratic Finance in the Sixteenth and Seventeenth Centuries* (1973), pp. 158–9; Thompson, *English Landed Society in the Nineteenth Century*, pp. 19, 212; P.R. Roberts, 'The

Landed Gentry in Merioneth, c. 1660–
1832, with Special Reference to the
Estates of Hengwrt, Nannau, Rug and
Ynysymaengwyn' (M.A. dissertation, Uni-
versity of Wales, 1963), pp. 119–20; D.W.
Howell, 'The Economy of the Landed
Estates of Pembrokeshire, c.1680–1830',
Welsh History Review, III (1966–7), 280–2;
C. Shrimpton, 'The Landed Society and
Farming Community in Essex in the Late
Eighteenth and early Nineteenth Centuries'
(Ph.D. dissertation, University of Cam-
bridge, 1965), pp. 52–5, 62–4, 82–4, 110–
11, 135–40; C.R. Strutt, *The Strutt Family of
Terling, 1650–1873* (privately printed, 1939),
pp. 24, 36–8.

11. T.J. Raybould, *The Economic Emergence of the
Black Country: A Study of the Dudley Estate*
(1973), pp. 18–22; R. Perren, 'The Effects
of the Agricultural Depression on the Eng-
lish Estates of the Dukes of Sutherland,
1870–1900' (Ph.D. dissertation, University
of Nottingham, 1967), pp. 87–8; M.J.
Hazelton-Swales, 'Urban Aristocrats: The
Grosvenors and the Development of
Belgravia and Pimlico in the Nineteenth
Century' (Ph.D. dissertation, University of
London, 1981), pp. 78–179.

12. D. & E. Spring, 'The Fall of the Grenvilles,
1844–48', *Huntington Library Quarterly*, XIX
(1956), pp. 165–90; Thompson, 'The End
of the Great Estate', pp. 36–52.

13. Kitson Clark, *Victorian England*, p. 217;
D. Sutherland, *The Yellow Earl: The Life of
Hugh Lowther, 5th Earl of Lonsdale, K.G.
G.C.V.O. 1857–1944* (1965), pp. 19–20,
109; J.T. Ward, 'Ayrshire Landed Estates in
the Nineteenth Century', *Ayrshire Collection*,
VIII (1967–9), p. 105; Thompson, *English
Landed Society in the Nineteenth Century*, p.
286; J. Vincent, *The Formation of the Liberal
Party, 1857–68* (1967), p. 12. For a more
detailed treatment of the Newcastles'
finances see: R.A. Kelch, *Newcastle: A Duke
without Money: Thomas Pelham-Holles, 1693–
1768* (1979), passim; F. Darrell Munsell, *The
Unfortunate Duke: Henry Pelham, Fifth Duke
of Newcastle, 1811–1864* (1985), esp. pp. 5,
17–18, 34–5, 47–9, 275.

14. A.S. Turberville, *A History of Welbeck Abbey
and its Owners* (2 vols., 1938–9), vol. II, pp.
345–6; R.A.C. Parker, *Coke of Norfolk: A
Financial and Agricultural Study, 1707–1842*
(1975), pp. 129, 188–98; Bedford MSS,
annual reports, 1839–55; Spring, *English
Landed Estate*, pp. 35–40; Spring, 'The Earls
of Durham', pp, 250–3.

15. A. Adonis, 'Aristocracy, Agriculture and

Liberalism: The Politics, Finances and Estates of the Third Lord Carrington', *HJ*,
XXXI (1988), pp. 882–5; Adonis, 'The
Survival of the Great Estates: Henry,
Fourth Earl of Carnarvon and His Disposi-
tion in the Eighteen Eighties', *Historical Research*, LXIV, (1991), pp. 61–2; A.L. Rowse,
The Later Churchills (1971), pp. 237–40,
249–50, 274–7; D. Cannadine, *The Decline
and Fall of the British Aristocracy* (1990), pp.
112–13.

16. For the detailed figures see Appendix A.

17. For discussions of the aggregate level of
debt, see: Beckett, *Aristocracy in England*, pp.
314–15; A. Offer, *Property and Politics: Landownership, Law, Ideology and Urban Development* (1991), pp. 138–40; D. Spring, 'Land
and Politics in Edwardian England', *Agricultural History*, LVIII (1984), pp. 28–9.

18. L.P. Curtis, Jr., 'Incumbered Wealth:
Landed Indebtedness in Post-Famine Ire-
land', *American Historical Review*, LXXXV
(1980), pp. 332–67; R.J. Colyer, 'The Pryse
Family of Gogerddan and the Decline of the
Great Estate, 1800–1960', *Welsh History Re-
view*, IX (1979), pp. 407–25; Colyer, 'The
Gentry and the County in Nineteenth-
Century Cardiganshire', *Welsh History Re-
view*, X (1981), pp. 519–35.

19. E. Richards, *The Leviathan of Wealth: The
Sutherland Fortune in the Industrial Revolution*
(1973), p. 289; Spring, 'The Earls of Durham', p. 250; Wentworth Woodhouse
MSS, Stw. 32 (2), List of Mortgages held by
Lord Fitzwilliam's Trustees on His Lord-
ship's Estates, 5 June 1907.

20. Beckett, *Aristocracy in England*, pp. 310–
11.

21. P. Mathias, 'The Lawyer as Businessman in
Eighteenth-Century England', in D.C.
Coleman & P. Mathias (eds.), *Enterprise and
History: Essays in Honour of Charles Wilson*
(1984), pp. 155–6, 162–4; R.A. Ward, *A
Treatise on Investments; Being a Popular Expo-
sition of the Advantages and Disadvantages of
each Kind of Investment, and of its Liability to
Depreciation and Loss* (1852), pp. 2, 98.

22. Thompson, 'The End of the Great Estate',
p. 49; B.E. Supple, *The Royal Exchange
Assurance: A History of British Insurance,
1720–1970*, (1970), pp. 336–7; A. Trollope,
The Last Chronicle of Barset (1958 edn),
p. 265.

23. W.A. Maguire, *The Downshire Estates in
Ireland, 1801–1845: The Management of Irish
Landed Estates in the Early Nineteenth Century*
(1972), pp. 101–6.

24. D. Cannadine, *Lords and Landlords: The*

Aristocracy in the Towns, 1774–1967 (1980), p. 130–1.

25. L.S. Pressnell, *Country Banking in the Industrial Revolution* (1956), pp. 344–9; Cannadine, *Lords and Landlords*, pp. 127–8.

26. R.W. Sturgess, *Aristocrat in Business: The Third Marquess of Londonderry as Coalowner and Portbuilder* (1925), pp. 20, 36, 84–84; S.G. Checkland, *Scottish Banking: A History, 1695–1973* (1975), pp. 226, 416–17.

27. J.H. Clapham, *The Bank of England: A History* (2 vols., 1944), vol. II, pp. 82–4, 193.

28. W. Bagehot, *Lombard Street* (1873), p. 270.

29. Unless otherwise stated, the rest of the paragraph is based on Hoare's Bank MSS, debt books, 1794–1805, 1805–23, 1823–43, 1843–77.

30. Thompson, 'English Landownership: The Ailesbury Trust', pp. 121–3.

31. A.H. John, 'Insurance Investment and the London Money Market of the Eighteenth Century', *Economica*, XX (1953), pp. 156–7.

32. Supple, *Royal Exchange Assurance*, pp. 318–20; Spring, *English Landed Estate*, p. 189; Spring, 'The Earls of Durham', p. 250; Spring, 'A Great Agricultural Estate', p. 76; J. Davies, 'Glamorgan and the Bute Estate, 1866–1947' (Ph.D. dissertation, University of Wales, 1969), p. 138.

33. Supple, *Royal Exchange Assurance*, pp. 330–48; P.G.M. Dickson, *The Sun Insurance Office, 1710–1960: The History of Two and a Half Centuries of British Insurance* (1960), pp. 250–1, 261–3; M.E. Ogborn, *Equitable Assurances, 1762–1961* (1962), pp. 243–4.

34. Supple, *Royal Exchange Assurance*, p. 318; Royal Exchange Assurance MSS, Register of Securities; Davies, 'Glamorgan and the Bute Estate', p. 371, n182.

35. In Ireland, the Representative Body of the recently-disestablished Church of Ireland also lent extensively in the 1870. See Curtis, 'Incumbered Wealth', pp. 340–1.

36. Supple, *Royal Exchange Assurance*, pp. 309–10; *RC on Agricultural Depression* (PP 1897, XV), p. 121. My italics.

37. Dickson, *Sun Insurance Office*, p. 250; Spring, 'A Great Agricultural Estate', p. 76.

38. Thompson, 'English Landownership: The Ailesbury Trust', pp. 122, 129.

39. Spring, 'The English Landed Estate in the Age of Coal and Iron', pp. 16–19; Spring, 'A Great Agricultural Estate', p. 81; Thompson, *English Landed Society in the Nineteenth Century*, pp. 290–1.

40. G.E. Mingay, *English Landed Society in the Eighteenth Century* (1963), pp. 32–6;

Beckett, *Aristocracy in England*, pp. 296–8.

41. T.W. Beastall, *A North Country Estate: The Lumleys and Sandersons as Landowners, 1600–1900* (1975), p. 109; J.M. Howells, 'The Crosswood Estate, 1547–1947', *Ceredigion*, III (1969), pp. 78–81.

42. R.W. Sturgess, 'Landownership, Mining and Urban Development in Nineteenth-Century Staffordshire', in J.T. Ward & R.G. Wilson (eds.), *Land and Industry: The Landed Estate and the Industrial Revolution* (1971), p. 199; Radnor MSS, T284, mortgage deed, 4 Aug. 1865.

43. Curtis, 'Incumbered Wealth', pp. 338–9; Colyer, 'Pryse Family', pp. 412–15; Spring, 'The English Landed Estate in the Age of Coal and Iron', p. 16; Wentworth Woodhouse MSS, T82, analytical table of debts, 1878.

44. M.W. Flinn, *The Origins of the Industrial Revolution* (1966), p. 48.

45. M. Girouard, *The Victorian Country House* (1971), pp. 5–6; J. Franklin, *The Gentleman's Country House and Its Plan, 1835–1914* (1981), pp. 24–38; L. & J.C.F. Stone, *An Open Elite? England 1540–1880* (1984), pp. 382–6.

46. Thompson, *English Landed Society in the Nineteenth Century*, p. 92.

47. Beckett, *Aristocracy in England*, p. 299; G. Cornwallis-West, *Edwardian Heydays* (1930), p. 12; H.M. Vaughan, *The South Wales Squires: A Welsh Picture of Social Life* (1926), pp. 64–5, 67.

48. Cannadine, *Lords and Landlords*, pp. 130–1; D.W. Howells, 'The Crosswood Estate: Its Growth and Economic Development' (M.A. dissertation, University of Wales, 1956), p. 244; T.W. Beastall, 'The History of the Earl of Scarbrough's Estate, 1860–1900' (M.A. dissertation, University of Manchester, 1954), pp. 156–8; M. Girouard, *Victorian Country House*, pp. 150–4.

49. Sturgess, 'Landowners, Mining and Urban Development', pp. 193–4; Davies, 'Glamorgan and the Bute Estate', pp. 135–6.

50. F.M. Reid, 'Economic and Social Aspects of Landownership in the Nineteenth Century' (B. Litt. dissertation, University of Oxford, 1956), pp. 48–54; Cannadine, *Lords and Landlords*, p. 130.

51. B.A. Holderness, 'Capital Formation in Agriculture', in J.P.P. Higgins & S. Pollard (eds.), *Aspects of Capital Investment in Great Britain, 1750–1850: A Preliminary Survey* (1971), p. 178; E.L. Jones, 'The Changing Basis of English Agricultural Prosperity,

1853–73', *AgHR*, x (1962), pp. 102–19; F.M.L. Thompson, 'The Second Agricultural Revolution, 1815–80', *EcHR*, 2nd ser., XXI (1968), 62–77.

52. R.W. Sturgess, 'The Agricultural Revolution on the English Clays', *AgHR*, XIV (1966), pp. 104–21; E.J.T. Collins & E.L. Jones, 'Sectoral Advance in English Agriculture, 1850–80', *AgHR*, XV (1967), pp. 65–89; R.W. Sturgess, 'The Agricultural Revolution of English Clays: A Rejoinder', *AgHR*, XV (1967), pp. 82–7; A.D. Phillips, 'Under-draining on the English Clay Lands, 1850–70', *AgHR*, XVII (1969), pp. 44–55; Thompson, *English Landed Society in the Nineteenth Century*, pp. 221, 235–7, 247–8.

53. J.D. Chambers & G.E. Mingay, *The Agricultural Revolution, 1750–1880* (1966), pp. 175–7; E.L. Jones, *The Development of English Agriculture, 1815–73* (1968), pp. 25–30; Colyer, 'Nineteenth-Century Cardiganshire', pp. 525–6.

54. J.H. Clapham, *An Economic History of Modern Britain* (3 vols., 1926–38), vol. II, pp. 271–2; D.W. Howell, *Land and People in Nineteenth-Century Wales* (1977), p. 52; C.O. Grada, 'The Investment Behaviour of Irish Landlords, 1850–75: Some Preliminary Findings', *AgHR*, XXII (1975), pp. 146–8.

55. Reid, 'Landownership in the Nineteenth Century', pp. 56–7; Beastall, 'Yorkshire Estates of the Earls of Scarbrough' p. 167; Howells, 'The Crosswood Estate: Its Growth and Economic Development', p. 244.

56. Stone, *Crisis of the Aristocracy*, pp. 335–84; Mingay, *English Landed Society in the Eighteenth Century*, pp. 189–201; Beckett, *Aristocracy in England*, pp. 206–86.

57. Spring, 'The Earls of Durham', p. 250; Sturgess, *Aristocrat in Business*, p. 37; J.T. Ward, 'The Earls Fitzwilliam and the Wentworth Estate in the Nineteenth Century', *Yorkshire Bulletin of Economic and Social Research*, XII (1960), p. 23; Radnor MSS, T284, mortgage documents, 4 Sept. 1867, 26 Nov. 1867.

58. Davies, 'Glamorgan and the Bute Estate', pp. 575–6, 678–9; M.J. Daunton, 'Aristocrat and Traders: The Bute Docks, 1839–1914', *JTH*, new ser., III (1975), pp. 73–4, 77; Sturgess, *Aristocrat in Business*, p. 76; for the Devonshires and Barrow, see below, pp. 174–7.

59. Jones, *Development of English Agriculture*, p. 30; Thompson, *English Landed Society in the Nineteenth Century*, pp. 247–52.

60. E. Richards, 'The Industrial Face of a Great Estate: Trentham and Lilleshall, 1780–1860', *EcHR*, 2nd ser., XXVII (1974), p. 430.

61. For the two sides of the debate, see: Beckett, *Aristocracy in England*, pp. 316–21; E. Richards, 'An Anatomy of the Sutherland Fortune: Income, Consumption, Investments and returns, 1780–1880', *Business History*, XXI (1979), pp. 46, 69–70.

62. Thompson, *English Landed Society in the Nineteenth Century*, pp. 310–11; P.J. Perry, *British Farming in the Great Depression, 1870–1914* (1974), pp. 69–76, 183; B.L. Solow, *The Land Question and the Irish Economy, 1870–1903* (1971), pp. 174–5.

63. Sturgess, 'Landowners, Mining and Urban Development', p. 200.

64. J.J. MacGregor, 'The Economic History of Two Rural Estates in Cambridgeshire, 1870–1934', *Journal of the Royal Agricultural Society*, XCVIII (1937) pp. 142, 150–1.

65. Thompson, *English Landed Society in the Nineteenth Century*, pp. 317–18; Perry, *British Farming in the Great Depression*, pp. 76–8; *The Economist*, 12 June 1897, pp. 839–40.

66. Supple, *Royal Exchange Assurance*, pp. 337–8; H. Rider Haggard, *Rural England* (2 vols., 1902), vol. I, pp. 320–1. See also the evidence of J. Francis to the *R C on Land in Wales and Monmouthshire* (PP 1894, XXXVII), Q32, 147.

67. D. Deuchar, 'Investments', *Journal of the Federation of Insurance Institutes*, I (1989), pp. 9–10. See also A.G. Mackenzie, 'On the Practice and Powers of Assurance Companies in Regard to the Investment of their Life Assurance Funds', *Journal of the Institute of Actuaries*, XXIX (1891), 198.

68. Sir Herbert Maxwell, *Annals of the Scottish Widows' Fund, 1815–1914* (1914), pp. 112–16. The advances to landowners by the Representative Body of the Church of Ireland also fell dramatically from the late 1870s. See Curtis, 'Incumbered Wealth', p. 341.

69. Thompson, *English Landed Society in the Nineteenth Century*, pp. 307, 320, 322, 329, 336–7; Michael Harrison, *Lord of London: A Biography of the Second Duke of Westminster* (1966), pp. 207–8; Duke of Sutherland, *Looking Back: The Autobiography of the Duke of Sutherland* (1957), pp. 86–7; Davies, 'Glamorgan and the Bute Estate', pp. 350–1; John, Duke of Bedford, *A Silver-Plated Spoon* (1959), pp. 8, 15. There is, apparently, no substance in the myth that the majority

of the £2 million obtained by the Bedfords for the sale of Covent Garden Estate in 1913 was invested in Russian bonds which subsequently became worthless: in the main, the proceeds were invested in British War Bonds and Canadian and Indian stock. See F.H.W. Sheppard (ed.), *Survey of London*, vol. XXXVI, *The Parish of St Paul Covent Garden* (1970), pp. 49–52. But cf. D. Spring, 'Landlords and Politics in Edwardian England', p. 24, n27.

70. It should be stressed how long this particular generation lasted, thereby postponing the payment of the next round of death duties, and winning a greater period of time in which to complete financial readjustment. The dates between which the heads of some of the wealthiest families held their titles in years after the First World War are as follows: sixth Duke of Portland, 1879–1943; eleventh Duke of Bedford, 1893–1940; second Duke of Westminster, 1899–1953; fourth Marquess of Bute, 1900–47; seventh Earl Fitzwilliam, 1902–43; seventeenth Earl of Derby, 1908–48; ninth Duke of Devonshire, 1908–38; fifth Duke of Sutherland, 1913–63; sixteenth Duke of Norfolk, 1917–75.

71. Cannadine, *Lords and Landlords*, pp. 170–3; Sturgess, 'Landowners, Mining and Urban Development', pp. 197–200.

72. Howells, 'The Crosswood Estate, 1547–1947', pp. 81–3; Cornwallis-West, *Edwardian Heydays*, p. 137; E.L. Jones, 'The Evolution of High Farming, 1815–65 with Reference to Herefordshire' (D. Phil. dissertation, University of Oxford, 1963), p. 443.

73. Thompson, *English Landed Society in the Nineteenth Century*, pp. 314–15, 342; Curtis, 'Incumbered Wealth', pp. 344–7, 350.

74. W.L. Guttsman, *The British Political Elite* (1963), p. 132; C.L. Mowat, *Britain Between the Wars, 1918–1940* (1971), p. 204.

75. D. Jenkins, *The Agricultural Community in South-West Wales at the Turn of the Twentieth Century* (1971), pp. 13–36; Colyer, 'Pryse Family of Gogerddan', pp. 413–25; Colyer, 'Nineteenth-Century Cardiganshire', pp. 529–35; Howell, *Land and People*, p. 57.

76. Cannadine, *Decline and Fall*, p. 127.

77. Cannadine, *Decline and Fall*, pp. 25–31.

3. Nobility and Mobility in Modern Britain

1. M. Bloch, *Feudal Society* (2 vols., trans. L.A. Manyon, 1965), vol. II, *Social Classes and Political Organisation*, pp. 290–1.

2. J.H. Kautsky, *The Politics of Aristocratic Empires* (1982), pp. 203–5, 346, 371; H.J. Perkin, *The Age of the Railway* (1971), pp. 35–6.

3. Lord Brabazon of Tara, *The Brabazon Story* (1956), pp. xii–xiv.

4. Perkin, *Age of the Railway*, pp. 171–2; J.V. Beckett, *The Aristocracy in England, 1660–1914* (1986), p. 243.

5. F.M.L. Thompson, *English Landed Society in the Nineteenth Century* (1963), pp. 190–1; D. Spring, 'English Landowners and Nineteenth-Century Industrialism', in J.T. Ward & R.G. Wilson (eds.), *Land and Industry: The Landed Estate and the Industrial Revolution* (1971), p. 53.

6. J. Simmons, *The Railway in Town and Country, 1830–1914* (1986), pp. 23–4; Spring, 'Landowners and Nineteenth-Century Industrialism', pp. 19–21.

7. Thompson, *English Landed Society*, pp. 259–60.

8. J.R. Kellett, *The Impact of Railways on Victorian Cities* (1969), pp. 251–2; D. Cannadine, *Lords and Landlords: The Aristocracy and the Towns, 1774–1967* (1980), pp. 176–80.

9. Simmons, *Railway in Town and Country*, pp. 245, 261–4; Kellett, *Impact of Railways*, p. 253.

10. R.J. Irving, 'The Capitalization of Britain's Railways, 1830–1914', *JTH*, 3rd ser., V (1984), pp. 6–8, 10–16; Beckett, *Aristocracy in England*, p. 246; Spring, 'Landowners and Nineteenth-Century Industrialism', p. 23.

11. J.T. Ward, 'West Riding Landowners and the Railways', *JTH*, IV (1959–60), pp. 243–4; Beckett, *Aristocracy in England*, p. 246.

12. Kellett, *Impact of Railways*, pp. 178–81, 246–7, 275–8; Spring, 'Landowners and Nineteenth-Century Industrialism', p. 23.

13. T.J. Raybould, *The Economic Emergence of the Black Country: A Study of the Dudley Estate* (1973), pp. 70–88; M.J. Daunton, 'Aristocrat and Traders: The Bute Docks, 1839–1914', *JTH*, new ser., III (1975), pp. 68–9; Thompson, *English Landed Society*, p. 263.

14. Perkin, *Age of the Railway*, pp. 126–30; Cannadine, *Lords and Landlords*, pp. 237–8, 269–71; S. Pollard, 'Barrow-in-Furness and the Seventh Duke of Devonshire', *EcHR*, 2nd ser., VIII (1955–6), p. 214.

15. S.W. Martins, *A Great Estate at Work: The Holkham Estate and Its Inhabitants in the Nineteenth Century* (1980), pp. 61–2; Simmons, *Railway in Town and Country* pp. 24, 308–10; Thompson, *English Landed Society*, p. 257.

16. E. Richards, 'An Anatomy of the Sutherland Fortune: Income, Consumption, Investments and Returns, 1780–1880', *Business History*, XXI (1979), pp. 54, 66–70.
17. Thompson, *English Landed Society*, p. 306.
18. Beckett, *Aristocracy in England*, p. 250; Simmons, *Railway in Town and Country*, pp. 311–12; Pollard, 'Barrow-in-Furness', p. 214.
19. Thompson, *English Landed Society*, p. 261; Beckett *Aristocracy in England*, pp. 254–5.
20. Richards, 'Anatomy of the Sutherland Fortune', pp. 51–3.
21. F.B. Heath, 'The Grenvilles in the Nineteenth Century: The Emergence of Commercial Affiliations', *Huntingdon Library Quarterly*, XXV (1961), pp. 40–9; T.C. Barker, 'Lord Salisbury, Chairman of the Great Eastern Railway, 1868–72', in S. Marriner (ed.), *Business and Businessmen: Studies in Banking, Economics and Accounting* (1979), pp. 81–103.
22. For the general background, see R.A. Buchannan, 'Gentlemen Engineers: The Making of a Profession', *Victorian Studies*, XXVI (1983), pp. 407–29.
23. H.C.B. Rogers, *G.J. Churchward: A Locomotive Biography* (1975), pp. 17–19, 86, 118, 123–30.
24. Lady Troubridge & A. Marshall, *John, Lord Montagu of Beaulieu: A Memoir* (1930), pp. 39, 41, 288–9; Lord Montagu of Beaulieu, *The Motoring Montagus* (1959), pp. 3–5.
25. For the general background, see D. Cannadine, *The Decline and Fall of the British Aristocracy* (1990), pp. 133–5.
26. Martins, *A Great Agricultural Estate*, pp. 61–5, 267–9; Thompson, *English Landed Society*, pp. 307–8.
27. Cannadine, *Decline and Fall*, pp. 406–17; P.S. Bagwell, 'The Railway Interest: Its Organisation and Influence, 1839–1914', *JTH*, VII (1965), p. 82.
28. K. Hoole (ed.), *Tomlinson's North Eastern Railway: Its Rise and Development* (1967), pp. 768–71; R.J. Irving, *The North Eastern Railway Company, 1870–1914: An Economic History* (1976), pp. 131–2.
29. Viscount Grey of Fallodon, *Twenty Five Years, 1892–1916* (2 vols., 1925), I, pp. 58–60; G.M. Trevelyan; *Grey of Fallodon* (1937), pp. 85, 157–8; K. Robbins, *Sir Edward Grey* (1971), pp. 102–4, 140.
30. C.J. Allen, *The Great Eastern Railway* (3rd edn, 1961), pp. 83, 127–38.
31. D.H. Aldcroft, 'The Efficiency and Enterprise of British Railways, 1870–1914', in

D.H. Aldcroft, *Studies in British Transport History, 1870–1970* (1974), pp. 31–51; P.J. Cain, 'Railway Combination and Government, 1900–1914', *EcHR*, 2nd ser., XXV (1972), pp. 623–41; R.J. Irving, 'The Efficiency and Enterprise of British Railways, 1870–1914: An Alternative Hypothesis', *EcHR*, 2nd ser., XXXI (1978), pp. 46–66; P.J. Cain, 'Private Enterprise or Public Utility? Output, Pricing and Investment on English and Welsh Railways, 1870–1914', *JTH*, 3rd ser., I (1980), pp. 9–28.
32. R.J. Irving, 'British Railway Investment and Innovation, 1900–1914', *Business History*, XIII (1971), pp. 58–9.
33. G. Alderman, *The Railway Interest* (1973), p. 227.
34. C.H. Grinling, *History of the Great Northern Railway, 1845–1922* (1966 edn.), pp. 425–7; Alderman, *Railway Interest*, p. 193.
35. C.J. Allen, *The London and North Eastern Railway* (1966), p. 23; *The Times*, 27 January 1925.
36. Bagwell, 'Railway Interest', p. 82; Sir John Elliot, 'Early Days of the Southern Railway', *JTH*, IV (1960), pp. 200–8.
37. Robbins, *Edward Grey*, pp. 364–6; Allen, *London and North Eastern*, pp. 60–1, 218–19; M. Bonavia, *The Four Great Railways* (1980), pp. 29, 50, 57–8, 72; F. Booker, *The Great Western Railway: A New History* (1977), pp. 140–3.
38. Allen, *London and North Eastern*, pp. 27, 60.
39. F.M.L. Thompson, 'Nineteenth-Century Horse Sense', *EcHR*, 2nd ser., XXIX (1976), p. 61.
40. H. Barty-King, *The AA: A History of the First Seventy Five Years of the Automobile Association, 1905–80* (1980), pp. 96–7; G.R. Searle, *Corruption in British Politics, 1895–1930* (1987), p. 25; R. Carr, *English Fox-Hunting: A History* (1976), p. 147.
41. Cannadine, *Decline and Fall*, pp. 359–60.
42. H. Langrishe, 'Motor Cars and Horses', in Lord Northcliffe (ed.), *Motors and Motor Driving* (1906 edn), pp. 344–9; Cannadine, *Decline and Fall*, p. 363.
43. B. Bond, *British Military Policy Between the Two Wars* (1980), pp. 64–6.
44. Brabazon of Tara, *The Brabazon Story*, pp. 29–30.
45. T.R. Nicholson, *The Birth of the British Motor Car, 1767–1897* (3 vols., 1982), vol. III, *The Last Battle, 1894–97*, p. 372; D. Sutherland, *The Yellow Earl* (1965), pp. 169–71; Barty-King, *The AA*, pp. 110, 190.
46. J.M. Lee, *Social Leaders and Public Persons* (1963), pp. 42–3; M. Harrison, *Lord of Lon-*

don (1966), pp. 96–7, 162–82.

47. K. Young, *Arthur James Balfour* (1963), pp. 459–60; K. Rose, *The Later Cecils* (1975), pp. 136, 254.

48. *The Times*, 8 Sept. 1913.

49. Nicholson, *The Last Battle*, pp. 338, 356–7.

50. Lord Montagu of Beaulieu, 'The Utility of Motor Vehicles', in Northcliffe, *Motors and Motor Driving*, pp. 25–37; P. Tritton, *John Montagu of Beaulieu, 1866–1929: Motoring Pioneer and Prophet* (1985), pp. 48–97; W. Plowden, *The Motor Car and Politics, 1896–1970* (1971), pp. 44–6.

51. Troubridge and Marshall, *John, Lord Montagu*, pp. 91, 216; Montagu of Beaulieu, *The Motoring Montagus*, pp. 10–12, 23–34.

52. W. Boddy, *The History of Brooklands Motor Course* (1957), pp. 5–17, 295, 353.

53. K. Richardson, *The British Motor Industry, 1896–1939* (1977), pp. 122–31; W. Boddy, 'The Motor Course', in C. Gardner (ed.), *Fifty Years of Brooklands* (1956), pp. 18–19.

54. S.B. Saul, 'The Motor Industry in Britain to 1914', *Business History*, v (1962), pp. 22–44; R. Church, 'Markets and Manufacturing in the British Motor Industry Before 1914, With Some French Comparisons', *JTH*, 3rd ser., iii (1982), pp. 1–20.

55. Richardson, *British Motor Industry*, pp. 29–30; *The Times*, 8 Sept. 1913; P.W.S. Andrews & E. Brunner, *The Life of Lord Nuffield: A Study in Enterprise and Benevolence* (1955), pp. 66–7, 89.

56. Nicholson, *The Last Battle*, pp. 361, 366, 383, 400, 415–16, 469.

57. A.E. Harrison, 'Joint Stock Company Flotation in the Cycle, Motor Vehicle and Related Industries, 1882–1914', *Business History*, xxiii (1981), pp. 174–7, 187; Richardson, *British Motor Industry*, p. 20; Saul, 'Motor Industry in Britain', p. 27; *The Times*, 18 May 1921.

58. C.S. Rolls, 'The Caprices of the Petrol Motor', in Northcliffe, *Motors and Motor Driving*, pp. 168–86.

59. I. Lloyd, *Rolls Royce: The Growth of a Firm* (1978), pp. 8–14, 22–36.

60. Richardson, *British Motor Industry*, pp. 29–35.

61. Earl of Cottenham, *Motoring Today and Tomorrow* (1928), pp. 116–17.

62. D.G. Rhys, 'Concentration in the Inter-War Motor Industry', *JTH*, new ser., iii (1976), pp. 241–64.

63. Andrews & Brunner, *Lord Nuffield*, p. 90; *The Times*, 19 June 1944; I. Lloyd, *Rolls Royce: The Years of Endeavour* (1978), pp. 147, 160–6.

64. Montagu of Beaulieu, *The Motoring Montagus*, pp. 43–8; Troubridge & Marshall, *John Lord Montagu*, pp. 245–50; Tritton, *John Montagu of Beaulieu*, pp. 237–45.

65. *The Times*, 21 July 1943.

66. Lord Howe (ed.), *Motor Racing* (Lonsdale Library, vol. xxvii) (1938); *The Times*, 27 July 1964.

67. *Daily Telegraph*, 23 May 1990.

68. Hon. Mrs Victor Bruce, *Nine Thousand Miles in Eight Weeks* (1927), passim; Bruce, *Nine Lives Plus* (1977), pp. 13, 24–33, 36–41, 57–7, 81–94.

69. Brabazon of Tara, *The Brabazon Story*, pp. 40, 48.

70. P. King, *Knights of the Air* (1989), pp. 75–6.

71. Brabazon of Tara, *The Brabazon Story*, pp. 1–21, 29–31, 43–6, 50–8, 66.

72. R. Dallas Brett, *History of British Aviation, 1908–1914* (2 vols., 1988 edn), vol. ii, pp. 174–92; 'L'Ancien', 'Brooklands as an Aerodrome', in Gardner, *Fifty Years of Brooklands*, pp. 63–84.

73. Tritton, *John Montagu of Beaulieu*, pp. 154–61, 203–15.

74. P. Fearon, 'The Formative Years of the British Aircraft Industry, 1913–1924', *Business History Review*, xliii (1969), pp. 476–95.

75. King, *Knights of the Air*, pp. 39–40; M. Howard de Walden, *Pages From My Life* (1963), p. 82.

76. Brabazon of Tara, *The Brabazon Story*, pp. 86–98; Rose, *Later Cecils*, pp. 254–8; *The Times*, 27 Aug. 1929; R. Skidelsky, *Oswald Mosley* (1975), pp. 62–4.

77. W.E. Burrows, *Richthofen: A True History of the Red Baron* (1970), pp. 25–8, 111–15, 130, 205.

78. P. Fearon, 'The British Airframe Industry and the State, 1918–35', *EcHR*, 2nd ser., xxvii (1974), pp. 236–51; Fearon, 'The Vicissitudes of a British Aircraft Company: Handley Page Ltd Between the Wars', *Business History*, xx (1978), pp. 63–85.

79. John, Duke of Bedford, *A Silver-Plated Spoon* (1959), pp. 3–5, 23–5, 71–2; C. Seebohm, *The Country House in Wartime, 1939–45* (1989), pp. 168–9.

80. *Daily Telegraph*, 23 May 1990; Bruce, *Nine Lives Plus*, pp. 102–49; Bruce, *The Bluebird's Flight* (1931), passim.

81. *DNB, 1961–1970* (1981), pp. 377–9; *The Times*, 31 Dec. 1965.

82. *The Times*, 2 Apr. 1973; P.F.M. Fellowes et al, *First Over Everest: The Houston Mount Everest Expedition* (1933); Lord Clydesdale & D.F. McIntyre, *The Pilot's Book of Everest*

(1936).

83. M. Smith, *British Air Strategy Between the Wars* (1984), p. 34.

84. J.A. Cross, *Sir Samuel Hoare: A Political Biography* (1977), pp. 2–4, 10, 83–124.

85. Cross, *Lord Swinton* (1982), pp. 135–219.

86. Cross, *Hoare*, pp. 86–8.

87. Cannadine, *Decline and Fall*, p. 219; Cross, *Swinton*, pp. 202, 213–17; Smith, *Air Strategy*, pp. 35–7; Sir Maurice Dean, *The Royal Air Force and Two World Wars* (1979), pp. 56, 74, 85.

88. M. Howard, 'Per Ardua', *New Statesman*, 26 Jan. 1957, pp. 106–7.

89. Duke of Sutherland, *Looking Back* (1957), pp. 108–13; Cross, *Hoare*, pp. 101–7; Viscount Templewood, *Empire of the Air: The Advent of the Air Age, 1922–1929* (1957), pp. 12, 115–16, 173, 181, 187.

90. Marquess of Londonderry, 'Foreword' to F. Young, *Growing Wings* (1936), pp. 11–18; Londonderry, *Airways of the Empire: Their History and Development* (1936), passim; Londonderry, *Wings of Destiny* (1943), p. 82.

91. Brabazon of Tara, *The Brabazon Story*, pp. 201–6.

92. J. Douglas-Hamilton, *Motive for a Misson: The Story Behind Hess's Flight to Britain* (1971), pp. 152–64.

93. Bruce, *Nine Lives Plus*, pp. 180–6.

94. Dean, *The Royal Air Force*, p. 181; Brabazon of Tara, *The Brabazon Story*, pp. 107–10.

95. Lord Douglas of Kirtleside, *Years of Combat* (1963), pp. 17–19, 37; Douglas, *Years of Command* (1966), pp. 362–3; R.J. Overy, *The Air War, 1939–1945* (1980), pp. 138–47; J.R. Colville, *The Fringes of Power: 10 Downing Street Diaries, 1939–1955* (1985), p. 278; G.M. Trevelyan, *Ilustrated English Social History* (1964 edn, 4 vols.), IV, p. 228.

96. Thompson, 'Nineteenth-Century Horse Sense'; p. 62.

97. M. Asquith, *Myself When Young: by Famous Women of Today* (1938), p. 232.

98. Lord Dunraven, *Past Times and Pastimes* (2 vols., 1922), vol. I, p. 6.

99. T.R. Gourvish, *British Railways, 1948–73: A Business History* (1986), pp. 144–5, 162–6; W. Whitelaw, *The Whitelaw Memoirs* (1989), pp. 1–7, 33–4.

100. Boddy, *History of Brooklands*, p. 232; Montagu of Beaulieu, *The Motoring Montagus*, pp. 61–6; the Duke of Richmond and Gordon, 'Motor Race Promotion', in S.C.H. Davies (ed.), *Motor Racing* (Lonsdale Library, vol. XXXIII) (1957), pp. 302–13.

101. F.M.L. Thompson, 'Britain', in D. Spring (ed.), *European Landed Elites in the Nineteenth*

Century (1977), p. 23.

4. Lord Curzon as Ceremonial Impressario

1. For a general discussion of these developments, see E.J. Hobsbawm & T. Ranger (eds.), *The Invention of Tradition* (1983).

2. Curzon MSS, FIII/153, Lord George Hamilton to Curzon, 1 Oct. 1902.

3. Curzon MSS, FI12/601, *Gossip*, 26 Dec. 1902; Sir J.A.R. Marriott, 'Lord Curzon of Kedleston', *Fortnightly Review*, CXVII (1925), p. 583.

4. *DNB, 1922–30* (1937), p. 223; K. Rose, *King George V* (1983), p. 104; Curzon MSS, FI12/531/1, 'The Ceremonial to be Observed at the Royal Coronation of their Majesties King George V and Queen Mary ... on 22 June 1911.'

5. Marchioness Curzon of Kedleston, *Reminiscences* (1955), pp. 99–109, 152–61.

6. Curzon MSS, FI12/187, Correspondence and Committees re the Setting Up of the Order of the British Empire, 1917; FI12/194, Court Functionaries, 1919–23; Rose, *King George V*, p. 256.

7. Lord Curzon, *Subjects of the Day* (1915), p. 77.

8. Curzon, *Subjects of the Day*, p. 14.

9. Lord Ronaldshay, *The Life of Lord Curzon* (3 vols., 1928), vol. I, p. 64.

10. Lord Curzon, *Tales of Travel* (1923), pp. 125–6, 130–1, 139.

11. G.N. Curzon, *Problems of the Far East* (1894), pp. 1–3.

12. Ronaldshay, *Curzon*, vol. I, p. 153; G.N. Curzon, *Problems of the Far East*, pp. 38–40, 130–68, 244–7, 254–62, 292–5; G.N. Curzon, *Russia in Central Asia* (1889), pp. xii, 200–1; G.N. Curzon, *Persia and the Persian Question* (2 vols., 1892), vol. I, pp. 312–21, 396–408; Lord Curzon, *Leaves From a Viceroy's Notebook* (1926), pp. 231–42.

13. G.N. Curzon, *Russia in Central Asia*, p. 244; Lord Curzon, *Subjects of the Day*, p. 30. See also Hardinge MSS 92 pt I, Curzon to Hardinge, 8 Jan. 1911.

14. Ronaldshay, *Curzon*, vol. I, pp. 55, 84; D.G. Hogarth, 'George Nathaniel Curzon, Marquess Curzon of Kedleston, 1859–1925', *Proceedings of the British Academy*, XI (1924–5), pp. 502–24.

15. Ronaldshay, *Curzon*: vol. I, p. 17; vol. III, pp. 72–8; Lord Curzon, *Subjects of the Day*, pp. 70–1; idem, *British Government in India* (2 vols., 1925), vol. I, pp. 93–4; idem,

Kedleston Church: An Account Historical, Descriptive and Archaeological (1922); idem, *Bodiam Castle, Sussex: An Historical and Descriptive Survey* (1926); idem, *The Personal History of Walmer Castle and Its Lords Warden* (1927); idem, *Tattershall Castle, Lincolnshire: An Historical and Descriptive Survey* (1929). See also Curzon MSS, F112/652, Correspondence re books on houses, 1919–25.

16. Curzon, *Tattershall*, pp. 142–60; idem, *Bodiam*, pp. 80–114; idem, *Subjects of the Day*, pp. 120–6, 134–9, 166–70.

17. Ronaldshay, *Curzon*, vol. II, pp. 155–62, 330–9; Curzon, *Kedleston*, pp. 25–88; idem, *British Government in India*, vol. I, pp. 177–201.

18. Ronaldshay, *Curzon*, vol. I, p. 73; Curzon, *Bodiam*, p. xii.

19. Curzon, *Subjects of the Day*, pp. 70–1; idem, *British Government in India*, vol. I, p. xvii.

20. Ronaldshay, *Curzon*, vol. I, pp. 40–5, 173–86; W.S. Churchill, *Great Contemporaries* (1942 edn), pp. 206–10; Lord Curzon, *Modern Parliamentary Eloquence* (1913), pp. 12, 47–8.

21. Ronaldshay, *Curzon*, vol. I, pp. 197–9; S. Leslie, *Studies in Sublime Failure* (1932), p. 242.

22. Ronaldshay, *Curzon*: vol. I, p. 179; vol. III, p. 389.

23. Ronaldshay, *Curzon*, vol. III, p. 394; Curzon, *Modern Parliamentary Eloquence*, p. 45; idem, *Tales of Travel*, p. 262.

24. M.V. Brett (ed.), *Journals and Letters of Reginald, Viscount Esher*, vol. I, *1870–1903* (1934), p. 321.

25. Curzon MSS, F111/154, Lord George Hamilton to Curzon, 6 Jan. 1903.

26. Leslie, *Studies in Sublime Failure*, p. 202; Marchioness Curzon, *Reminiscences*, pp. 77, 100–1, 154.

27. Curzon, *British Government in India*, vol. I, p. 208.

28. Ronaldshay, *Curzon*, vol. I, p. 250; Curzon MSS, F112/229, Lord Selborne to Curzon, 4 Jan. 1903.

29. Curzon, *Subjects of the Day*, p. 43.

30. Curzon MSS, F112/231, Knollys to Curzon: 1 Mar. 1901, 25 Apr. 1901, 9 May 1901, 28 June 1901, 15 Aug. 1901, 9 Jan. 1902.

31. Curzon MSS, F112/231, Knollys to Curzon: 11 July 1902, 23 Sept. 1902, 1 Oct. 1902; F111/152, Lord George Hamilton to Curzon, 13 Aug. 1902; F111/182, Curzon to George Wyndham, 7 May 1902.

32. There is a growing literature on the establishment of the ceremonial image of the British Raj. I found the following to be especially helpful: B.S. Cohn, 'Representing Authority in Victorian India', in Hobsbawm & Ranger, *Invention of Tradition*, pp. 165–210; M.H. Fisher, 'The Resident in Court Ritual, 1764–1858', *Modern Asian Studies*, XXIV (1990), pp. 419–58; E.S. Haynes, 'Rajput Ceremonial Interactions as a Mirror of a Dying Indian State System, 1820–1947', *Modern Asian Studies*, XXIV (1990), pp. 459–92; D. Haynes, 'Imperial Ritual in a Local Setting: The Ceremonial Order in Surat, 1890–1939', *Modern Asian Studies*, XXIV (1990), pp. 493–527; C.W. Nuckolls, 'The Durbar Incident', *Modern Asian Studies*, XXIV (1990), pp. 529–59; A. Trevithick, 'Some Structural and Sequential Aspects of the British Imperial Assemblages at Delhi: 1877–1911', *Modern Asian Studies*, XXIV (1990), pp. 561–78.

33. Cohn, 'Representing Authority', pp. 185–207; J. Talboys Wheeler, *The History of the Imperial Assemblage at Delhi* (1877); Lady B. Balfour, *History of Lord Lytton's Indian Administration* (1899), pp. 106–33; M. Lutyens, *The Lyttons in India: Lord Lytton's Viceroyalty* (1979), pp. 74–88.

34. Sir I. de la Bere, *The Queen's Orders of Chivalry* (1964), pp. 177–81.

35. Ronaldshay, *Curzon*, vol. II, pp. 222–3; M. Edwardes, *High Noon of Empire: India Under Curzon* (1965), p. 169.

36. Curzon MSS, F111/151, Lord George Hamilton to Curzon, 9 Jan. 1902; F111/153, Lord George Hamilton to Curzon, 24 Sept. 1902, 6 and 20 Nov. 1902; F111/161, Curzon to A.J. Balfour, 20 Nov. 1902; Curzon to Lord George Hamilton, 27 Nov. 1902, 11 and 18 Dec. 1902.

37. Curzon MSS, F111/153, Lord George Hamilton to Curzon, 13 Nov. 1902; D. Dilks, *Curzon in India* (2 vols., 1969), vol. I, pp. 249–60, provides the fullest account of the controversy.

38. Curzon MSS, F112/600, *Manchester Guardian*, 8 Nov. 1902; F112/601, *Westminster Gazette*, 9 Sept. 1902; *Daily News*, 11 Sept. 1902.

39. Dilks, *Curzon in India*, vol. I, p. 290; Curzon MSS, F111/232, Curzon to Lord Percy, 1 Oct. 1902; F111/161, Curzon to Lord George Hamilton, 10 Sept. 1902; F111/162 pt I, Curzon to Lord George Hamilton, 19 Mar. 1903.

40. Cohn, 'Representing Authority', p. 208.

41. Ronaldshay, *Curzon*, vol. II, p. 229; Curzon MSS, F111/161, Curzon to Lord George Hamilton, 22 Oct. 1902.

42. Curzon MSS, FIII/161, Curzon to Lord George Hamilton, 23 Apr. 1902.

43. Curzon MSS, FIII/274A, Lord Curzon's handwritten notes [undated]; 'Minute by His Excellency the Viceroy on the Proposed Coronation Durbar at Delhi on January 1st, 1903', dated 11 May 1902; FIII/274B, 'Supplementary Minute by His Excellency the Viceroy on the Coronation Durbar at Delhi on 1st January 1903', dated 21 Oct. 1903. See also Curzon's speech to the Legislative Council at Simla, 5 Sept. 1902, printed in Sir T. Raleigh (ed.), Lord Curzon in India (1906), pp. 289–300.

44. Curzon MSS, FIII/161, Curzon to Lord George Hamilton, 26 Oct. 1902.

45. Curzon MSS, FIII/161, Curzon to Lord George Hamilton, 16 July 1902.

46. There are many accounts of Curzon's Durbar. For the official view, see: Curzon MSS, FI12/465, E. Baring, Description of the Viceroy's Camp, Delhi, 1903; FI12/466, The Coronation Durbar Delhi, 1903: Official Directory. For newspaper reports, see especially The Times, 29–31 Dec. 1902, 1–13 Jan. 1903. For contemporary accounts, see: M. Menpes, The Durbar (1903); L. Fraser, At Delhi (1903); V. Steer, The Delhi Durbar, 1902–03 (Madras, 1903); J.O. Hobbes, Imperial India: Letters from the East (1903); S. Wheeler, History of the Delhi Coronation Durbar (1904). For more recent studies, see: Ronaldshay, Curzon, vol. II, pp. 221–34, 252–60; Dilks, Curzon in India, vol. II, pp. 249–66; Edwardes, High Noon of Empire, pp. 169–81; N. Nicolson, Mary Curzon (1977), pp. 160–7.

47. The Times, 30 Dec. 1902.

48. For Curzon's account, see Curzon, Leaves From a Viceroy's Notebook, pp. 32–6.

49. The Times, 2 Jan. 1903.

50. Curzon, Leaves From a Viceroy's Notebook, p. 50.

51. The Times, 12 Jan. 1903.

52. Raleigh, Curzon in India, pp. 306–9; Curzon MSS, FIII/162, pt II, Curzon to Lord George Hamilton, 13 Jan. 1903.

53. Ronaldshay, Curzon, vol. II, pp. 254–5; Menpes, The Durbar, p. 188.

54. Curzon MSS, FI12/231, Knollys to Curzon, 8 Jan. 1903, 5 Feb. 1903, 6 Mar. 1903; FI12/577, King Edward VII to Curzon, 16 and 29 Jan. 1903; FIII/154, Lord George Hamilton to Curzon, 6 and 28 Jan. 1903, 5 Feb. 1903.

55. Dilks, Curzon in India, vol. I, p. 264; C. Vanderbilt Balsan, The Glitter and the Gold (New York, 1952), p. 175; Curzon MSS, FIII/154, A. Godley to Curzon, 1 Jan. 1903.

56. Menpes, The Durbar, pp. 113–19, 306; Fraser, At Delhi, p. 170; Curzon MSS, FI12/600, Daily Telegraph, 22 Dec. 1902.

57. Fraser, At Delhi, p. 169; Steer, Delhi Durbar, p. 3; Curzon MSS, FI12/600, Morning Leader, 4 Feb. 1903.

58. Menpes, Delhi Durbar, pp. 203–10; Fraser, At Delhi, pp. 170–7; The Times, 13 Jan. 1903; Curzon MSS, FI12/601, The Statesman, 31 Dec. 1902.

59. The Times, 30 Dec. 1902.

60. Curzon MSS, FI12/600, Daily News, 30 Dec. 1902; South Wales Daily News, 31 Dec. 1902; Yorkshire Herald, 17 Jan. 1903.

61. Curzon MSS, FI12/601, Newcastle Daily Leader, 30 Dec. 1902; Pall Mall Gazette, 30 Dec. 1902; Yorkshire Daily Observer, 31 Dec. 1902.

62. Curzon MSS, FIII/154. Lord George Hamilton to Curzon, 23 Jan. 1903; FIII/161, Curzon to Lord George Hamilton, 22 Oct. 1902; S. Gopal, British Policy in India, 1858–1905 (1965), pp. 297–8.

63. Curzon MSS, FI12/600, Morning Leader, 4 Oct. 1902; FI12/601, Daily Chronicle, 6 Sept. 1902; Wheeler, Delhi Coronation Durbar, pp. 211–17, 288–9.

64. Curzon MSS, FI12/600, Morning Leader, 4 Feb. 1903; Trevithick, 'British Imperial Assemblages at Delhi', pp. 568–9.

65. Curzon MSS, FI12/600, Morning Leader, 4 Feb. 1903.

66. Hardinge MSS, 92 pt 1, Curzon to Hardinge, 28 Dec. 1910, 8 Jan. 1911, 10 Feb. 1911, 21 Apr. 1911, 28 May 1911, 24 July 1911; 92 pt II, Hardinge to Curzon, 19 Jan. 1911, 2 Feb. 1911, 8 May 1911, 1 June 1911, 3 July 1911, 16 Aug. 1911. Curzon's tone was ill-judged throughout, a characteristic combination of interference and self-effacement, but his letters once again bear witness to his astonishing capacity to visualise a pageant.

67. For Hardinge's Durbar, see: J.W. Fortescue, Narrative of. . . . the Coronation Durbar held at Delhi on 12th December 1911 (1912); B.C. Busch, Hardinge of Penshurst: A Study in the Old Diplomacy (1980), pp. 163–90; R.E. Frykenberg, 'The Coronation Durbar of 1911: Some Implications', in R.E. Frykenberg (ed.), Delhi Through the Ages: Essays in Urban History, Culture and Society (Delhi, 1986), pp. 369–90.

68. Trevithick, 'British Imperial Assemblages at Delhi', pp. 575–6.

69. Curzon MSS, FI12/429, 'Letters Patent Granting the Office of Lord Warden of the

Cinque Ports and Constable of Dover Castle to Lord Curzon of Kedleston, 6 June 1904.'

70. Curzon, *Walmer Castle*, p. 268.

71. Curzon, *Walmer Castle*, pp. 260–72.

72. E. Knocker, *On The Antiquities of Dover: A Lecture* (1871).

73. Cinque Ports MSS, CPW/RPS 1, E. Knocker to Evelyn Ashley, 9 May 1861; Ashley to E. Knocker, 16 May 1861; E. Knocker to G.M. Underdown, 8 July 1861; Underdown to E. Knocker, 6 and 11 July 1861; Ashley to E. Knocker, 24 July 1861.

74. E. Knocker, *An Account of the Grand Court of Shepway, Holden on the Bredenstone Hill at Dover for the Installation of The Rt. Hon. Henry John Temple, Viscount Palmerston* . . . (1862), pp. 90, 154; E. Walford, 'The Cinque Ports and the Bredenstone at Dover', *Once a Week*, v (1861), pp. 320–32; Cinque Ports MSS, CPW/RPS 3, bundle C, 'Recollections of the Installation of Lord Palmerston as Lord Warden of the Cinque Ports by one who was present'; Curzon, *Walmer Castle*, pp. 273–6.

75. Cinque Ports MSS, CPW/RPS 2, Installation of Earl Granville; Curzon, *Walmer Castle*, pp. 276–80.

76. Sir W. Knocker, *An Account of the Dover Corporation Insignia* . . . (1898); Knocker, *The Coronation of Their Majesties King Edward VII and Queen Alexandra.* . . . (1902). For the growing interest in the history of the Cinque Ports at this time, see: M. Burrows, *Historic Towns: Cinque Ports* (1888); F.M. Hueffer [Ford Madox Ford], *The Cinque Ports: A Historical and Descriptive Record* (1900); M.F. Johnson, 'The Barons of the Cinque Ports', *Macmillans Magazine*, XCII (1905), pp. 130–8.

77. Cinque Ports MSS, CPW/RPS 3, bundle A, Dufferin to W. Knocker, 12 and 21 Apr. 1892, 9 June 1892.

78. Cinque Ports MSS, CPW/RPS 4, bundle A, Dufferin to W. Knocker, 19 Aug. 1896.

79. Cinque Ports MSS, CPW/RPS 5, bundles A, B and D.

80. Cinque Ports MSS, CPW/RPS 5, bundle C, Curzon to W. Knocker, 3, 17 and 25 May 1904, 4, 15, 21, 22, 25, 30 June 1904.

81. *Dover Standard*, 9 July 1904. See also *The Times*, 4 July 1904.

82. Curzon, *Subjects of the Day*, pp. 79–83.

83. Cinque Ports MSS, CPW/RPS 5, bundle E, A.M. Wollaston to W. Knocker, 4 July 1904; *The Times*, 4 July 1905; *Dover Standard*, 9 July 1904.

84. Cinque Port MSS, CPW/RPS 5, bundle C, Curzon to W. Knocker, 2 July 1904.

85. Hueffer, *The Cinque Ports*, p. 270.

86. Curzon, *Walmer Castle*, pp. 266–80; Rose, *King George V*, pp. 70–1.

87. Curzon, *Walmer Castle*, pp. 291–318; Cinque Ports MSS, CPW/RPS 7, Installation of Lord Brassey; CPW/RPS 8, Installation of Lord Beauchamp; CPW/RPS 10, Installation of Lord Reading.

88. L.S. Sutherland, 'The Administration of the University', in L.S. Sutherland & L.G. Mitchell (eds.), *The History of the University of Oxford*, vol. V, *The Eighteenth Century* (1986), pp. 212–13; M.G. Brock, 'The University Chancellorship', *The American Oxonian*, XLVII (1960), pp. 105–9; L.H.D. Buxton & S. Gibson, *Oxford University Ceremonies* (1935), pp. 129–33.

89. H. Warren, 'Chancellor of Oxford', in Ronaldshay, *Curzon*, vol. III, p. 93.

90. Warren, 'Chancellor of Oxford', pp. 89–93.

91. *The Times*, 25 and 27 Feb. 1907.

92. *The Times*, 5, 6, 9, 14 and 15 Mar. 1907.

93. *DNB, 1922–30* (1937), pp. 891–3; L. Magnus, *Herbert Warren of Magdalen: President and Friend, 1853–1930* (1932), pp. 79–80, 121–33, 181–6; G. Kendall, *A Headmaster Remembers* (1933), pp. 88–9.

94. Warren, 'Chancellor of Oxford', p. 93.

95. D.W. Rannie (ed.), *Remarks and Collections of Thomas Hearne*, vol. V (*December 1 1714– December 31 1716*) (1901), pp. 116–19; *Oxford Magazine*, 1 May 1907, pp. 297–8. For the broader historical background, see W.R. Ward, *Georgian Oxford: University Politics in the Eighteenth Century* (1958), pp. 52–68.

96. Magnus, *Herbert Warren*, p. 128.

97. The two fullest accounts are: *The Times*, 13 May 1907; *Oxford Magazine*, 15 May 1907, pp. 331–2.

98. *The Times*, 13 May 1907; *Oxford Magazine*, 15 May 1907, p. 332; *Jackson's Oxford Journal*, 18 May 1907.

99. Curzon to Warren, 12 May 1907, quoted in Magnus, *Herbert Warren*, p. 135.

100. *The Oxford Historical Pageant, June 27–July 3 1907: Book of Words* (1907).

101. Warren, 'Chancellor of Oxford', pp. 94–116.

102. Curzon's immediate successor, Lord Cave, was installed in private in a committee room of the House of Lords. Since then, all installations have been public. Buxton & Gibson, *Oxford University Ceremonies*, pp. 133–6; *The Times*, 13 and 16 July 1925, 30 June 1928, 8 Dec. 1933, 7 and 8 Mar. 1960, 25 June 1987.

103. Marriott, 'Curzon of Kedleston', p. 583.

104. E.J. Hobsbawm, 'Mass-Producing Traditions: Europe, 1870–1914', in Hobsbawm &
Ranger, *Invention of Tradition*, pp. 303–4.
105. The majority of this section is based on D.
Cannadine, 'War and Death, Grief and
Mourning in Modern Britain', in J. Whaley
(ed.), *Mirrors of Mortality: Studies in the Social
History of Death* (1981), pp. 219–25, though
I have naturally changed the emphasis to lay
more stress on Curzon's role in events.
106. Marchioness Curzon, *Reminiscences*, pp. 85–
6.
107. PRO CAB, 23/9, 19 Feb. 1919.
108. Curzon MSS, F112/316, Peace Celebrations
Committee, 9 May 1919.
109. Curzon MSS, F112/316, Peace Celebrations
Committee, 18 June 1919.
110. PRO CAB, 23/10, 15 May 1919, 30 June
1919; Curzon MSS, F112/316, Peace Celebrations Committee, 1 July 1919.
111. PRO CAB, 23/11, 1 July 1919.
112. PRO CAB, 23/11, 4 July 1919.
113. *The Times*, 8 July 1919; S.M. Alsop, *Lady
Sackville: A Biography* (1978), p. 221; C.
Hussey, *The Life of Sir Edwin Lutyens* (1953),
pp. 386–95; A.S.G. Butler, *The Architecture
of Sir Edwin Lutyens* (3 vols., 1950), vol. III,
pp. 37–8.
114. Curzon MSS, F112/686, 'Official Programme of the National Peace Celebrations,
19 July 1919'.
115. *The Times*, 21 July 1919; PRO CAB, 23/11,
22 July 1919.
116. *The Times*, 31 July 1919, 14 Jan. 1920; PRO
CAB, 23/11, 29 and 30 July 1919.
117. PRO CAB, 23/22, 14 Oct. 1920.
118. Ronaldshay, *Curzon*, vol. III, p. 200.
119. M.H. Fitzgerald, *A Memoir of H.E. Ryle*
(1928), p. 311.
120. PRO CAB, 23/22, 15 and 26 Oct. 1920.
121. Curzon MSS, F112/318, Unveiling Ceno-
taph/Unknown Warrior Committee, 19
Oct. 1920.
122. Curzon MSS, F112/318, Unveiling Ceno-
taph/Unknown Warrior Committee, 3
Nov. 1920.
123. Curzon MSS, F112/318, Unveiling Ceno-
taph/Unknown Warrior Committee, 19
Oct. 1920.
124. *The Times*, Armistice Day Supplement, 12
Nov. 1920.
125. Fitzgerald, *Ryle*, pp. 311–12.
126. *The Times*, 15 Nov. 1920.
127. Curzon MSS, F112/318, Observance of
Armistice Day (Nov. 11) Committee, 12
Oct. 1921.
128. Curzon MSS, F112/318, Observance of Armistice Day (Nov. 11) Committee, 12 Oct.

1921.
129. *The Times*, 23 Oct. 1923.
130. PRO CAB, 23/23, 17 Jan. 1921.
131. Curzon MSS, F112/318, Stamfordham to
Curzon, 13 Nov. 1920.
132. Ronaldshay, *Curzon*, vol. III, p. 200.
133. Curzon MSS, F112/318, Storr to Curzon,
13 Nov. 1920. The articles he referred to
were published in the *Pall Mall Gazette*, 11
and 12 Nov. 1920.
134. Raleigh, *Curzon in India*, p. 308; Curzon
MSS, F111/162, pt II, Curzon to Lord
George Hamilton, 13 Jan. 1903.
135. Marchioness Curzon, *Reminiscences*, p. 98.
136. *The Times*, 21 Mar. 1925.
137. Curzon, *Tales of Travel*, pp. 217–19, 228–30,
231–6, 239–42, 247–50; idem, *Leaves from a
Viceroy's Notebook*, pp. 3–8, 18–31, 37–40,
71–5.
138. Marchioness Curzon, *Reminiscences*, pp.
180–1; Hardinge MSS, 92 pt I, Curzon to
Hardinge, 26 June 1911.
139. *The Times*, 24, 26 and 27 Mar. 1925.
140. Ronaldshay, *Curzon*, vol. III, p. 380; R.
Rhodes James (ed.), *'Chips': The Diaries of
Sir Henry Channon* (1967), p. 7.

5. Lord Strickland: Imperial Aristocrat and Aristocratic Imperialist

1. S.W. Martins, *A Great Estate at Work: The
Holkham Estate and Its Inhabitants in the Nine-
teenth Century* (1980), pp. 63–5, 267–9; A.
Offer, 'Empire and Social Reform: British
Overseas Investment and Domestic Politics,
1908–1914', *HJ*, XXVI (1983), p. 124; A.
Adonis, 'The Survival of Great Estates:
Henry, Fourth Earl of Carnarvon and His
Dispositions in the 1880s', *Historical Re-
search*, LXIV (1991), pp. 54–62.
2. D. Cannadine, *The Decline and Fall of the
British Aristocracy* (1990), pp. 133–5, 420–43,
558–602; A.J.P. Taylor, *English History,
1914–1945* (1965), pp. 172–3; A. Adonis,
*Making Aristocracy Work; The Peerage and the
Political System in Britain, 1884–1914* (1993),
pp. 210–39.
3. *Burke's Peerage* (101st edn, 1956), pp. 2390–
2400; B. Cohn, 'Representing Authority in
Victorian India', in E.J. Hobsbawm & T.
Ranger (eds.), *The Invention of Tradition*
(1983), pp. 165–210.
4. Sir Bernard Burke, *A Genealogical and Heraldic History of the Colonial Gentry* (2 vols.,
1891–95); H. Reynolds, "Men of Substance
and Deservedly Good Repute": The Tas-
manian Gentry, 1856–1875', *Australian Journal of Politics and History*, XV (1969), pp.

61–72; G. Bolton, 'The Idea of a Colonial Gentry', *Historical Studies*, XIII (1968), pp. 307–28. For earlier and unsuccessful efforts to export the House of Lords to Canada and Australia, see G. Martin, *Bunyip Aristocracy: The New South Wales Constitutional Debates and Hereditary Institutions in the British Colonies* (1986).

5. Lord Meath, 'Shall Indian Princes Sit in the House of Lords?', *Nineteenth Century*, XXXV (1894), pp. 710–16; J.A.R. Marriott, 'The House of Lords as an Imperial Senate', *Fortnightly Review*, LXXXVII (1907), pp. 1003–17; S.M. Mitra, 'The House of Lords and the Indian Princes', *Fortnightly Review*, XCIII (1910), pp. 1090–9.

6. [Sir] R. Syme, *The Roman Revolution* (1939), pp. 10–27, 78–96, 350–68, 500–8; Syme, *Rome, Spain and the Americas* (1958), pp. 4, 13. For more general speculations on the connections between aristocracies and empires, see: J.A. Schumpeter, *Imperialism and Social Class* (1951); J.H. Kautsky, *The Politics of Aristocratic Empires* (1982).

7. There are two brief obituary notices: *The Times*, 23 Aug. 1940; *DNB, 1931–40* (1949), pp. 838–9. The authoritative life is H. Smith & A. Koster, *Lord Strickland: Servant of the Crown* (2 vols., Malta, 1986), to which I must acknowledge my overriding indebtedness throughout this essay, even though I have only given detailed references to specific quotations from that work.

8. For the earliest accounts of the family history, see: J. Nicolson & R. Burn, *The History and Antiquities of Westmorland and Cumberland* (2 vols., 1777), vol. I, pp. 86–103; J. Burke, *A Genealogical and Heraldic History of the Commoners of Great Britain and Ireland* (4 vols., 1833–8), vol. I, pp. 55–9; W. Whellan, *The History and Topography of the Counties of Cumberland and Westmorland* (1860), pp. 860–2.

9. E. Bellasis, 'Strickland of Sizergh', *Transactions of the Cumberland and Westmorland Antiquarian and Archaeological Society*, X (1889), pp. 75–94; Lady Edeline Strickland, *Sizergh Castle, Westmorland, and Notes on Twenty Five Generations of the Strickland Family* (1898); D. Scott, *The Stricklands of Sizergh Castle: The Records of Twenty Five Generations of a Westmorland Family* (1908); H. Hornyold, *Genealogical Memoirs of the Family of Strickland of Sizergh* (1928). I have drawn extensively on these authorities for the next four paragraphs.

10. Hornyold, *Genealogical Memoirs*, p. xi.

11. M.W. Taylor, 'Sizergh, no. 1', *Transactions of the Cumberland and Westmorland Antiquarian and Archaeological Society*, X (1889), pp. 48–65; J.F. Curwen, 'Sizergh, no. 2', *Transactions of the Cumberland and Westmorland Antiquarian and Archaeological Society*, X (1889), pp. 66–74; Anon., 'Sizergh Castle, Westmorland: the Seat of Sir Gerald Strickland, KCMG', *Country Life*, XIX (30 June 1906), pp. 942–50; Royal Commission on Historical Monuments, *Westmorland* (1936), pp. 106–8; N. Pevsner, *The Buildings of England: Cumberland and Westmorland* (1967), pp. 289–91.

12. Anon., 'The Inlaid Room from Sizergh Castle', *The House*, III (May 1898), pp. 81–4; Victoria and Albert Museum, Dept of Woodwork [H. Clifford Smith], *The Panelled Rooms, IV, The Inlaid Room of Sizergh Castle* (rev. edn, 1928). See also M. Girouard, 'Comment', *Country Life*, CLXXXV (9 May 1991), p. 63, and the letters in reply in *Country Life*, CLXXXV (6 June 1991), p. 130.

13. British Library, SC 1909, 'Catalogue of the Stuart and Strickland Family Portraits from Sizergh Castle, 1896'.

14. H. Frendo, 'Maltese Colonial Identity: Latin Mediterranean or British Empire?', in V. Mallia-Milanes (ed.), *The British Colonial Experience, 1800–1964: The Impact on Maltese Society* (Malta, 1988), pp. 195–7. Despite evidence to the contrary, Strickland was convinced that the British and the Maltese were both descended from the Phonecians: see G. Strickland, *Malta and the Phonecians* (1925); Strickland, 'Malta', *Encyclopaedia Britannica* (13th edn, 32 vols., 1926), vol. XVII, pp. 507–14.

15. Smith & Koster, *Lord Strickland*, vol. I, p. 90.

16. Smith & Koster, *Lord Strickland*, vol. I, pp. 92, 118, 121.

17. For a general discussion of indebted proconsuls, see Cannadine, *Decline and Fall*, pp. 594–9.

18. *The Times*, 14 Sept. 1886. For the broader historical background, see: H. Smith, *Britain in Malta* (2 vols., 1953); H.I. Lee, *Malta, 1813–1914: A Study in Constitutional and Strategic Development* (Malta, 1973), pp. 194–215; E. Dobie, *Malta's Road to Independence* (Oklahoma, 1967), pp. 38–60.

19. Strickland, 'Malta', p. 513.

20. Sir I. de la Bere, *The Queen's Orders of Chivalry* (1964), pp. 139–43; A.E. Abela, *The Order of St Michael and St George in Malta, and Maltese Knights of the British Realm* (Malta, 1988), esp. pp. 1–106. For Strickland's comments on the Order, see

Hansard, HL, 5 Nov. 1930, col. 61.

21. Dobie, *Malta's Road to Independence*, p. 59; Lee, *Malta, 1813–1914*, pp. 216–32; J.L. Garvin & J. Amery, *The Life of Joseph Chamberlain* (6 vols., 1932–69), vol. IV, pp. 176–8.
22. Smith & Koster, *Lord Strickland*, vol. I, p. 48.
23. Smith & Koster, *Lord Strickland*, vol. I, p. 146.
24. Smith & Koster, *Lord Strickland*, vol. I, p. 216.
25. *The Times*, 9 June 1904.
26. Smith & Koster, *Lord Strickland*, vol. I, pp. 226, 243.
27. Smith & Koster, *Lord Strickland*, vol. I, pp. 258, 283; C. Cunneen, *Kings' Men: Australia's Governors General* (1983), pp. 48–71.
28. Cunneen, *Kings' Men*, p. 77.
29. Cunneen, *Kings' Men*, pp. 89–105.
30. *The Times*, 3 June 1913.
31. *The Times*, 15 Mar. 1913; Cunneen, *Kings' Men*, pp. 106–9.
32. Cunneen, *Kings' Men*, pp. 126–7, 211–12.
33. Smith & Koster, *Lord Strickland*, vol. I, p. 347.
34. H.A. Evatt, *Australian Labour Leader: The Story of W.A. Holman and the Labour Movement* (1954 edn), pp. 300–24. See also the vivid, critical and affectionate portrait of Strickland in A.A. Holman, *Memoirs of a Premier's Wife* (1947), pp. 18–30.
35. *The Times*, 13 Sept. 1917.
36. *The Times*, 18–28 Sept. 1917; A.B. Keith, 'Ministerial Responsibility in the Dominions', *Journal of the Society of Comparative Legislation*, XVII (1917), pp. 227–32; Keith, *Responsible Government in the Dominions* (2nd edn, 2 vols., 1928), vol. I, pp. 81, 106, 176–7; R.F. Shinn, *Arthur Berriedale Keith, 1879–1944: The Chief Ornament of Scottish Learning* (1990), pp. 134–5, 179–80; H.V. Evatt, *The King and the Dominion Governors: A Study of the Reserve Powers of the Crown in Great Britain and the Dominions* (1936), pp. 146–52.
37. Smith & Koster, *Lord Strickland*, vol. II, p. 368.
38. L. Amery, *My Political Life* (3 vols., 1953–5), vol. II, pp. 188–96; J. Barnes & D. Nicholson (eds.), *The Leo Amery Diaries*, vol. I, *1896–1929* (1980), pp. 244, 261–4.
39. *The Times*, 16 Aug. 1927; Frendo, 'Maltese Colonial Identity', pp. 195–6.
40. *The Times*, 13 Apr. 1927; Smith & Koster, *Lord Strickland*, vol. II, pp. 402–5.
41. *The Times*, 30 June 1904, 10 Oct. 1950; Smith & Koster, *Lord Strickland*, vol. II, p. 414.
42. Smith & Koster, *Lord Strickland*, vol. II, p. 416.
43. D. Austin, *Malta and the End of Empire* (1971), p. 121, n22. For Strickland's interventions, see *Hansard*, HC: 23 Feb. 1925, col. 1578; 11 May 1925, col. 1428; 13 May 1925, cols. 1991–92; 18 May 1925, cols. 16–17, 194–202; 23 June 1925, cols. 1086–90; 13 July 1925, cols. 864–5; 27 July 1925, cols. 8–9; 30 July 1925, col. 649; 3 Aug. 1925, cols. 942–3; 5 Aug. 1925, col. 1351; 6 Aug. 1925, col. 1552; 7 Aug. 1925, cols. 1865–72; 29 July 1926, cols. 2436–47; 9 Feb. 1927, cols. 230–4; 15 Feb. 1927, cols. 756–7; 17 Feb. 1927, cols. 1116–17; 28 Feb. 1927, cols. 50–1; 3 May 1927, cols. 1440–1; 5 May 1927, cols. 1763–4; 9 May 1927, col. 46; 10 May 1927, cols. 351–6; 16 May 1927, col. 905.
44. Smith & Koster, *Lord Strickland*, vol. II, p. 416.
45. *The Times*: 9, 13 May 1927; 2, 21 Jan. 1928.
46. Bellasis, 'Strickland of Sizergh', p. 94.
47. J. Jackson Howard (ed.), *Genealogical Collections Illustrating the History of Roman Catholic Families of England Based on the Lawson Manuscript*, part IV, Hornyold (1892).
48. H. Hornyold-Strickland, *Biographical Sketches of the Members of Parliament of Lancashire (1290–1550)* (1935); idem (ed.), *Index to Nicolson and Burn's History and Antiquities of the Counties of Westmorland and Cumberland, Abridged and Revised from the Manuscript of the Late Daniel Scott* (1934). He also contributed the notice of his father-in-law in *DNB, 1931–40*, pp. 838–9. For the Gandolfi Dukedom, see *Burke's Peerage* (71st edn, 1909), pp. 2542–3, and (97th edn, 1939), p. 2676.
49. For Strickland's words on Death Duties, see *Hansard*, HL, 4 Nov. 1938, col. 1558.
50. *The Times*, 20 Nov. 1928.
51. *The Times*, 30 Nov. 1988.
52. For detailed treatment of this protracted dispute, see: W.K. Hancock, *Survey of British Commonwealth Affairs*, vol. I, *Problems of Nationality, 1918–1936* (1937), pp. 406–28; J. Bezzina, 'Church and State in an Island Colony', in Mallia-Milanes, *The British Colonial Experience*, pp. 65–9; A. Koster, *Prelates and Politicians in Malta: Changing Power-Balances between Church and State in a Mediterranean Island Fortress (1800–1976)* (The Netherlands, 1984), pp. 93–119.
53. *The Times*: 29 Apr. 1930; 24, 26 May 1930; 5 June 1930; 3 July 1930; Hancock, *Survey of Commonwealth Affairs*, p. 411.
54. *Hansard*, HL: 25 June 1830, cols. 129–62; 5 Nov. 1930, cols. 44–62; 3 Mar. 1931, cols. 216–23.

55. Smith & Koster, *Lord Strickland*, vol. II, p. 496; *Hansard*, HC, 1 Aug. 1930, cols. 1005–6.

56. *The Times*, 1, 4, 6, 18 June 1932.

57. *The Times*, 3, 6 Nov. 1933; Smith & Koster, *Lord Strickland*, vol. II, p. 559. See also: D.B. Swinfen, 'Lord Strickland, the *Ultra Vires* Cases and the Maltese Constitution, 1934–39', *Journal of Imperial and Commonwealth History*, XVII (1988–9), pp. 413–32.

58. *Hansard*, HL: 29 Nov. 1933, cols. 193–277; 1 Nov. 1934, cols. 65–90; 22 Nov. 1934, cols. 77–110; 30 July 1935, cols. 926–53; 10 Dec. 1935, cols. 130–45; 5 May 1936, cols. 748–84; 13 May 1936, cols. 960–99; 13 July 1936, cols. 730–8; 30 July 1936, cols. 449–60; 2 Dec. 1936, cols. 564–79.

59. *Hansard*, HL: 29 July 1930, cols. 995–1001; 17 Nov. 1931, cols. 53–66; 15 July 1935, cols. 380–7; 4 Dec. 1935, cols. 60–5; 15 July 1936, cols. 854–68; 18 Nov. 1936, cols. 260–6; 3 Nov. 1937, cols. 55–87; 4 Nov. 1938, cols. 1553–64.

60. *Hansard*, HL: 17 Nov. 1931, col. 65; 4 Dec. 1935, cols. 65–73; 12 Dec. 1935, col. 226; 24 Mar. 1937, cols. 783–92, 802–3; 28 Apr. 1937, cols. 43–50, 64–6.

61. *The Times*: 28, 30 July 1939; 17 Aug. 1939; 24, 27, 28 Aug. 1940; 12 Oct. 1940.

62. *Hansard*, HL, 25 June 1930, cols. 138–9.

63. Holman, *Memoirs of a Premier's Wife*, pp. 18–19; Hornyold-Strickland in *DNB, 1931–40*, p. 839; G. Martin, 'Colonial Peerage and Bunyip Aristocracy', in *The Diaspora of the British* (University of London, Institute of Commonwealth Studies, Collected Seminar Papers no. 31, 1982), p. 105, n5. Even A.B. Keith thought Strickland 'amusingly conceited': see Shinn, *Berriedale Keith*, pp. 179–80.

64. *Hansard*, HL, 4 Nov. 1938, col. 1559.

65. *Hansard*, HL, 4 Nov. 1938, col. 1558.

66. Lord Strickland's will, dated 3 July 1939.

67. *The Times*: 20 Jan. 1970; 2 Feb. 1970; 26 Sept. 1975; 4, 5 Nov. 1975.

68. Dobie, *Malta's Road to Independence*, pp. 116–19, 123.

69. *The Times*: 11, 12 Sept. 1950; 30 Nov. 1988; Dobie, *Malta's Road to Independence*, pp. 123, 152–5, 200, 208, 227; Austin, *Malta and the End of Empire*, pp. 28, 45–6, 121.

70. *The Times*, 7 Oct. 1949. The National Trust Guide Book, *Sizergh Castle, Westmorland* (1951), was written by Henry Hornyold-Strickland.

71. Dobie, *Malta's Road to Independence*, pp. 190–1; S. Howe, 'British Decolonisation and Malta's Imperial Role', in Mallia-Milanes, *The British Colonial Experience*, p. 357.

72. Cannadine, *Decline and Fall*, pp. 673, 684–5.

73. Anon., 'Canada Spurns Titles', *Literary Digest*, LIV (1917), pp. 1985–6; anon., 'Titles to Go in Canada', *Literary Digest*, LVII (1918), p. 17; D.W. Thomson, 'The Fate of Titles in Canada', *Canadian Historical Review*, X (1929), pp. 236–46; Martin, *Bunyip Aristocracy*, pp. 182–8.

6. Winston Churchill as an Aristocratic Adventurer

1. C.V. Balsan, *The Glitter and the Gold* (New York, 1952), p. 72; D. Cannadine, *The Decline and Fall of the British Aristocracy* (1990), p. 680.

2. C.P. Snow, *Variety of Men* (1969), pp. 125, 131; J.R. Colville, *The Churchillians* (1981), pp. 4, 10, 20. For Churchill's relatives, see Appendix B, tables 1 and 2.

3. P. Addison, 'Winston Churchill and the Working Class, 1990–14', in J. Winter (ed.), *The Working Class in Modern British History: Essays in Honour of Henry Pelling* (1983), p. 46; Lord Moran, *Churchill: Taken from the Diaries of Lord Moran: The Struggle for Survival, 1940–1965* (Boston, 1966), p. 334.

4. V. Bonham Carter, *Winston Churchill: An Intimate Portrait* (New York, 1965), p. 107; Moran, *Struggle for Survival*, pp. 13, 265; Lord Butler, *The Art of the Possible* (1971), p. 156.

5. W.S. Churchill, *My Early Life* (New York, 1939 edn), pp. 62, 151–2, 162–3.

6. *WSC*, vol. I, p. 517.

7. Cannadine, *Decline and Fall*, pp. 707–8.

8. R. Rhodes James, *Churchill: A Study in Failure, 1900–1939* (1973), p. 16.

9. R.F. Foster, *Lord Randolph Churchill: A Political Life* (1981), p. 127.

10. A.L. Rowse, *The Later Churchills* (1971), pp. 237–40, 249–50.

11. P. Magnus, *King Edward VII* (1967), pp. 185–93; P. Churchill & J. Mitchell, *Jennie, Lady Randolph Churchill: A Portrait with Letters* (1974), pp. 87–104; Foster, *Lord Randolph Churchill*, pp. 9–16; Rowse, *Later Churchills*, pp. 274–9.

12. Foster, *Lord Randolph Churchill*, pp. 122–4, 376; Marquess of Blandford, 'The Limits of English Revolution', *Fortnightly Review*, XL (1883), pp. 72–84; idem, 'The Break-Up of the Land Monopoly', *Nineteenth Century*, IX (1881), pp. 249–68; idem, 'Reform of Feudal Laws', *Nineteenth Century*, IX (1881), pp. 664–80; idem, 'Hereditary Rulers', *Nine-*

teenth Century, x (1881), pp. 216–34; Duke of Marlborough, 'On the Cross Benches', *Fortnightly Review*, XLII (1884), pp. 45–56; idem, 'The Transfer of Land', *Fortnightly Review*, XLIII (1885), pp. 544–56.

13. *WSC CV*, vol, II, pt I, pp. 487–90; M. Ashley, *Churchill as Historian* (1968), pp. 1–5.

14. Balsan, *Glitter and the Gold*, pp. 42–54, 187–212; H. Vickers, *Gladys, Duchess of Marlborough* (1979), pp. 51, 69, 106–7, 134, 172, 213, 223, 225–33.

15. S. Leslie, *Long Shadows* (1966), pp. 236–9; Magnus, *Edward VII*, p. 497; Vickers, *Duchess of Marlborough*, pp. 187–8, 196–9, 208–11, 214.

16. Foster, *Lord Randolph Churchill*, pp. 24, 30, 59, 96–7, 217–19, 349; R.G. Martin, *Jennie: The Life of Lady Randolph Churchill*, vol. I, *The Romantic Years, 1854–1895* (1969), pp. 56–7, 110–11, 152–3, 177–8, 307–8, 321–35.

17. Magnus, *Edward VII*, pp. 191–3; Rhodes James, *Study in Failure*, p. 22.

18. Mrs George Cornwallis-West, *The Reminiscences of Lady Randolph Churchill* (New York, 1908), preface, pp. 362–85.

19. R.G. Martin, *Jennie: The Life of Lady Randolph Churchill*, vol. II, *The Dramatic Years, 1895–1921* (1971), pp. 190–1, 389.

20. M. Soames, *Clementine Churchill* (1979), pp. 1–11, 26–7, 199, 213.

21. Lord Birkenhead, *Churchill, 1874–1922* (1989), p. 179.

22. *The Times*, 25 Feb. 1947; R. Hough, *Winston and Clementine: The Triumphs and Tragedies of the Churchills* (New York, 1991), pp. 26, 47, 150, 372, 422.

23. *WSC CV*, vol. II, pt II, pp. 695–7, 704, 728, 736; J.R. Colville, *The Fringes of Power: 10 Downing Street Diaries, 1939–1955* (1985), p. 210.

24. Birkenhead, *Churchill*, pp. 552–62.

25. D. Irving, *Churchill's War*, vol. I, *The Struggle For Power* (Bullsbrook, Western Australia, 1987), p. 169.

26. Rhodes James, *Study in Failure*, p. 272; *WSC*, vol. v, pp. 592–3.

27. B. Roberts, *Randolph: A Study of Churchill's Son* (1984), pp. 130–9, 140–2, 153–6.

28. Colville, *Fringes of Power*, p. 125; Bonham Carter, *Intimate Portrait*, p. 116.

29. *WSC CV*, vol. II, pt I, p. 437; *WSC CV*, vol. III, pt II, pp. 1078–9.

30. *WSC*, vol. v, pp. 422 n2, 559 n2, 592–3.

31. Foster, *Lord Randolph Churchill*, p. 177; *WSC CV*, vol. III, pt II, p. 1545; R. Hyam, *Elgin and Churchill at the Colonial Office,*

1905–08: The Watershed of Empire-Commonwealth (1968), p. 502.

32. Irving, *Churchill's War*, p. 33.

33. *WSC CV*, vol. II, pt I, pp. 239, 393; Foster, *Lord Randolph Churchill*, p. 16.

34. J.R. Vincent (ed.), *The Crawford Papers: The Journals of David Lindsay, Twenty Seventh Earl of Crawford, and Tenth Earl of Balcarres, 1871–1940, During the Years 1882–1940* (1984), p. 73; N. Blewett, *The Peers, the Parties and the People: The General Elections of 1910* (1972), pp. 374–6, 465 n1, 478 n68–70; H. Pelling, *Social Geography of British Elections, 1885–1910* (1967), pp. 135–6.

35. *The Times*, 15 June 1939; M. & E. Brock (eds.), *H.H. Asquith: Letters to Venetia Stanley* (1982), pp. 161, 162 n2.

36. *WSC CV*, vol. II, pt III, p. 1393; *WSC CV*, vol. III, pt I, p. 268; Brocks, *Asquith Letters*, pp. 254, 273, 278, 313, 377, 637.

37. T. Cullen, *Maundy Gregory: Purveyor of Honours* (1974), pp. 93–5, 103–5, 107–9; Brocks, *Asquith Letters*, p. 383.

38. G. Searle, *Corruption in British Politics, 1895–1930* (1987), p. 382; *The Times*, 29 Apr. 1937. But cf. Churchill's genuine sorrow at his death: *WSC*, vol. v, pp. 855–6.

39. H.M. Hyde, *The Londonderrys: A Family Chronicle* (1979), pp. 109–10, 136–43, 157, 163, 170–9, 208–9, 213, 217–18, 238, 253, 256, 261; *WSC CV*, vol. II, pt III, pp. 1382–7.

40. M. Cowling, *The Impact of Hitler: British Politics and British Policy, 1933–1940* (1975), pp. 240–1; *WSC*, vol. v, pp. 191–204, 217–18, 635–40, 731–3, 873, 1019–20.

41. Cannadine, *Decline and Fall*, pp. 416–17.

42. Viscount Churchill, *Be All My Sins Remembered* (New York, 1965), pp. 11, 40–3, 51, 85–126, 138–56.

43. A. Leslie, *Mr Frewen of England* (1966), p. 202; A. Andrews, *The Splendid Pauper* (1968), p. 215.

44. S. Leslie, *Studies in Sublime Failure* (1932), pp. 247–95. Clare Frewen married Wilfred Sheridan (who died in action in the First World War). She visited Russia in 1920, and was briefly (and publicly) friends with Lenin and Trotsky, much to Churchill's embarrassment. See J. Pearson, *Citadel of the Heart: Winston and the Churchill Dynasty* (1991), pp. 173–8.

45. S. Leslie, *The End of a Chapter* (1916), pp. iii, 16, 164–6, 183; Leslie, *The Irish Tangle for English Readers* (1943), pp. 11–13, 146–52.

46. *DNB, 1971–80* (1983), pp. 501–2; S. Leslie, *The Fulness of Memory* (1938), pp. 118–19, 145, 373–6.

47. *WSC CV*, vol. II, pt I, pp. 591–4.
48. G. Cornwallis-West, *Edwardian Hey-Days: or, A Little About a Lot of Things* (1930), pp. 118–27, 158–69; E. Quelch, *Perfect Darling: the Life and Times of George Cornwallis-West* (1972), pp. 81–3, 102–4, 128–9, 144, 149–51, 164–72, 188, 192–6.
49. Cannadine, *Decline and Fall*, p. 387.
50. M. Harrison, *Lord of London: A Biography of the Second Duke of Westminster* (1966), pp. 1–8, 70–7, 183–91, 212, 224–7; G.D. Phillips, *The Diehards: Aristocratic Society and Politics in Edwardian England* (1979), pp. 91, 107–8.
51. *The Times*, 22 July 1953; R. Rhodes James (ed.), *'Chips': The Diaries of Sir Henry Channon* (1967), p. 477.
52. K. Ingram, *Rebel: The Short Life of Esmond Romilly* (1985), pp. 1–3, 9–15, 17–18, 42–6, 64–73, 146–8, 154–5.
53. Hough, *Winston and Clementine*, pp. 4–5.
54. Cannadine, *Decline and Fall*, pp. 550–4.
55. D. Pryce-Jones, *Unity Mitford: A Quest* (1976), pp. 114–15, 169–70, 178; Colville, *Fringes of Power*, p. 177; Vincent, *Crawford Papers*, pp. 604–5. For the most recent account of Churchill and the Mosleys in wartime, see A.W.B. Simpson, *In the Highest Degree Odious: Detention Without Trial in Wartime Britain* (1992), esp. pp. 143–5, 164–6, 274–9, 388–92.
56. Andrews, *Splendid Pauper*, pp. 238–9; Ingram, *Rebel*, p. 193.
57. *WSC CV*, vol. III, pt I, p. 27.
58. Rhodes James, *Study in Failure*, p. 195; C.E. Lysaght, *Brendan Bracken* (1979), p. 66.
59. *WSC*, vol. I, p. 527.
60. *WSC*, vol. I, pp. 247, 316–17, 319, 357–8.
61. *WSC*, vol. I, p. 428; *WSC*, vol. II, p. 2; *WSC CV*, vol. II, pt I, pp. 102–3.
62. Churchill, *My Early Life*, p. 361; *WSC*, vol. II, pp. 541–2; *WSC CV*, vol. II, pt II, p. 746.
63. Soames, *Clementine*, pp. 93, 97; *WSC*, vol. II, p. 351; *WSC CV*, vol. II, pt III, pp. 1741–5.
64. *WSC*, vol. III, p. 493; *WSC CV*, vol. III, pt II, pp. 1097–8, 1279.
65. Searle, *Corruption*, pp. 90–1, 271.
66. H.M. Hyde, *Lord Alfred Douglas: A Biography* (1984), pp. 251–6; Searle, *Corruption*, p. 123.
67. *WSC*, vol. V, pp. 11–12.
68. Soames, *Clementine*, pp. 219–31.
69. *WSC*, vol. V, pp. 844, 919–20.
70. Bonham Carter, *Intimate Portrait*, pp. 209–22.
71. Searle, *Corruption*, pp. 133–5; *WSC CV*, vol. II, pt III, p. 1739.
72. *WSC*, vol. V, pp. 346–9. See also R. Elegant, 'Churchill Slept Here', *New York Times Magazine*, 4 Mar. 1990, pp. 32–3, 73–6.
73. Soames, *Clementine*, pp. 257–70, 277–81.
74. Searle, *Corruption*, p. 315; Cannadine, *Decline and Fall*, p. 324.
75. J. Campbell, *F.E. Smith: First Earl of Birkenhead* (1983), pp. 334–6, 472, 625, 719–20, 804.
76. Searle, *Corruption*, pp. 306–7, 318–23.
77. Cannadine, *Decline and Fall*, pp. 327–8.
78. Lysaght, *Bracken*, pp. 67–75, 129–39.
79. Lysaght, *Bracken*, pp. 58, 66–9.
80. Soames, *Clementine*, pp. 250–2; Rhodes James, *Study in Failure*, pp. 372–9; Lysaght, *Bracken*, pp. 136–8.
81. Searle, *Corruption*, p. 123; Lysaght, *Bracken*, p. 69.
82. Birkenhead, *Churchill*, pp. 536–7; Irving, *Churchill's War*, p. 145.
83. F. Harris, *My Life and Loves*, vol. II (1925), pp. 252–69.
84. Rhodes James, *Study in Failure*, pp. 388–9; Hough, *Winston and Clementine*, pp. 378, 505; Irving, *Churchill's War*, pp. 225–8.
85. *WSC*, vol. II, p. 132; *WSC*, vol. V, pp. 319, 441. For Churchill's full literary earnings between 1929 and 1937, see *WSC*, vol. V, p. 835, n1.
86. Cannadine, *Decline and Fall*, pp. 399–400.
87. Phillips, *The Diehards*, pp. 17–18; Churchill, *My Early Life*, p. 364.
88. W.S. Churchill, *Lord Randolph Churchill* (2 vols., 1906), vol. I, pp. 1–2; *WSC CV*, vol. II, pt II, p. 477.
89. Foster, *Lord Randolph Churchill*, pp. 394–7.
90. Foster, *Lord Randolph Churchill*, pp. 383–92, 401.
91. Ashley, *Churchill as Historian*, pp. 34–7, 138–40, 156–7; *WSC*, vol. V, pp. 319, 333.
92. W.S. Churchill, *Marlborough: His Life and Times*, vol. I, *1650–1688* (1933), pp. 3–8.
93. H.S. Commager, 'Introduction', to W.S. Churchill, *Marlborough: His Life and Times*, (New York, 1968, one-vol. edn), p. xxiii.
94. Rhodes James, *Study in Failure*, pp. 395–9; Irving, *Churchill's War*, p. 148.
95. Cannadine, *Decline and Fall*, p. 395.
96. Vincent, *Crawford Papers*, p. 544.
97. *WSC*, vol. V, pp. 410 n3, 412.
98. *WSC*, vol. V, pp. 423, 438–9, 559 n2, 592.
99. F. Woods, *A Bibliography of the Works of Sir Winston Churchill, KG, OM, CH* (1969 edn), pp. 237, 251.
100. Soames, *Clementine*, p. 197.
101. *WSC*, vol. V, p. 434.
102. Foster, *Lord Randolph Churchill*, p. 400;

G.M. Trevelyan, letter to *The Times Literary Supplement*, 19 Oct. 1993. For Trevelyan's general distrust of Churchill's politics during the 1930s, see D. Cannadine, *G.M. Trevelyan: A Life in History* (1992), pp. 130–4.

103. *WSC*, vol. V, p. 1089 n1; *WSC*, vol. VI, p. 56.

104. J.H. Plumb, 'Churchill: The Historian', in *The Collected Essays of J.H. Plumb*, vol. I, *The Making of an Historian* (1988), pp. 226–30.

105. Vincent, *Crawford Papers*, p. 319; Addison, 'Churchill and the Working Class', pp. 52–5, 63.

106. Bonham Carter, *Intimate Portrait*, p. 129; A.J.P. Taylor (ed.), *W.P. Crozier: Off the Record: Political Interviews, 1933–43* (1973), p. 323.

107. Bonham Carter, *Intimate Portrait*, pp. 116, 147; *WSC CV*, vol. II, pt II, pp. 904–5, 909, 968; W.S. Churchill, *The People's Rights* (1970 edn), pp. 20–54, 116–30.

108. Addison, 'Churchill and the Working Class', p. 56.

109. M. Cowling, *Religion and Public Doctrine in Modern England* (1980), pp. 320–8; *WSC*, vol. IV, pp. 914–15; W.S. Churchill, 'Sport as a Stimulant in our Workaday World', *News of the World*, 4 Sept. 1938.

110. W.S. Churchill, *The World Crisis*, vol. I, *1911–1914* (1923), p. 188; idem, *The World Crisis*, vol. VI, *The Eastern Front* (1931), pp. 17–32; idem, 'Will the World Swing Back to Monarchies?', *Pearson's Magazine*, January 1934, pp. 16–22.

111. Churchill, *My Early Life*, pp. 89–92, 122; idem, *Marlborough*, vol. I, pp. 37–40.

112. W.S. Churchill, 'A Friend's Tribute', *The Times*, 2 July 1934.

113. Colville, *Fringes of Power*, p. 278; Moran, *Struggle for Survival*, p. 351; H. Laski, *Reflections on the Revolution of Our Time* (1943), p. 197.

114. W.S. Churchill, *Great Contemporaries* (New York, 1937), pp. 8, 25–6, 82; idem, 'Penny in the Slot Politics', *Answers*, 31 Mar. 1934.

115. W.S. Churchill, *The World Crisis*, vol. V, *The Aftermath* (1929), pp. 32–51; idem, *Thoughts and Adventures* (1932), pp. 256–7, 278–9; idem, *My Early Life*, pp. 357, 368–9.

116. W.S. Churchill, 'Parliamentary Government and the Economic Problem', reprinted in *Thoughts and Adventures*, pp. 229–41.

117. Rhodes James, *Study in Failure*, pp. 384–6; W.S. Churchill, 'Whither Britain?', *The Listener*, 17 Jan. 1934; idem, 'How Can We Restore the Lost Glory to Democracy?', *Evening Standard*, 24 Jan. 1934; 'What's Wrong with Parliament?', *Answers*, 5 May 1934; idem, 'Elections Ahead – and the Same Old Voting System', *Daily Mail*, 29 May 1935.

118. Rhodes James, *Study in Failure*, p. 155.

119. Churchill, *Great Contemporaries*, p. 256; Ashley, *Churchill as Historian*, p. 2; Rhodes James, *Study in Failure*, p. 197.

120. Rhodes James, *Study in Failure*, pp. 329–30; W.S. Churchill, 'Introduction' to O.F. de Battaglia (ed.), *Dictatorship on its Trial* (1930), pp. 7–10.

121. Soames, *Clementine*, pp. 211–12; W.S. Churchill, 'This Age of Government by Great Dictators', *News of the World*, 10 Oct. 1937; A.G. Gardiner, *Portraits and Portents* (1926), p. 59.

122. *WSC*, vol. III, p. 478.

123. R. Skidelsky, *Oswald Mosley* (1975), pp. 227–8, 236, 286, 288, 329; N. Mosley, *Rules of the Game: Sir Oswald and Lady Cynthia Mosley, 1896–1933* (1982), pp. 150–1, 188, 203; the Duke of Manchester, *My Candid Recollections* (1932), pp. 254–64.

124. Lord Beaverbrook, *Politicians and the War* (1959 edn), p. 284.

125. W. Manchester, *The Last Lion: Winston Spencer Churchill*, vol. II, *Alone, 1932–1940* (Boston, 1988), p. 87.

126. Cannadine, *Decline and Fall*, p. 556.

127. Leslie, *Long Shadows*, p. 18.

128. P. Addison, 'The Political Beliefs of Winston Churchill', *Transactions of the Royal Historical Society*, 5th ser., XXX (1980), pp. 28, 46.

129. Vincent, *Crawford Papers*, pp. 83, 101, 153, 179; Addison, 'Political Beliefs of Winston Churchill', p. 25.

130. Moran, *Struggle for Survival*, p. 772; Lord Birkenhead, *Halifax* (Boston, 1966), pp. 533–8; Lord Home of the Hirsel, *The Way the Wind Blows* (1976), pp. 50–5, 63, 67.

131. P. Addison, *Churchill on the Home Front, 1900–1955* (1992), p. 440.

132. A.J.P. Taylor, *Beaverbrook* (1974), pp. 532–3; Colville, *Fringes of Power*, pp. 122, 129; A. Roberts, 'The Holy Fox': A Biography of Lord Halifax* (1991), p. 209; R. Blake, 'How Churchill Became Prime Minister', in R. Blake & W.R. Louis (eds.), *Churchill* (1993), p. 273.

133. E.g. Evelyn Waugh to Lady Diana Cooper,

7 February 1965: 'I suppose you all mourn Sir Winston. I never had any esteem for him. Interesting how all his crook associates began with B – Birkenhead, Baruch, Beaverbrook, Bracken, Boothby. The Sutherland caricature caught the Tammany Hall aspect very well.' A. Cooper (ed.), *The Letters of Evelyn Waugh and Diana Cooper* (New York, 1992), p. 316.

7. The Landowner as Millionaire: The Finances of the Dukes of Devonshire

1. D. Rush, *The Court of London from 1819 to 1825* (1873), p. 9. In the light of recent research, Rush's figure of £100,000 seems an exaggeration. See G.E. Mingay, *English Landed Society in the Eighteenth Century* (1963), p. 58; E. Richards, *The Leviathan of Wealth: The Sutherland Fortune in the Industrial Revolution* (1973), p. 13; F.C. Mather, *After the Canal Duke: a study of the Estates Administered by the Trustees of the Third Duke of Bridgewater in the Age of Railway Building 1825–1872* (1970), pp. xviii, 358–9; F.M.L. Thompson, 'The Economic and Social Background of the English Landed Interest: 1840–70, with particular reference to the Estates of the Dukes of Northumberland' (D.Phil. dissertation, Oxford University, 1956), appendix VIII.
2. H.A. Taine, *Notes on England, 1860–70* (trans. E. Hyams, New Jersey, 1958), p. 181.
3. A.C. Ewald, *The Crown and its Advisers* (1870), p. 129.
4. T.H.S. Escott, *Society in the English Country House* (1907), p. 50.
5. The figures for these two peers were:

	Acres	Gross annual value
Lord Leicester	44,090	£59,578
Lord Overstone	30,849	£58,098

Overstone claimed his entry was 'so fearfully incorrect that it is impossible to correct it': J. Bateman, *The Great Landowners of Great Britain and Ireland* (4th edn, 1883, ed. D. Spring, 1971), pp. 263, 348. For more recent detailed estimates see: S.W. Martins, *A Great Estate at Work: The Holkham Estate and its Inhabitants in the Nineteenth Century* (1980), p. 272; R.C. Mitchie 'Income, Expenditure and Investment of a Victorian Millionaire: Lord Overstone, 1823–83', *Bulletin of the Institute of Historical Research*, LVIII (1985), pp. 61–2.
6. See Appendix C, table 1.
7. Lord Calthorpe's gross income from his Edgbaston building estate was £37,000 in 1914. In 1893, his gross income from all sources was £42,000. See D. Cannadine, *Lords and Landlords: The Aristocracy and the Towns, 1774–1967* (1980), pp. 159–62, 432.
8. See Appendix C, table 2.
9. W.D. Rubinstein, 'British Millionaires, 1809–1949', *Bulletin of the Intitute of Historical Research*, XLVII (1974), pp. 219, 222. For estimates of the Cadogan, Portman and Westminster incomes, see Rubinstein, *Men of Property: The Very Wealthy in Britain Since the Industrial Revolution* (1981), pp. 194–5.
10. J.L. Sandford & M. Townsend, *The Great Governing Families of England* (2 vols, 1865), vol. I, p. 112; R. Colby, *Mayfair: A Town Within London* (1966), p. 46.
11. The Cadogan family does not appear at all. The figures for the other two are as follows:

	Acres	Gross annual value
Viscount Portman	33,891	£45,972
Duke of Westminster	19,749	£38,994

See: Bateman, *Great Landowners*, pp. 365, 472.
12. Rubinstein, 'British Millionaires', p. 213, n2; Rubinstein, *Men of Property*, p. 228.
13. W. Bagehot, *The English Constitution* (ed. R.H.S. Crossman, 1968), p. 124; J.F.C. Harrison, *The Early Victorians, 1832–51* (1971), pp. 98–9; H. Perkin, *The Age of the Railway* (1970), p. 196.
14. W.L. Burn, *The Age of Equipoise: A Study of the Mid-Victorian Generation* (1968), p. 196.
15. G.M. Young, *Victorian England: Portrait of an Age* (2nd edn, 1960), p. 145; O.F. Christie, *The Transition to Democracy, 1867–1914* (1934), pp. 148, 172; G.S.R. Kitson Clark, *The Making of Victorian England* (1962), pp. 215–16, 251; F.M.L. Thompson, *English Landed Society in the Nineteenth Century* (1963), pp. 256, 268, 317; H. Perkin, *The Origins of Modern English Society, 1780–1880* (1969), p. 435.
16. T.H.S. Escott, *England: Its People, Polity and Pursuits* (1885), pp. 314–15.
17. Appendix C, table 1; D. Spring, 'English Landowners and Nineteenth-Century Industrialism' in J.T. Ward & R.G. Wilson (eds.), *Land and Industry; The Landed Estates and the Industrial Revolution* (1971), pp. 16–52; Rubinstein, *Men of Property*, pp. 193–213; Thompson, *English Landed Society*, pp. 306–8, 320, 322, 329, 336–7.
18. See above, pp. 37–54.

19. So as to avoid unnecessary interruptions in the text, the essential information about the Devonshires and their finances is displayed in the tables and graphs collected in Appendix C, 3–5. For a detailed study of the family's Irish estates see L. Proudfoot, 'The Management of a Great Estate: Patronage, Income and Expenditure on the Dukes of Devonshires' Irish Property, c.1816 to 1891', *Irish Economic and Social History*, XIII (1986), pp. 32–55.

20. Thompson, *English Landed Society*, pp. 76–9.

21. Chatsworth MSS, fifth Duke's ser.: 1997, John Heaton to Thomas Knowlton, 18 Apr. 1811; 2005, Knowlton to Heaton, 23 May 1811; 2006, Knowlton to Marquess of Hartington, 27 May 1811; 2009, Knowlton to Hartington, 17 June 1811.

22. F. Leveson Gower, *Bygone Years* (1905), p. 41.

23. L. Stone, *The Crisis of the Aristocracy, 1558–1641* (1965), pp. 193–4; J.H. Plumb, *Men and Places* (1966), pp. 113–21; F. Bickley, *The Cavendish Family* (1911), p. 210.

24. Chatsworth MSS, accounts 1813–15. 'Current Income', the description used throughout this essay, is the gross agricultural rent, less arrears, tithes, taxes and cost-improvements. From 1858 onwards it also includes dividend income.

25. Sir A.W. Cavendish, *A Sketch of the Life of the Sixth Duke of Devonshire* (3rd edn, 1870), p. 5.

26. Chatsworth MSS L/60/20, Compendious Account of the Paternal Estates of the Duke of Devonshire, 1792. The spending of the fifth Duke on Buxton was in excess of £120,000. See R.G. Heape, *Buxton Under the Dukes of Devonshire* (1948), pp. 28–30, 35.

27. Chatsworth MSS L/24/105, Statement of the Duchess of Devonshire's Debts, Dec. 1804.

28. Chatsworth MSS L/24/106, Report Respecting the Late Duchess of Devonshire's Debts, 26 July 1806. For a full account of Georgiana's career see I. Leveson Gower, *The Face Without a Frown: Georgiana, Duchess of Devonshire* (1944), esp. pp. 30–1; 46, 85–7, 112–14, 128–30, 136–43, 151–3, 162–3, 225–7; the Earl of Bessborough (ed.), *Georgiana: Extracts From the Correspondence of Georgiana, Duchess of Devonshire* (1955), esp. pp. 30–46, 167–74, 194–206.

29. Chatsworth MSS, accounts 1812–15. For most years of the sixth Duke's tenure of the title, the only figure available for fixed charges is a combined total of interest payments and annuities, whereas, from 1858 onwards, the figure is for interest payments alone. Accordingly, the two series are not exactly comparable; but as indicators of general trends they should be reliable.

30. L. Strachey & R. Fulford (eds.), *The Greville Memoirs, 1814–60* (8 vols., 1938), vol. VII, p. 333.

31. Thompson, *English Landed Society*, p. 68.

32. Cavendish, *Sixth Duke of Devonshire*, pp. 6–7.

33. The best contemporary description is by Greville. See Strachey & Fulford, *Greville Memoirs*, vol. VII, p. 332.

34. D. Spring: 'The English Landed Estate in the Age of Coal and Iron, 1830–80', *JEH*, XI (1951), p. 14; idem, 'English Landownership in the Nineteenth Century: A Critical Note', *EcHR* 2nd ser., IX (1957), p. 473; idem, 'Aristocracy, Social Structure and Religion in the Early Victorian Period', *Victorian Studies*, VI (1963), p. 271; E.J. Hobsbawm, *Industry and Empire* (1969), p. 107.

35. D. Linstrum, *Sir Jeffry Wyatville: Architect to the King* (1972), pp. 141–62; F. Thompson, *A History of Chatsworth* (1949), pp. 102–3; M. Girouard, *The Victorian Country House* (1971), p. 192.

36. The two best accounts of the Devonshire-Paxton partnership are in: V. Markham, *Paxton and the Bachelor Duke* (1935) and G.F. Chadwick, *The Works of Sir Joseph Paxton* (1961).

37. Chatsworth MSS L/83/2, Heaton to Devonshire, 25 Mar. 1812. See also Plumb, *Men and Places*, p. 89.

38. Chatsworth MSS, sixth Duke's ser. 3889, I, Countess of Malmesbury to Devonshire, April 1838; Leveson Gower, *Bygone Years*, pp. 47–8; Chadwick, *Joseph Paxton*, p. 98; Strachey & Fulford, *Greville Memoirs*, vol. V, pp. 147–8; E. Longford, *Victoria RI* (1966), p. 219.

39. Chatsworth MSS, accounts: 1812–15, 1917–29.

40. Chatsworth MSS, L/83/2, Heaton to Devonshire, 16 Feb. 1813; 6th Duke's ser. 344, J. Abercrombie to Devonshire, 9 Dec. 1819.

41. Chatsworth MSS, accounts, 1817–29.

42. Chatsworth MSS L/83/2, General Abstract of Sales at Nottingham (undated); sixth Duke's ser. 1069, Abercrombie to Devonshire, 21 Nov. 1842; R.W. Unwin, 'A Nineteenth-Century Estate Sale: Wetherby 1824', *AgHR*, XXIII (1975), p. 118; F.H.W. Sheppard (ed.) *The Survey of London*, vol. XXXII, *The Parish of St James Westminster*, pt

II, *North of Piccadilly* (1963), pp. 407, 412.

43. Strachey & Fulford, *Greville Memoirs*, vol. III, p. 157. For the extent of the Duke of Bedford's indebtedness, and successful attempts at reduction, see D. Spring, *The English Landed Estate in the Nineteenth Century: Its Administration* (1963), pp. 21–40, 189–90; Spring, 'English Landowners and Nineteenth–Century Industrialism', pp. 52, 62.

44. Chatsworth MSS, sixth Duke's ser.: 861, Abercrombie to Devonshire, 11 Nov. 1823; 896, Benjamin Currey to Pinder Simpson, 20 Jan. 1824.

45. Earl Fitzwilliam urged strongly against the sale of the Irish estates, on the grounds that the Duke would 'lose greatly in station'. See: Chatsworth MSS, sixth Duke's ser: 180.0, Fitzwilliam to Devonshire, 2 July 1845; 180.1, Devonshire to Fitzwilliam, 8 July 1845 (both quoted in Spring, 'English Landed Estate in the Age of Coal and Iron', p. 17).

46. Chadwick, *Joseph Paxton*, p. 241; Markham, *Bachelor Duke*, pp. 156–61.

47. Chatsworth MSS, 7 DDD, 25 Sept. 1844.

48. J.T. Ward, 'Landowners and Mining', in Ward & Wilson, *Land and Industry*, p. 88; Currey MSS, sixth Duke's executors account, 19 June 1860.

49. Chatsworth MSS, 2nd ser. 25.70, William Currey to Devonshire, 28 Feb. 1849.

50. Chatsworth MSS, 2nd ser. 25.90, Benjamin Currey to Devonshire, 4 Sept. 1855.

51. S. Pollard & J.D. Marshall, 'The Furness Railway and the Rise of Barrow', *JTH*, I (1953), pp. 115–18; J.C. Wright, *Bygone Eastbourne* (1920), pp. 77–81; Cannadine, *Lords and Landlords*, pp. 236–8.

52. Chatsworth MSS, sixth Duke's ser. 3326, Lord Burlington to Mrs William Cavendish, 20 May 1835; Currey MSS, seventh Duke's accounts, 1858–72.

53. H. Leach, *The Duke of Devonshire: A Personal and Political Biography* (1904), p. 23; Burn, *Age of Equipoise*, pp. 310–11.

54. *Vanity Fair*, 6 June 1874.

55. Chadwick, *Joseph Paxton*, pp. 68–9; Markham, *Bachelor Duke*, pp. 117–18, 308–9.

56. *DNB*, vol. XXII, *Supplement* (1901), pp. 400–1.

57. J.G. Crowther, *Statesmen of Science* (1965), p. 217; Bickley, *The Cavendish Family*, p. 311; Leach, *Duke of Devonshire*, p. 26; *Proceedings of the Royal Society*, LI (1892), obituary notices, p. xli.

58. Spring, 'English Landed Estate in the Age of Coal and Iron', p. 19; Spring, 'English Landowners and Nineteenth–Century Industrialism', 43–8; S. Pollard, 'Barrow-in-Furness and the Seventh Duke of Devonshire', *EcHR*, 2nd ser., VIII (1955), p. 221; Hobsbawm, *Industry and Empire*, p. 107; W.A. Maguire, *The Downshire Estates in Ireland, 1801–1845: The Management of Irish Landed Estates in the Early Nineteenth Century* (1972), p. 84.

59. Chatsworth MSS, 7 DDD, 26 Jan. 1858.

60. Chatsworth MSS, 7 DDD, 17 Feb. 1858; Chatsworth MSS, 2nd ser., 4.53, Devonshire to the Duke of Bedford, 17 May 1858; Markham, *Bachelor Duke*, pp. 310–13.

61. Chatsworth MSS, 7 DDD: 8 Apr. 1840; 6 Aug. 1840; 10 Oct. 1840; 25 May 1842; 21 Aug. 1842.

62. Chatsworth MSS, 7 DDD: 2 Mar. 1858; 23 Apr. 1858.

63. Chatsworth MSS, 2nd ser.: 4.52, Bedford to Devonshire, 15 May 1858; 4.53 Devonshire to Bedford, 17 May 1858; 4.54, Bedford to Devonshire, 21 May 1858; 4.55, Bedford to Devonshire, 22 May 1858. Much of this correspondence has already been published in Spring, 'English Landed Estate in the Age of Coal and Iron', p. 19.

64. Chatsworth MSS, 7 DDD, 15, 21 May 1858.

65. Granville to Gladstone, 26 May 1869. Quoted in A. Ramm (ed.), *The Political Correspondence of Mr. Gladstone and Lord Granville, 1868–1876* (2 vols., 1952), vol. I, p. 23.

66. As well as the articles by Pollard and Marshall already cited, see J. Melville & J.L. Hobbs, *Early Railway History in Furness*, (*Cumberland & Westmorland Antiquarian & Archaeological Society*, Tract Series, XIII (1951)); J.D. Marshall, *Furness and the Industrial Revolution* (1958); S. Pollard, 'North-West Coast Railway Politics in the 1860', *Transactions of the Cumberland & Westmorland Antiquarian and Archaeological Society*, LII (1952), pp. 160–77; Pollard, 'Town Planning in the Nineteenth Century: The Beginnings of Modern Barrow-in-Furness', *Transactions of the Lancashire and Cheshire Antiquarian Society*, LXIII (1952–3), pp. 87–116.

67. By comparison, Eastbourne had reached only 10,342 by 1871, and Buxton a mere 6021 ten years later; see Wright, *Eastbourne*, p. 66; Heape, *Buxton*, p. 123.

68. Chatsworth MSS, 7 DDD: 27 July 1863; 22 Mar. 1870; 11 Mar. 1871; 17 Feb. 1872; 3 Apr. 1872; 12 Jan. 1873; 15 Feb. 1873; 17 Feb. 1873; 11 June 1873.

69. Chatsworth MSS, 7 DDD, 31 Mar. 1871.

70. Girouard, *Victorian Country House*, p. 182.

71. For Buxton, see Heape, *Buxton*, pp. 88–108; T. Marchinton, 'The Development of Buxton and Matlock since 1800' (M.A. dissertation, London University, 1961), pp. 97–130. For Eastbourne, see Cannadine, *Lords and Landlords*, pp. 288–92.

72. For a more detailed breakdown of the Devonshires' precise holdings in individual companies, see the tables in Pollard's articles: 'The Beginnings of Modern Barrow', p. 102; 'Barrow-in-Furness and the Seventh Duke', pp. 216, 218.

73. Between 1858 and 1884, £260,000 was also obtained for investment purposes from the more extensive sale than purchase of land: Chatsworth MSS 73. L/60/40, summary of accounts, 1858–84.

74. Chatsworth MSS, box 10, Banker's memoranda, Feb. 1888.

75. Chatsworth MSS, box 10, William Currey to Devonshire, 5 Apr. 1875.

76. Pollard, 'Barrow-in-Furness and the Seventh Duke', pp. 216–17.

77. Currey MSS, seventh Duke's accounts, 1873–88.

78. Chatsworth MSS, 7 DDD, 1 Jan. 1879.

79. Chatsworth MSS, 7 DDD, 17 June 1879.

80. Chatsworth MSS, 7 DDD, 9 Mar. 1886, 25 July 1886.

81. Chatsworth MSS, 7 DDD, 13 and 23 Mar. 1877.

82. Chatsworth MSS, box 10: F.A. Currey to Devonshire, 15 Jan. 1887, 11 Jan. 1889.

83. An unsuccessful attempt was made to sell it to the Barking Jute Co. in 1889: Chatsworth MSS, box 10, F.A. Currey to Devonshire, 8 Apr. 1890.

84. Pollard, 'Barrow-in-Furness and the Seventh Duke', pp. 217–20.

85. Chatsworth MSS, box 10, F.A. Currey to Devonshire, 15 Jan. 1887.

86. Chatsworth MSS, 7 DDD, 29 Mar. 1879, 13 May 1879, 1 Oct. 1879, 1 May 1885, 1 Dec. 1885, 2 Nov. 1887, 2 Dec. 1887; Chatsworth MSS, box 10, Sussex Estate: statement of Rents, Nov. 1892.

87. The income from the Grassington Mines also declined in the 1870s: Ward, 'Landowners and Mining', p. 88.

88. Chatsworth MSS, box 10, F.A. Currey to Devonshire, 15 Jan. 1887.

89. Chatsworth MSS, F.A. Currey to Devonshire, 11 Nov. 180: Sir H. Maxwell, *Annals of the Scottish Widows' Fund, 1815–1914* (1914), pp. 112–16.

90. Chatswoth MSS, 7 DDD: 27 Apr. 1885,

1886; 4 Feb. 1888; 27 Mar. 1888.

91. Bickley, *Cavendish Family*, p. 301.

92. Leach, *Duke of Devonshire*, pp. 300–7; B. Holland, *The Life of Spencer Compton, Eighth Duke of Devonshire* (2 vols., 1911), vol. II, pp. 223–5, 239–41.

93. *DNB, Supplement 1901–1911* (1912), p. 328; A. Jones, *The Politics of Reform 1884* (1972), p. 253. See also H. Blyth, *Skittles, The Last Victorian Courtesan; The Life and Times of Catherine Walters* (1970), pp. 73–95, 101–5.

94. A.B. Cooke & J. Vincent, *The Governing Passion: Cabinet Government and Party Politics in Great Britain, 1885–89* (1974), pp. 10, 15, 24, 88–9.

95. Chatsworth MSS, 2nd ser., 340.2537A, Lady L. Egerton to Devonshire, 25 Jan. 1894.

96. Chatsworth MSS, 2nd ser., 340.2551, Devonshire to Lady Egerton, 6 Apr. 1894.

97. Chatsworth MSS, 2nd ser., 340.2553, Devonshire to Lady Egerton, 23 Apr. 1894.

98. Chatsworth MSS, 2nd ser., 340.2556, Devonshire to Sir William Harcourt, 11 May 1894. See also Devonshire's speech at Buxton, 13 June 1894, in which he warned that he might be forced to close Chatsworth, Lismore, Hardwick and Bolton: Heape, *Buxton*, p. 121.

99. Chatsworth MSS, 2nd ser., 340.2557, Harcourt to Devonshire, 15 May 1894.

100. Christie, *Transition to Democracy*, p. 172.

101. Chatsworth MSS, 2nd ser., 340.2553, Devonshire to Lady Egerton, 23 Apr. 1894.

102. Pollard & Marshall, 'Furness Railway and the Growth of Barrow', pp. 112–13.

103. Cannadine, *Lords and Landlords*, pp. 323–8.

104. Cannadine, *Lords and Landlords*, pp. 328–30.

105. Pollard & Marshall, 'Furness Railway and Growth of Barrow', p. 124; Currey MSS, eighth and ninth Dukes' accounts, 1900–25.

106. Chatsworth MSS, W.F. Egerton to Hamilton, 12 Apr. 1896.

107. J.D. Scott, *Vickers: A History* (1962), p. 44; Chatsworth MSS, Bryce to Hamilton, 24 Nov. 1896.

108. Chatsworth MSS, Price Waterhouse to Devonshire, 8 Aug. 1901.

109. Pollard & Marshall, 'Furness Railway and the Growth of Barrow'. p. 125. The eighth Duke also sold his holdings in the Waterford, Dungavron and Lismore Railway, and in the Buxton Baths, and his successor tried (without success) to sell the Devonshire Parks and Baths Co. to Eastbourne Corporation in 1912–14. See Holland, *Eighth Duke of Devonshire*, vol. II, p. 223; Heape, *Buxton*, p. 123; H.W. Fovargue, *Municipal East-*

bourne (1956), pp. 76–8, 80.

110. Currey MSS, Duke of Devonshire and Equitable Assurance Co., mortgage, 7 Nov. 1894; Duke of Devonshire and Scottish Widows' Fund and Life Assurance Co. mortgage, 30 Aug. 1897.

111. Chatsworth MSS, eighth and ninth Dukes' accounts, 1900–25. Succession and estate duty for the seventh Duke had been a mere £40,000.

112. Chatsworth MSS, eighth and ninth Dukes' accounts, 1892–9, 1900–25.

113. Scott, *Vickers*, p. 390.

114. Currey MSS, eighth and ninth Dukes' accounts, 1900–25. For similar behaviour by other aristocrats, see Thompson, *English Landed Society*, pp. 329–33, 335–7; D. Cannadine, *The Decline and Fall of the British Aristocracy* (1990), pp. 132–6.

115. Currey MSS, eighth and ninth Dukes' accounts, 1900–25.

116. For another example of the transformation and rehabilitation of an aristocratic family's finances, see A. Adonis 'Aristocracy, Agriculture and Liberalism: The Politics, Finances and Estates of the Third Lord Carrington', *HJ*, xxxi (1988), pp. 880–7.

117. R. Rhodes James (ed.) *'Chips': The Diaries of Sir Henry Channon* (1967), p. 346; W.L. Guttsman, *The British Political Elite* (1965), p. 224; H. Nicolson, *King George V: His Life and Reign* (1967), p. 676; H. Macmillan, *Winds of Change, 1914–1939* (1966), pp. 189–94.

118. *HND* I, p. 418.

119. Rhodes James, *'Chips'*, pp. 450, 475.

120. Cannadine, *Decline and Fall*, pp. 641, 645; The Duchess of Devonshire, *The House: Living at Chatsworth* (1982), pp. 76–7.

121. Cannadine, *Decline and Fall*, pp. 660, 665; *The Spectator*, 1 Jan. 1977.

122. For other studies of super-rich landed fortunes, see the works cited in note 5 above, and E. Richards, 'An Anatomy of the Sutherland Fortune: Income, Consumption, Investments and Returns, 178–1880', *Business History*, xxi (1979), pp. 45–78.

8. Landowners, Lawyers and Litterateurs: The Cozens-Hardys of Letheringsett

1. F.M.L. Thompson, *English Landed Society in the Nineteenth Century* (1963), pp. 30–2; P.A. Barnes, 'The Economic History of Landed Estates in Norfolk since 1880', (Ph.D. dissertation, University of East Anglia, 1984), pp. 9–16.

2. M. Lascelles, 'R.W. Ketton-Cremer, 1906–1969', *Proceedings of the British Academy*, LVI (1972), pp. 403–14; J.R. Gretton, 'A Bibliography of the Printed Works of R.W. Ketton-Cremer', *Norfolk Archaeology*, XXXXVI (1977), pp. 85–96; *DNB, 1981–85* (1990), pp. 19–20; D. Lindsay, *Sir Edmund Bacon: A Norfolk Life*: (1988); *The Times*, 15 Mar. 1990, 2 Apr. 1990, 11 Dec. 1990.

3. EDP MSS, letter books, AC-H to L.B. Lister, 4 Mar. 1930.

4. J.K. Edwards, 'Industrial Development of the City, 1800–1914', in C. Barringer (ed.), *Norwich in the Nineteenth Century* (1984), pp. 154–8; P. Mathias, *The Brewing Industry in England, 1700–1830* (1959), pp. 287–99; H.F. Barclay & A.W. Fox, *History of the Barclay Family* (1924); P.W. Matthews & A.W. Tuke, *A History of Barclays Bank* (1928); W.H. Bidwell, *Annals of an East Anglian Bank* (1900); A.J.C. Hare, *The Gurneys of Earlham* (1895); Sir R. Bignold, *Five Generations of the Bignold Family, 1761–1947, and Their Connection with the Norwich Union* (1948); Viscount Templewood [Sir Samuel Hoare], *The Unbroken Thread* (1949). In describing these Norfolk families as 'gentlemanly capitalists', I am deliberately borrowing a term, recently applied in a metropolitan context, which might be at least as appropriately used to describe those who lived in the countryside yet were simultaneously landowners and businessmen. For the broader issues see: P.J. Cain & A.G. Hopkins, 'Gentlemanly Capitalism and British Expansion Overseas: I: The Old Colonial System, 1688–1850', *EcHR*, 2nd ser., xxxix (1986), pp. 501–25; Cain & Hopkins, 'Gentlemanly Capitalism and British Expansion Overseas: II: The New Imperialism, 1850–1945', *EcHR*, 2nd ser., XL (1987), pp. 1–26; M.J. Daunton, 'Gentlemanly Capitalism and British Industry, 1820–1914', *Past & Present*, no. 122 (1989), pp. 119–58.

5. Sir L. Jones, *Georgian Afternoon* (1958), pp. 209–12.

6. BC-H, *The History of Letheringsett . . .* (1957), pp. 64–72, 78–80. See the genealogical table in Appendix D.1.

7. BC-H, *Letheringsett*, pp. 104–13.

8. For a brief glimpse of him, see Mathias, *Brewing Industry*, p. 463.

9. D. Watkin, 'Letheringsett Hall, Norfolk', *Country Life*, 5 Jan. 1967, pp. 18–21.

10. N. Pevsner, *The Buildings of England: North-East Norfolk and Norwich* (1962), p. 183.

11. BC-H, *Letheringsett*, p. 114.

12. BC-H, *Letheringsett*, pp. 115–20 for this and the next two paragraphs.

13. S. Cozens-Hardy (ed.), *Memorials of William Hardy Cozens-Hardy of Letheringsett, Norfolk* (1936), pp. 7–8.

14. J. Bateman, *The Great Landowners of Great Britain and Ireland* (4th edn, 1883, ed. D. Spring, 1971), p. 207.

15. Cozens-Hardy, *William Hardy Cozens-Hardy*, pp. 12–16.

16. *The Wesleyan Conference v. Cozens-Hardy and Others, A Report of the Proceedings in Chancery. . . . With an Introduction by W.H. Cozens-Hardy* (1852), pp. v–xxxi.

17. W.H. Cozens-Hardy, *A Lecture on the Life and Character of Johnson Jex* (1855).

18. *EDP*, 30 Apr. 1895, 4 May 1895.

19. C. Colman, *In Memoriam: Sarah Cozens-Hardy* (1892), pp. 5–8.

20. BC-H, *Letheringsett*, p. 117.

21. Sir L.E. Jones, *A Victorian Boyhood* (1955), p. 82; V. Berry, *The Rolfe Papers: The Chronicle of a Norfolk Family, 1559–1908* (1979), pp. 193–206; P.J. Roe, 'The Development of Norfolk Agriculture in the Nineteenth Century, 1815–1914' (Ph.D. dissertation, University of East Anglia, 1975), pp. 103–9, 226–7; Barnes, 'Economic History of Landed Estates in Norfolk', pp. 44–52, 82–3.

22. BC-H, *Letheringsett*, pp. 120, 154; Barnes, 'Economic History of Landed Estates in Norfolk', pp. 218–22; Norwich City Library, Local Collection, c658.844, 'Particulars of the Valuable Estate of the Late William Hardy Cozens-Hardy Situate at Sprowston. . . . to be sold 30 June 1896 in Norwich under the will of the late William Hardy Cozens-Hardy in 79 lots'.

23. *EDP*, 28 Apr. 1906, 2 May 1906.

24. *EDP*, 31 Oct. 1925, 2 Nov. 1925.

25. *EDP*, 19 and 23 Oct. 1917.

26. G.F. Holtblack to Mr and Mrs Cozens-Hardy, 20 Jan. 1918, in M. Cozens-Hardy, *A Blessed Memory: Raven Cozens-Hardy* (1918), unpaginated.

27. BC-H to Mr and Mrs Cozens-Hardy, in M. Cozens-Hardy, *A Blessed Memory*, undated and unpaginated.

28. BC-H, 'Some Norfolk Halls', *Norfolk Archaeology*, XXXII (1961), p. 175.

29. *The Times*, 19 June 1920; *DNB, 1912–21* (1927), pp. 130–1; *EDP*, 19 June 1920; *East Anglian Daily Times*, 19 June 1920.

30. R.W. Ketton-Cremer, *Felbrigg: The Story of a House* (1976 edn), p. 273; H. Pelling, *Social Geography of British Elections, 1885–1910*

31. (1967), pp. 98–9.

31. *EDP*, 28 Sept. 1885, 9, 14, 15 and 26 Oct. 1885, 25 and 30 Nov. 1885, 2 and 3 Dec. 1885.

32. *EDP*, 8 and 17 June 1886.

33. *EDP*, 5, 6, 7, 8 and 13 July 1886.

34. *EDP*, 16 June 1892, 7, 18 and 19 July 1892.

35. *EDP*, 1, 3, 17, 18, 22, 24 July 1895.

36. *EDP*, 24 Feb. 1899.

37. *Hansard*: HC: 20 June 1887, cols. 1497–1500; 20 June 1889, col. 313; 7 July 1890, cols. 921–2; 1 June 1891, col. 1372; 24 Apr. 1893, cols. 1025–6; 26 July 1894, col. 951; 9 Mar. 1897, col. 283.

38. *EDP*, 23 Feb. 1899.

39. BC-H, *Letheringsett*, p. 120.

40. *EDP*, 2 and 7 May 1918, 23 June 1920.

41. *The Times*, 27 May 1924.

42. W.B. Harris & the Hon. W. Cozens-Hardy, *Modern Morocco: A Report on Trade Prospects, with some Geographical and Historical Notes* (1919).

43. E. Goldstein, 'Historians Outside the Academy: G.W. Prothero and the Experience of the Foreign Office Historical Section', *Bulletin of the Institute of Historical Research*, LXIII (1990), pp. 196–99; *The Times*, 29 May 1924.

44. Reading MSS, FI18/12, ff. 26–7, W. Cozens-Hardy to Reading, 14 Aug. 1918, 1 Oct. 1918.

45. *EDP*, 25, 28 and 29 Nov. 1918, 5, 6, 7, 11, 12, 30 Dec. 1918.

46. *Hansard*: HC: 12 Mar. 1919, col. 1282; 18 June 1919, col. 676; HL: 20 Dec. 1920, cols. 680–1; 28 July 1921, cols. 81–3; *The Times*, 28 May 1924.

47. *EDP*, 27 and 30 May 1924, 23 Aug. 1933; *Norfolk Chronicle*, 6 June 1924; *Norwich Mercury*, 7 June 1924.

48. L. Stuart, *In Memoriam: Caroline Colman* (1896), pp. 18–32.

49. H.C. Colman, *Jeremiah James Colman: A Memoir* (1905), pp. 107–8, 381–2; P. Palgrave-Moore, *The Mayors and Lord Mayors of Norwich, 1836–1974* (1978), pp. 4–7.

50. Stuart, *Caroline Colman*, pp. 38–56; Colman, *Jeremiah James Colman*, p. 239.

51. Palgrave-Moore, *Mayors and Lord Mayors of Norwich*, pp. 39, 54–5.

52. S. Koss, *The Rise and Fall of the Political Press in Britain* (1990 edn), pp. 217, 308–10, 328, 332, 478.

53. *EDP*, 18 Feb. 1910.

54. This and the next paragraph owe much to the *EDP Centenary Supplement*, 10 Oct. 1970.

55. EDP MSS, letter books, AC-H to L.B.

Lister, 20 Nov. 1930, 12 Sept. 1932.

56. *EDP*, 5 July 1937, 27 Sept. 1937; EDP MSS, letter books, AC-H to E.J. Tillett, 30 June 1937.

57. EDP MSS, letter books, AC-H to Edith Colman, 2 May 1929; AC-H to E.C. Randolph, 28 Sept. 1931, 12 and 20 Oct. 1931, 13 Nov. 1931.

58. EDP MSS, letter books, AC-H to E.W. Betts, 8 Aug. 1934; AC-H to W.H. Besant, 7 Sept. 1934; AC-H to R.G. Dingle, 16 Nov. 1934, 12 July 1935; AC-H to P.C. Loftus, 19 Dec. 1935.

59. *EDP*, 27 Sept. 1937; Templewood MSS: IX: 2, S. Hoare to AC-H, 28 May 1937; X: 1, AC-H to S. Hoare, 30 May 1937.

60. EDP MSS, letter books, AC-H to W. Blackley, 15 Apr. 1929; AC-H to E.A. Harvey, 6 June 1929; AC-H to E.B. Gee, 25 March 1930; AC-H to Mrs Dennis, 3 Dec. 1930; AC-H to Councillor F.L. Browne, 29 May 1933.

61. EDP MSS, letter books, AC-H to H. Clough, 19 Feb. 1929; AC-H to H.E. Hurrell, 6 Mar. 1929; AC-H to R. Dingle, 3 July 1937.

62. *EDP*, 5 July 1948.

63. *EDP*, 21 and 25 Apr. 1955. The history of Norfolk County Council has yet to be written. For some suggestive hints, see C. Wilkins-Jones (ed.), *Centenary: A Hundred Years of County Government in Norfolk* (1989).

64. *EDP*, 11 Nov. 1949.

65. *The Times*, 14 Mar. 1957; *EDP*, 11 and 14 Mar. 1957.

66. Harry Cozens-Hardy, *The Glorious Years* (1953), p. 5; idem (ed.), *Broad Norfolk: being a series of articles and letters republished from the Eastern Daily Press* (1893).

67. EDP MSS, letter books, AC-H to R. Stannard, 4 July 1930; *Norfolk News*, 10 June 1955.

68. H.C. Colman, *Sydney Cozens-Hardy: A Memoir* (1944), pp. 19–27.

69. Colman, *Sydney Cozens-Hardy*, pp. 28–34, 50–2.

70. For the broader background, see J. Hooper, *Norwich Charities: Short Sketches of their Origins and History* (1888).

71. Report of the Select Committee on the Endowed Schools Acts, 11 June 1886, QQ 1953–2132.

72. Norwich City Library, Local Collections N361, Sydney Cozens-Hardy, 'To the Trustees of the Norwich Municipal (General) Charities', report, 29 Feb. 1892; 'City and County of Norwich: Proposed Amalgamation of Charities Under the Administration of a Central Body: Transcript of Shorthand Notes of a Conference at the Technical Institute, Norwich, 13 January 1909'; 'An Act to Confirm a Scheme of the Charity Commissioners for the Management of Various Charities in the City and County of Norwich', 26 July 1910.

73. E. Griffiths & H. Smith, *'Buxom to the Mayor': A History of the Norwich Freemen and the Town Close Estate* (1987), pp. 27–37, 39–48.

74. Sydney Cozens-Hardy, *Norwich Charities: A Retrospect, 1880–1934* (1935).

75. Colman, *Sydney Cozens-Hardy*, pp. 34–49.

76. Ketton-Cremer MSS, 6/476, correspondence between R. Ketton and Sydney Cozens-Hardy, June–Aug. 1886.

77. Colman, *Sydney Cozens-Hardy*, pp. 62–70.

78. Sydney Cozens-Hardy, *Glavenside* (1936), pp. 2–3, 6–8, 11; Colman, *Sydney Cozens-Hardy*, pp. 54, 56, 60, 75–7.

79. *EDP*, 17 Aug. 1932; EDP MSS, letter books, AC-H to BC-H, 11 Oct. 1933.

80. *Eastern Evening News*, 14 Jan. 1976.

81. EDP MSS, letter books, AC-H to BC-H, 11 Oct. 1935; *EDP*, 5 Feb. 1960, 18 Apr. 1963.

82. *EDP*, 11 Nov. 1935; I. Cresswell, 'Obituary: Basil Cozens-Hardy, DL, MA, FSA, Hon. Life Fellow', *Norfolk Archaeology*, XXXVI (1976), pp. 283–4.

83. He also helped Nikolaus Pevsner with his volumes on Norfolk; see Pevsner, *North-East Norfolk and Norwich*, p. 10.

84. A full list is given in Appendix D.2.

85. *EDP*, 8 Feb. 1975.

86. *Eastern Evening News*, 26 Oct. 1956; Hornor MSS, Conveyance of Letheringsett Estate from Arthur Wrigley Cozens-Hardy to the Hon. Edward Herbert Cozens-Hardy, 21 Feb. 1919.

87. Hornor MSS, Letheringsett Hall Estate rent book, 1918–51; Letheringsett Hall Estate accounts, 1932–43. For the generally depressed condition of agriculture in the county during the inter-war years, see A. Donet, 'Norfolk Agriculture, 1914–1972' (Ph.D. dissertation, University of East Anglia, 1989), pp. 134–42.

88. T.C. Barker, *The Glassmakers: Pilkington: the rise of an international company, 1826–1976* (1977), pp. 220–2, 233–6.

89. Barker, *Pilkington*, pp. 240–1, 259–63, 316–19.

90. Barker, *Pilkington*, pp. 321–35.

91. Hornor MSS, Letheringsett Hall Estate accounts, 1932–43; Barker, *Pilkington*, p. 320.

92. Hornor MSS, F. Hornor to Lord Cozens-Hardy, 20 Aug. 1951; F. Hornor to the Hon. H.A. Cozens-Hardy, 22 Oct. 1951; Barker, *Pilkington*, pp. 257–8, 393–4.
93. For another impoverished Norfolk landowner going into business, see Jones, *Georgian Afternoon*, pp. 154–223.
94. *The Times*, 24 and 30 Oct. 1956.
95. *EDP*, 23 Oct. 1956, 21 June 1975.
96. Barker, *Pilkington*, pp. 323–4, 461.
97. Barker, *Pilkington*, pp. 416–25.
98. *The Times*, 13 Sept. 1975; *EDP*, 18 Sept. 1975.
99. Stuart, *Caroline Colman*, p. 87.
100. EDP MSS, letter books, AC-H to E.M. Colman, 9 Mar. 1931; AC-H to BC-H, 4 Jan. 1935.
101. The debate as to whether the British landed elite was open or closed continues. For the most recent contributions, see: F.M.L. Thompson, 'Life After Death: How Successful Nineteenth-Century Businessmen Disposed of Their Fortunes', *EcHR*, 2nd ser., XLIII (1990), pp. 40–61; W.D. Rubinstein, 'Cutting Up Rich: A Reply to F.M.L. Thompson', *EcHR*, 2nd ser., XLV (1992), pp. 350–61; F.M.L. Thompson, 'Stitching It Together Again', *EcHR*, 2nd ser., XLV (1992), pp. 362–75.
102. For some suggestive hints, see F.M.L. Thompson, 'Desirable Properties: The Town and Country Connection in British Society Since the Late Eighteenth Century', *Historical Research*, LXIV (1991), pp. 156–71.
103. BC-H, 'Cley Next-the-Sea and its Marshes', *Transactions of the Norfolk and Norwich Naturalists' Society*, XII (1924–9), p. 373.
104. E. Gundrey, *Staying Off the Beaten Track* (9th edn, 1989), p. 124.
105. Private information.
106. *John Betjeman's Collected Poems*, ed. Lord Birkenhead (1979 edn), pp. 282–3.

9. Portrait of More Than a Marriage: Harold Nicolson and Vita Sackville-West Revisited

1. J. Lees-Milne, *Harold Nicolson: A Biography*, vol. I, *1886–1929* (1980); vol. II, *1930–1968* (1983); V. Glendinning, *Vita: The Life of V. Sackville-West* (1983); *DNB, 1961–70* (1981), pp. 793–6, 931–5.
2. *HND; HND* I– III; N. MacKnight (ed.), *'Dearest Andrew': Letters from V. Sackville-West to Andrew Reiber, 1951–1962* (1980); L. de Salvo & M.A. Leaska (eds.), *The Letters of Vita Sackville-West to Virginia Woolf* (1985); M.A. Leaska & J. Phillips (eds.), *Violet to Vita: The Letters of Violent Trefusis to Vita Sackville-West* (1989); N. Nicolson (ed.), *Vita and Harold: The Letters of Vita Sackville-West and Harold Nicolson* (1992).
3. N. Nicolson, *Portrait of a Marriage* (1973); Nicolson, 'Portrait of a Love Betrayed?', *The Times*, 22 Sept. 1990.
4. S.R. Watson, *V. Sackville-West* (1972); M. Stevens, *V. Sackville-West: A Critical Biography* (1973); N. Nicolson (ed.), *'A Change of Perspective': The Letters of Virginia Woolf*, vol. III, *1923–1928* (1977), p. 150; *HND* II, pp. 350–1.
5. A. Scott-James, *Sissinghurst: The Making of a Garden* (1975); J. Brown, *Vita's Other World: A Gardening Biography of V. Sackville-West* (1985).
6. V. Cunningham, 'A Prideful Pair of the Terribly Self-Possessed', *The Observer*, 2 Aug. 1992.
7. Lees-Milne, *Harold Nicolson*, vol. I, pp. 20–1.
8. HN, *The Spectator*, 5 Jan. 1940.
9. Glendinning, *Vita*, p. 186. For VS-W's hostility to the working class, see her two early novels: *Heritage* (1919), and *The Dragon in Shallow Waters* (1921). See also S. Raitt, *Vita and Virginia: The Work and Friendship of V. Sackville-West and Virginia Woolf* (1993), pp. 41–51.
10. Throughout this section, see the genealogical table of the Nicolsons and the Sackville-Wests, printed as Appendix E.
11. VS-W, *Knole and the Sackvilles* (1922); C.J. Phillips, *A History of the Sackville Family* (2 vols., 1929).
12. The National Trust, *Knole* (1986 edn); J. Newman, *The Buildings of England: West Kent and the Weald* (1969), pp. 342–9.
13. D.L. Smith, ' "The More Posed and Wise Advice": The Fourth Earl of Dorset and the English Civil Wars', *HJ*, XXXIV (1991), pp. 797–829.
14. For the general background, see C. Clay, 'Marriage, Inheritance and the Rise of Large Estates in England', *EcHR*, 2nd ser., XXI (1968), pp. 515–17; L. Bonfield, 'Marriage Settlements and the "Rise of Great Estates": The Demographic Aspect', *EcHR*, 2nd ser., XXXII (1979), pp. 486–7; L. & J.C.F. Stone, *An Open Elite?: England, 1540–1880* (1984), pp. 93–124.
15. J. Bateman, *The Great Landowners of Great Britain and Ireland* (4th edn, 1883, ed. D. Spring, 1971), p. 392.
16. T.C. Hinckley, 'George Osgoodby and the

Murchison Letter', *Pacific Historical Review*, XXVII (1958), pp. 359–70; C.S. Campbell, 'The Dismissal of Lord Sackville', *Mississippi Valley Historical Review*, XLIV (1958), pp. 635–48.

17. For a recent study, see S.M. Alsop, *Lady Sackville: A Biography* (1978).

18. *HND* I, pp. 274, 352; HN, *The Future of the English-Speaking World* (1949), p. 9; HN, *The Desire to Please* (1943), pp. 1–5.

19. L. Colley, *Britons: Forging the Nation, 1707–1837* (1992), pp. 155–64.

20. Lees-Milne, *Harold Nicolson*, vol. I, p. 2.

21. Z. Steiner, *The Foreign Office and Foreign Policy, 1898–1914* (1969), pp. 121–52; S.A. Cohen, 'Sir Arthur Nicolson and Russia: The Case of the Baghdad Railway', *HJ*, XVIII (1975), pp. 863–72; K. Neilson, ' "My Beloved Russians": Sir Arthur Nicolson and Russia, 1906–1916', *International History Review*, IX (1987), pp. 521–54.

22. Bateman, *Great Landowners*, p. 203.

23. Brown, *Vita's Other World*, p. 56; Lees-Milne, *Harold Nicolson*, vol. I, p. 65; Nicolson, *Portrait of a Marriage*, pp. 81–6.

24. Glendinning, *Vita*, pp. 44–5, 60, 329, 338, 368–9, 374; Lees-Milne, *Harold Nicolson*, vol. II, pp. 244–5, 271–2.

25. *The Times*, 30 Jan. 1928, 9 May 1962; *HND* I, p. 20.

26. *The Times*, 6 July 1975; *DNB, 1961–70*, pp. 912–13; M. De-la-Noy, *Eddy: The Life of Edward Sackville-West* (1988), p. 65.

27. *The Times*, 2 June 1952; Glendinning, *Vita*, p. 305; *HND* III, pp. 225, 231.

28. *The Times*, 16 Oct. 1998; De-la-Noy, *Eddy*, p. 55.

29. Bateman, *Great Landowners*, p. 125; D. Cannadine, *The Decline and Fall of the British Aristocracy* (1990), p. 413.

30. *The Times*, 29 Jan. 1976; *DNB, 1971–80* (1986), pp. 752–3; Cannadine, *Decline and Fall*, pp. 539–41.

31. *HND* I, p. 291.

32. Bateman, *Great Landowners*, p. 141; Sir A. Lyall, *The Life of the Marquis of Dufferin and Ava* (2 vols., 1905) remains the most detailed account.

33. Cannadine, *Decline and Fall*, pp. 413–14, 598.

34. *The Times*, 8 Feb. 1918, 22 July 1930, 5 Apr. 1945.

35. *HND*, II, p. 400.

36. HN, *The Spectator*, 3 Dec. 1943.

37. HN, *Desire to Please*, pp. 1–9; Lees-Milne, *Harold Nicolson*, vol. I, pp. 8, 18.

38. *HND* II, p. 240; HN, *The Spectator*, 27 Mar. 1942, 3 Sept. 1943, 20 Jan. 1950, 14 July 1950.

39. Cannadine, *Decline and Fall*, pp. 280–2; HN, *The Spectator*, 29 June 1951.

40. HN, *The Evolution of Diplomatic Method* (1954), p. 57.

41. *HND*, p. 37; *HND* I, pp. 210, 212–13; Cannadine, *Decline and Fall*, pp. 289–90.

42. HN, 'The Foreign Service', in W.A. Robson et al, *The British Civil Servant* (1936), pp. 47–63; HN, *Diplomacy* (1939), passim; *Hansard*: HC: 19 Dec. 1935, col. 2080; 29 June 1936, cols. 131–2; *HND* I, pp. 53, 291; *HND* II, p. 323.

43. Lees-Milne, *Harold Nicolson*, vol. II, pp. 34–7, 51–2; Nicolson, *Vita and Harold*, pp. 239, 242, 333; *HND* I, pp. 183, 139–40, 262; *HND* II, p. 137; HN, *The Spectator*, 16 June 1944, 8 Mar. 1946, 24 Aug. 1951.

44. *HND* I, p. 203; *HND* II, p. 323; D.C.M. Platt, *Finance, Trade and Politics in British Foreign Policy, 1815–1914* (1968), p. xviii.

45. Nicolson, *Vita and Harold*, pp. 218–25; K. Young (ed.), *The Diaries of Sir Robert Bruce Lockhart*, vol. I, *1915–1938* (1973), pp. 99–100, 103–4, 107, 160, 174–6. HN's broadcast talks were published as *People and Things* (1931).

46. Lees-Milne, *Harold Nicolson*, vol. II, pp. 2–3; *HND* I, pp. 36, 44, 55–7.

47. *HND* I, pp. 187, 189, 204; *HND* II, p. 207.

48. HN, *Desire to Please*, p. 191.

49. *DNB, 1961–70*, p. 796.

50. *HND*, pp. 259, 298; *HND* I, p. 157; *HND* II, pp. 350–2; Lees-Milne, *Harold Nicolson*, vol. II, pp. 169–70; E. Wilson, 'Through The Embassy Window', *The New Yorker*, 1 Jan. 1944, pp. 63–7.

51. *HND*, p. 205.

52. HN, *Politics in the Train* (1936), passim; *HND*, p. 37; *HND* II, p. 256; *HND* III, pp. 33–4; Lees-Milne, *Harold Nicolson*, vol. II, p. 189.

53. *HND* I, pp. 59, 61, 216; *HND* II, p. 383.

54. *HND* I, p. 114; R. Skidelsky, *Oswald Mosley* (1975), pp. 249–50.

55. *HND*, p. 38; Lees-Milne, *Harold Nicolson*, vol. II, p. 24.

56. Cannadine, *Decline and Fall*, pp. 545–7, 556; *HND* I, p. 207.

57. Lees-Milne, *Harold Nicolson*, vol. II, pp. 62–3; *HND* I, pp. 214, 216, 222–4.

58. *HND* I, pp. 122, 301, 329, 402.

59. *HND* II, pp. 55, 147.

60. HN, *The Spectator*, 28 Apr. 1950; Lees-Milne, *Harold Nicolson*, vol. II, pp. 170–1; L. Wolff, 'The Public Faces of Harold Nicolson: The Thirties', *Biography*, V (1982), pp. 240–52.

61. For disparaging views by contemporaries of Nicolson's political and administrative skills, see: O. Mosley, *My Life* (1968), pp. 80, 285–6; B. Pimlott (ed.), *The Second World War Diaries of Hugh Dalton, 1940–45* (1986), p. 215; Lees-Milne, *Harold Nicolson*, vol. II, pp. 144–5.

62. J. Lees-Milne, *People and Places: Country House Donors and the National Trust* (1992), p. 168; *Glendinning*, Vita, p. 12.

63. VS-W, *Pepita* (1937), p. 181; Glendinning, *Vita*, pp. 22, 26–7; Nicolson, *Portrait of a Marriage*, p. 80.

64. Nicolson, *Portrait of a Marriage*, pp. 57–8.

65. Alsop, *Lady Sackville*, pp. 126–40, 161–82; Nicolson, *Portrait of a Marriage*, pp. 65–73.

66. Lees-Milne, *Harold Nicolson*, vol. I, pp. 53, 355–6.

67. Nicolson, *Portrait of a Marriage*, pp. 68, 73; Glendinning, *Vita*, p. 58.

68. Lees-Milne, *Harold Nicolson*, vol. I, pp. 79–81; Glendinning, *Vita*, pp. 76–80.

69. F.M.L. Thompson, *English Landed Society in the Nineteenth Century* (1963), pp. 332–3; Cannadine, *Decline and Fall*, pp. 110–11.

70. VS-W, *Knole and the Sackvilles*, pp. 2, 18.

71. Glendinning, *Vita*, p. 124; VS-W, *Knole and the Sackvilles*, p. 29; De-la-Noy, *Eddy*, p. 66.

72. See also VS-W (ed.), *The Diary of Lady Anne Clifford* (1923), esp. the intro., pp. ix–lvi.

73. VS-W, *Knole and the Sackvilles*, p. 193.

74. Raitt, *Vita and Virginia*, p. 12; R. Williams, *The Country and the City* (1985), pp. 248, 254.

75. VS-W, *The Land and The Garden* (1988 edn), intro. by N. Nicolson), pp. 15, 16, 31.

76. VS-W explored the same anti-modernistic themes in her two travel books on Persia, where she visited her husband *en poste* in 1926, where the last lines of *The Land* were written, and where she deplored the incursion of oil wells and twentieth-century capitalism: see VS-W, *Passenger to Teheran* (1926), pp. 121–3; VS-W, *Twelve Days* (1928), pp. 23, 27–8, 68, 80, 117–30.

77. Glendinning, *Vita*, pp. 188–9; Brown, *Vita's Other World*, p. 99.

78. There is a vast literature on *Orlando*. I have found the following especially helpful and suggestive: Glendinning, *Vita*, pp. 202–5; VS-W, 'Virginia Woolf and Orlando', *The Listener*, 27 Jan. 1955, pp. 157–8; F. Baldanza, '*Orlando* and the Sackvilles', *Proceedings of the Modern Languages Association*, LXX (1955), pp. 274–9; M. Philipson, 'Virginia Woolf's *Orlando*: Biography as a Work of Fiction', in D.B. Weiner & W.R. Keylor (eds.), *From Parnassus: Essays in Honor of*

Jacques Barzun (New York, 1977), pp. 237–48; F. Kellerman, 'A New Key to Virginia Woolf's *Orlando*', *English Studies*, LIX (1978), pp. 138–50; L.A. DeSalvo, 'Lighting the Cave: The Relationship Between Vita Sackville-West and Virginia Woolf', *Signs*, VIII (1982–3), pp. 197–205.

79. V. Woolf, *Orlando* (1977 edn), p. 199.

80. Glendinning, *Vita*, pp. 213–14.

81. Brown, *Vita's Other World*, p. 110; Glendinning, *Vita*, p. 224; *HND* I, pp. 47–8; Nicolson, *Vita and Harold*, pp. 227–8; Newman, *West Kent and the Weald*, pp. 508–9.

82. Brown, *Vita's Other World*, p. 219; Nicolson, *Vita and Harold*, p. 373; Glendinning, *Vita*, p. 347.

83. Glendinning, *Vita*, p. 268.

84. Brown, *Vita's Other World*, p. 42; Glendinning, *Vita*, p. 275; VS-W, *The Death of Noble Godavary* (1932), p. 1.

85. VS-W, *Country Notes* (1939), p. 97; *HND* III, p. 352; Glendinning, *Vita*, pp. 246, 281; Lees-Milne, *Harold Nicolson*, vol. II, p. 113.

86. VS-W, *Anne Clifford*, p. xliv; *HND* I, p. 109; Glendinning, *Vita*, pp. 283, 355–6.

87. VS-W, 'Kent', in H.J. Massingham (ed.), *English Country* (1934), pp. 201–12; Glendinning, *Vita*, pp. 281–2, 288; VS-W, *Country Notes*, pp. 11–12, 59, 70, 96, 119, 146, 180.

88. Brown, *Vita's Other World*, pp. 15, 134–5; *HND* I, p. 422.

89. *HND* I, p. 416; *HND* II, pp. 57, 99.

90. HN, *The Spectator*, 21 Nov. 1941, 2 Jan. 1942, 25 Feb. 1944; *HND* II, p. 170; *HND*, pp. 288–9.

91. Glendinning, *Vita*, p. 320; *HND* II, pp. 57, 264–5.

92. *HND* II, pp. 350, 432–3.

93. *HND*, p. 289.

94. Lees-Milne, *Harold Nicolson*, vol. II, p. 206; *HND* III, pp. 90–1, 94.

95. Lees-Milne, *Harold Nicolson*, vol. II, pp. 216–20; *HND*, p. 331; *HND* III, pp. 125–9, 133–7; HN, *The Spectator*, 19 Mar. 1948.

96. Lees-Milne, *Harold Nicolson*, vol. II, pp. 190–2, 196, 215, 219–21; *HND* III, pp. 80–1, 157.

97. *HND* III, pp. 35, 140–1.

98. *HND*, p. 357; *HND* III, pp. 228–9, 235–6.

99. Lees-Milne, *Harold Nicolson*, vol. II, pp. 176–7, 208–10; J. Gaze, *Figures in a Landscape: A History of the National Trust* (1988), pp. 137, 150–1; HN, *The Spectator*, 15 Aug. 1947, 18 Nov. 1949, 23 June 1950; *HND* III, pp. 102–6, 171.

100. *HND* II, pp. 55, 139, 178, 191.

101. HN, *The Spectator*, 17 May 1946, 1 July 1949, 20 Jan. 1950, 13 Oct. 1950, 30 Nov. 1951, 8 Feb. 1952, 6 June 1952, 18 July 1952, 24 Oct. 1952.

102. HN, *The Age of Reason* (1960), pp. 211, 417, 442–4. HN was especially ill-disposed to the citizens of Bournemouth since his son Nigel had been forced to stand down as the Conservative MP because his Tory supporters disapproved of his anti-Eden attitudes during the Suez crisis, attitudes which HN wholeheartedly shared.

103. *HND* III, pp. 93, 110, 149, 176, 196.

104. MacKnight, *'Dearest Andrew'*, p. 122.

105. VS-W, *The Land and The Garden*, pp. 11–12.

106. ibid., pp. 92, 104, 106, 131.

107. VS-W, 'Outdoor Life', in E. Barker (ed.), *The Character of England* (1947), pp. 408–24.

108. VS-W, *In Your Garden* (1951), pp. 46, 69, 123, 204; idem, *In Your Garden Again* (1953), pp. 27, 46, 58, 67, 75, 102, 122, 133, 145; idem, *More For Your Garden* (1955), pp. 27, 41–2, 44, 48–9, 74, 77, 101, 117, 139–40, 145; idem, *Even More For Your Garden* (1958), pp. 47, 80, 143, 150, 163.

109. *HND* III, pp. 152, 212, 339.

110. *HND*, p. 386; Nicolson, *Vita and Harold*, pp. 344–5; HN, *Desire to Please*, p. 201; Lees-Milne, *Harold Nicolson*, vol. II, pp. 82, 226–7, 261–2.

111. Lees-Milne, *People and Places*, pp. 166–83; Gaze, *Figures in a Landscape*, pp. 131–2, 291–2; Nicolson, *Vita and Harold*, p. 425; *HND* III, pp. 24, 268.

112. Lees-Milne, *Harold Nicolson*, vol. II, pp. 278–9, 345, 350, 354.

113. Glandinning, *Vita*, p. 186; *HND* III, p. 352.

114. *HND*, p. 259.

115. Thompson, *English Landed Society*, pp. 18–19.

116. R. Gill, *Happy Rural Seat: The Country House and the Literary Imagination* (1972), esp. pp. 133–63.

117. Nicolson, *Portrait of a Marriage*, p. 80; Nicolson, *Vita and Harold*, pp. 12–13; *HND* III, pp. 16–17. Lees-Milne was unable to make up his mind whether HN was a snob or not: Lees-Milne, *Harold Nicolson*, vol. I, pp. 20–1; vol. II, p. 190.

118. J. Carey, 'Darling, We're Wonderful', *Sunday Times*, 14 June 1992; Nicolson, *Vita and Harold*, pp. 167–8, 312–13, 352, 356–7; Lees-Milne, *Harold Nicolson*, vol. II, p. 337.

Conclusion

1. M. Girouard, *Town and Country* (1992), p. 9.

2. D. Cannadine, *The Pleasures of the Past* (1989), pp. 256–71; Cannadine, *The Decline and Fall of the British Aristocracy* (1990) pp. 691–6.

Index

Photographic Acknowledgements

THE FOLLOWING INDIVIDUALS AND INSTITUTIONS kindly supplied photographs for inclusion in the book: The British Library 19, 25, 27; Country Life 28, 41, 49; Cumbria County Council, Barrow-in-Furness Library 39; Currey & Co. (photograph Eileen Tweedy) 40; Fitzwilliam Museum, Cambridge 36; *Harold Nicolson's Diaries and Letters 1930–1964* ed. Stanley Olson (Harper Collins Publishers Ltd.) 50; The Hulton Deutsch Collection 34; A.F. Kersting 8, 20, 21, 22, 23, 31, 45; the Lord Bishop of Durham, the Church Commissioners for England and the Courtauld Institute of Art 3; the Marquess of Tavistock and Trustees of the Bedford Estates 18; The National Gallery of Ireland 1; The National Motor Museum, Beaulieu 14, 16, 17; The National Museum of Wales 9; The National Portrait Gallery, London 2, 5, 6, 10, 32, 33, 35; The National Railway Museum 11, 12, 13, 15; The National Trust, Sizergh Castle (photograph Courtauld Institute of Art) 29; Norwich Library 42; The Provost and Fellows of Eton College (photograph Courtauld Institute of Art) 26; The Royal Ulster Yacht Club 47; The Victoria and Albert Museum 30; The Yale Centre for British Art, Paul Mellon Collection 4.